Beowulf Cluster Computing with Linux

Scientific and Engineering Computation
Janusz Kowalik, editor

Beowulf Cluster Computing with Linux

Thomas Sterling

The MIT Press
Cambridge, Massachusetts
London, England

This book was set in LaTeX by the author and was printed and bound in the United States of America.

Library of Congress Control Number 2001095383
ISBN: 0–262–69274–0

Dedicated with respect and appreciation to the memory of
Seymour R. Cray
1925–1996

Contents

Series Foreword

The world of modern computing potentially offers many helpful methods and tools to scientists and engineers, but the fast pace of change in computer hardware, software, and algorithms often makes practical use of the newest computing technology difficult. The Scientific and Engineering Computation series focuses on rapid advances in computing technologies, with the aim of facilitating transfer of these technologies to applications in science and engineering. It will include books on theories, methods, and original applications in such areas as parallelism, large-scale simulations, time-critical computing, computer-aided design and engineering, use of computers in manufacturing, visualization of scientific data, and human-machine interface technology.

The series is intended to help scientists and engineers understand the current world of advanced computation and to anticipate future developments that will affect their computing environments and open up new capabilities and modes of computation.

This volume in the series describes the increasingly successful distributed/parallel system called Beowulf. A Beowulf is a cluster of PCs interconnected by network technology and employing the message-passing model for parallel computation. Key advantages of this approach are high performance for low price, system scalability, and rapid adjustment to new technological advances.

This book includes how to build, program, and operate a Beowulf system based on the Linux operating system. A companion volume in the series provides the same information for Beowulf clusters based on the Microsoft Windows operating system.

Beowulf hardware, operating system software, programming approaches and libraries, and machine management software are all covered here. The book can be used as an academic textbook as well as a practical guide for designing, implementing, and operating a Beowulf for those in science and industry who need a powerful system but are reluctant to purchase an expensive massively parallel processor or vector computer.

Janusz S. Kowalik

Foreword

We know two things about progress in parallel programming:

1. Like nearly all technology, progress comes when effort is headed in a common, focused direction with technologists competing and sharing results.

2. Parallel programming remains very difficult and should be avoided if at all possible. This argues for a single environment and for someone else to do the programming through built-in parallel function (e.g., databases, vigorous applications sharing, and an applications market).

After 20 years of false starts and dead ends in high-performance computer architecture, "the way" is now clear: Beowulf clusters are becoming the platform for many scientific, engineering, and commercial applications. Cray-style supercomputers from Japan are still used for legacy or unpartitionable applications code; but this is a shrinking fraction of supercomputing because such architectures aren't scalable or affordable. But if the code cannot be ported or partitioned, vector supercomputers at larger centers are required. Likewise, the Top500 share of proprietary MPPs[1] (massively parallel processors), SMPs (shared memory, multiple vector processors), and DSMs (distributed shared memory) that came from the decade-long government-sponsored hunt for *the* scalable computer is declining. Unfortunately, the architectural diversity created by the hunt assured that a standard platform and programming model could not form. Each platform had low volume and huge software development costs and a lock-in to that vendor.

Just two generations ago based on Moore's law (1995[2]), a plethora of vector supercomputers, nonscalable multiprocessors, and MPP clusters built from proprietary nodes and networks formed the market. That made me realize the error of an earlier prediction that these exotic shared-memory machines were supercomputing's inevitable future. At the time, several promising commercial off-the-shelf (COTS) technology clusters using standard microprocessors and networks were beginning to be built. Wisconsin's Condor to harvest workstation cycles and Berkeley's NOW (network of workstations) were my favorites. They provided one to two orders of

---

[1] MPPs are a proprietary variant of clusters or multicomputers. Multicomputers is the name Allen Newell and I coined in our 1971 book, *Computer Structures*, to characterize a single computer system comprising connected computers that communicate with one another via message passing (versus via shared memory). In the 2001 list of the world's Top500 computers, all except a few shared-memory vector and distributed shared-memory computers are multicomputers. "Massive" has been proposed as the name for clusters over 1,000 computers.

[2] G. Bell, "1995 Observations on Supercomputing Alternatives: Did the MPP Bandwagon Lead to a Cul-de-Sac?", *Communications of the ACM* 39, no. 3 (March 1996) 11–15.

magnitude improvement in performance/price over the proprietary systems, including their higher operational overhead.

In the past five years, the "Beowulf way" has emerged. It developed and integrated a programming environment that operates on scalable clusters built on commodity parts—typically based on Intel but sometimes based on Alphas or PowerPCs. It also leveraged a vendor-neutral operating system (Linux) and helped mature tools such as GNU, MPI, PVM, Condor, and various schedulers. The introduction of Windows Beowulf leverages the large software base, for example, applications, office and visualization tools, and clustered SQL databases.

Beowulf's lower price and standardization attracted a large user community to a common software base. Beowulf follows the personal computer cycle of innovation: platform availability attracts applications; applications attract users; user demand attracts platform competition and more applications; lower prices come with volume and competition. Concurrently, proprietary platforms become less attractive because they lack software, and hence live in niche markets.

Beowulf is the hardware vendor's worst nightmare: there is little profit in Beowulf clusters of commodity nodes and switches. By using COTS PCs, networks, *free* Linux/GNU-based operating systems and tools, or Windows, Beowulf enables any group to buy and build its own supercomputer. Once the movement achieved critical mass, the world *tipped* to this new computing paradigm. No amount of government effort to prop up the ailing domestic industry, and no amount of industry lobbying, could reverse that trend. Today, traditional vector supercomputer companies are gone from the United States, and they are a vanity business in Japan, with less than 10% of the Top500 being vector processors. Clusters beat vector supercomputers, even though about eight scalar microprocessors are still needed to equal the power of a vector processor.

The Beowulf movement unified the cluster community and changed the course of technical computing by "commoditizing" it. Beowulf enabled users to have a common platform and programming model independent of proprietary processors, interconnects, storage, or software base. An applications base, as well as an industry based on many low-cost "killer microprocessors," is finally forming.

You are the cause of this revolution, but there's still much to be done! There is cause for concern, however. Beowulf is successful because it is a common base with critical mass.

There will be considerable pressure to create Linux/Beowulf dialects (e.g., 64-bit flavor and various vendor binary dialects), which will fragment the community, user attention span, training, and applications, just as proprietary-platform Unix dialects sprang from hardware vendors to differentiate and lock in users. The community must balance this pseudo- and incremental innovation against standardization, because standardization is what gives the Beowulf its huge advantage.

Having described the inevitable appearance of Linux/Beowulf dialects, and the associated pitfalls, I am strongly advocating Windows Beowulf. Instead of fragmenting the community, Windows Beowulf will significantly increase the Beowulf community. A Windows version will support the large community of people who want the Windows tools, layered software, and development style. Already, most users of large systems operate a heterogeneous system that runs both, with Windows (supplying a large scalable database) and desktop Visual-X programming tools. Furthermore, competition will improve both. Finally, the big gain will come from cross-fertilization of .NET capabilities, which are leading the way to the truly distributed computing that has been promised for two decades.

Beowulf Becomes a Contender

In the mid-1980s an NSF supercomputing centers program was established in response to Digital's VAX minicomputers.[3] Although the performance gap between the VAX and a Cray could be as large as 100,[4] the performance per price was usually the reverse: VAX gave much more bang for the buck. VAXen soon became the dominant computer for researchers. Scientists were able to own and operate their own computers and get more computing resources with their own VAXen, including those that were operated as the first clusters. The supercomputer centers were used primarily to run jobs that were too large for these personal or departmental systems.

In 1983 ARPA launched the Scalable Computing Initiative to fund over a score of research projects to design, build, and buy scalable, parallel computers. Many of these were centered on the idea of the emerging "killer microprocessor." Over forty startups were funded with venture capital and our tax dollars to build different parallel computers. *All of these efforts failed.* (I estimate these efforts cost between one and three billion dollars, plus at least double that in user programming that is best written off as training.) The vast funding of all the different species, which varied only superficially, guaranteed little progress and no applications market. The user community did, however, manage to *defensively* create lowest common

---

[3]The VAX 780 was introduced in 1978.

[4]VAXen lacked the ability to get 5–20 times the performance that a large, shared Cray provided for single problems.

denominator standards to enable programs to run across the wide array of varying architectures.

In 1987, the National Science Foundation's new computing directorate established the goal of achieving parallelism of 100X by the year 2000. The goal got two extreme responses: Don Knuth and Ken Thompson said that parallel programming was too hard and that we shouldn't focus on it; and others felt the goal should be 1,000,000X! Everyone else either ignored the call or went along quietly for the funding. This call was accompanied by an offer (by me) of yearly prizes to reward those who achieved extraordinary parallelism, performance, and performance/price. In 1988, three researchers at Sandia obtained parallelism of 600X on a 1000-node system, while indicating that 1000X was possible with more memory. The announcement of their achievement galvanized others, and the Gordon Bell prizes continue, with gains of 100% nearly every year.

Interestingly, a factor of 1000 scaling seems to continue to be the limit for most scalable applications, but 20–100X is more common. In fact, at least half of the Top500 systems have fewer than 100 processors! Of course, the parallelism is determined largely by the fact that researchers are budget limited and have only smaller machines costing \$1,000–\$3,000 per node or parallelism of < 100. If the nodes are in a center, then the per node cost is multiplied by at least 10, giving an upper limit of 1000–10,000 nodes per system. If the nodes are vector processors, the number of processors is divided by 8–10 and the per node price raised by 100X.

In 1993, Tom Sterling and Don Becker led a small project within NASA to build a gigaflops workstation costing under \$50,000. The so-called Beowulf project was outside the main parallel-processing research community: it was based instead on commodity and COTS technology and publicly available software. The Beowulf project succeeded: a 16-node, \$40,000 cluster built from Intel 486 computers ran in 1994. In 1997, a Beowulf cluster won the Gordon Bell Prize for performance/price. The recipe for building one's own Beowulf was presented in a book by Sterling et al. in 1999.[5] By the year 2000, several thousand-node computers were operating. In June 2001, 33 Beowulfs were in the Top500 supercomputer list (`www.top500.org`). Today, in the year 2001, technical high schools can buy and assemble a supercomputer from parts available at the corner computer store.

Beowulfs formed a do-it-yourself cluster computing community using commodity microprocessors, local area network Ethernet switches, Linux (and now Windows 2000), and tools that have evolved from the user community. This vendor-neutral

---

[5] T. Sterling, J. Salmon, D. J. Becker, and D. V. Savarese, *How to Build a Beowulf: A Guide to the Implementation and Application of PC Clusters,* MIT Press, Cambridge, MA, 1999.

platform used the MPI message-based programming model that scales with additional processors, disks, and networking.

Beowulf's success goes beyond the creation of an "open source" model for the scientific software community. It utilizes the two decades of attempts by the parallel processing community to apply these mutant multicomputers to a variety of applications. Nearly all of these efforts, like Beowulf, have been created by researchers outside the traditional funding stream (i.e., "pull" versus "push" research). Included among these efforts are the following:

- Operating system primitives in Linux and GNU tools that support the platform and networking hardware to provide basic functions
- Message Passing Interface (MPI) programming model
- Various parallel programming paradigms, including Linda, the Parallel Virtual Machine (PVM), and Fortran dialects.
- Parallel file systems, awaiting transparent database technology
- Monitoring, debugging, and control tools
- Scheduling and resource management (e.g., Wisconsin's Condor, the Maui scheduler)
- Higher-level libraries (e.g., LINPACK, BLAS)

Challenges of "Do-It-Yourself Supercomputers"

Will the supercomputer center's role change in light of personal Beowulfs? Beowulfs are even more appealing than VAXen because of their ubiquity, scalability, and extraordinary performance/price. A supercomputer center user usually gets no more than 64–128 nodes[6] for a single problem—comparable to the size that researchers have or can build up in their labs. At a minimum, centers will be forced to rethink and redefine their role.

An interesting scenario arises when Gigabit and 10 Gigabit Ethernets become the de facto LAN. As network speed and latency increase more rapidly than processing, message passing looks like memory access, making data equally accessible to all nodes within a local area. These match the speed of the next-generation Internet. This would mean any LAN-based collection of PCs would become a de facto Beowulf! Beowulfs and Grid computing technologies will become more closely

---

[6]At a large center with over 600 processors, the following was observed: 65%, of the users were assigned < 16 processors; 24%<32; 4%<64; 4%<128; and 1%<256.

related to each other than they are now. I can finally see the environment that I challenged the NSF computer science research community to build in 1987!

By 2010 we can expect several interesting paths that Beowulf could host for more power through parallelism:

• In situ Condor-scheduled workstations providing de facto clusters, with scaleup of 100–10,000X in many environments
• Large on-chip caches, with multiple processors to give much more performance for single nodes
• Disks with embedded processors in a network attached storage architecture, as opposed to storage area networking that connects disks to nodes and requires a separate system area network to interconnect nodes

Already in 2001, a relatively large number of applications can utilize Beowulf technology by "avoiding" parallel programming, including the following:

• Web and Internet servers that run embarrassingly parallel to serve a large client base
• Commercial transaction processing, including inherent, parallelized databases
• Monte Carlo simulation and image rendering that are embarrassingly parallel

Great progress has been made in parallelizing applications (e.g., n-body problems) that had challenged us in the past. The most important remaining challenge is to continue on the course to parallelize those applications heretofore deemed the province of shared-memory multiprocessors. These include problems requiring random variable access and adaptive mesh refinement. For example, automotive and aerodynamic engineering, climate and ocean modeling, and applications involving heterogeneous space remain the province of vector multiprocessors. We need to have a definitive list of challenges to log progress; but, unfortunately, the vector supercomputer community have not provided this list.

Another challenge must be to make the use of multicomputers for parallel operation as easy as scalar programming. Although great progress has been made by computational scientists working with computer scientists, the effort to adopt, understand, and train computer scientists in this form of parallelism has been minimal. Few computer science departments are prepared to take on this role.

Based on two decades of "no surprises" in overall architectures, will there be any unforeseen advances outside of Moore's law to help achieve petaflops? What will high-performance systems look like in two or four more generations of Moore's law, considering processing, storage, networking, and user connections? Will Beowulf evolve to huge (100,000-node) clusters built from less costly nodes? Or will clusters be just part of the international computing "Grid"?

Gordon Bell
Microsoft Research

Preface

Within the past three years, there has been a rapid increase in the deployment and application of computer clusters to expand the range of available system capabilities beyond those of conventional desktop and server platforms. By leveraging the development of hardware and software for these widely marketed and heavily used mainstream computer systems, clusters deliver order of magnitude or more scaling of computational performance and storage capacity without incurring significant additional R&D costs. Beowulf-class systems, which exploit mass-market PC hardware and software in conjunction with cost-effective commercial network technology, provide users with the dual advantages of unprecedented price/performance and configuration flexibility for parallel computing. Beowulf-class systems may be implemented by the end users themselves from available components. But with their growth in popularity, so has evolved industry support for commercial Beowulf systems. Today, depending on source and services, Beowulf systems can be installed at a cost of between one and three dollars per peak megaflops and of a scale from a few gigaflops to half a teraflops. Equally important is the rapid growth in diversity of application. Originally targeted to the scientific and technical community, Beowulf-class systems have expanded in scope to the broad commercial domain for transaction processing and Web services as well as to the entertainment industry for computer-generated special effects. Right now, the largest computer under development in the United States is a commodity cluster that upon completion will be at a scale of 30 teraflops peak performance. It is quite possible that, by the middle of this decade, commodity clusters in general and Beowulf-class systems in particular may dominate middle and high-end computing for a wide range of technical and business workloads. It also appears that for many students, their first exposure to parallel computing is through hands-on experience with Beowulf clusters.

The publication of *How to Build a Beowulf* by MIT Press marked an important milestone in commodity computing. For the first time, there was an entry-level comprehensive book showing how to implement and apply a PC cluster. The initial goal of that book, which was released almost two years ago, was to capture the style and content of the highly successful tutorial series that had been presented at a number of conferences by the authors and their colleagues. The timeliness of this book and the almost explosive interest in Beowulf clusters around the world made it the most successful book of the MIT Press Scientific and Engineering Computation series last year. While other books have since emerged on the topic of assembling clusters, it still remains the most comprehensive work teaching hardware, software, and programming methods. Nonetheless, in spite of its success, *How to Build a Beowulf* addressed the needs of only a part of the rapidly growing commodity cluster community. And because of the rapid evolution in hardware and software, aspects of its contents have grown stale in a very short period of time. *How to Build a Beowulf* is still a very useful introduction to commodity clusters and has been widely praised for its accessibility to first-time users. It has even found its way into a number of high schools across the country. But the community requires a much more extensive treatment of a topic that has changed dramatically since that book was introduced.

In addition to the obvious improvements in hardware, over the past two years there have been significant advances in software tools and middleware for managing cluster resources. The early Beowulf systems ordinarily were employed by one or a few closely associated workers and applied to a small easily controlled workload, sometimes even dedicated to a single application. This permitted adequate supervision through direct and manual intervention, often by the users themselves. But as the user base has grown and the nature of the responsibilities for the clusters has rapidly diversified, this simple "mom-and-pop" approach to system operations has proven inadequate in many commercial and industrial-grade contexts. As one reviewer somewhat unkindly put it, *How to Build a Beowulf* did not address the hard problems. This was, to be frank, at least in part true, but it reflected the state of the community at the time of publication. Fortunately, the state of the art has progressed to the point that a new snapshot of the principles and practices is not only justified but sorely needed.

The book you are holding is far more than a second addition of the original *How to Build a Beowulf;* it marks a major transition from the early modest experimental Beowulf clusters to the current medium- to large-scale, industrial-grade PC-based clusters in wide use today. Instead of describing a single depth-first minimalist path to getting a Beowulf system up and running, this new reference work reflects a range of choices that system users and administrators have in programming and managing what may be a larger user base for a large Beowulf clustered system. Indeed, to support the need for a potentially diverse readership, this new book comprises three major parts. The first part, much like the original *How to Build a Beowulf,* provides the introductory material, underlying hardware technology, and assembly and configuration instructions to implement and initially use a cluster. But even this part extends the utility of this basic-level description to include discussion and tutorial on how to use existing benchmark codes to test and evaluate new clusters. The second part focuses on programming methodology. Here we have given equal treatment to the two most widely used programming frameworks: MPI and PVM. This part stands alone (as do the other two) and provides detailed presentation of parallel programming principles and practices, including some of the most widely used libraries of parallel algorithms. The largest and third part of the new book describes software infrastructure and tools for managing cluster resources. This includes some of the most popular of the readily available software packages for distributed task scheduling, as well as tools for monitoring and administering system resources and user accounts.

To provide the necessary diversity and depth across a range of concepts, topics, and techniques, I have developed a collaboration among some of the world's experts in cluster computing. I am grateful to the many contributors who have added their expertise to the body of this work to bring you the very best presentation on so many subjects. In many cases, the contributors are the original developers of the software component being described. Many of the contributors have published earlier works on these or other technical subjects and have experience conveying sometimes difficult issues in readable form. All are active participants in the cluster community. As a result, this new book is a direct channel to some of the most influential drivers of this rapidly moving field.

One of the important changes that has taken place is in the area of node operating system. When Don Becker and I developed the first Beowulf-class systems in 1994, we adopted the then-inchoate Linux kernel because it was consistent with other Unix-like operating systems employed on a wide range of scientific compute platforms from workstations to supercomputers and because it provided a full open source code base that could be modified as necessary, while at the same time providing a vehicle for technology transfer to other potential users. Partly because of these efforts, Linux is the operating system of choice for many users of Beowulf-class systems and the single most widely used operating system for technical computing with clusters. However, during the intervening period, the single widest source of PC operating systems, Microsoft, has provided the basis for many commercial clusters used for data transaction processing and other business-oriented workloads. Microsoft Windows 2000 reflects years of development and has emerged as a mature and robust software environment with the single largest base of targeted independent software vendor products. Important path-finding work at NCSA and more recently at the Cornell Theory Center has demonstrated that scientific and technical application workloads can be performed on Windows-based systems. While heated debate continues as to the relative merit of the two environments, the market has already spoken: both Linux and Windows have their own large respective user base for Beowulf clusters.

As a result of attempting to represent the PC cluster community that clearly embodies two distinct camps related to the node operating system, my colleagues and I decided to simultaneously develop two versions of the same book. *Beowulf*

Cluster Computing with Linux and *Beowulf Cluster Computing with Windows* are essentially the same book except that, as the names imply, the first assumes and discusses the use of Linux as the basis of a PC cluster while the second describes similar clusters using Microsoft Windows. In spite of this marked difference, the two versions are conceptually identical. The hardware technologies do not differ. The programming methodologies vary in certain specific details of the software packages used but are formally the same. Many but not all of the resource management tools run on both classes of system. This convergence is progressing even as the books are in writing. But even where this is not true, an alternative and complementary package exists and is discussed for the other system type. Approximately 80 percent of the actual text is identical between the two books. Between them, they should cover the vast majority of PC clusters in use today.

On behalf of my colleagues and myself, I welcome you to the world of low-cost Beowulf cluster computing. This book is intended to facilitate, motivate, and drive forward this rapidly emerging field. Our fervent hope is that you are able to benefit from our efforts and this work.

Acknowledgments

I thank first the authors of the chapters contributed to this book:

David Bailey, Lawrence Berkeley National Laboratory
Peter H. Beckman, Turbolinux
Remy Evard, Argonne National Laboratory
Al Geist, Oak Ridge National Laboratory
William Gropp, Argonne National Laboratory
David B. Jackson, University of Utah
James Patton Jones, Veridian
Jim Kohl, Oak Ridge National Laboratory
Walt Ligon, Clemson University
Miron Livny, University of Wisconsin
Ewing Lusk, Argonne National Laboratory
Karen Miller, University of Wisconsin
Bill Nitzberg, Veridian
Rob Ross, Argonne National Laboratory
Daniel Savarese, University of Maryland
Stephen Scott, Oak Ridge National Laboratory
Todd Tanenbaum, University of Wisconsin

Derek Wright, University of Wisconsin

Many other people helped in various ways to put this book together. Thanks are due to Michael Brim, Philip Carns, Anthony Chan, Andreas Dilger, Michele Evard, Tramm Hudson, Andrew Lusk, Richard Lusk, John Mugler, Thomas Naughton, John-Paul Navarro, Daniel Savarese, Rick Stevens, and Edward Thornton.

Jan Lindheim of Caltech provided substantial information related to networking hardware. Narayan Desai of Argonne provided invaluable help with both the node and network hardware chapters. Special thanks go to Rob Ross and Dan Nurmi of Argonne for their advice and help with the cluster setup chapter.

Paul Angelino of Caltech contributed the assembly instructions for the Beowulf nodes. Susan Powell of Caltech performed the initial editing of several chapters of the book.

The authors would like to respectfully acknowledge the important initiative and support provided by George Spix, Svetlana Verthein, and Todd Needham of Microsoft that were critical to the development of this book. Dr. Sterling would like to thank Gordon Bell and Jim Gray for their advice and guidance in its formulation.

Gail Pieper, technical writer in the Mathematics and Computer Science Division at Argonne, was an indispensable guide in matters of style and usage and vastly improved the readability of the prose.

Beowulf Cluster Computing with Linux

1 Introduction

Thomas Sterling

Clustering is a powerful concept and technique for deriving extended capabilities from existing classes of components. In nature, clustering is a fundamental mechanism for creating complexity and diversity through the aggregation and synthesis of simple basic elements. The result is no less than the evolution and structure of the universe, the compound molecules that dictate the shape and attributes of all materials and the form and behavior of all multicellular life, including ourselves. To accomplish such synthesis, an intervening medium of combination and exchange is required that establishes the interrelationships among the constituent elements and facilitates their cooperative interactions from which is derived the emergent behavior of the compound entity. For compound organizations in nature, the binding mechanisms may be gravity, coulombic forces, or synaptic junctions. In the field of computing systems, clustering is being applied to render new systems structures from existing computing elements to deliver capabilities that through other approaches could easily cost ten times as much. In recent years clustering hardware and software have evolved so that today potential user institutions have a plethora of choices in terms of form, scale, environments, cost, and means of implementation to meet their scalable computing requirements. Some of the largest computers in the world are cluster systems. But clusters are also playing important roles in medium-scale technical and commerce computing, taking advantage of low-cost, mass-market PC-based computer technology. These Beowulf-class systems have become extremely popular, providing exceptional price/performance, flexibility of configuration and upgrade, and scalability to provide a powerful new tool, opening up entirely new opportunities for computing applications.

1.1 Definitions and Taxonomy

In the most general terms, a cluster is any ensemble of independently operational elements integrated by some medium for coordinated and cooperative behavior. This is true in biological systems, human organizations, and computer structures. Consistent with this broad interpretation, computer clusters are ensembles of independently operational computers integrated by means of an interconnection network and supporting user-accessible software for organizing and controlling concurrent computing tasks that may cooperate on a common application program or workload. There are many kinds of computer clusters, ranging from among the world's largest computers to collections of throwaway PCs. Clustering was among the first computer system architecture techniques for achieving significant improvements in overall performance, user access bandwidth, and reliability. Many research clusters have been implemented in industry and academia, often with proprietary networks and/or custom processing nodes.

Commodity clusters are local ensembles of computing nodes that are commercially available systems employed for mainstream data-processing markets. The interconnection network used to integrate the compute nodes of a commodity cluster is dedicated to the cluster system and is also commercially available from its manufacturer. The network is dedicated in the sense that it is used internally within the cluster supporting only those communications required between the compute nodes making up the cluster, its host or master nodes, which are themselves "worldly," and possibly the satellite nodes responsible for managing mass storage resources that are part of the cluster. The network of a commodity cluster must not be proprietary to the cluster product of a single vendor but must be available for procurement, in general, for the assembly of any cluster. Thus, all components of a commodity cluster can be bought by third-party systems integrators or the end-user installation site itself. Commodity clusters employ software, which is also available to the general community. Software can be free, repackaged and distributed for modest cost, or developed by third-party independent software vendors (ISVs) and commercially marketed. Vendors may use and distribute as part of their commodity cluster products their own proprietary software as long as alternate external software is available that could be employed in its place. The twin motivating factors that drive and restrict the class of commodity computers is (1) their use of nonspecialty parts that exploits the marketplace for cost reduction and stable reliability and (2) the avoidance of critical unique solutions restricted to a specific cluster product that if unavailable in the future would disrupt end-user productivity and jeopardize user investment in code base.

Beowulf-class systems are commodity clusters that exploit the attributes derived from mass-market manufacturing and distribution of consumer-grade digital electronic components. Beowulfs are made of PCs, sometimes lots of them; cheap EIDE (enchanced integrated drive electronics) (usually) hard disks; and low-cost DIMMs (dual inline memory modules) for main memory. A number of different microprocessor families have been used successfully in Beowulfs, including the long-lasting Intel X86 family (80386 and above), their AMD binary compatible counterparts, the Compaq Alpha 64-bit architecture, and the IBM PowerPC series. Beowulf systems deliver exceptional price/performance for many applications. They use low cost/no cost software to manage the individual nodes and the ensemble as a whole. A large part of the scientific and technical community using Beowulf has employed the Linux open source operating system, while many of the business and commercial users of Beowulf support the widely distributed commercial Microsoft Windows operating system. Both types of Beowulf system use middleware that is a combination of free open software and commercial ISV products. Many of these tools have been ported to both environments, although some still are restricted to one or the other environment. The nodes of Beowulfs are either uniprocessor or symmetric multiprocessors (SMPs) of a few processors. The price/performance sweet spot appears to be the dual-node SMP systems, although performance per microprocessor is usually less than for single-processor nodes. Beowulf-class systems are by far the most popular form of commodity cluster today.

At the other end of the cluster spectrum are the constellations. A constellation is a cluster of large SMP nodes scaled such that the number of processors per node is greater than the number of such nodes making up the entire system. This is more than an arbitrary distinction. Performance of a cluster for many applications is derived through program and system parallelism. For most commodity clusters and Beowulf systems, the primary parallelism exploited is the internode parallelism. But for clusters, the primary parallelism is intranode, meaning most of the parallelism used is within the node. Generally, processors within an SMP node are more tightly coupled through shared memory and can exploit finer-grained parallelism than can Beowulf clusters. But shared-memory systems require the use of a different programming model from that of distributed-memory systems, and therefore programming constellations may prove rather different from programming Beowulf clusters for optimal performance. Constellations are usually restricted to the largest systems.

1.2   Opportunities and Advantages

Commodity clusters and Beowulf-class systems bring many advantages to scalable parallel computing, opening new opportunities for users and application domains. Many of these advantages are a consequence of superior price/performance over many other types of system of comparable peak capabilities. But other important attributes exhibited by clusters are due to the nature of their structure and method of implementation. Here we highlight and expand on these, both to motivate the deployment and to guide the application of Beowulf-class systems for myriad purposes.

Capability Scaling. More than even cost effectiveness, a Beowulf system's principle attribute is its scalability. Through the aggregation of commercial off-the-shelf components, ensembles of specific resources deemed critical to a particular mode of operation can be integrated to provide a degree of capability not easily acquired through other means. Perhaps most well known in high-end computing circles is peak performance measured in flops (floating-point operations per second). Even modest Beowulf systems can attain a peak performance between 10 and 100 gigaflops. The largest commodity cluster under development will achieve 30 teraflops peak performance. But another important capability is mass storage, usually through collections of hard disk drives. Large commodity disks can contain more than 100 gigabytes, but commercial database and scientific data-intensive applications both can demand upwards of 100 terabytes of on-line storage. In addition, certain classes of memory intensive applications such as those manipulating enormous matrices of multivariate data can be processed effectively only if sufficient hardware main memory is brought to bear on the problem. Commodity clusters provide one method of accumulating sufficient DRAM (dynamic random access memory) in a single composite system for these large datasets. We note that while clusters enable aggregation of resources, they do so with limited coupling, both logical and physical, among the constituent elements. This fragmentation within integrated systems can negatively impact performance and ease of use.

Convergence Architecture. Not anticipated by its originators, commodity clusters and Beowulf-class systems have evolved into what has become the de facto standard for parallel computer structure, having converged on a communitywide system architecture. Since the mid-1970s, the high-performance computing industry has dragged its small user and customer base through a series of often-disparate parallel architecture types, requiring major software rework across successive generations. These changes were often a consequence of individual vendor decisions and resulted in low customer confidence and a strong reticence to invest in porting codes to a system that could easily be obsolete before the task was complete and incompatible with any future generation systems. Commodity clusters employing communitywide message-passing libraries offer a common structure that crosses vendor boundaries and system generations, ensuring software investment longevity and providing customer confidence. Through the evolution of clusters, we have witnessed a true convergence of parallel system architectures, providing a shared framework in which hardware and software suppliers can develop products with the assurance of customer acceptance and application developers can devise advanced user programs with the confidence of continued support from vendors.

Price/Performance. No doubt the single most widely recognized attribute of Beowulf-class cluster systems is their exceptional cost advantage compared with other parallel computers. For many (but not all) user applications and workloads,

Beowulf clusters exhibit a performance-to-cost advantage of as much as an order of magnitude or more compared with massively parallel processors (MPPs) and distributed shared-memory systems of equivalent scale. Today, the cost of Beowulf hardware is approaching one dollar per peak megaflops using consumer-grade computing nodes. The implication of this is far greater than merely the means of saving a little money. It has caused a revolution in the application of high-performance computing to a range of problems and users who would otherwise be unable to work within the regime of supercomputing. It means that for the first time, computing is playing a role in industry, commerce, and research unaided by such technology. The low cost has made Beowulfs ideal for educational platforms, enabling the training in parallel computing principles and practices of many more students than previously possible. More students are now learning parallel programming on Beowulf-class systems than all other types of parallel computer combined.

Flexibility of Configuration and Upgrade. Depending on their intended user and application base, clusters can be assembled in a wide array of configurations, with very few constraints imposed by commercial vendors. For those systems configured at the final site by the intended administrators and users, a wide choice of components and structures is available, making possible a broad range of systems. Where clusters are to be dedicated to specific workloads or applications, the system structure can be optimized for the required capabilities and capacities that best suit the nature of the problem being computed. As new technologies emerge or additional financial resources are available, the flexibility with which clusters are imbued is useful for upgrading existing systems with new component technologies as a midlife "kicker" to extend the life and utility of a system by keeping it current.

Technology Tracking. New technologies most rapidly find their way into those products likely to provide the most rapid return: mainstream high-end personal computers and SMP servers. Only after substantial lag time might such components be incorporated into MPPs. Clustering, however, provides an immediate path to integration of the latest technologies, even those that may never be adopted by other forms of high-performance computer systems.

High Availability. Clusters provide multiple redundant identical resources that, if managed correctly, can provide continued system operation through graceful degradation even as individual components fail.

Personal Empowerment. Because high-end cluster systems are derived from readily available hardware and software components, installation sites, their system administrators, and users have more control over the structure, elements, operation, and evolution of this system class than over any other system. This sense of control and flexibility has provided a strong attractor to many, especially those in the research community, and has been a significant motivation for many installations.

Development Cost and Time. The emerging cluster industry is being fueled by the very low cost of development and the short time to product delivery. Based on existing computing and networking products, vendor-supplied commodity clusters can be developed through basic systems integration and engineering, with no component design required. Because the constituent components are manufactured for a much larger range of user purposes than is the cluster market itself, the cost to the supplier is far lower than custom elements would otherwise be. Thus commodity clusters provide vendors with the means to respond rapidly to diverse customer needs, with low cost to first delivery.

1.3   A Short History

Cluster computing originated within a few years of the inauguration of the modern electronic stored-program digital computer. SAGE was a cluster system built for NORAD under Air Force contract by IBM in the 1950s based on the MIT Whirlwind computer architecture. Using vacuum tube and core memory technologies, SAGE consisted of a number of separate standalone systems cooperating to manage early warning detection of hostile airborne intrusion of the North American continent. Early commercial applications of clusters employed paired loosely coupled computers, with one computer performing user jobs while the other managed various input/output devices.

Breakthroughs in enabling technologies occurred in the late 1970s, both in hardware and software, which were to have significant long-term effects on future cluster computing. The first generations of microprocessors were designed with the initial development of VLSI (very large scale integration) technology, and by the end of the decade the first workstations and personal computers were being marketed. The advent of Ethernet provided the first widely used local area network technology, creating an industry standard for a modestly priced multidrop interconnection medium and data transport layer. Also at this time, the multitasking Unix operating system was created at AT&T Bell Labs and extended with virtual memory and network interfaces at the University of California–Berkeley. Unix was adopted in its various commercial and public domain forms by the scientific and technical computing community as the principal environment for a wide range of computing system classes from scientific workstations to supercomputers.

During the decade of the 1980s, increased interest in the potential of cluster computing was marked by important experiments in research and industry. A collection of 160 interconnected Apollo workstations was employed as a cluster to perform certain computational tasks by the National Security Agency. Digital Equipment Corporation developed a system comprising interconnected VAX 11/750 computers, coining the term "cluster" in the process. In the area of software, task management tools for employing workstation farms were developed, most notably the Condor software package from the University of Wisconsin. Different strategies for parallel processing were explored during this period by the computer science research community. From this early work came the communicating sequential processes model more commonly referred to as the message-passing model, which has come to dominate much of cluster computing today.

An important milestone in the practical application of the message-passing model was the development of PVM (Parallel Virtual Machine), a library of linkable functions that could allow routines running on separate but networked computers to exchange data and coordinate their operation. PVM (developed by Oak Ridge National Laboratory, Emery University, and the University of Tennessee) was the first widely deployed distributed software system available across different platforms. By the beginning of the 1990s, a number of sites were experimenting with clusters of workstations. At the NASA Lewis Research Center, a small cluster of IBM workstations was used to simulate the steady-state behavior of jet aircraft engines in 1992. The NOW (network of workstations) project at UC Berkeley began operating the first of several clusters there in 1993, which led to the first cluster to be entered on the Top500 list of the world's most powerful computers. Also in 1993, Myrinet, one of the first commercial system area networks, was introduced for commodity clusters, delivering improvements in bandwidth and latency an order of magnitude better than the Fast Ethernet local area network (LAN) most widely used for the purpose at that time.

The first Beowulf-class PC cluster was developed at the NASA Goddard Space Flight center in 1994 using early releases of the Linux operating system and PVM running on 16 Intel 100 MHz 80486-based personal computers connected by dual 10 Mbps Ethernet LANs. The Beowulf project developed the necessary Ethernet driver software for Linux and additional low-level cluster management tools and demonstrated the performance and cost effectiveness of Beowulf systems for real-world scientific applications. That year, based on experience with many other message-passing software systems, the first Message-Passing Interface (MPI) standard was adopted by the parallel computing community to provide a uniform set of message-passing semantics and syntax. MPI has become the dominant parallel computing programming standard and is supported by virtually all MPP and cluster system vendors. Workstation clusters running Sun Microsystems Solaris operating system and NCSA's PC cluster running the Microsoft NT operating system were being used for real-world applications.

In 1996, the DOE Los Alamos National Laboratory and the California Institute of Technology with the NASA Jet Propulsion Laboratory independently demonstrated sustained performance of over 1 Gflops for Beowulf systems costing under $50,000 and was awarded the Gordon Bell Prize for price/performance for this accomplishment. By 1997, Beowulf-class systems of over a hundred nodes had demonstrated sustained performance of greater than 10 Gflops, with a Los Alamos system making the Top500 list. By the end of the decade, 28 clusters were on the Top500 list with a best performance of over 200 Gflops. In 2000, both DOE and NSF announced awards to Compaq to implement their largest computing facilities, both clusters of 30 Tflops and 6 Tflops, respectively.

1.4   Elements of a Cluster

A Beowulf cluster comprises numerous components of both hardware and software. Unlike pure closed-box turnkey mainframes, servers, and workstations, the user or hosting organization has considerable choice in the system architecture of a cluster, whether it is to be assembled on site from parts or provided by a systems integrator or vendor. A Beowulf cluster system can be viewed as being made up of four major components, two hardware and two software. The two hardware components are the compute nodes that perform the work and the network that interconnects the node to form a single system. The two software components are the collection of tools used to develop user parallel application programs and the software environment for managing the parallel resources of the Beowulf cluster. The specification of a Beowulf cluster reflects user choices in each of these domains and determines the balance of cost, capacity, performance, and usability of the system.

The hardware node is the principal building block of the physical cluster system. After all, it is the hardware node that is being clustered. The node incorporates the resources that provide both the capability and capacity of the system. Each node has one or more microprocessors that provide the computing power of the node combined on the node's motherboard with the DRAM main memory and the I/O interfaces. In addition the node will usually include one or more hard disk drives for persistent storage and local data buffering although some clusters employ nodes that are diskless to reduce both cost and power consumption as well as increase reliability.

The network provides the means for exchanging data among the cluster nodes and coordinating their operation through global synchronization mechanisms. The subcomponents of the network are the network interface controllers (NIC), the network channels or links, and the network switches. Each node contains at least one NIC that performs a series of complex operations to move data between the external network links and the user memory, conducting one or more transformations on the data in the process. The channel links are usually passive, consisting of a single wire, multiple parallel cables, or optical fibers. The switches interconnect a number of channels and route messages between them. Networks may be characterized by their topology, their bisection and per channel bandwidth, and the latency for message transfer.

The software tools for developing applications depend on the underlying programming model to be used. Fortunately, within the Beowulf cluster community, there has been a convergence of a single dominant model: communicating sequential processes, more commonly referred to as message passing. The message-passing model implements concurrent tasks or processes on each node to do the work of the application. Messages are passed between these logical tasks to share data and to synchronize their operations. The tasks themselves are written in a common language such as Fortran or C++. A library of communicating services is called by these tasks to accomplish data transfers with tasks being performed on other nodes. While many different message-passing languages and implementation libraries have been developed over the past two decades, two have emerged as dominant: PVM and MPI (with multiple library implementations available for MPI).

The software environment for the management of resources gives system administrators the necessary tools for supervising the overall use of the machine and gives users the capability to schedule and share the resources to get their work done. Several schedulers are available and discussed in this book. For coarse-grained job stream scheduling, the popular Condor scheduler is available. PBS and the Maui scheduler handle task scheduling for interactive concurrent elements. For lightweight process management, the new Scyld Bproc scheduler will provide efficient operation. PBS also provides many of the mechanisms needed to handle user accounts. For managing parallel files, there is PVFS, the Parallel Virtual File System.

1.5   Description of the Book

Beowulf Cluster Computing is offered as a fully comprehensive discussion of the foundations and practices for the operation and application of commodity clusters with an emphasis on those derived from mass-market hardware components and readily available software. The book is divided into three broad topic areas. Part I describes the hardware components that make up a Beowulf system and shows how to assemble such a system as well as take it out for an initial spin using some readily available parallel benchmarks. Part II discusses the concepts and techniques for writing parallel application programs to run on a Beowulf using the two dominant communitywide standards, PVM and MPI. Part III explains how to manage the resources of Beowulf systems, including system administration and task scheduling. Each part is standalone; any one or pair of parts can be used without the need of the others. In this way, you can just jump into the middle to get to the necessary information fast. To help in this, Chapter 2 (the next chapter) provides an overview and summary of all of the material in the book. A quick perusal of that chapter should give enough context for any single chapter to make sense without your having to have read the rest of the book.

The Beowulf book presents three kinds of information to best meet the requirements of the broad and varied cluster computing community. It includes foundation material for students and people new to the field. It also includes reference material in each topic area, such as the major library calls to MPI and PVM or the basic controls for PBS. And, it gives explicit step-by-step guidance on how to accomplish specific tasks such as assembling a processor node from basic components or installing the Maui scheduler.

This book can be used in many different ways. We recommend just sitting down and perusing it for an hour or so to get a good feel for where the information is that you would find most useful. Take a walk through Chapter 2 to get a solid overview. Then, if you're trying to get a job done, go after that material germane to your immediate needs. Or if you are a first-time Beowulf user and just learning about cluster computing, use this as your guide through the field. Every section is designed both to be interesting and to teach you how to do something new and useful.

One major challenge was how to satisfy the needs of the majority of the commodity cluster community when a major division exists across the lines of the operating system used. In fact, at least a dozen different operating systems have been used for cluster systems. But the majority of the community use either Linux or Windows. The choice of which of the two to use depends on many factors, some of them purely subjective. We therefore have taken the unprecedented action of offering a choice: we've crafted two books, mostly the same, but differing between the two operating systems. So, you are holding either *Beowulf Cluster Computing with Windows* or *Beowulf Cluster Computing with Linux*. Whichever works best for you, we hope you find it the single most valuable book on your shelf for making clusters and for making clusters work for you.

I ENABLING TECHNOLOGIES

2 An Overview of Cluster Computing

Thomas Sterling

Commodity cluster systems offer an alternative to the technical and commercial computing market for scalable computing systems for medium- and high-end computing capability. For many applications they replace previous-generation monolithic vector supercomputers and MPPs. By incorporating only components already developed for wider markets, they exploit the economy of scale not possible in the high-end computing market alone and circumvent significant development costs and lead times typical of earlier classes of high-end systems resulting in a price/performance advantage that may exceed an order of magnitude for many user workloads. In addition, users have greater flexibility of configuration, upgrade, and supplier, ensuring longevity of this class of distributed system and user confidence in their software investment. Beowulf-class systems exploit mass-market components such as PCs to deliver exceptional cost advantage with the widest space of choice for building systems. Beowulfs integrate widely available and easily accessible low-cost or no-cost system software to provide many of the capabilities required by a system environment. As a result of these attributes and the opportunities they imply, Beowulf-class clusters have penetrated almost every aspect of computing and are rapidly coming to dominate the medium to high end.

Computing with a Beowulf cluster engages four distinct but interrelated areas of consideration:

1. hardware system structure,

2. resource administration and management environment,

3. distributed programming libraries and tools, and

4. parallel algorithms.

Hardware system structure encompasses all aspects of the hardware node components and their capabilities, the dedicated network controllers and switches, and the interconnection topology that determines the system's global organization. The resource management environment is the battery of system software and tools that govern all phases of system operation from installation, configuration, and initialization, through administration and task management, to system status monitoring, fault diagnosis, and maintenance. The distributed programming libraries and tools determine the paradigm by which the end user coordinates the distributed computing resources to execute simultaneously and cooperatively the many concurrent logical components constituting the parallel application program. Finally, the domain of parallel algorithms provides the models and approaches for organizing a user's application to exploit the intrinsic parallelism of the problem while operating within the practical constraints of effective performance.

This chapter provides a brief and top-level overview of these four main domains that constitute Beowulf cluster computing. The objective is to provide sufficient context for you to understand any single part of the remaining book and how its contribution fits in to the broader form and function of commodity clusters.

2.1   A Taxonomy of Parallel Computing

The goal of achieving performance through the exploitation of parallelism is as old as electronic digital computing itself, which emerged from the World War II era. Many different approaches and consequent paradigms and structures have been devised, with many commercial or experimental versions being implemented over the years. Few, however, have survived the harsh rigors of the data processing marketplace. Here we look briefly at many of these strategies, to better appreciate where commodity cluster computers and Beowulf systems fit and the tradeoffs and compromises they represent.

A first-tier decomposition of the space of parallel computing architectures may be codified in terms of coupling: the typical latencies involved in performing and exploiting parallel operations. This may range from the most tightly coupled fine-grained systems of the systolic class, where the parallel algorithm is actually hard-wired into a special-purpose ultra-fine-grained hardware computer logic structure with latencies measured in the nanosecond range, to the other extreme, often referred to as distributed computing, which engages widely separated computing resources potentially across a continent or around the world and has latencies on the order of a hundred milliseconds. Thus the realm of parallel computing structures encompasses a range of 10^8, when measured by degree of coupling and, by implication, granularity of parallelism. In the following list, the set of major classes in order of tightness of coupling is briefly described. We note that any such taxonomy is subjective, rarely orthogonal, and subject to debate. It is offered only as an illustration of the richness of choices and the general space into which cluster computing fits.

Systolic computers are usually special-purpose hardwired implementations of fine-grained parallel algorithms exploiting one-, two-, or three-dimensional pipelining. Often used for real-time postsensor processors, digital signal processing, image processing, and graphics generation, systolic computing is experiencing a revival through adaptive computing, exploiting the versatile FPGA (field programmable gate array) technology that allows different systolic algorithms to be programmed into the same FPGA medium at different times.

Vector computers exploit fine-grained vector operations through heavy pipelining of memory bank accesses and arithmetic logic unit (ALU) structure, hardware support for gather-scatter operations, and amortizing instruction fetch/execute cycle overhead over many basic operations within the vector operation. The basis for the original supercomputers (e.g., Cray), vector processing is still a formidable strategy in certain Japanese high end systems.

SIMD (single instruction, multiple data) architecture exploits fine-grained data parallelism by having many (potentially thousands) or simple processors performing the same operation in lock step but on different data. A single control processor issues the global commands to all slaved compute processors simultaneously through a broadcast mechanism. Such systems (e.g., MasPar-2, CM-2) incorporated large communications networks to facilitate massive data movement across the system in a few cycles. No longer an active commercial area, SIMD structures continue to find special-purpose application for postsensor processing.

Dataflow models employed fine-grained asynchronous flow control that depended only on data precedence constraints, thus exploiting a greater degree of parallelism and providing a dynamic adaptive scheduling mechanism in response to resource loading. Because they suffered from severe overhead degradation, however, dataflow computers were never competitive and failed to find market presence. Nonetheless, many of the concepts reflected by the dataflow paradigm have had a strong influence on modern compiler analysis and optimization, reservation stations in out-of-order instruction completion ALU designs, and multithreaded architectures.

PIM (processor-in-memory) architectures are only just emerging as a possible force in high-end system structures, merging memory (DRAM or SRAM) with processing logic on the same integrated circuit die to expose high on-chip memory bandwidth and low latency to memory for many data-oriented operations. Diverse structures are being pursued, including system on a chip, which places DRAM banks and a conventional processor core on the same chip; SMP on a chip, which places multiple conventional processor cores and a three-level coherent cache hierarchical structure on a single chip; and Smart Memory, which puts logic at the sense amps of the DRAM memory for in-place data manipulation. PIMs can be used as standalone systems, in arrays of like devices, or as a smart layer of a larger conventional multiprocessor.

MPPs (massively parallel processors) constitute a broad class of multiprocessor architectures that exploit off-the-shelf microprocessors and memory chips in custom designs of node boards, memory hierarchies, and global system area networks. Ironically, "MPP" was first used in the context of SIMD rather than MIMD (multiple instruction, multiple data) machines. MPPs range from distributed-memory machines such as the Intel Paragon, through shared memory without coherent caches such as the BBN Butterfly and CRI T3E, to truly CC-NUMA (non-uniform memory access) such as the HP Exemplar and the SGI Origin2000.

Clusters are an ensemble of off-the-shelf computers integrated by an interconnection network and operating within a single administrative domain and usually within a single machine room. Commodity clusters employ commercially available networks (e.g., Ethernet, Myrinet) as opposed to custom networks (e.g., IBM SP-2). Beowulf-class clusters incorporate mass-market PC technology for their compute nodes to achieve the best price/performance.

Distributed computing, once referred to as "metacomputing", combines the processing capabilities of numerous, widely separated computer systems via the Internet. Whether accomplished by special arrangement among the participants, by means of disciplines referred to as Grid computing, or by agreements of myriad workstation and PC owners with some commercial (e.g., DSI, Entropia) or philanthropic (e.g., SETI@home) coordinating host organization, this class of parallel computing exploits available cycles on existing computers and PCs, thereby getting something for almost nothing.

In this book, we are interested in commodity clusters and, in particular, those employing PCs for best price/performance, specifically, Beowulf-class cluster systems. Commodity clusters may be subdivided into four classes, which are briefly discussed here.

Workstation clusters — ensembles of workstations (e.g., Sun, SGI) integrated by a system area network. They tend to be vendor specific in hardware and software. While exhibiting superior price/performance over MPPs for many problems, there can be as much as a factor of 2.5 to 4 higher cost than comparable PC-based clusters.

Beowulf-class systems — ensembles of PCs (e.g., Intel Pentium 4) integrated with commercial COTS local area networks (e.g., Fast Ethernet) or system area networks (e.g., Myrinet) and run widely available low-cost or no-cost software for managing system resources and coordinating parallel execution. Such systems exhibit exceptional price/performance for many applications.

Cluster farms — existing local area networks of PCs and workstations serving either as dedicated user stations or servers that, when idle, can be employed to perform pending work from outside users. Exploiting job stream parallelism, software systems (e.g., Condor) have been devised to distribute queued work while precluding intrusion on user resources when required. These systems are of lower performance and effectiveness because of the shared network integrating the resources, as opposed to the dedicated networks incorporated by workstation clusters and Beowulfs.

Superclusters — clusters of clusters, still within a local area such as a shared machine room or in separate buildings on the same industrial or academic campus, usually integrated by the institution's infrastructure backbone wide area netork. Although usually within the same internet domain, the clusters may be under separate ownership and administrative responsibilities. Nonetheless, organizations are striving to determine ways to enjoy the potential opportunities of partnering multiple local clusters to realize very large scale computing at least part of the time.

2.2   Hardware System Structure

The most visible and discussed aspects of cluster computing systems are their physical components and organization. These deliver the raw capabilities of the system, take up considerable room on the machine room floor, and yield their excellent price/performance. The two principal subsystems of a Beowulf cluster are its constituent compute nodes and its interconnection network that integrates the nodes into a single system. These are discussed briefly below.

2.2.1   Beowulf Compute Nodes

The compute or processing nodes incorporate all hardware devices and mechanisms responsible for program execution, including performing the basic operations, holding the working data, providing persistent storage, and enabling external communications of intermediate results and user command interface. Five key components make up the compute node of a Beowulf cluster: the microprocessor, main memory, the motherboard, secondary storage, and packaging.

The *microprocessor* provides the computing power of the node with its peak performance measured in Mips (millions of instructions per second) and Mflops (millions of floating-point operations per second). Although Beowulfs have been implemented with almost every conceivable microprocessor family, the two most prevalent today are the 32-bit Intel Pentium 3 and Pentium 4 microprocessors and the 64-bit Compaq Alpha 21264 family. We note that the AMD devices (including the Athlon), which are binary compatible with the Intel Pentium instruction set, have also found significant application in clusters. In addition to the basic floating-point and integer arithmetic logic units, the register banks, and execution pipeline and control logic, the modern microprocessor, comprising on the order of 20 to 50 million transistors, includes a substantial amount of on-chip high-speed memory called cache for rapid access of data. Cache is organized in a hierarchy usually with two or three layers, the closest to the processor being the fastest but smallest and the most distant being relatively slower but with much more capacity. These caches buffer data and instructions from main memory and, where data reuse or spatial locality of access is high, can deliver a substantial percentage of peak performance. The microprocessor interfaces with the remainder of the node usually by two external buses: one specifically optimized as a high-bandwidth interface to main memory, and the other in support of data I/O.

Main memory stores the working dataset and programs used by the microprocessor during job execution. Based on DRAM technology in which a single bit is stored as a charge on a small capacitor accessed through a dedicated switching transistor, data read and write operations can be significantly slower to main memory than to cache. However, recent advances in main memory design have improved memory access speed and have substantially increased memory bandwidth. These improvements have been facilitated by advances in memory bus design such as RAMbus.

The *motherboard* is the medium of integration that combines all the components of a node into a single operational system. Far more than just a large printed circuit board, the motherboard incorporates a sophisticated chip set almost as complicated as the microprocessor itself. This chip set manages all the interfaces between components and controls the bus protocols. One important bus is PCI, the primary interface between the microprocessor and most high-speed external devices. Initially a 32-bit bus operating at 33 MHz, the most recent variation operates at 66 MHz on 64-bit data, thus quadrupling its potential throughput. Most system area network interface controllers are connected to the node by means of the PCI bus. The motherboard also includes a substantial read-only memory (which can be updated) containing the system's BIOS (basic input/output system), a set of low-level services, primarily related to the function of the I/O and basic bootstrap tasks, that defines the logical interface between the higher-level operating system software and the node hardware. Motherboards also support several other input/output ports such as the user's keyboard/mouse/video monitor and the now-ubiquitous universal serial bus (USB) port that is replacing several earlier distinct interface types. Nonetheless, the vestigial parallel printer port can still be found, whose specification goes to the days of the earliest PCs more than twenty years ago.

Secondary storage provides high-capacity persistent storage. While main memory loses all its contents when the system is powered off, secondary storage fully retains its data in the powered-down state. While many standalone PCs include several classes of secondary storage, some Beowulf-systems may have nodes that keep only something necessary for holding a boot image for initial startup, all other data being downloaded from an external host or master node. Secondary storage can go a long way to improving reliability and reducing per node cost. However, it misses the opportunity for low-cost, high-bandwidth mass storage. Depending on how the system ultimately is used, either choice may be optimal. The primary medium for secondary storage is the hard disk, based on a magnetic medium little different from an audio cassette tape. This technology, almost as old as digital computing itself, continues to expand in capacity at an exponential rate, although access speed and bandwidths have improved only gradually. Two primary contenders, SCSI (small computer system interface) and EIDE (enhanced integrated dual electronics), are differentiated by somewhat higher speed and capacity in the first case, and lower cost in the second case. Today, a gigabyte of EIDE disk storage costs the user a few dollars, while the list price for SCSI in a RAID (redundant array of independent disks) configuration can be as high as $100 per gigabyte (the extra cost does buy more speed, density, and reliability). Most workstations use SCSI, and most PCs employ EIDE drives, which can be as large as 100 GBytes per drive. Two other forms of secondary storage are the venerable floppy disk and the optical disk. The modern 3.5-inch floppy (they don't actually flop anymore, since they now come in a hard rather than a soft case), also more than twenty years old, holds only 1.4 MBytes of data and should have been retired long ago. Because of its ubiquity, however, it continues to hang on and is ideal as a boot medium for Beowulf nodes. Largely replacing floppies are the optical CD (compact disk), CD-RW (compact disk-read/write), and DVD (digital versatile disk). The first two hold approximately 600 MBytes of data, with access times of a few milliseconds. (The basic CD is read only, but the CD-RW disks are writable, although at a far slower rate.) Most commercial software and data are now distributed on CDs because they are very cheap to create (actually cheaper than a glossy one-page double-sided commercial flyer). DVD technology also runs on current-generation PCs, providing direct access to movies.

Packaging for PCs originally was in the form of the "pizza boxes": low, flat units, usually placed on the desk with a fat monitor sitting on top. Some small early Beowulfs were configured with such packages, usually with as many as eight of these boxes stacked one on top of another. But by the time the first Beowulfs were implemented in 1994, tower cases—vertical floor-standing (or sometimes on the desk next to the video monitor) components—were replacing pizza boxes because of their greater flexibility in configuration and their extensibility (with several heights available). Several generations of Beowulf clusters still are implemented using this low-cost, robust packaging scheme, leading to such expressions as "pile of PCs" and "lots of boxes on shelves" (LOBOS). But the single limitation of this strategy was its low density (only about two dozen boxes could be stored on a floor-to-ceiling set of shelves) and the resulting large footpad of medium- to large-scale Beowulfs. Once the industry recognized the market potential of Beowulf clusters, a new generation of rack-mounted packages was devised and standardized (e.g., 1U, 2U, 3U, and 4U, with 1U boxes having a height of 1.75 inches) so that it is possible to install a single floor-standing rack with as many as 42 processors, coming close to doubling the processing density of such systems. Vendors providing complete turnkey systems as well as hardware system integrators ("bring-your-own software") are almost universally taking this approach. Yet for small systems where cost is critical and simplicity a feature, towers will pervade small labs, offices, and even homes for a long time. (And why not? On those cold winter days, they make great space heaters.)

Beowulf cluster nodes (i.e., PCs) have seen enormous, even explosive, growth over the past seven years since Beowulfs were first introduced in 1994. We note that the entry date for Beowulf was not arbitrary: the level of hardware and software technologies based on the mass market had just (within the previous six months) reached the point that ensembles of them could compete for certain niche applications with the then-well-entrenched MPPs and provide price/performance benefits (in the very best cases) of almost 50 to 1. The new Intel 100 MHz 80486 made it possible to achieve as much as 5 Mflops per node for select computationally intense problems and the cost of 10 Mbps Ethernet network controllers and network hubs had become sufficiently low that their cost permitted them to be employed as dedicated system area networks. Equally important was the availability of the inchoate Linux operating system with the all-important attribute of being free and open source and the availability of a good implementation of the PVM message-passing library. Of course, the Beowulf project had to fill in a lot of the gaps, including writing most of the Ethernet drivers distributed with Linux and other simple tools, such as channel bonding, that facilitated the management of these early modest systems. Since then, the delivered floating-point performance per processor has grown by more than two orders of magnitude while memory capacity has grown by more than a factor of ten. Disk capacities have expanded by as much as 1000X. Thus, Beowulf compute nodes have witnessed an extraordinary evolution in capability. By the end of this decade, node floating-point performance, main memory size, and disk capacity all are expected to grow by another two orders of magnitude.

One aspect of node structure not yet discussed is symmetric multiprocessing. Modern microprocessor design includes mechanisms that permit more than one processor to be combined, sharing the same main memory while retaining full coherence across separate processor caches, thus giving all processors a consistent view of shared data in spite of their local copies in dedicated caches. While large industrial-grade servers may incorporate as many as 512 processors in a single SMP unit, a typical configuration for PC-based SMPs is two or four processors per unit. The ability to share memory with uniform access times should be a source of improved performance at lower cost. But both design and pricing are highly complicated, and the choice is not always obvious. Sometimes the added complexity of SMP design offsets the apparent advantage of sharing many of the node's resources. Also, performance benefits from tight coupling of the processors may be outweighed by the contention for main memory and possible cache thrashing. An added difficulty is attempting to program at the two levels: message passing between nodes and shared memory between processors of the same node. Most users don't bother, choosing to remain with a uniform message-passing model even between processors within the same SMP node.

2.2.2 Interconnection Networks

Without the availability of moderate-cost short-haul network technology, Beowulf cluster computing would never have happened. Interestingly, the two leaders in cluster dedicated networks were derived from very different precedent technologies. Ethernet was developed as a local area network for interconnecting distributed single user and community computing resources with shared peripherals and file servers. Myrinet was developed from a base of experience with very tightly coupled processors in MPPs such as the Intel Paragon. Together, Fast and Gigabit Ethernet and Myrinet provide the basis for the majority of Beowulf-class clusters.

A network is a combination of physical transport and control mechanisms associated with a layered hierarchy of message encapsulation. The core concept is the "message." A message is a collection of information organized in a format (order and type) that both the sending and the receiving processes understand and can correctly interpret. One can think of a message as a movable record. It can be as short as a few bytes (not including the header information) or as long as many thousands of bytes. Ordinarily, the sending user application process calls a library routine that manages the interface between the application and the network. Performing a high-level send operation causes the user message to be packaged with additional header information and presented to the network kernel driver software. Additional routing information and additional converges are performed prior to actually sending the message. The lowest-level hardware then drives the communication channel's lines with the signal, and the network switches route the message appropriately in accordance with the routing information encoded bits at the header of the message packet. Upon receipt at the receiving node, the process is reversed and the message is eventually loaded into the user application name space to be interpreted by the application code.

The network is characterized primarily in terms of its bandwidth and its latency. Bandwidth is the rate at which the message bits are transferred, usually cited in terms of peak throughput as bits per second. Latency is the length of time required to sends the message. Perhaps a fairer measure is the time from sending to receiving an application process, taking into consideration all of the layers of translation, conversions, and copying involved. But vendors often quote the shorter time between their network interface controllers. To complicate matters, both bandwidth and latency are sensitive to message length and message traffic. Longer messages make better use of network resources and deliver improved network throughput. Shorter messages reduce transmit, receive, and copy times to provide an overall lower transfer latency but cause lower effective bandwidth. Higher total network traffic (i.e., number of messages per unit time) increases overall network throughput, but the resulting contention and the delays they incur result in longer effective message transfer latency.

More recently, an industrial consortium has developed a new networking model known as VIA. The goal of this network class is to support a zero-copy protocol, avoiding the intermediate copying of the message in the operating system space and permitting direct application-to-application message transfers. The result is significantly reduced latency of message transfer. Emulex has developed the cLAN network product, which provides a peak bandwidth in excess of 1 Gbps and for short messages exhibits a transfer latency on the order of 7 microseconds.

2.3   Node Software

A node in a cluster is often (but not always) an autonomous computing entity, complete with its own operating system. Beowulf clusters exploit the sophistication of modern operating systems both for managing the node resources and for communicating with other nodes by means of their interconnection network.

Linux has emerged as the dominant Unix-like operating system. Its development was anything but traditional; it was started by a graduate student (Linus Tovald) in Finland and contributed to by a volunteer force of hundreds of developers around the world via the Internet. Recently Linux has received major backing from large computer vendors including IBM, Compaq, SGI, and HP. Linux is a full-featured multiuser, multitasking, demand-paged virtual memory operating system with advanced kernel software support for high-performance network operation.

2.4   Resource Management

Except in the most restrictive of cases, matching the requirements of a varied workload and the capabilities of the distributed resources of a Beowulf cluster system demands the support and services of a potentially sophisticated software system for resource management. The earliest Beowulfs were dedicated systems used by (at most) a few people and controlled explicitly, one application at a time. But today's more elaborate Beowulf clusters, possibly comprising hundreds or even thousands of processors and shared by a large community of users, both local and at remote sites, need to balance contending demands and available processing capacity to achieve rapid response for user programs and high throughput of cluster resources. Fortunately, several such software systems are available to provide systems administrators and users alike with a wide choice of policies and mechanisms by which to govern the operation of the system and its allocation to user tasks.

The challenge of managing the large set of compute nodes that constitute a Beowulf cluster involves several tasks to match user-specified workload to existing resources.

Queuing. User jobs are submitted to a Beowulf cluster by different people, potentially from separate locations, who are possibly unaware of requirements being imposed on the same system by other users. A queuing system buffers the randomly submitted jobs, entered at different places and times and with varying requirements, until system resources are available to process each of them. Depending on priorities and specific requirements, different distributed queues may be maintained to facilitate optimal scheduling.

Scheduling. Perhaps the most complex component of the resource manager, the scheduler has to balance the priorities of each job, with the demands of other jobs, the existing system compute and storage resources, and the governing policies dictated for their use by system administrators. Schedulers need to contend with such varied requirements as large jobs needing all the nodes, small jobs needing only one or at most a few nodes, interactive jobs during which the user must be available and in the loop for such things as real-time visualization of results or performance debugging during program development, or high-priority jobs that must be completed quickly (such as medical imaging). The scheduler determines the order of execution based on these independent priority assessments and the solution to the classic bin-packing problem: What jobs can fit on the machine at the same time?

Resource Control. A middleware component, resource control puts the programs on the designated nodes, moves the necessary files to the respective nodes, starts jobs, suspends jobs, terminates jobs, and offloads result files. It notifies the scheduler when resources are available and handles any exception conditions across the set of nodes committed to a given user job.

Monitoring. The ongoing status of the Beowulf cluster must be continuously tracked and reported to a central control site such as a master or host node of the system. Such issues as resource availability, task status on each node, and operational health of the nodes must be constantly monitored to aid in the successful management of the total system in serving its incident user demand. Some of this information must continuously update the system operators status presentation, while other statistics and status parameters must be directly employed by the automatic resource management system.

Accounting. In order to assess billing or at least to determine remaining user allocation of compute time (often measured in node hours), as well as to assess overall system utilization, availability, and demand response effectiveness, records must be automatically kept of user accounts and system work. This is the primary tool by which system administrators and managers assess effectiveness of scheduling policies, maintenance practices, and user allocations.

While no single resource management system addresses all of these functions optimally for all operational and demand circumstances, several tools have proven useful in operational settings and are available to users and administrators of Beowulf-class cluster systems. An entire chapter is dedicated to each of these in Part III of this book; here they are discussed only briefly.

Condor supports distributed job stream resource management emphasizing capacity or throughput computing. Condor schedules independent jobs on cluster nodes to handle large user workloads and provides many options in scheduling policy. This venerable and robust package is particularly well suited for managing both workloads and resources at remote sites.

PBS is a widely used system for distributing parallel user jobs across parallel Beowulf cluster resources and providing the necessary administrative tools for professional systems supervision. Both free and commercially supported versions of this system are available, and it is professionally maintained, providing both user and administrator confidence.

Maui is an advanced scheduler incorporating sophisticated policies and mechanisms for handling a plethora of user demands and resource states. This package actually sits on top of other lower-level resource managers, providing added capability.

PVFS manages the secondary storage of a Beowulf cluster, providing parallel file management shared among the distributed nodes of the system. It can deliver faster response and much higher effective disk bandwidth than conventional use of NFS (network file system).

2.5   Distributed Programming

Exploitation of the potential of Beowulf clusters relies heavily on the development of a broad range of new parallel applications that effectively takes advantage of the parallel system resources to permit larger and more complex problems to be explored in a shorter time. Programming a cluster differs substantially from that of programming a uniprocessor workstation or even an SMP. This difference is in part due to the fact that the sharing of information between nodes of a Beowulf cluster can take a lot longer than between the nodes of a tightly coupled system, because the fragmented memory space reflected by the distributed-memory Beowulfs imposes substantially more overhead than that required by shared-memory systems, and because a Beowulf may have many more nodes than a typical 32-processor SMP. As a consequence, the developer of a parallel application code for a Beowulf must take into consideration these and other sources of performance degradation to achieve effective scalable performance for the computational problem.

A number of different models have been employed for parallel programming and execution, each emphasizing a particular balance of needs and desirable traits. The models differ in part by the nature and degree of abstraction they present to the user of the underlying parallel system. These vary in generality and specificity of control. But one model has emerged as the dominant strategy. This is the "communicating sequential processes" model, more often referred to as the message-passing model. Through this methodology, the programmer partitions the problem's global data among the set of nodes and specifies the processes to be executed on each node, each working primarily on its respective local data partition. Where information from other nodes is required, the user establishes logical paths of communication between cooperating processes on separate nodes. The application program for each process explicitly sends and receives messages passed between itself and one or more other remote processes. A message is a packet of information containing one or more values in an order and format that both processes involved in the exchange understand. Messages are also used for synchronizing concurrent processes in order to coordinate the execution of the parallel tasks on different nodes.

Programmers can use low-level operating system kernel interfaces to the network, such as Unix sockets or remote procedure calls. Fortunately, however, an easier way exists. Two major message-passing programming systems have been developed to facilitate parallel programming and application development. These are in the form of linkable libraries that can be used in conjunction with conventional languages such as Fortran or C. Benefiting from prior experiences with earlier such tools, PVM has a significant following and has been used to explore a broad range of semantic constructs and distributed mechanisms. PVM was the first programming system to be employed on a Beowulf cluster and its availability was critical to this early work. MPI, the second and more recently distributed programming system, was developed as a product of a communitywide consortium. MPI is the model of choice for the majority of the parallel programming community on Beowulf clusters and other forms of parallel computer as well, even shared-memory machines. There are a number of open and commercial sources of MPI with new developments, especially in the area of parallel I/O, being incorporated in implementations of MPI-2. Together, MPI and PVM represent the bulk of parallel programs being developed around the world, and both languages are represented in this book.

Of course, developing parallel algorithms and writing parallel programs involves a lot more than just memorizing a few added constructs. Entire books have been dedicated to this topic alone (including threein this series), and it is a focus of active research. A detailed and comprehensive discourse of parallel algorithm design is beyond the scope of this book. Instead, we offer specific and detailed examples that provide templates that will satisfy many programming needs. Certainly not exhaustive, these illustrations nonetheless capture many types of problem.

2.6 Conclusions

Beowulf cluster computing is a fascinating microcosm of parallel processing, providing hands-on exposure and experience with all aspects of the field, from low-level hardware to high-level parallel algorithm design and everything in between. While many solutions are readily available to provide much of the necessary services required for effective use of Beowulf clusters in many roles and markets, many challenges still remain to realizing the best of the potential of commodity clusters. Research and advanced development is still an important part of the work surrounding clusters, even as they are effectively applied to many real-world workloads. The remainder of this book serves two purposes: it represents the state of the art for those who wish ultimately to extend Beowulf cluster capabilities, and it guides those who wish immediately to apply these existing capabilities to real-world problems.

3 Node Hardware

Thomas Sterling

Beowulf is a network of nodes, with each node a low-cost personal computer. Its power and simplicity is derived from exploiting the capabilities of the mass-market systems that provide both the processing and the communication. This chapter explores all of the hardware elements related to computation and storage. Communication hardware options will be considered in detail in Chapter 5.

Few technologies in human civilization have experienced such a rate of growth as that of the digital computer and its culmination in the PC. Its low cost, ubiquity, and sometimes trivial application often obscure its complexity and precision as one of the most sophisticated products derived from science and engineering. In a single human lifetime over the fifty-year history of computer development, performance and memory capacity have grown by a factor of almost a million. Where once computers were reserved for the special environments of carefully structured machine rooms, now they are found in almost every office and home. A personal computer today outperforms the world's greatest supercomputers of two decades ago at less than one ten-thousandth the cost. It is the product of this extraordinary legacy that Beowulf harnesses to open new vistas in computation.

Hardware technology changes almost unbelievably rapidly. The specific processors, chip sets, and three-letter acronyms (TLAs) we define today will be obsolete in a very few years. The prices quoted will be out of date before this book reaches bookstore shelves. On the other hand, the organizational design of a PC and the functions of its primary components will last a good deal longer. The relative strengths and weaknesses of components (e.g., disk storage is slower, larger, cheaper and more persistent than main memory) should remain valid for nearly as long. Fortunately, it is now easy to find up-to-date prices on the Web; see Appendix C for some places to start.

This chapter concentrates on the practical issues related to the selection and assembly of the components of a Beowulf node. You can assemble the nodes of the Beowulf yourself, let someone else (a system integrator) do it to your specification, or purchase a turnkey system. In either case, you'll have to make some decisions about the components. Many system integrators cater to a know-nothing market, offering a few basic types of systems, for example, "office" and "home" models with a slightly different mix of hardware and software components. Although these machines would work in a Beowulf, with only a little additional research you can purchase far more appropriate systems for less money. Beowulf systems (at least those we know of) have little need for audio systems, speakers, joysticks, printers, frame grabbers, and the like, many of which are included in the standard "home" or "office" models. High-performance video is unnecessary except for specialized applications where video output is the primary function of the system. Purchasing just the components you need, in the quantity you need, can be a tremendous advantage. Fortunately, customizing your system this way does not mean that you have to assemble the system yourself. Many system integrators, both large and small, will assemble custom systems for little or no price premium. In fact, every system they assemble is from component parts, so a custom system is no more difficult for them than a standard one.

An enormous diversity of choice exists both in type and quantity of components. More than one microprocessor family is available, and within each family are multiple versions. There is flexibility in both the amount and the type of main memory. Disk drives, too, offer a range of interface, speed, capacity, and number. Choices concerning ancillary elements such as floppy disk drives and CD-ROM drives have to be considered. Moreover, the choice of the motherboard and its chip set provide yet another dimension to PC node implementation. This chapter examines each of these issues individually and considers their interrelationships. A step-by-step procedure for the assembly of a processor node is provided to guide the initiate and protect the overconfident.

We reiterate that we make no attempt to offer a complete or exhaustive survey. Far more products are available than can be explicitly presented in any single book, and new products are being offered all the time. In spite of the impossibility of exhaustive coverage, however, the information provided here should contain most of what is required to implement a Beowulf node. Final details can be acquired from documentation provided by the parts vendors.

3.1   Overview of a Beowulf Node

The Beowulf node is responsible for all activities and capabilities associated with executing an application program and supporting a sophisticated software environment. These fall into four general categories:

1. instruction execution,
2. high-speed temporary information storage,
3. high-capacity persistent information storage, and
4. communication with the external environment, including other nodes.

The node is responsible for performing a set of designated instructions specified by the application program code or system software. The lowest-level binary encoding of the instructions and the actions they perform are dictated by the microprocessor instruction set architecture (ISA). Both the instructions and the data upon which they act are stored in and loaded from the node's random access memory (RAM). The speed of a processor is often measured in megahertz, indicating that its clock ticks so many million times per second. Unfortunately, data cannot be loaded into or stored in memory at anywhere near the rate necessary to feed a modern microprocessor (1 GHz and higher rates are now common). Thus, the processor often waits for memory, and the overall rate at which programs run is usually governed as much by the memory system as by the processor's clock speed.

Microprocessor designers employ numerous ingenious techniques to deal with the problem of slow memories and fast processors. Usually, a memory hierarchy is incorporated that includes one or more layers of very fast but very small and very expensive cache memories, which hold copies of the contents of the slower but much larger main memory. The order of instruction execution and the access patterns to memory can profoundly affect the performance impact of the small high-speed caches. In addition to holding the application dataset, memory must support the operating system and provide sufficient space to keep the most frequently used functions and system management tables and buffers coresident for best performance.

Except for very carefully designed applications, a program's entire dataset must reside in RAM. The alternative is to use disk storage either explicitly (out-of-core calculations) or implicitly (virtual memory swapping), but this usually entails a severe performance penalty. Thus, the size of a node's memory is an important parameter in system design. It determines the size of problem that can practically be run on the node. Engineering and scientific applications often obey a rule of thumb that says that for every floating-point operation per second, one byte of RAM is necessary. This is a gross approximation at best, and actual requirements can vary by many orders of magnitude, but it provides some guidance; for example, a 1 GHz processor capable of sustaining 200 Mflops should be equipped with approximately 200 MBytes of RAM.

Information stored in RAM is not permanent. When a program finishes execution, the RAM that was assigned to it is recovered by the operating system and reassigned to other programs. The data is not preserved. Thus, if one wishes to permanently store the results of a calculation, or even the program itself, a persistent storage device is needed. Hard disk devices that store data on a rotating magnetic medium are the most common storage device in Beowulf nodes. Data stored on hard disk is persistent even under power failures, a feature that makes the hard disk the preferred location for the operating system and other utilities that are required to restart a machine from scratch. A widely held guideline is that the local disk capacity be at least ten times the main memory capacity to provide an adequate area for virtual-memory swap space; more room is required for software and user-generated data. With the low cost of hard disk, a single drive can provide this capacity at a small fraction of the overall system cost. An alternative is to provide permanent storage capability off-node, providing access via the system area network to remote storage resources (e.g., an NFS server on one of the nodes). This may be a practical solution for small Beowulf systems, but as the system grows, a single server can easily be overwhelmed.

The results of computational activities performed on a Beowulf node must be presented to the node's external environment during and after a computation. This requires communication with peripheral devices such as video monitors, printers, and external networks. Furthermore, users need access to the system to start jobs and to monitor and control jobs in progress. System managers may need console access, the ability to install software distributions on CD-ROMs or other media, or backup data to tape or other archival storage. The requirements are served by the I/O subsystem of the node. On today's PCs, these devices usually share the PCI bus, with some low-performance devices using the older ISA bus. In fact, some systems no longer have an ISA bus.

In a Beowulf system typically only one or two nodes have extensive I/O capabilities beyond communication on the system area network. All external interaction is then funneled through these *worldly* nodes. The specific I/O requirements vary greatly from installation to installation, so a precise specification of the peripherals attached to a worldly node is impossible. We can, however, make firm recommendations about the I/O requirements of internal or *compute* nodes. The majority of nodes in a Beowulf system lack the personality of a worldly node. They have one major I/O requirement, which is to communicate with one another. The hardware and software involved in interprocessor communication are discussed in Chapters 5 and 6, respectively. For now, we will simply observe that the processor communicates with the network through the network interface controller attached to a high-speed bus.

3.1.1   Principal Specifications

In selecting the proper node configuration for a new Beowulf, the choices can appear overwhelming. Fortunately, only a small number of critical parameters largely characterize a particular Beowulf node. These parameters usually relate to a few peak capabilities or capacities and are only roughly predictive of the performance of any given application or workload. Nonetheless, they are widely used and provide a reasonable calibration of the price/performance tradeoff space.

Processor clock rate — the frequency (MHz or GHz) of the primary signal within the processor that determines the rate at which instructions are issued

Peak floating-point performance — the combination of the clock rate and the number of floating-point operations that can be issued and/or retired per instruction (Mflops)

Cache size — the storage capacity (KBytes) of the high-speed buffer memory between the main memory and the processor

Main memory capacity — the storage capacity (MBytes) of the primary system node memory in which resides the global dataset of the applications as well as myriad other supporting program, buffering, and argument data

Disk capacity — the storage capacity (GBytes) of the permanent secondary storage internal to the processing node

SAN network port peak bandwidth — the bandwidth (Mbps) of the network control card and system area network communication channel medium

Other parameters that are sometimes of interest are the number of processors included in symmetric multiprocessing configurations, memory latency and bandwidth, measured performance of various benchmarks, and seek and access times to disks.

3.1.2   Basic Elements

The general Beowulf node is a complex organization of multiple subsystems that support the requirements for computation, communication, and storage discussed above. Figure 3.1 shows a block diagram of a node architecture representative of the general structures found in today's PCs adapted to the purpose of Beowulf-class computing.

Microprocessor — all of the logic required to perform instruction execution, memory management and address translation, integer and floating-point operations, and cache management. Processor clock speeds can be as low as 100 MHz found on previous-generation Intel Pentium processors to as high as 1.7 GHz on the Intel Pentium 4 with an 800 MHz Pentium 3 representing near the sweet spot in price/performance.

Cache — a small but fast buffer for keeping recently used data. Cache provides the illusion of a much higher-speed memory than is actually available. Multiple

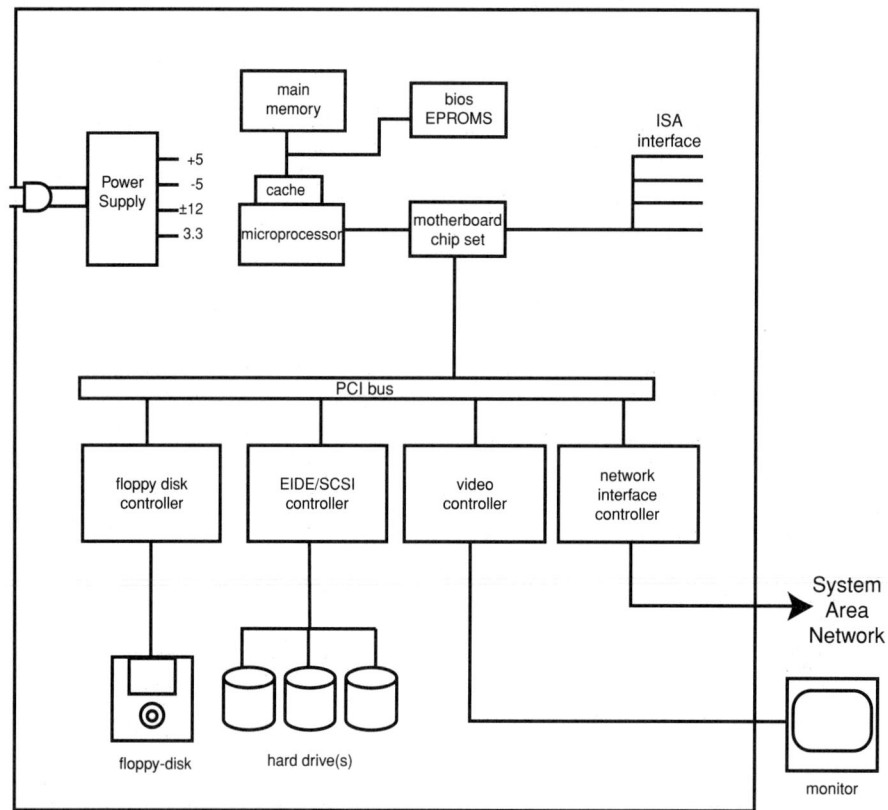

Figure 3.1
Block diagram of a typical Beowulf node. Some additional components, e.g., keyboard, mouse,
additional network interfaces, graphics adaptors, CD-ROM drive, will be necessary on nodes
responsible for I/O services.

layers of cache may be employed; 16 KBytes of Level 1 (L1) and 256 KBytes of
Level 2 (L2) cache are common. The effect of cache can be dramatic, but not all
programs will benefit. Memory systems are so complex that often the only reliable
way to determine the effectiveness of cache for a given application is to test the
application on machines with different amounts of cache.

Main memory — high-density storage with rapid read/write access. Typical
access times of 70 nanoseconds can be found with DIMM memory modules with
memory capacities between 64 MBytes and 512 MBytes. This memory is often
optimized for throughput, delivering successive data items every 10 nanoseconds or

less after an initial setup step.

EIDE/SCSI disk controller — a sophisticated unit that manages the operation of the hard disk and CD-ROM drives, buffers data blocks, and controls the transfer of data directly to or from main memory.

Hard drive — persistent storage, even after processor power cycling, and backing store to the main memory for problems requiring datasets larger than the main memory can hold. Disk capacities range from 1 GByte to over 100, but the most common and cost effective sizes today are between 20 and 80 GBytes. Hard disks conform to either the EIDE or SCSI interface standards. Access times of a few milliseconds are usual for these electromechanical rotating magnetic storage devices.

Floppy disk controller — a very low cost and low capacity storage medium of nominally 1.4 MBytes capacity (double sizes are available). Floppies are used primarily at boot time to install a minimal system capable of bootstrapping itself into a full configuration. Access times are long, and the small capacity makes them unsuitable for other data storage roles. Nevertheless, their historical role as a boot medium makes them a valuable part of every Beowulf node.

Motherboard chip set — a sophisticated special-purpose controller that manages and coordinates the interactions of the various components of the PC through PCI, USB, and other interfaces. It plays an important role in memory management, especially for symmetric multiprocessors where cache coherence is maintained through snooping cache protocols.

BIOS ROM memory — the minimum set of functional binary routines needed to perform rudimentary functionality of the motherboard and its interfaces, including bootstrap and diagnostic functions. Modern systems include writable BIOS EEPROMs (electronically erasable, programmable ROMs) that can have their contents directly upgraded from newer versions of the BIOS programs with replacement on the actual chips.

PCI bus — the universal industry standard for high-speed controllers. The common PCI bus operates a 32-bit data path at 33 MHz; PCI buses with 64-bit data paths at 66 MHz are also available.

Video controller — a card that converts digital signals from the processor into analog signals suitable for driving a video display. Modern high-end video cards contain powerful on-board processors and often have many megabytes of memory and sophisticated programmable interfaces. Such a card might be appropriate for an I/O or interactive node intended to drive a high-resolution monitor for data visualization and interactive display. Other Beowulf nodes, however, have little need for video output. Indeed, were it were not for the fact that most BIOS software will not boot without a video card, such cards would be unnecessary on the majority of Beowulf nodes. Video cards are available with either PCI or AGP connections.

Network interface controller — an interface that provide communication access to the node's external environment. One or more such interfaces couple the node to the Beowulf's system area network. A second network interface card (not shown) on a worldly node can provide the link between the entire Beowulf machine and the local area network that connects it to other resources in the user's environment, such as file servers, printers, terminals, and the Internet.

Power supply — not part of the logical system, but an important component to the overall operation. It provides regulated output voltages of 5 volts, −5 volts, 12 volts, and −12 volts to support system operation. Power supplies are rated in watts and have a general range of between 200 and 400 watts per node.

Cooling systems — typically a fan mounted on the CPU carrier itself, for dissipating heat from the processor. Other fans cool the rest of a node. Because fans are mechanical devices, they are among the most likely components to fail in a Beowulf cluster.

3.2   Processors

The microprocessor is the critical computational component of the PC-based node and Beowulf-class systems. In the seven-year period since the first Beowulf was completed in early 1994, central processing unit (CPU) clock speed has increased by a factor of 16. More impressive is the single-node floating-point performance sustained on scientific and engineering problems which has improved by two orders of magnitude during the same period. A single PC today outperforms the entire 16-processor first-generation Beowulf of 1994.

With the proliferation of Linux ports to a wide array of processors, Beowulf-like clusters are being assembled with almost every conceivable processor type. Primary attention has been given to Intel processors and their binary compatible siblings from AMD. The Compaq Alpha family of processors has also been effectively applied in this arena. Compaq has recently announced that development of the Alpha family will continue only through 2003, with Compaq contributing the Alpha technology to the development of future Intel IA64 processors.

This section presents a brief description of the most likely candidates of microprocessors for future Beowulf-class systems. The choice is constrained by three factors: performance, cost, and software compatibility. Raw performance is important to building effective medium- and high-end parallel systems. To build an effective parallel computer, you should start with the best uniprocessor. Of course, this tendency must be tempered by cost. The overall price/performance ratio for your favorite application is probably the most important consideration. The highest performance processor at any point in time rarely has the best price/performance ratio. Usually it is the processor one generation or one-half generation behind the cutting edge that is available with the most attractive ratio of price to performance. Recently, however, the Compaq Alpha has delivered both best performance and best price/performance for many applications. The third factor of software compatibility is an important practical consideration. If a stable software environment is not available for a particular processor family, even if it is a technical pacesetter, it is probably inappropriate for Beowulf. Fortunately, Linux is now available on every viable microprocessor family, and this should continue to be the case into the foreseeable future. Some key features of current processors are summarized in Table 3.1.

3.2.1 Intel Pentium Family

The Pentium 4 implements the IA32 instruction set but uses an internal architecture that diverges substantially from the old P6 architecture. The internal architecture is geared for high clock speeds; it produces less computing power per clock cycle but is capable of extremely high frequencies.

The Pentium III is based on the older Pentium Pro architecture. It is a minor upgrade from the Pentium II; it includes another optimized instruction set called SSE for three-dimensional instructions and has moved the L2 cache onto the chip, making it synchronized with the processor's clock. The Pentium III can be used within an SMP node with two processors; a more expensive variant, the Pentium III Xeon, can be used in four-processor SMP nodes.

3.2.2 AMD Athlon

The AMD Athlon platform is similar to the Pentium III in its processor architecture but similar to the Compaq Alpha in its bus architecture. It has two large 64 KByte L1 caches and a 256 KByte L2 cache that runs at the processor's clock speed. The

Chip	Vendor	Speed (MHz)	L1 Cache Size I/D (KBytes)	L2 Cache Size (KBytes)
Pentium III	Intel	1000	16K/16K	256K
Pentium 4	Intel	1700	12K/8K	256K
Itanium	Intel	800	16K/16K	96K
Athlon	AMD	1330	64K/64K	256K
Alpha 21264B	Compaq	833	64K	64K

Table 3.1
Key features of selected processors, mid-2001.

performance is a little ahead of the Pentium III in general, but either can be faster (at the same clock frequency) depending on the application. The Athlon supports dual-processor SMP nodes.

3.2.3   Compaq Alpha 21264

The Compaq Alpha processor is a true 64-bit architecture. For many years, the Alpha held the lead in many benchmarks, including the SPEC benchmarks, and was used in many of the fastest supercomputers, including the Cray T3D and T3E, as well as the Compaq SC family.

The Alpha uses a Reduced Instruction Set Computer (RISC) architecture, distinguishing it from Intel's Pentium processors. RISC designs, which have dominated the workstation market of the past decade, eschew complex instructions and addressing modes, resulting in simpler processors running at higher clock rates, but executing somewhat more instructions to complete the same task.

3.2.4   IA64

The IA64 is Intel's first 64-bit architecture. This is an all-new design, with a new instruction set, new cache design, and new floating-point processor design. With clock rates approaching 1 GHz and multiway floating-point instruction issue, Itanium should be the first implementation to provide between 1 and 2 Gflops peak performance. The first systems with the Itanium processor were released in the middle of 2001 and have delivered impressive results. For example, the HP Server rx4610, using a single 800 MHz Itanium, delivered a SPECfp2000 of 701, comparable to recent Alpha-based systems. The IA64 architecture does, however, require significant help from the compiler to exploit what Intel calls EPIC (explicitly parallel instruction computing).

3.3   Motherboard

The motherboard is a printed circuit board that contains most of the active electronic components of the PC node and their interconnection. The motherboard provides the logical and physical infrastructure for integrating the subsystems of the Beowulf PC node and determines the set of components that may be used. The motherboard defines the functionality of the node, the range of performance that can be exploited, the maximum capacities of its storage, and the number of subsystems that can be interconnected. With the exception of the microprocessor itself, the selection of the motherboard is the most important decision in determining the qualities of the PC node to be used as the building block of the Beowulf-class system. It is certainly the single most obvious piece of the Beowulf node other than the case or packaging in which it is enclosed.

While the motherboard may not be the most interesting aspect of a computer, it is, in fact, a critical component. Assembling a Beowulf node primarily involves the insertion of modules into their respective interface sockets, plugging power and signal cables into their ports, and placing configuration jumpers across the designated posts. The troubleshooting of nonfunctioning systems begins with verification of these same elements associated with the motherboard.

The purpose of the motherboard is to integrate all of the electronics of the node in a robust and configurable package. Sockets and connectors on the motherboard include the following:

- Microprocessor(s)
- Memory
- Peripheral controllers on the PCI bus
- AGP port
- Floppy disk cables
- EIDE cables for hard disk and CD-ROM
- Power
- Front panel LEDs, speakers, switches, etc.
- External I/O for mouse, keyboard, joystick, serial line, USB, etc.

Other chips on the motherboard provide

- the system bus that links the processor(s) to memory,
- the interface between the peripheral buses and the system bus, and
- programmable read-only memory (PROM) containing the BIOS software.

The motherboard restricts as well as enables functionality. In selecting a motherboard as the basis for a Beowulf node, several requirements for its use should be considered, including

- processor family,
- processor clock speed,
- number of processors,
- memory capacity,
- memory type,
- disk interface,
- required interface slots, and
- number of interface buses (32- and 64-bit PCI).

Currently the choice of processor is likely to be the Intel Pentium III, AMD Athlon, or the Compaq Alpha 21264B. More processors, including native 64-bit processors, will continue to be released. In most cases, a different motherboard is required for each choice. Clock speeds for processors of interest range from 733 MHz to almost 2 GHz, and the selected motherboard must support the desired speed. Motherboards containing multiple processors in symmetric multiprocessor configurations are available, adding to the diversity of choices. Nodes for compute intensive problems often require large memory capacity with high bandwidth. Motherboards have a limited number of memory slots, and memory modules have a maximum size. Together, these will determine the memory capacity of your system. Memory bandwidth is a product of the width and speed of the system memory bus.

Several types of memory are available, including conventional DRAM, EDO RAM (extended data output RAM), SDRAM (synchronous DRAM), and RDRAM (Rambus DRAM). The choice of memory type depends on your application needs. While RDRAM currently provides the highest bandwidth, other types of memory, such as SDRAM and DDR SDRAM (double data rate SDRAM) can provide adequate bandwidth at a significantly reduced cost. The two disk interfaces in common use are EIDE and SCSI. Both are good with the former somewhat cheaper and the latter slightly faster under certain conditions. Most motherboards come with EIDE interfaces built in, and some include an SCSI interface as well, which can be convenient and cost effective if you choose to use SCSI. On the other hand, separate SCSI controllers may offer more flexibility and options. Motherboards have a fixed number of PCI slots, and it is important to select one with enough slots to meet your needs. This is rarely a consideration in Beowulf compute nodes but can become an issue in a system providing I/O services.

3.4 Memory

The memory system of a personal computer stores the data upon which the processor operates. We would like a memory system to be fast, cheap, and large, but available components can simultaneously deliver only two (any two) of the three. Modern memory systems use a hierarchy of components implemented with different technologies that together, under favorable conditions, achieve all three. When purchasing a computer system, you must select the size and type of memory to be used. This section provides some background to help with that choice.

3.4.1 Memory Capacity

Along with processor speed, memory capacity has grown at a phenomenal rate, quadrupling in size approximately every three years. Prices for RAM have continued to decline and now are about ten cents per megabyte (a little more for higher-speed/capacity SDRAMs). A general principle is that faster processors require more memory. With increasingly sophisticated and demanding operating systems, user interfaces, and advanced applications such as multimedia, there is demand for ever-increasing memory capacity. As a result of both demand and availability, the size of memory in Beowulf-class systems has progressively expanded. Today, a typical Beowulf requires at least 256 MBytes of main memory, and this can be expected to grow to 2 GBytes within the next two to three years.

3.4.2 Memory Speed

In addition to the capacity of memory, the memory speed can significantly affect the overall behavior and performance of a Beowulf node. Speed may be judged by the latency of memory access time and the throughput of data provided per unit time. While capacities have steadily increased, access times have progressed only slowly. However, new modes of interfacing memory technology to the processor managed system bus have significantly increased overall throughput of memory systems. This increase is due to the fact that the memory bandwidth internal to the memory chip is far greater than that delivered to the system bus at its pins. Significant advances in delivering these internal acquired bits to the system bus in rapid succession have been manifest in such memory types as EDO-DRAM, SDRAM, and Rambus DRAM. Further improvement to the apparent performance of the entire memory system as viewed by the processor comes from mixing small memories of fast technology with high-capacity memory of slower technology.

3.4.3   Memory Types

Semiconductor memory is available in two fundamental types. Static random access memory (SRAM) is high speed but moderate density, while dynamic random access memory (DRAM) provides high-density storage but operates more slowly. Each plays an important role in the memory system of the Beowulf node.

SRAM   is implemented from bit cells fabricated as multitransistor flipflop circuits. These active circuits can switch state and be accessed quickly. They are not as high density as are DRAMs and consume substantially more power. They are reserved for those parts of the system principally requiring high speed and are employed regularly in L1 and L2 caches. Current-generation processors usually include SRAMs directly on the processor chip. L2 caches may be installed on the motherboard of the system or included as part of the processor module.

Earlier SRAM was asynchronous (ASRAM) and provided access times of between 12 and 20 nanoseconds. Motherboards operating up to 66 MHz or better use synchronous burst SRAM (SBSRAM) providing access times on the order of ten nanoseconds.

DRAM   is implemented from bit cells fabricated as a capacitor and a single bypass transistor. The capacitor stores a charge passively. The associated switching transistor deposits the state of the capacitor's charge on the chip's internal memory bus when the cell is addressed. Unlike SRAM, reading a DRAM cell is destructive, so after a bit is accessed, the charged state has to be restored by recharging the capacitor to its former condition. As a consequence, DRAM can have a shorter access time (the time taken to read a cell) than cycle time (the time until the same cell may be accessed again). Also, isolation of the cell's storage capacitor is imperfect and the charge leaks away, requiring it to be refreshed (rewritten) every few milliseconds. Finally, because the capacitor is a passive, nonamplifying device, it takes longer to access a DRAM than an SRAM cell. However, the benefits are substantial. DRAM density can exceed ten times that of SRAM, and its power consumption is much lower. Also, new techniques for moving data from the DRAM internal memory row buffers to the system bus have narrowed the gap in terms of memory bandwidth between DRAM and SRAM. As a result, main memory for all Beowulf nodes is provided by DRAM in any one of its many forms.

Of the many forms of DRAM, the two most likely to be encountered in Beowulf nodes are EDO DRAM and SDRAM. Both are intended to increase memory throughput. EDO DRAM provides a modified internal buffering scheme that maintains data at the output pins longer than conventional DRAM, improving memory data transfer rates. While many current motherboards support EDO DRAM, the higher-speed systems likely to be used as Beowulf nodes in the immediate future will employ SDRAM instead. SDRAM is a significant advance in memory interface design. It supports a pipeline burst mode that permits a second access cycle to begin before the previous one has completed. While one cycle is putting output data on the bus, the address for the next access cycle is simultaneously applied to the memory. Effective access speeds of 10 nanoseconds can be achieved with systems using a 100 MHz systems bus; such memory is labeled PC100 SDRAM. Faster versions are available, including PC133 SDRAM.

Other, even higher-performance forms of DRAM memory are appearing. Two of the most important are Rambus DRAM and DDR SDRAM. These may be described as "PC1600" or "PC2100" memory. These are not 16 or 21 times as fast as PC100; in these cases, the number refers to the peak transfer rate (in Mbps) rather than the system bus clock speed. It is important to match both the memory type (e.g., SDRAM or RDRAM) and the system bus speed (e.g., PC133) to the motherboard.

3.4.4 Memory Hierarchy and Caches

The modern memory system is a hierarchy of memory types. Figure 3.2 shows a typical memory hierarchy. Near the processor at the top of the memory system are the high-speed Level-1 (L1) caches. Usually a separate cache is used for data and instructions for high bandwidth to load both data and instructions into the processor on the same cycle. The principal requirement is to deliver the data and instruction words needed for processing on every processor cycle. These memories run fast and hot, are relatively expensive, and now often incorporated directly on the processor chip. For these reasons, they tend to be very small, with a typical size of 16 KBytes. Because L1 caches are so small and the main memory requires long access times, modern architectures usually include a second-level (L2) cache to hold both data and instructions. Access time to acquire a block of L2 data may take several processor cycles. A typical L2 cache size is 256 KBytes. Some systems add large external caches (either L2 or L3) with sizes of up to 8 MBytes.

Cache memory is usually implemented in SRAM technology, which is fast (a few nanoseconds) but relatively low density. Only when a datum required by the processor is not in cache does the processor directly access the main memory. Main memory is implemented in one of the DRAM technologies. Beowulf nodes will often include between 256 MBytes and 512 MBytes of SDRAM memory.

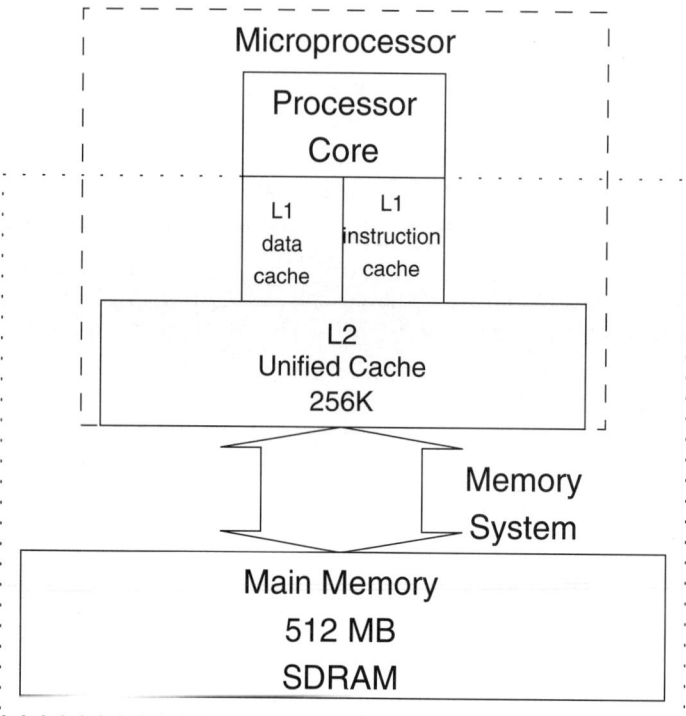

Figure 3.2
A node memory hierarchy with sizes typical of Beowulf nodes in 2001.

3.4.5 Package Styles

The packaging of memory has evolved along with the personal computers in which they were installed and has converged on a few industrywide standards. Dual Inline Memory Modules (DIMMs) are the primary means of packaging DRAMs, and most modern motherboards use one or more of these forms. The most common form factors are 168-pin and 184-pin DIMMs.

3.5 BIOS

Even with effective industrywide standardization, hardware components will differ in detail. In order to avoid the necessity of customizing a different operating system for each new hardware system, a set of low-level service routines is provided, incorporated into read-only memory on the motherboard. This basic I/O system

(BIOS) software is a logical interface to the hardware, giving a layer of abstraction that facilitates and makes robust higher-level support software. Besides the system BIOS that is hardwired to the motherboard, additional BIOS ROMs may be provided with specific hardware peripherals. These include the video BIOS, the drive controller BIOS, the network interface controller BIOS, and the SCSI drive controller BIOS. The BIOS contains a large number of small routines organized in three groups: startup or POST (for power-on self-test), setup, and system services.

The POST startup BIOS routines manage initialization activities, including running diagnostics, setting up the motherboard chip set, organizing scratchpad memory for the BIOS data area (BDA), identifying optional equipment and their respective BIOS ROMs, and then bootstrapping the operating system. The CMOS (complementary metal oxide semiconductor) setup routine provides access to the system configuration information, which is stored in a small CMOS RAM. The system services routines are called through interrupts directly from hardware on the motherboard, from the processor itself, or from software. They allow access to low-level services provided by the system including the CPU, memory, motherboard chip set, integrated drive electronics, PCI, USB, boot drives, plug-n-play capability, and power control interfaces.

3.6   Secondary Storage

With the exception of the BIOS ROM, all information in memory is lost during power cycling except for that provided by a set of external (to the motherboard) devices that fall under the category of secondary storage. Of these, disk drives, floppy drives, and CD-ROM drives are most frequently found on Beowulf nodes. Disk and floppy drives are spinning magnetic media, while CD-ROM drives (which are also spinning media) use optical storage to hold approximately 650 MBytes of data. The newer DVD technology is replacing CD-ROMs with greater storage capacity. Besides persistence of storage, secondary storage is characterized by very high capacity and low cost per bit. While DRAM may be purchased at about ten cents per megabyte, disk storage costs less than half a cent per megabyte, and the price continues to fall. For the particular case of Beowulf, these three modes of secondary storage play very different roles.

CD-ROMs provide an easy means of installing large software systems but are used for little else. Even for this purpose, only one or two nodes in a system are likely to include a CD-ROM drive because installation of software on most of the nodes is performed over the system area network.

Floppy discs are fragile and slow and don't hold very much data (about 1.44 MBytes). They would be useless except that they were the primary means of persistent storage on early PCs, and PC designers have maintained backward compatibility that allows systems to boot from a program located on floppy disk. Occasionally, something goes terribly wrong with a node (due either to human or to system error), and it is necessary to restore the system from scratch. A floppy drive and an appropriate "boot floppy" can make this a quick, painless, and trouble-free procedure. Although other means of recovery are possible, the small price of about $15 per node for a floppy drive is well worth the investment.

The hard drive serves three primary purposes. It maintains copies of system wide programs and data so that these do not have to be repeatedly acquired over the network. It provides a large buffer space to hold very large application datasets. And it provides storage space for demand paging as part of the virtual memory management system. When the user or system memory demands exceed the available primary memory, page blocks can be automatically migrated to hard disk, making room in memory for other information to be stored.

Between the hard disk drive and the motherboard are two dominant interface types: EIDE and SCSI. The earlier IDE interface evolved from the PC industry, while SCSI was a product of the workstation and server industry. Today, both are available. In the past, SCSI performance and cost were both significantly greater than those of IDE. The EIDE standard closed the performance gap a few years ago, but the price difference still exists. Perhaps equally important is that many motherboards now include EIDE interfaces as integral components so that no separate control card is required to be purchased or to take up a PCI socket. SCSI drive capacities can run a little higher than IDE drives, a factor that may be important for some installations. Several different SCSI standards exist, including Wide, UltraWide, SCSI-2, and SCSI-3. Systems are usually downwards compatible, but it is safest to match the drive's capabilities with that of your SCSI controller. Beowulf-class systems have been implemented with both types, and your needs or preferences should dictate your choice. (We have continued to rely on EIDE drives because of their lower cost.)

The primary performance characteristic of a hard drive is its capacity. EIDE hard drives with 80 GByte capacities are available for under $300, and 40 GByte drives cost around $100. Also of interest is the rotation speed, measured in revolutions per minute, which governs how quickly data can be accessed. The fastest rotation speeds are found on SCSI drives, and are now around 15000 rpm and deliver transfer rates in excess of 50 MBytes per second.

3.7   PCI Bus

While the PC motherboard determines many of the attributes of the PC node, it also provides a means for user-defined configuration through the Peripheral Component Interconnect. This interface is incorporated as part of virtually every modern motherboard, providing a widely recognized standard for designing separate functional units. PCI is replacing the ISA and EISA buses as the principal means of adding peripherals to personal computers.

The PCI standard permits rapid data transfer of 132 MBytes per second peak using a 33 MHz clock and 32-bit data path. A 64-bit extension is defined, enabling peak throughput of 264 MBytes per second when used. A extension with a bus clock rate of 66 MHz provides a peak transfer bandwidth of 528 MBytes per second. A new version, PCI-X, is expected toward the end of 2001.

The PCI bus permits direct interconnection between any pair of PCI devices, between a PCI device and the system memory, or between the system processor and the PCI devices. PCI supports multiple bus masters, allowing any PCI device to take ownership of the bus and permitting (among other things) direct memory access transfers without processor intervention. Arbitration among the pending PCI masters for the next transfer action can be overlapped with the current PCI bus operation, thereby hiding the arbitration latency and ensuring high sustained bus throughput.

High throughput is enabled by a process called linear burst transfer. A block of data being sent from one device to another on the PCI bus is moved without having to send the address of each word of data. Instead, the length of the block is specified along with the initial address of the location where the block is to be moved. Each time a word is received, the accepting unit increments a local address register in preparation for the next word of the block. PCI bus transfers can be conducted concurrently with operation of the processor and its system bus to avoid processor delays caused by PCI operation.

Although bus loading limits the number of PCI sockets to three or four, each connected board can logically represent as many as eight separate PCI functions for a total of 32. Up to 256 PCI buses can be incorporated into one system, although rarely are more than two present.

The PCI standard includes complete bit-level specification of configuration registers. This makes possible the automatic configuration of connected peripheral devices for plug-n-play reconfigurability.

3.8   Example of a Beowulf Node

The majority of Beowulfs (over five generations of systems in the past seven years) have employed microprocessors from Intel or AMD. This is because they have been among the least expensive systems to build, the system architectures are open providing a wealth of component choices, and the Linux operating system was first available on them. While not the fastest processors in peak performance, their overall capability has been good, and their price/performance ratios are excellent. The most recent microprocessors in this family and their motherboards support clock speeds of over 1 GHz.

The following table shows a snapshot of current costs for an AMD Athlon-based node and illustrates the amazing value of commodity components. These prices were taken from a variety of sources, including online retailers and Web pages about recent Beowulf clusters. We note that, as discussed earlier, a CD-ROM is not included in the list because it is assumed that system installation will be performed over the network. A floppy drive is included to facilitate initial installation and crash recovery. Moreover, since the BIOS requires a video card to boot, a very inexpensive one is included on every system.

Many other choices exist, of course, and the products of other vendors in many cases are as worthy of consideration as the ones listed here.

Processor	AMD Athlon 1GHz	$102
Processor Fan		$8.50
Motherboard	Generic	$117.50
Memory	512 MB PC100 SDRAM	$74
Hard Disk	40GB	$141
Floppy Disk	Sony 1.44MB	$13.50
Network Interface Controller	100Mb/s Ethernet	$16.50
Video Card	Generic VGA	$25
Package	Generic tower case with power supply and cables	$58
Total		$556

3.9   Boxes, Shelves, Piles, and Racks

A review of Beowulf hardware would be incomplete without some mention of the technology used to physically support (i.e., keep it off the floor) a Beowulf system. Packaging is an important engineering domain that can significantly influence the cost and practical aspects of Beowulf implementation and operation. Packaging of Beowulfs has taken two paths: the minimalist "lots of boxes on shelves" strategy, captured so well by the acronym of the NIH LOBOS system, and the "looks count" strategy, adopted by several projects including the Hive system at NASA Goddard Space Flight Center and the Japanese Real World Computing Initiative. The minimalist approach was driven by more than laziness. It is certainly the most economical approach and is remarkably reliable as well. This is due to the same economies of scale that enable the other low-cost, high-reliability subsystems in Beowulf. In the minimalist approach, individual nodes are packaged in exactly the same "towers" that are found deskside in homes and offices. These towers incorporate power supplies, fan cooling, and cabling and cost less than a hundred dollars. Towers provide uniform configuration, standardized interface cabling, effective cooling, and a structurally robust component mounting framework but are flexible enough to support a variety of internal node configurations. Industrial-grade shelving, usually of steel framework and particle board shelves, is strong, readily available, easily assembled, and inexpensive. It is also flexible, extensible, and easily reconfigured. You can find it at your nearest home and garden center.

When assembling such a system, care should be taken to design tidy power distribution and networking wire runs. Extension cords and power strips work fine but should be physically attached to the shelving with screws or wire-ties so that the system does not become an unmaintainable mess. Similar considerations apply to the Ethernet cables. Labeling cables so the ends can be identified without laboriously tracing the entire run can save hours of headache.

Different approaches are possible for video and keyboard cables. In our systems, most nodes do not have dedicated keyboard and video cables. Instead, we manually attach cables to nodes in the very rare circumstances when necessary maintenance cannot be carried out remotely. Linux's powerful networking capabilities makes it unnecessary to maintain constant console video and keyboard access to each and every node of the system.

Rack mounting is considerably more expensive but offers the possibility of much higher physical densities. New motherboards with rack-mountable form factors that incorporate a Fast Ethernet controller, SCSI controller, and video controller offer the possibility of building Beowulf nodes that can be packaged very tightly because they don't require additional daughter cards. These systems probably will be important in the future, as larger Beowulf systems are deployed and machine room space becomes a major consideration.

3.10   Node Assembly

We conclude this chapter with a checklist for building a Beowulf node. Building Beowulf nodes from component parts may not be the right choice for everyone. Some will feel more comfortable with systems purchased from a system integrator, or they simply won't have the manpower or space for in-house assembly. Nevertheless, the cost should not be overlooked; a node can be several hundred dollars. You should carefully weigh the luxury of having someone else wield the screwdriver vs. owning 25 percent more computer power. Keep in mind that cables often come loose in shipping, and there is no guarantee that the preassembled system will not require as much or more on-site troubleshooting as the homemade system.

Although targeted at the reader who is building a Beowulf node from parts, this checklist will also be useful to those who purchase preassembled systems. Over the lifetime of the Beowulf system, technology advances will probably motivate upgrades in such things as memory capacity, disk storage, or improved networking. There is also the unavoidable problem of occasional maintenance. Yes, once in a while, something breaks. Usually it is a fan, a memory module, a power supply, or a disk drive, in that order of likelihood. More often than not, such a break will occur in the first few weeks of operation. With hundreds of operational nodes in a large Beowulf, some parts replacement will be required. The checklist below will get you started if you decide to replace parts of a malfunctioning node.

To many, the list below will appear obvious, but, in fact, experience has shown that a comprehensive list of steps is not only convenient but likely to simplify the task and aid in getting a system working the first time. Many sites have put together such procedures, and we offer the one used at Caltech as a helpful example.

Before you initiate the actual assembly, it helps to get organized. Five minutes of preparation can save half an hour during the process. If you're assembling a Beowulf, you will probably build more than one unit at one time, and the preparation phase is amortized over the number of units built.

- Collect and organize the small set of tools you will be using:
  - #2 Phillips head screwdriver
  - Antistatic wrist strap
  - Antistatic mat on which to place assembly
  - Needlenose pliers
  - 1/8-inch blade flat blade screwdriver
  - Small high-intensity flashlight

- Organize all parts to be assembled. If more than one unit is to be built, collect like parts together bin-style.
- Provide sufficient flat space for assembly, including room for keyboard, mouse, and monitor used for initial check-out.
- Work in a well-lighted environment.
- Follow the same order of tasks in assembling all units; routine leads to reliability.
- Have a checklist, like this one, handy, even if it is used only as a reference.
- When first opening a case, collect screws and other small items in separate containers.
- Keep food and drink on another table to avoid the inevitable accident.

After you have done one or two systems, the process becomes much quicker. We find that we can assemble nodes in well under an hour once we become familiar with the idiosyncrasies of any particular configuration.

Many of the instructions below may not apply in every case. Included are directions for such subassemblies as monitors, keyboards, and sound cards that rarely show up in the majority of Beowulf nodes. Usually, however, at least one such node is more heavily equipped to support user interface, operations support, and external connections for the rest of the system.

In a number of cases, the specific action is highly dependent on the subsystems being included. Only the documentation for that unit can describe exactly what actions are to be performed. For example, every motherboard will have a different set and positioning of jumpers, although many of the modern boards are reducing or almost eliminating these. In these instances, all we can say is: "do the right thing," but we still indicate in general terms the class of action to take place.

3.10.1 Motherboard Preassembly

- Set every jumper on the motherboard properly.
- Look through your motherboard manual and verify every setting, since the default may not work for your CPU, memory, or cache configuration.
- Locate every jumper and connector: floppy, hard drive, PS/2, COM port, LPT port, sound connectors, speaker connector, hard disk LED, power LED, reset switch, keyboard lock switch, and so forth.
- Install the CPU.
  - Processors are designed so that they can only be inserted correctly. Don't force.
  - Whatever the chip, match the notched corner of the CPU with the notched corner of the socket.

- When using a ZIF socket, lift the handle 90 degrees, insert the CPU, and then return the handle back to its locked position.
- Install the memory.
  - Main memory DIMM. Note pin 1 on the DIMM, and find the pin 1 mark on the motherboard. It is difficult to install 164-pin DIMMs incorrectly, but it is possible. Begin by placing the DIMM at a 45 degree angle to the socket of bank 0. The DIMM will be angled toward the rest of the DIMM sockets (and away from any DIMMs previously installed). Insert the DIMM firmly into the socket; then rotate the DIMM until it sits perpendicular to the motherboard and the two clips on each edge have snapped around the little circuit board. There may or may not be a "snap," but you should verify that the two clips are holding the DIMM fast and that it doesn't jiggle in the socket. Repeat this until you fill one, two, or more banks.
  - Cache memory (if so equipped). Some older units may have L2 caches on the motherboard, while newer processors include them within the processor module. Cache memory may be DIMM or SIMM; in any case, install it now.

3.10.2   The Case

- Open the case, remove all the internal drive bays, and locate all the connectors: speaker, hard disk LED, power LED, reset switch, keyboard lock switch, mother board power, peripheral power, and so forth.
- Mount the motherboard in the case.
  - ATX-style cases use only screws to mount the motherboard, and it is very straightforward.
- Plug in the keyboard, and see whether it fits.
- Plug in an adapter card, and see whether it fits.
- Start connecting the case cables to the motherboard.
  - Pull out floppy cables, hard disk cables, PS/2 mouse cable, and lights. Line up each pin 1 to the red side of cables.
  - Install the speaker. It usually is a 4-pin connector with two wires (one red, one black, which can be installed either way on the motherboard).
  - If your case has holes for COM ports and LPT ports, punch these out, and save a card slot by unscrewing the connectors that came on the slot-filler strip of metal, removing the connector, and mounting it directly on the case.
  - Attach power cables to the motherboard.
    - ATX-style cases have only one power connector, which is keyed to only fit one way.

- The AT-style power connector comes in two pieces and must be connected properly. The black wires *must be placed together* when they are plugged into the motherboard.
- Ensure that the CPU cooling fan is connected to the power supply. This is usually a 4-pin male connector that goes to one of the power supply connectors.

3.10.3 Minimal Peripherals

- Floppy disk drive
  - Mechanical
    - It may be necessary to reinstall the floppy mounting bay (if it was taken out previously).
    - The floppy drive must protrude from the front of the case. Take off one of the 3.5 inch plastic filler panels from the front of the case. Then slide the floppy drive in from the front until the front of the drive is flush with the front of the case. Using two small screws that are supplied with the case, attach the floppy drive's left side. If the floppy drive bay is detachable, remove the bay with the floppy half installed, and with the drive bay out, install the screws for the right side.
    - If the drive bay is going to contain hard disks in addition to floppy drives, leave the drive bay out for now, and go to the hard disk installation section before putting the drive bay back into the case.
  - Electrical
    - The floppy disk needs two connections: one to the power supply, and one to the motherboard or floppy controller. The power supply connector is shaped to prevent you from getting it backwards.
    - Some floppy power connectors are smaller than the standard connector, and most power supplies come with one of these plugs. These connectors can be installed in only one way.
    - For data, a flat ribbon cable is needed. It is gray with 34 conductors and a red stripe to indicate pin 1. One end of the cable will usually have a twist in it. The twisted portion connects to a second floppy drive (drive B:). The end farthest from the twist connects to the motherboard or floppy controller.
- VGA card installation
  - If the motherboard has an integrated video adapter, skip the next step.
  - Plug the VGA card into the appropriate slot, depending on the type of card purchased (PCI slot for a PCI card, ISA slot for an ISA card).
  - Screw the top of the metal bracket that is attached to the adapter into the case, using one of the screws supplied with the case.

- Monitor
  - Plug the monitor into a wall power outlet.
  - Plug the video input plug, which is a 15-pin connector, into the back of the video card.

3.10.4   Booting the System

Setup involves configuring the motherboard's components, peripherals, and controllers. The setup program is usually in ROM and can be run by pressing a certain key during POST. Check the CMOS settings using the setup program before booting for the first time. If you make changes, you will need to exit setup and save changes to CMOS for them to take effect. You will be able to change the date and time kept by the real time clock. Memory configuration such as shadow RAM and read/write wait states can be changed from their defaults. IDE hard disks can be detected and configured. Boot sequence and floppy drives can be configured and swapped. PCI cards and even ISA cards can be configured, and plug-n-play disabled (which should be done if running a non-Windows operating system). ISA bus speed can be changed and ports can be enabled or disabled.

IDE disks are almost always configured as auto detect or user-defined type. Use shadow video unless you have problems. Shadow the ROM of your network interface card (NIC) or SCSI card for better speed. For better speed and if you have EDO memory, you can usually use the most aggressive memory settings—just try it out before you stick with it to avoid corrupting data files.

Minimum requirements for booting the system are as follows:

- A bootable floppy disk
- Motherboard with CPU and memory installed
- Video card on the motherboard
- Floppy drive with one cable connected to it and power to it
- Monitor plugged into the wall and the video card
- Keyboard attached

To boot the system, proceed as follows:

- Making sure that the power switch is off, attach a power cord from the case to the wall.
- Turn on the monitor.
- Turn on the power to the PC, and get ready to shut it off if you see, hear, or smell any problems.
- Look for signs that all is working properly:

- The speaker may make clicks or beeps.
- The monitor should fire up and show something.
- Make sure all of the memory counts.
- The floppy drive light should come on one time during POST.

To set up the system, proceed as follows:

- Enter setup by hitting the appropriate key (delete, F1, F10, Esc, or whatever the motherboard manual specifies), and check the CMOS settings.
- Change the CMOS settings, and see whether the computer will remember them.
- Update the date and time.
- View every setup screen, and look at each of the settings.
- Make sure the first boot device is set to be the floppy drive.
- If you have EDO RAM, optimize the memory settings (if you wish) or make any other changes you see fit.
- Save your changes and reboot; rerun setup, and make sure the updates were made.
- Save any changes after the rerun. Make sure the bootable floppy is in the drive, and let it try to boot from the floppy. If it does not boot, or there is some error message—or nothing—on the screen, go to the troubleshooting section (Section 3.10.6).

3.10.5   Installing the Other Components

If your PC boots and runs setup, you're almost done. Now you can install all of the other components. First, unplug your PC and wait a few minutes. You should begin to mount the drives if you have not already done so.

IDE Hard disk installation

- Mechanical. This is similar to the floppy installation above, with the exception that the drive will not be visible from outside of the case.
- Electrical
  - Most motherboard BIOS systems today can read the IDE drive's specifications and automatically configure them. If it does not, you will have to get the drive's parameters (usually written on the drive), which include number of cylinders, number of heads, and number of sectors per track, and enter them in the drive parameter table in the CMOS setup.
  - A ribbon cable and power connector attach to each hard disk. The power cable has four wires in it and is keyed so it cannot be installed incorrectly.

- The documentation that came with the hard disk indicates how the jumpers are set, if you are installing one disk and no other IDE device, the jumpers can usually be removed. If you are installing more than one disk, decide which disk will be booted. The boot disk should go on the primary hard disk controller. Move the jumper(s) on the hard disk to make it a MASTER or PRIMARY. Many newer hard disks will use pins labeled MA, SL, and CS; you will jumper the MA pins. The second hard disk or CD-ROM will be configured as a SLAVE or SECONDARY drive. You will jumper the SL pins on this device. Use your drive's manual or call the manufacturer's 800 number for proper jumper settings. If the CD-ROM drive will be alone on its own controller, follow the manufacturer's directions (usually it is okay to jumper it as a slave). Once jumpered properly, the drives can be connected with the 18-inch 40-pin ribbon cables and powered up. Pin 1 usually goes next to the power connector.

SCSI hard disk installation

- Mechanical. Follow the floppy installation above, with the exception that the drive will not be visible from outside of the case.
- Electrical
  - Unless the motherboard has the SCSI controller built in, the BIOS will not read a SCSI drive, and the drive table should be set up with "not installed."
  - A ribbon cable and power connector attach to each hard disk. The power cable has four wires in it and is keyed so it cannot be installed incorrectly. The other end of the ribbon cable plugs into the SCSI controller itself.
  - The documentation that came with the hard disk explains how the jumpers are set. If you are installing one disk and no other SCSI devices, the jumpers can usually be removed so that the disk will be set to ID 0. Each SCSI device on the chain (ribbon cable) must have its own unique ID number, usually 0 through 7, with 7 being reserved for the controller itself.
  - The last physical device on the cable has to be terminated, depending on the device, either with a jumper or with some type of resistor networks that are plugged in. This is very important.

NIC installation

- This is similar to the VGA card installation described previously. If any jumpers are to be set, do that now, and write the settings down. Read the installation manual that came with the card.

Sound card installation

• See NIC installation above. If you are setting jumpers, make sure you don't set two cards to the same resource (interrupt request, direct memory access, or port address). Keep all settings distinct.

At this point, you are ready to begin installing the operating system. Don't forget to connect the mouse and external speakers and to make a network hookup, if you have these options installed.

3.10.6   Troubleshooting

Each time you boot, you should connect at least the following four components to your PC:

• Speaker
• Keyboard
• Floppy drive
• Monitor

What should a normal boot look and sound like?

• First, LEDs will illuminate everywhere—the motherboard, the hard disks, the floppy drive, the case, the NIC, the printer, the CD-ROM, the speakers, the monitor, and the keyboard.
• The hard disks usually spin up, although some disks, especially SCSIs, may wait for a cue from the controller or may simply wait a fixed amount of time to begin spinning to prevent a large power surge during boot.
• The P/S and CPU fans will start to spin.
• The first thing displayed on the monitor usually will be either memory counting or a video card BIOS display.
• During the memory count, the PC speaker may click.
• When the memory is done counting, the floppy disk often screeches as its LED comes on (called floppy seek).
• The monitor may have messages from the BIOS, including BIOS version, number of CPUs, a password prompt, and nonfatal error messages.
• The last part of the power-on self-test is often a chart that lists the components found during POST, such as CPU and speed, VGA card, serial ports, LPT ports, IDE hard disks, and floppy disks. If no system files are found, either on a bootable floppy or hard disk, you may get a message from the BIOS saying, "Insert Boot disk and press any key" or something similar. This is a nonfatal error, and you can put a bootable floppy in the drive and press a key.

If the above happens, you will know that your motherboard is at least capable of running the ROM's POST. The POST has many potential problems, most of which are nonfatal errors. Any consistent error, however, is a cause for concern. The fatal POST errors will normally generate no video, so you need to listen to the speaker and count beeps. The number of beeps and their length indicate codes for a technician to use in repairing the PC.

At this point, the POST is done, and the boot begins.

What should I do if there is no video or bad video during boot?

- Check the monitor's power and video connection.
- Try reseating the video card or putting it in a new socket (turn off the system first!).
- Make sure the speaker is connected, in case you are getting a fatal POST message that could have nothing to do with video.
- Swap out the video card and/or the monitor.

The two most notable and common POST messages are as follows:

- HDD (or FDD) controller error. Usually this is a cabling issue, such as a reversed connector.
- Disk drive 0 failure. You forgot power to the hard disk, or you've got the wrong drive set in CMOS (rerun setup). Also make sure the disk is properly connected to the controller.

What about floppy problems?

- If the light stays on continuously after boot, you probably have the connector on backwards.

If you are still experiencing problems, try the following:

- Check the cables or try someone else's cables.
- Recheck all the jumper settings on the motherboard.
- Remove secondary cache, or disable it in setup. This can fix many problems.
- Slow down the CPU: it may have been sold to you at the wrong speed.
- Replace SIMMs with known working ones.
- Replace the video card.
- Remove unnecessary components such as extra RAM, sound card, mouse, modem, SCSI card, extra hard disks, tape drives, NIC, or other controller card.
- Remove all hard disks, and try booting from floppy.
- Remove the motherboard from the case, and run it on a piece of cardboard. This will fix a problem caused by a motherboard grounded to the case.

4 Linux

Peter H. Beckman

Since the original AT&T and Berkeley Unix operating systems of the early 1970s, many variants of the operating system have been launched. Some have prospered, while others have fallen into obscurity. Have you ever heard of Concentrix or nX? Many customized Unix derivatives are no doubt still occupying obsolete Winchester drives and 8-inch floppies in the dusty storage rooms of businesses and laboratories, right there next to the paper tape readers and acoustic modem couplers. Even Microsoft tried its hand and sold a Unix back in 1980, when it released XENIX.

4.1 What Is Linux?

Simply put, Linux^{TM} is a flavor (clone) of the original Unix^{TM} operating systems. While Linux is relatively new on the operating system scene, arriving about two decades after Ken Thompson and Dennis Ritchie of AT&T presented the first Unix paper at a Purdue University symposium in 1973, it has rapidly become one of the most widely known and used Unix derivatives. Ever since Linus Torvalds, the creator of Linux, released it in October 1991, developers from all over the world have been improving, extending, and modifying the source code. Linus has remained the godfather of the Linux source code, ensuring that it does not get overwhelmed with useless features, code bloat, and bad programming. As a result, Linux has become so popular that International Data Corporation (IDC) reported that Linux was the fastest-growing server operating system in both 1999 and 2000 and, after Microsoft Windows, is the most-used server operating system.

4.1.1 Why Use Linux for a Beowulf?

Linux users tend to be some of the most fervent, inspired, and loyal computer users in the world—probably in the same league as Apple Macintosh users. Both groups of users are likely to rebut any criticism with a prolonged, sharp-tongued defense of the capabilities of their system. For scientific computational clusters, however, a cute penguin named Tux and lots of enthusiasm are insufficient; some pragmatism is required.

Linux is the most popular open source operating system in the world. Its success is the result of many factors, but its stability, maturity, and straightforward design have certainly been keys to its growth and market share. The stability and availability of Linux have also created a booming commercial marketplace for products, unmatched by any other open source operating system. Companies such as IBM, Fujitsu, NEC, Compaq, and Dell have all incorporated Linux into their business model, creating a marketplace around a distribution of kernel source code that is free. Other companies are simply using Linux because it makes practical business sense.

The enthusiastic backing of multibillion dollar companies is certainly a vote of confidence for Linux, but it is by no means sufficient for deciding to choose Linux. Probably the most important reason for using Linux to build a Beowulf is its flexibility. Because Linux is open source, it can easily be modified, rearranged, and tweaked for whatever the task. Some individuals may grow pale at the idea of modifying the operating system, but never fear: Linux is actually very friendly. Because of the distributed development environment that has helped it become so successful, it is also easily modified and tweaked. Later in this chapter, some simple instructions will show just how easy modifying Linux can be.

Does Linux really need to be modified before you can use it to build a Beowulf? Well, no. However, scientists are generally by their very nature extremely curious, and even though a wonderfully fast and easy-to-use Beowulf can be constructed with "stock" kernels, most cluster builders will soon give in to the nearly irresistible urge to roll up their sleeves and pop the hood to see what is really inside the Linux kernel. Be warned: many a plasma physicist or molecular biologist, fully intending to spend all of her time solving the mysteries of the universe and writing technical papers, has instead become completely drawn into the wonderful and creative release that comes from modifying the source code. You can often see these expatriates roaming the HPC and Beowulf mailing lists answering questions about the latest kernel and support for new chip sets or features.

Another reason to choose Linux is that you will not be alone. The available talent pool for knowledgeable system administrators that have Linux experience and actually enjoy working with Linux is large. System administrators are scrambling to find excuses for building a Beowulf with Linux. The same cannot often be said for other operating systems. Furthermore, remote administration has been a part of all Unix derivatives for decades. Many simple interfaces are available for updating the configuration of remote machines and organizing a room full of servers. The talent pool of Beowulf builders is growing. Linux clusters are popping up in every nook and cranny, from small departments on campus to the world's most prestigious laboratories. A quick look at the Top500 list (`www.top500.org`) shows that Linux is the unchallenged champion for building compute engines with commodity parts.

Google (`www.google.com`), one of the most popular and acclaimed search engines, is now using more than 8,000 Linux nodes for its search engine server farm [38]. While Google is not a scientific computing cluster, its size demonstrates the flexibility and adaptability of Linux. From an embedded palm-sized computer to running on an 8,000-processor cluster, Linux has demonstrated its utility and stability for nearly any task. There are even real-time versions of the Linux operating system. No legacy operating system can even come close to such flexibility and dominance among the largest clusters in the world.

Another reason to choose Linux is its support for many types of processors. Alpha, PowerPC, IA32, IA64, and many others are all supported in Linux. You can choose to build your Beowulf from the fastest Apple Macintosh servers or IBM pSeries servers, or you can buy the biggest and hottest (literally) chip on the market, the Intel IA64. As an example of the flexibility and speed with which the Linux community ports to new hardware, take a quick look at the Intel IA64. The IA64 is already available in many places, and the operating system of choice is Linux. Several distributions have already been released, and for many users, removing Linux and installing a legacy operating system (should it become widely available) is certainly not in their plans.

Finally, many people choose Linux for what it does not have, or what can be removed. Linux is a sophisticated multitasking virtual memory kernel. However, it can be trimmed down to a very small set of functions representing the bare necessities. In fact, Linux can easily be compiled to use as little as 600 KBytes of compressed disk space on a floppy. Linux can be made small. It can fit on embedded devices. Although counterintuitive to some legacy companies, where adding a new feature and urging all the users to upgrade are the status quo, smaller and simpler is better when it comes to operating system kernels for a Beowulf. The first reason that smaller is better comes from decades of experience with source code development and stability. Whenever a line of code is added to a source tree, the probability increases that a hidden bug has been introduced. For a kernel that controls the memory system and precious data on disk, robustness is vital. Having fewer functions running in privileged mode makes for a more stable environment. A small kernel is a kernel that is more likely to be stable. Although it did not run Linux, the NASA Sojourner that traveled to Mars was also designed with the "smaller and simpler is better" mantra. The Sojourner sported a 2 MHz CPU and less than 1 MByte of combined RAM and nonvolatile data storage. While NASA certainly could have afforded a larger computer, as well as a large commercial operating system, simpler was better. Making a service call to Mars to press Ctrl-Alt-Del was not an option.

More down to earth, although nearly as cold, the NSF-funded Anubis project uses Linux machines to monitor seismic conditions at unmanned monitoring stations on Antartica [1]. The stations upload their data via ARGOS satellite transmitters. The average annual temperature for the stations is –28 degrees Celsius to –54 degrees Celsius. Linux was chosen for its stability, robustness, and the ease with which it could be modified for the task. Traveling hundreds of miles across an ice sheet to repair a blue screen of death was not seriously considered.

The second reason for a small kernel is that the most stable code path is the most used code path. Bugs tend to congregate in out-of-the-way locations, away from the well-worn code paths. The smaller the kernel, the fewer the hidden and rarely tested code paths. Finally, smaller is better when it comes to kernel memory and CPU cycles on a Beowulf. For scientific computing, nearly every instruction not being performed by the scientific application, usually in the form of a floating-point operation, is overhead. Every unnecessary kernel data structure that is walked by the kernel pollutes the precious cache values intended for the scientific application. Because kernel operations such as task switching are run extremely often, even a small amount of additional kernel overhead can noticeably impact application performance. Linux's heritage of development on small machines forced developers to pay extremely close attention to performance issues. For Beowulfs, a small kernel is advantageous.

With its modular and easy-to-modify code base, support for a wide variety of the hottest CPUs on the planet, and incredibly enthusiastic talent pool, Linux is a winner for building Beowulfs.

4.1.2   A Kernel and a Distribution

The term "Linux" is most correctly applied to the name for the Unix-like kernel, the heart of an operating system that directly controls the hardware and provides true multitasking, virtual memory, shared libraries, demand loading, shared copy-on-write executables, TCP/IP networking, and file systems. The kernel is lean and mean. It contains neither an integrated Web browser nor a graphic windowing system. Linux, in keeping with its Unix heritage, follows the rule that smaller and simpler should be applied to every component in the system and that components should be easily replaceable. However, the term "Linux" has also been applied in a very general way to mean the entire system, the Linux kernel combined will all of the other programs that make the system easy to use, such as the graphic interface, the compiler tools, the e-mail programs, and the utilities for copying and naming files. Strictly speaking, Linux is the kernel. Nevertheless, most users refer to a "Linux system" or "Linux CD-ROM" or "Linux machine" when they really mean the Linux kernel packaged up with all of the tools and components that work with the kernel—a *distribution*.

A Linux distribution packages up all the common programs and interfaces that most users think of when they imagine Linux, such as the desktop icons or the

Apache Web server or, more important, for scientific users, compilers, performance monitoring tools, and the like. Many Linux distribution companies exist. They take the freely available Linux kernel and add an "installer" and all the other goodies just described. In fact, those companies (Red Hat, Turbolinux, Caldera, SuSE, and a host of smaller companies) have the freedom to customize, optimize, support, and extend their Linux distribution to satisfy the needs of their users. Several volunteer efforts also bundle up all the software packages with the kernel and release a distribution. Understanding how the Linux kernel and Linux distributions are developed and maintained is key to understanding how to get support and how to get a Beowulf cluster up and running on the network as quickly as possible.

4.1.3 Open Source and Free Software

Of course, before getting very far in any discussion about the Linux kernel or Linux CD-ROM distributions, some time must be spent on the topic of open source and free software. Several well-written books on the topic have already been published. The book *Open Sources* [7] details the many intertwined and fascinating stories of how the code bases that began as research projects or simply hobby tinkering become the fundamental standards that are the lifeblood of the Internet. It is important, however, to understand some of the basic concepts of freely distributable software for building a Beowulf with Linux. Of course, the most important reason for understanding some of the fundamental licensing issues surrounding the Linux kernel is so that they can be adhered to. Even though the term "free" is cavalierly used within the community, there can often be strict rules and practices that must be followed. Another reason why it is important to understand these basic issues is so that you can understand how the code base came to exist in the form it is today and how you can contribute back to the community that provided the software for your use.

The open source software movement has gathered both publicity and credibility over the past couple of years. Richard Stallman began work in 1984 on creating a free, publicly available set of Unix-compatible tools. He uses the term "free software" to describe the freedom users have to modify it, not the price. Several years later, the GNU General Public License (GPL) was released. The GPL (sometimes called the "copyleft") became the license for all of the GNU products, such as gcc (a C compiler) and emacs (a text editor). The GPL strives to ensure that nobody can restrict access to the original source code of GPL licensed software or can limit other rights to using the software. Anyone may sell a copy of GPL software for as much as people are willing to pay (without any obligation to give money back to the original author), but nothing prevents the person who bought the software from doing the same. Moreover, all users must be given a copy of the source code so that those users are able to fix and enhance the software to suit their needs. However, probably the most important aspect of the GPL is that any modifications to GPLed source code must also be GPLed.

For most Beowulf users, the strict rules for how free software may be distributed will never come up. However, if code licensed under the GPL is modified, its binary-only distribution is forbidden under the license. For example, if a Beowulf user extends or patches one of Donald Becker's Ethernet drivers or uses it as the basis for writing a driver, that driver cannot be redistributed in binary-only form. The Linux kernel also uses a clarified GPL license. Therefore, modifying the Linux kernel for private use is fine, but users may not modify the kernel and then make binary-only versions of the kernel for distribution. Instead, they must make the source code available if they intend to share their changes with the rest of the world.

More recently, Eric Raymond and others coined the term "open source" to refer to freely distributable software (`www.opensource.org`). There are, however, differences between the two monikers associated with freely distributable software. GPLed source code cannot be the basis for a privately developed set of enhancements that are then sold in binary-only shrink-wrapped form. Derived software must remain essentially free. On the other hand, licenses that follow the open source definition but are not the GPL are not so restricted. An open source–compliant license that is not using the GPL permits programmers and users greater flexibility in what they do with the code. They are free to use the source code however they wish. They may develop private, "closed" code repositories and then sell products that may be distributed in binary-only form.

Many licenses conform to the open source definition: Mozilla Public License (Netscape), MIT License (used for the X-Windows Consortium), and the amended BSD License. A company can enhance an open source–licensed program that is not using the GPL and then sell a binary-only version. In fact, software developed by the X-Windows Consortium and the BSD project was commercialized and used as the basis for a wide range of products. For the Beowulf user, this means that code licensed with a BSD or X-Windows–style license give the users the freedom to use the software in whatever manner they see fit. Specifically, the MPICH version of MPI, available from Argonne National Laboratory and explained in greater detail in Chapter 9 of this book, is licensed using a non-GPL open source license. Beowulf users may make changes to the source code and distribute binary-only versions, or even create products based on the work done by the original authors. Many people believe the careful choice of license for the MPICH project helped make the MPI standard as successful as it is today.

Of course "giving back" to the community that has worked collectively to provide the sophisticated toolset that makes Beowulf computation possible is part of the scientific process and is highly encouraged by the authors of this book regardless of what kind of license a particular piece of software uses. The scientific process demands repeatability, and the freely distributable nature of most Beowulf software provides an ideal environment for extending and corroborating other scientists results. Whenever possible, changes to the source code should be sent back to the authors or maintainers, so the code can continue to grow and improve.

4.1.4 A Linux Distribution

A Linux distribution generally arrives on one or more CD-ROMs, with the Linux kernel actually using a very small portion of that CD-ROM. Since a distribution can be fashioned around a Linux kernel in practically any manner, Linux distributions can vary quite widely in form and function. Since the Linux kernel is probably the most portable kernel on the planet, it is running on an amazing array of CPUs and devices, everything from handheld devices such as the Compaq iPAQ and the IBM Linux wrist watch to the IBM S390, a large corporate enterprise server getting a new lease on life with Linux. With such an incredible range of users and hardware devices that can run Linux comes a plethora of distributions built around those kernels and their target users. It can be quite daunting to choose among the dozens of popular (and hundreds of specialized) Linux distributions. Linux Web sites list dozens of distributions created with the Linux kernel. Of course, not all such distributions are suitable for use in a Beowulf. Many are designed for the embedded market, while others are built for a single-purpose appliance server, such as a firewall or a file/print server.

One of the first steps to using Linux to build your Beowulf Linux cluster is to pick a distribution and get comfortable with it. While it is beyond the scope of this book to help you become a rabid Linux user, there are plenty of books on the topic that can help guide you through the different installers and different graphic desktops optimized for each distribution. The list below shows some of the most popular Linux distribution companies or groups and where to find more information about them.

Which distribution is best for building a Beowulf? Unfortunately, there is no easy answer. Usually, the choice comes down to three factors: support, language, and ease of use. While the core of all Linux distributions are, by nature of the GPL, available for free and may downloaded from the Internet, the question of support is very important, especially to the new user. Most commercial distributions include

Company	URL
Red hat	`www.redhat.com`
Turbolinux	`www.turbolinux.com`
Mandrake	`www.mandrake.com`
Debian	`www.debian.org`
SuSE	`www.suse.com`
Slackware	`www.slackware.com`
Caldera	`www.caldera.com`

Table 4.1
Some companies or groups that release Linux distributions.

access to either phone or e-mail support. Some include the option of purchasing additional support. Some integrate software that is not freely distributable. Other companies, such as LinuxCare, do not produce a Linux distribution but simply support all of them.

Local familiarity and popularity can be a factor in your choice. If everyone else in your office or on your campus or at your laboratory is using the same Linux distribution, getting their help when things go awry may be easiest if you share a common distribution. Another consideration is support for your native language and e-mail support in that language. The SuSE distribution is very popular in Germany, and naturally has very good support for the German language. Certainly, you can e-mail your questions in German to their support staff. Likewise, the Turbolinux distribution is very popular in Japan and China and supports double-byte characters and special input methods for typing in Japanese or Chinese. Naturally, your choice of distribution may also be influenced by what the hardware company can preload on your Beowulf nodes if you are not building them from scratch. Having your nodes arrive preloaded with a Linux distribution can save a lot of time.

Another key detail for building a Beowulf with Linux is the licensing of the distribution. Almost every commercial vendor, has, at times, included software that could not be freely distributed. In some cases, a portion of the purchase price is used to pay royalties for the software that is not freely distributable. Using such a distribution to install 16 nodes would violate the licensing unless you actually purchased 16 copies. Luckily, most distribution companies try to make it very clear whether their distribution can be freely distributed and, in many cases, offer a freely distributable version of the distribution on the Web site.

4.1.5 Version Numbers and Development Methods

The Linux kernel, Linux applications, and even the Linux distributions have different development models, different version numbers, and different schedules. While picking a Linux distribution for your Beowulf, a basic understanding of version numbers and distribution versions is required. A relatively small team of core developers develops the Linux kernel. Yes, many many people from around the world, representing more than fifty different countries, have contributed to the Linux kernel, but its stability and the organized introduction of new features are made possible by a well-coordinated band of core programmers. With Linus Torvalds sometimes called the "benevolent dictator," core developers such as Donald Becker, Alan Cox, Stephen Tweedie, and David Miller maintain and extend sections of the kernel with the help of hundreds of programmers who send in contributions to the kernel. This hierarchical model is clearly more efficient than everyone sending Linus their patches and new ideas for how the kernel can be extended (not that they don't try). Of course, not all patches and extensions are included in the main line, or "stock" kernel, no matter who sent them. Significant restraint and conservatism are used for most sections of the code. Some programmers must lobby Linus or other code developers for extended periods of time before their improvements are incorporated. In some cases, the suggestions are never accepted and are therefore made available only as a patch and not part of the "official" kernel tree.

Your Linux distribution will, of course, arrive with a Linux kernel, but upgrading the kernel is one of the most common ways to update a Beowulf node, and will be discussed later. It is important to understand that the version number of the kernel and the version number of the distribution are in no way related. At any point in time the Linux kernel has two most-up-to-date kernels: the "stable" release and the "development" release. Stable kernels use an even minor kernel number, such as 2.0, 2.2, or 2.4. Similarly, development kernels use odd minor kernel numbers, such as 2.1 or 2.3. As work on a development kernel becomes more stable, the rate of change begins to slow, and finally the core kernel developers stop adding new features. There exists no definitive set of tests that indicate when a development kernel is ready for general use, but at some point, Linus will "release" a new stable kernel. After that, patches and updates take the form of incremental versions, such as 2.4.9 or 2.4.11. With few exceptions, a kernel that is part of a popular CD-ROM distribution comes from the "stable" kernel releases. Of course, nothing prevents a would-be Beowulf builder from using the latest, most unstable versions of the development kernel. However, the main kernel developers take the stability of the Linux kernel very seriously, and it would be wise to be conservative in choosing a kernel.

Linux distributions, on the other hand, can create version numbers for their distribution however they please. Red Hat 7.0 simply means that it is newer than Red Hat 6.0. Since distribution companies are separate, they use completely different versioning schemes. Red Hat 7.0 is not necessarily any newer than Turbolinux 6.5. In fact, because it is clearly to their advertising advantage, don't be surprised to find out that the distribution on the shelf with the highest version number is in fact not the most recent release. Furthermore, distributions are free to use whatever basic version of the Linux kernel they believe will make their end-users most satisfied. Then, they often add in a couple more changes to the kernel that may not be in the mainline kernel. For example, a hardware company working with a distribution company may ask for some special drivers or special options be added to the kernel, so their hardware can work well with Linux. While certainly common practice, it can lead to some confusion in infrequent cases because upgrading the kernel for such a distribution may not always work unless the upgraded kernel came from the distribution's Web site and therefore contained the special additions, or the special additions are added to the basic main-line kernel that can be downloaded from `www.kernel.org`.

For the Beowulf user, this situation means that getting help with kernel issues may involve some investigation. Generally, the distribution companies support their product, or you can purchase support from a company such as LinuxCare. However, that does not mean they wrote the code or are on a first-name basis with the person who did. The commercial support company can certainly provide front-line support, but what the industry often calls level-3 support requires some extra work. Generally, open source programmers such as Donald Becker make a portion of their time available to answer questions about the code they authored. However, the author of the code could also have moved on to other endeavors, leaving the source code behind. Kernel and Beowulf mailing lists help, but the burden can often be on you to find the problem or find the person who can help you. When trying to track down what you believe to be a kernel or driver issue, please follow these guidelines:

1.   Read the documentation. Because Linux support has traditionally been ad hoc in nature, a large number of `HOWTO` documents have been written, ranging from ones that are probably very important to you like the `Kernel-HOWTO`, the `Beowulf-HOWTO`, and the `Parallel-Processing-HOWTO`, to more specific ones like the `Slovenian-HOWTO`,the `Kodak-Digitalcam-HOWTO`, the `Quake-HOWTO`, and the

`Coffee-mini-HOWTO`. These documents are located under `/usr/doc/HOWTO` on most distributions.

2. Second, search the Web. Google `www.google.com` is amazing. Many a perplexing, nasty bug or software incompatibility has been easily solved with fifteen or twenty minutes of Web surfing.

3. Get some help from local Linux users. Often, there is a very simple answer or widely known work-around for a problem. Talking to someone can also help you better understand the problem, so Google can once again be queried or intelligent e-mail sent.

4. Read the relevant mailing lists, and search for your topic of interest on the mailing list. Several archives of Linux-specific mailing lists exist, such as can be found at `marc.theaimsgroup.com`.

5. After the difficulty has been narrowed down to a very clear, reproducible example, mail the appropriate mailing list, and ask for help. To make your bug report useful to the readers (and get you a fix much faster), follow the guidelines given in the kernel sources as `REPORTING-BUGS`, `Documentation/BUG-HUNTING`, and `Documentation/oops-tracing`.

6. If you don't make any progress, try looking at the source code and mailing the author directly. Naturally, this should be used as a last resort. Authors of key portions can often get dozens or hundreds of e-mail messages a day about their code.

4.2   The Linux Kernel

As mentioned earlier, for the Beowulf user, a smaller, faster, and leaner kernel is a better kernel. This section describes the important features of the Linux kernel for Beowulf users and shows how a little knowledge about the Linux kernel can make the cluster run faster and more smoothly.

What exactly does the kernel do? Its first responsibility is to be an interface to the hardware and provide a basic environment for processes and memory management. When user code opens a file, requests 30 megabytes of memory for user data, or sends a TCP/IP message, the kernel does the resource management. If the Linux server is a firewall, special kernel code can be used to filter network traffic. In general, there are no additives to the Linux kernel to make it better for scientific clusters—usually, making the kernel smaller and tighter is the goal. However, sometimes a virtual memory management algorithm can be twiddled to improve cache locality, since the memory access patterns of scientific applications are often much different from the patterns common Web servers and desktop workstations, the applications for which Linux kernel parameters and algorithms are generally tuned. Likewise, occasionally someone creates a TCP/IP patch that makes message passing for Linux clusters work a little better. Before going that deep into Linux kernel tuning, however, the kernel must first simply be compiled.

4.2.1   Compiling a Kernel

Almost all Linux distributions ship with a kernel build environment that is ready for action. The transcript below shows how you can learn a bit about the kernel running on the system.

```
% ls -l /proc/version
-r--r--r-- 1 root root 0 Jun 9 23:32 /proc/version
% cat /proc/version
Linux version 2.2.14-3 (support@kernel.turbolinux.com) (gcc driver
version 2.95.2 19991024 (release) executing gcc version 2.7.2.3)
#1 Wed Feb 23 14:09:33 PST 2000

% cd /usr/src
% ls -ld linux
lrwxrwxrwx 1 root root 12 May 16 2000 linux -> linux-2.2.14
```

The /proc file system is not really a file system in the traditional meaning. It is not used to store files on the disk or some other secondary storage; rather, it is a pseudo-file system that is used as an interface to kernel data structures—a window into the running kernel. Linus likes the file system metaphor for gaining access to the heart of the kernel. Therefore, the /proc file system does not really have disk filenames but the names of parts of the system that can be accessed. In the example above, we read from the handle /proc/version using the Unix cat command. Notice that the file size is meaningless, since it is not really a file with bytes on a disk but a way to ask the kernel "What version are you currently running?" We can see the version of the kernel and some information about how it was built.

The source code for the kernel is often kept in /usr/src. Usually, a symbolic link from /usr/src/linux points to the kernel currently being built. Generally, if you want to download a different kernel and recompile it, it is put in /usr/src, and the symlink `/usr/src/linux` is changed to point to the new directory while you work on compiling the kernel. If there is no kernel source in `/usr/src/linux`, you probably did not select "kernel source" when you installed the system for the first time, so in an effort to save space, the source code was not installed on the machine. The remedy is to get the software from the company's Web site or the original installation CD-ROM.

The kernel source code often looks something like the following:

```
% cd /usr/src/linux
% ls
COPYING          README                  configs  init     modules
CREDITS          README.kernel-sources   drivers  ipc      net
Documentation    REPORTING-BUGS          fs       kernel   pcmcia-cs-3.1.8
MAINTAINERS      Rules.make              ibcs     lib      scripts
Makefile         arch                    include  mm
```

If your Linux distribution has provided the kernel source in its friendliest form, you can recompile the kernel, as it currently is configured, simply by typing

```
% make clean ; make bzImage
```

The server will then spend anywhere from a few minutes to twenty or more minutes depending on the speed of the server and the size of the kernel. When it is finished, you will have a kernel.

```
% ls -l /usr/src/linux-2.2.14/arch/i386/boot/bzImage
-rw-r--r-- 1 root root 574272 Jun 10 00:13
              /usr/src/linux-2.2.14/arch/i386/boot/bzImage
```

4.2.2   Loadable Kernel Modules

For most kernels shipped with Linux distributions, the kernel is built to be modular. Linux has a special interface for loadable kernel modules, which provides a convenient way to extend the functionality of the kernel in a dynamic way, without maintaining the code in memory all the time, and without requiring the kernel be recompiled every time a new or updated module arrived. Modules are most often used for device drivers, file systems, and special kernel features. For example, Linux can read and write MSDOS file systems. However, that functionality is usually not required at all times. Most often, it is required when reading or writing from an MSDOS floppy disk. The Linux kernel can dynamically load the MSDOS file system kernel module when it detects a request to mount an MSDOS file system. The resident size of the kernel remains small until it needs to dynamically add more functionality. By moving as many features out of the kernel core and into dynamically loadable modules, the legendary stability of Linux compared with legacy operating systems is achieved.

Linux distributions, in an attempt to support as many different hardware configurations and uses as possible, ship with as many precompiled kernel modules as possible. It is not uncommon to receive five hundred or more precompiled kernel modules with the distribution. In the example above, the core kernel was recompiled. This does not automatically recompile the dynamically loadable modules.

4.2.3   The Beowulf Kernel Diet

It is beyond the scope of this book to delve into the inner workings of the Linux kernel. However, for the Beowulf builder, slimming down the kernel into an even leaner and smaller image can be beneficial and, with a little help, is not too difficult.

In the example above, the kernel was simply recompiled, not configured. In order to slim down the kernel, the configuration step is required. There are several interfaces to configuring the kernel. The README file in the kernel source outlines the steps required to configure and compile a kernel. Most people like the graphic interface and use `make xconfig` to edit the kernel configuration for the next compilation.

Removing and Optimizing.   The first rule is to start slow and read the documentation. Plenty of documentation is available on the Internet that discusses the Linux kernel and all of the modules. However, probably the best advice is to start slow and simply remove a couple unneeded features, recompile, install the kernel, and try it. Since each kernel version can have different configuration options and module names, it is not possible simply to provide the Beowulf user a list of kernel configuration options in this book. Some basic principles can be outlined, however.

Think compute server: Most compute servers don't need support for amateur radio networking. Nor do most compute servers need sound support, unless of course your Beowulf will be used to provide a new type of parallel sonification. The list for what is really needed for a compute server is actually quite small. IrDA (infrared), quality of service, ISDN, ARCnet, Appletalk, Token ring, WAN, AX.25, USB support, mouse support, joysticks, and telephony are probably all useless for a Beowulf.

Optimize for your CPU: By default, many distributions ship their kernels compiled for the first-generation Pentium CPUs, so they will work on the widest range of machines. For your high-performance Beowulf, however, compiling the kernel to use the most advanced CPU instruction set available for your CPU can be an important optimization.

Optimize for the number of processors: If the target server has only one CPU, don't compile a symmetric multiprocessing kernel, because this adds unneeded locking overhead to the kernel.

Remove firewall or denial-of-service protections: Since Linux is usually optimized for Web serving or the desktop, kernel features to prevent or reduce the severity of denial-of-services attacks are often compiled into the kernel. Unfortunately, an extremely intense parallel program that is messaging bound can flood the interface with traffic, often resembling a denial-of-service attack. Indeed, some people have said that many a physicist's MPI program is actually a denial-of-service attack on the Beowulf cluster. Removing the special checks and detection algorithms can make the Beowulf more vulnerable, but the hardware is generally purchased with the intent to provide the most compute cycles per dollar possible, and putting it behind a firewall is relatively easy compared with securing and hampering every node's computation to perform some additional security checks.

Other Considerations.   Many Beowulf users slim down their kernel and even remove loadable module support. Since most hardware for a Beowulf is known, and scientific applications are very unlikely to require dynamic modules be loaded and unloaded while they are running, many administrators simply compile the required kernel code into the core. Particularly careful selection of kernel features can trim the kernel from a 1.5-megabyte compressed file with 10 megabytes of possible loadable modules to a 600-kilobyte compressed kernel image with no loadable modules. Some of the kernel features that should be considered for Beowulfs include the following:

- *NFS:* While NFS does not scale to hundreds of node, it is very convenient for small clusters.
- *Serial console:* Rather than using KVM (Keyboard, Video, Mouse) switches or plugging a VGA (video graphics array) cable directly into a node, it is often very convenient to use a serial concentrator to aggregate 32 serial consoles into one device that the system administrator can control.
- *Kernel IP configuration:* This lets the kernel get its IP address from BOOTP or DHCP, often convenient for initial deployment of servers.
- *NFS root:* Diskless booting is an important configuration for some Beowulfs. NFS root permits the node to mount the basic distribution files such as /etc/passwd from an NFS server.

- *Special high-performance network drivers:* Often, an extreme performance Beowulf will use high-speed networking, such as Gigabit Ethernet or Myrinet. Naturally, those specialized drivers as well as the more common 100BT Ethernet driver can be compiled into the kernel.
- *A file system:* Later in this chapter a more thorough discussion of file systems for Linux will be presented. It is important the kernel is compiled to support the file system chosen for the compute nodes

Network Booting. Because of the flexibility of Linux, many options are available to the cluster builder. While certainly most clusters are built using a local hard drive for booting the operating system, it is certainly not required. Network booting permits the kernel to be loaded from a network-attached server. Generally, a specialized network adapters or system BIOS is required. Until recently, there were no good standards in place for networking booting commodity hardware. Now, however, most companies are offering network boot-capable machines in their high-end servers. The most common standard is the Intel PXE 2.0 net booting mechanism. On such machines, the firmware boot code will request a network address and kernel from a network attached server, and then receive the kernel using TFTP (Trivial File Transfer Protocol). Unfortunately, the protocol is not very scalable, and attempting to boot more than a dozen or so nodes simultaneously will yield very poor results. Large Beowulfs attempting to use network boot protocols must carefully consider the number of simultaneously booting nodes or provide multiple TFTP servers and separate Ethernet collision domains. For a Linux cluster, performing a network boot and then mounting the local hard drive for the remainder of the operating system does not seem advantageous; it probably would have been much simpler to store the kernel on hard drive. However, network booting can be important for some clusters if it is used in conjunction with diskless nodes.

4.2.4   Diskless Operation

Some applications and environments can work quite well without the cost or management overhead of a hard drive. For example, in secure or classified computing environments, secondary storage can require special, labor-intensive procedures. In some environments, operating system kernels and distributions may need to be switched frequently, or even between runs of an application program. Reinstalling the operating system on each compute node to switch over the system would be impractical, as would maintaining multiple hard disk partitions with different operating systems or configurations. In such cases, building the Beowulf without the operating system on the local hard drive, if it even exists, can be a good solution. Diskless operation also has the added benefit of making it possible to maintain only one operating system image, rather than having to propagate changes across the system to all of the Beowulf nodes.

For diskless operations, naturally, Linux can accommodate where other systems may not be so flexible. A complete explanation of network booting and NFS-root mechanisms is beyond the scope of this book (but they are documented in the `Diskless-HOWTO` and `Diskless-root-NFS-HOWTO`) and certainly is a specialty area for Beowulf machines. However, a quick explanation of the technology will help provide the necessary insight to guide your decision in this regard.

In addition to hardware that is capable of performing a network boot and a server to dole out kernels to requesting nodes, a method for accessing the rest of the operating system is required. The kernel is only part of a running machine. Files such as `/etc/passwd` and `/etc/resolv.conf` also need to be available to the diskless server. In Linux, *NFS root* provides this capability. A kernel built with NFS root capability can mount the root file system from a remote machine using NFS. Operating system files such as dynamic libraries, configuration files, and other important parts of the complete operating system can be accessed transparently from the remote machine via NFS. As with network booting, there are certain limitations to the scalability of NFS root for a large Beowulf. In Section 4.2.6, a more detailed discussion of NFS scalability is presented. In summary, diskless operation is certainly an important option for a Beowulf builder but remains technically challenging.

4.2.5 Downloading and Compiling a New Kernel

For most users, the kernel shipped with their Linux distribution will be adequate for their Beowulf. Sometimes, however, there are advantages to downloading a newer kernel. Occasionally a security weakness has been solved, or some portion of TCP/IP has been improved, or a better, faster, more stable device driver arrives with the new kernel. Downloading and compiling a new kernel may seem difficult but is really not much harder than compiling the kernel that came with the distribution.

The first step is to download a new kernel from `www.kernel.org`. The importance of reading the online documents, readme files, and instructions cannot be overstated. As mentioned earlier, sticking with a "stable" (even minor version) kernel is recommended over the "development" (odd minor version) kernel. It is also important to understand how far forward you can move your system simply by adding a new kernel. The kernel is not an isolated piece of software. It interfaces with a myriad of program and libraries. For example, the Linux mount command file system interfaces to the kernel; should significant changes to the kernel occur, a newer, compatible mount command may also need to be upgraded. Usually, however, the most significant link between the kernel and the rest of the operating system programs occurs with what most people call `libc`. This is a library of procedures that must be linked with nearly every single Linux program. It contains everything from the `printf` function to routines to generate random numbers. The library `libc` is tied very closely to the kernel version, and since almost every program on the system is tied closely to `libc`, the kernel and LibC must be in proper version synchronization. Of course, all of the details can be found at `www.kernel.org`, or as a link from that site.

The next step is to determine whether you can use a "stock" kernel. While every major distribution company uses as a starting point a stock kernel downloaded from `kernel.org`, companies often apply patches or fixes to the kernel they ship on the CD-ROM. These minor tweaks and fixes are done to support the market for which the distribution is targeted or to add some special functionality required for their user base or to distinguish their product. For example, one distribution company may have a special relationship with a RAID device manufacturer and include a special device driver with their kernel that is not found in the stock kernel. Or a distribution company may add support for a high-performance network adapter or even modify a tuning parameter deep in the kernel to achieve higher performance over the stock kernels. Since the distribution company often modifies the stock kernel, several options are available for upgrading the kernel:

- Download the kernel from the distribution company's Web site instead of `kernel.org`. In most cases, the distribution company will make available free, upgraded versions of the kernel with all of their distribution-specific modifications already added.
- Download the kernel from `kernel.org`, and simply ignore the distribution-dependent modifications to the kernel. Unless you have a special piece of hardware not otherwise supported by the stock kernel, it is usually safe to use the stock kernel. However, any performance tuning performed by the distribution company would not have been applied to the newly download kernel.
- Port the kernel modification to the newer kernel yourself. Generally, distribution companies try to make it very clear where changes have been made. Normally, for example, you could take a device driver from the kernel that shipped with your distribution and add it to the newer stock kernel if that particular device driver was required.

Of course, all of this may sound a little complicated to the first-time Beowulf user. However, none of these improvements or upgrades are required. They are by the very nature of Linux freely available to users to take or leave as they need or see fit. Unless you know that a new kernel will solve some existing problem or security issue, it is probably good advice to simply trim the kernel down, as described earlier, and use what was shipped with your distribution.

4.2.6   Linux File Systems

Linux supports an amazing number of file systems. Because of its modular kernel and the virtual file system interface used within the kernel, dynamically loaded modules can be loaded and unloaded on the fly to support whatever file system is being mounted. For Beowulf, however, simplicity is usually a good rule of thumb. Even through there are a large number of potential file systems to compile into the kernel, most Beowulf users will require only one or two.

The de facto standard file system on Linux is the second extended file system, commonly called EXT2. EXT2 has been performing well as the standard file system for years. It is fast and extremely stable. Every Beowulf should compile the EXT2 file system into the kernel. It does, unfortunately, have one drawback, which can open the door to including support for (and ultimately choosing) another file system. EXT2 is not a "journaling" file system.

Journaling File Systems. The idea behind a journaling file system is quite simple: Make sure that all of the disk writes are performed in such a way as to ensure the disk always remains in a consistent state or can easily be put in a consistent state. That is usually not the case with nonjournaling file systems like EXT2. Flipping off the power while Linux is writing to an EXT2 file system can often leave it in an inconsistent state. When the machine reboots, a file system check, or "fsck," must be run to put the disk file system back into a consistent state. Performing such a check is not a trivial matter. It is often very time consuming. One rule of thumb is that it requires one hour for every 100 gigabytes of used disk space. If a server has a large RAID array, it is almost always a good idea to use a journaling file system, to avoid the painful delays that can occur when rebooting from a crash or power outage. However, for a Beowulf compute node, the choice of a file system is not so clear.

Journaling file systems are slightly slower than nonjournaling file systems for writing to the disk. Since the journaling file system must keep the disk in a consistent state even if the machine were to suddenly crash (although not likely with Linux), the file system must write a little bit of extra accounting information, the "journal," to the disk first. This information enables the exact state of the file system to be tracked and easily restored should the node fail. That little bit of extra writing to the disk is what makes journaling file systems so stable, but it also slows them down a little bit.

If a Beowulf user expects many of the programs to be disk-write bound, it may be worth considering simply using EXT2, the standard nonjournaling file system. Using EXT2 will eke out the last bit of disk performance for a compute node's local file writes. However, as described earlier, should a node fail during a disk write, there is a chance that the file system will be corrupt or require an fsck that could take several minutes or several hours depending on the size of the file system. Many parallel programs use the local disk simply as a scratch disk to stage output files that then must be copied off the local node and onto the centralized, shared file system. In those cases, the limiting factor is the network I/O to move the partial results from the compute nodes to the central, shared store. Improving disk-write performance by using a nonjournaling file system would have little advantage in such cases, while the improved reliability and ease of use of a journaling file system would be well worth the effort.

Which Journaling File System?   Once, unlike other legacy operating systems, Linux is blessed with a wide range of journaling file systems from which to choose. The most common are EXT3, ReiserFS, IBM's JFS, and SGI's XFS. EXT3 is probably the most convenient file system for existing Linux to tinker with. EXT3 uses the well-known EXT2 file formatting but adds journaling capabilities; it does not improve upon EXT2, however. ReiserFS, which was designed and implemented using more sophisticated algorithms than EXT2, is being used in the SuSE distribution. It generally has better performance characteristics for some operations, especially systems that have many, many small files or large directories. IBM's Journaling File System (JFS) and SGI's XFS files systems had widespread use with AIX and IRIX before being ported to Linux. Both file systems not only do journaling but were designed for the highest performance achievable when writing out large blocks of data from virtual memory to disk. For the user not highly experienced with file systems and recompiling the kernel, the final choice of journaling file system should be based not on the performance characteristics but on the support provided by the Linux distribution, local Linux users, and the completeness of Linux documentation for the software.

Networked and Distributed File Systems.   While most Linux clusters use a local file system for scratch data, it is often convenient to use network-based or distributed file systems to share data. A network-based file system allows the node to access a remote machine for file reads and writes. Most common and most popular is the network file system, NFS, which has been around for about two decades. An NFS client can mount a remote file system over an IP (Internet Protocol) network. The NFS server can accept file access requests from many remote clients and store the data locally. NFS is also standardized across platforms, making it convenient for a Linux client to mount and read and write files from a remote server, which could be anything from a Sun desktop to a Cray supercomputer.

Unfortunately, NFS does have two shortcomings for the Beowulf user: scalability and synchronization. Most Linux clusters find it convenient to have each compute node mount the user's home directory from a central server. In this way, a user in the typical edit, compile, and run development loop can recompile the parallel program and then spawn the program onto the Beowulf, often with the use of an *mpirun* or *PBS* command, which are covered in Chapters 9 and 16, respectively. While using NFS does indeed make this operation convenient, the result can be a B3 (big Beowulf bottleneck). Imagine for a moment that the user's executable was 5 megabytes, and the user was launching the program onto a 256-node Linux cluster. Since essentially every single server node would NFS mount and read the single executable from the central file server, 1,280 megabytes would need to be sent across the network via NFS from the file server. At 50 percent efficiency with 100-baseT Ethernet links, it would take approximately 3.4 minutes simply to transfer the executable to the compute nodes for execution. To make matters worse, NFS servers generally have difficulty scaling to that level of performance for simultaneous connections. For most Linux servers, NFS performance begins to seriously degrade if the cluster is larger than 64 nodes. Thus, while NFS is extremely convenient for smaller clusters, it can become a serious bottleneck for larger machines. Synchronization is also an issue with NFS. Beowulf users should not expect to use NFS as a means of communicating between the computational nodes. In other words, compute nodes should not write or modify small data files on the NFS server with the expectation that the files can be quickly disseminated to other nodes.

The best technical solution would be a file system or storage system that could use a tree-based distribution mechanism and possibly use available high-performance network adapters such as Myrinet or Gigabit Ethernet to transfer files to and from the compute nodes. Unfortunately, while several such systems exist, they are research projects and do not have a pervasive user base. Other solutions such as shared global file systems, often using expensive fiber channel solutions, may increase disk bandwidth but are usually even less scalable. For generic file server access from the compute nodes to a shared server, NFS is currently the most common option.

Experimental file systems are available, however, that address many of the short-comings described earlier. Chapter 17 discusses PVFS, the Parallel Virtual File System. PVFS is different from NFS because it can distribute parts of the operating system to possibly dozens of Beowulf nodes. When done properly, the bottleneck is no longer an Ethernet adapter or hard disk. Furthermore, PVFS provides parallel access, so many readers or writers can access file data concurrently. You are encouraged to explore PVFS as an option for distributed, parallel access to files.

4.3   Pruning Your Beowulf Node

Even if recompiling your kernel, downloading a new one, or choosing a journaling file system seems too adventuresome at this point, you can some very simple things to your Beowulf node that can increase performance and manageability. Remember that just as the kernel, with its nearly five hundred dynamically loadable modules, provides drivers and capabilities you probably will never need, so too your Linux distribution probably looks more like a kitchen sink than a lean and mean computing machine. While you may now be tired of the Linux Beowulf adage "a smaller operating system is a better operating system," it must be once again applied to the auxiliary programs often run with a conventional Linux distribution. If we look at the issue from another perspective, every single CPU instruction performed by the kernel or operating system daemon not directly contributed to the scientific calculation is a wasted CPU instruction. Fortunately, with Linux you can understand and modify any daemon or process as you convert your kitchen sink of useful utilities and programs into a designed-for-computation roadster. For a Beowulf, eliminating useless tasks delivers more megaflop per dollar to the end user.

The first step to pruning the operating system daemons and auxiliary programs is to find out what is running on the system. For most Linux systems there are at least two standard ways to start daemons and other processes, which may waste CPU resources as well as memory bandwidth (often the most precious commodity on a cluster).

inetd: This is the "Internet superserver". Its basic function is to wait for connections on a set of ports and then spawn and hand off the network connection to the appropriate program when an incoming connection is made. The configuration for what ports `inetd` is waiting as well as what will get spawned can been determined by looking at `/etc/inetd.conf` and `/etc/services`.

/etc/rc.d/init.d: This special directory represents the scripts that are run during the booting sequence and that often launch daemons that will run until the machine is shut down.

4.3.1 inetd.conf

The file `inetd.conf` is a simple configuration file. Each line in the file represents a single service, including the port associated with that service and the program to launch when a connection to the port is made. Below are some simple examples:

```
ftp      stream  tcp     nowait  root    /usr/sbin/tcpd  in.proftpd
finger   stream  tcp     nowait  root    /usr/sbin/tcpd  in.fingerd
talk     dgram   udp     wait    root    /usr/sbin/tcpd  in.talkd
```

The first column provides the name of the service. The file `/etc/services` maps the port name to the port number, for example,

```
% grep ^talk /etc/services
talk 517/udp # BSD talkd(8)
```

To slim down your Beowulf node, get rid of the extra services in `inetd.conf`; you probably will not require the `/usr/bin/talk` program on each of the compute nodes. Of course, what is required will depend on the computing environment. In many very secure environments, where ssh is run as a daemon and not launched from inetd.conf for every new connection, inetd.conf has *no* entries. In such extreme examples, the inetd process that normally reads inetd.conf and listens on ports, ready to launch services, can even be eliminated.

4.3.2 /etc/rc.d/init.d

The next step is to eliminate any daemons or processes that are normally started at boot. While occasionally Linux distributions differ in style, the organization of the files that launch daemons or run scripts during the first phases of booting up a system are very similar. For most distributions, the directory `/etc/rc.d/init.d` contains scripts that are run when entering or leaving a run level. Below is an example:

```
% cd /etc/rc.d/init.d
% ls
alsasound  functions  keytable  named    postgresql  snmpd   ypbind
apmd       gpm        killall   network  proftpd     squid   yppasswdd
atalk      halt       kparam    nfs      radiusd     sshd    ypserv
```

atd	httpd	kudzu	nfsfs	random	synctime
autofs	identd	ldap	nfslock	sendmail	syslog
canna	inet	lpd	nscd	serial	unicon
crond	innd	mars-nwe	pcmcia	single	xinetd
dhcpd	ipchains	mysql	portmap	smb	xntpd

However, the presence of the script does not indicate it will be run. Other directories and symlinks control which scripts will be run. Most systems now use the convenient `chkconfig` interface for managing all the scripts and symlinks that control when they get turned on or off. Not every script spawns a daemon. Some scripts just initialize hardware or modify some setting.

A convenient way to see all the scripts that will be run when entering run level 3 is the following:

```
% chkconfig --list | grep '3:on'
syslog 0:off 1:off 2:on 3:on 4:on 5:on 6:off
pcmcia 0:off 1:off 2:on 3:on 4:on 5:on 6:off
xinetd 0:off 1:off 2:off 3:on 4:on 5:on 6:off
lpd 0:off 1:off 2:off 3:on 4:on 5:on 6:off
mysql 0:off 1:off 2:on 3:on 4:on 5:on 6:off
httpd 0:off 1:off 2:off 3:on 4:on 5:on 6:off
sshd 0:off 1:off 2:off 3:on 4:on 5:on 6:off
atd 0:off 1:off 2:off 3:on 4:on 5:on 6:off
named 0:off 1:off 2:off 3:on 4:on 5:on 6:off
dhcpd 0:off 1:off 2:off 3:on 4:on 5:on 6:off
gpm 0:off 1:off 2:on 3:on 4:on 5:on 6:off
inet 0:off 1:off 2:off 3:on 4:on 5:on 6:off
network 0:off 1:off 2:on 3:on 4:on 5:on 6:off
nfsfs 0:off 1:off 2:off 3:on 4:on 5:on 6:off
random 0:off 1:off 2:on 3:on 4:on 5:on 6:off
keytable 0:off 1:off 2:on 3:on 4:on 5:on 6:off
nfs 0:off 1:off 2:off 3:on 4:on 5:on 6:off
nfslock 0:off 1:off 2:off 3:on 4:on 5:on 6:off
ntpd 0:off 1:off 2:off 3:on 4:on 5:on 6:off
portmap 0:off 1:off 2:off 3:on 4:on 5:on 6:off
sendmail 0:off 1:off 2:on 3:on 4:on 5:on 6:off
serial 0:off 1:off 2:on 3:on 4:on 5:on 6:off
squid 0:off 1:off 2:off 3:on 4:on 5:on 6:off
tltime 0:off 1:off 2:off 3:on 4:off 5:on 6:off
```

```
crond 0:off 1:off 2:on 3:on 4:on 5:on 6:off
```

Remember that not all of these spawn cycle-stealing daemons that are not required for Beowulf nodes. The "serial" script, for example, simply initializes the serial ports at boot time; its removal is not likely to reduce overall performance. However, in this example many things could be trimmed. For example, there is probably no need for `lpd`, `mysql`, `httpd`, `named`, `dhcpd`, `sendmail`, or `squid` on a compute node. It would be a good idea to become familiar with the scripts and use the "chkconfig" command to turn off unneeded scripts. With only a few exceptions, an X-Windows server should not be run on a compute node. Starting an X session takes ever-increasing amounts of memory and spawns a large set of processes. Except for special circumstances, run level 3 will be the highest run level for a compute node.

4.3.3 Other Processes and Daemons

In addition to `inetd.conf` and the scripts in `/etc/rc.d/init.d`, there are other common ways for a Beowulf node to waste CPU or memory resources. The `cron` program is often used to execute programs at scheduled times. For example, `cron` is commonly used to schedule a nightly backup or an hourly cleanup of system files. Many distributions come with some `cron` scripts scheduled for execution. The program `slocate` is often run as a nightly `cron` to create an index permitting the file system to be searched quickly. Beowulf users may be unhappy to learn that their computation and file I/O are being hampered by a system utility that is probably not useful for a Beowulf. A careful examination of `cron` and other ways that tasks can be started will help trim a Beowulf compute node.

The `ps` command can be invaluable during your search-and-destroy mission.

```
% ps -eo pid,pcpu,sz,vsize,user,fname --sort=vsize
```

This example command demonstrates sorting the processes by virtual memory size.

The small excerpt below illustrates how large server processes can use memory. The example is taken from a Web server, not a well-tuned Beowulf node.

```
  PID %CPU   SZ   VSZ  USER COMMAND
26593  0.0  804  3216   web httpd
26595  0.0  804  3216   web httpd
 3574  0.0  804  3216   web httpd
  506  0.0  819  3276  root squid
  637  0.0  930  3720  root AgentMon
```

```
  552  0.0 1158   4632 dbenl postmast
13207  0.0 1213   4852  root  named
13209  0.0 1213   4852  root  named
13210  0.0 1213   4852  root  named
13211  0.0 1213   4852  root  named
13212  0.0 1213   4852  root  named
  556  0.0 1275   5100 dbenl postmast
  657  0.0 1280   5120 dbenl postmast
  557  0.0 1347   5388 dbenl postmast
  475  0.0 2814  11256 mysql mysqld
  523  0.0 2814  11256 mysql mysqld
  524  0.0 2814  11256 mysql mysqld
  507  0.0 3375  13500 squid squid
```

In this example the proxy cache program `squid` is using a lot of memory (and probably some cache), even though the CPU usage is negligible. Similarly, the ps command can be used to locate CPU hogs. Becoming familiar with `ps` will help quickly find runaway processes or extra daemons competing for cycles with the scientific applications intended for your Beowulf.

4.4   Other Considerations

You can explore several other basic areas in seeking to understand the performance and behavior of your Beowulf node running the Linux operating system. Many scientific applications need just four things from a node: CPU cycles, memory, networking (message passing), and disk I/O. Trimming down the kernel and removing unnecessary processes can free up resources from each of those four areas.

Because the capacity and behavior of the memory system are vital to many scientific applications, it is important that memory be well understood. One of the most common ways an application can get into trouble with the Linux operating system is by using too much memory. Demand-paged virtual memory, where memory pages are swapped to and from disk on demand, is one of the most important achievements in modern operating system design. It permits programmers to transparently write applications that allocate and use more virtual memory than physical memory available on the system. The performance cost for declaring enormous blocks of virtual memory and letting the clever operating system sort out which virtual memory pages in fact get mapped to physical pages, and when, is usually very small. Most Beowulf applications will cause memory pages to be swapped in and out at very predictable points in the application. Occasionally, however, the worst can happen. The memory access patterns of the scientific application can cause a pathological behavior for the operating system.

The crude program below demonstrates this behavior:

```
#include <stdlib.h>
#include <stdio.h>
#define MEGABYTES 300
main() {
  int *x, *p, t=1, i, numints = MEGABYTES*1024*1024/sizeof(int);
  x = (int *) malloc(numints*sizeof(int));
  if (!x) { printf("insufficient memory, aborting\n"); exit(1); }
  for (i=1; i<=5; i++) {
    printf("Loop %d\n",i);
    for (p=x; p<x+numints-1; p+=1024) {
      *p = *p + t;
    }
  }
}
```

On a Linux server with 256 megabytes of memory, this program—which walks through 300 megabytes of memory, causing massive amounts of demand-paged swapping—can take about 5 minutes to complete and can generate 377,093 page faults. If, however, you change the size of the array to 150 megabytes, which fits nicely on a 256-megabyte machine, the program takes only a half a second to run and generates only 105 page faults.

While this behavior is normal for demand-paged virtual memory operating systems such as Linux, it can lead to sometimes mystifying performance anomalies. A couple of extra processes on a node using memory can push the scientific application into swapping. Since many parallel applications have regular synchronization points, causing the application to run as slow as the slowest node, a few extra daemons or processes on just one Beowulf node can cause an entire application to halt. To achieve predictable performance, you must prune the kernel and system processes of your Beowulf.

4.4.1 TCP Messaging

Another area of improvement for a Beowulf can be standard TCP messaging. As mentioned earlier, most Linux distributions come tuned for general-purpose networking. For high-performance compute clusters, short low-latency messages and very long messages are common, and their performance can greatly affect the overall speed of many parallel applications. Linux is not generally tuned for messages at the extremes. However, once again, Linux provides you the tools to tune it for nearly any purpose.

For 2.2.x kernels, a series of in-depth performance studies from NASA ICASE [20] detail the improvements made to the kernel for Beowulf-style messaging. In their results, significant and marked improvement could be achieved with some simple tweaks to the kernel. Other kernel modifications that improve performance of large messages over high-speed adapters such as Myrinet have also been made available on the Web. Since modifications and tweaks of that nature are very dependent on the kernel version, they are not outlined here. You are encouraged to browse the Beowulf mailing lists and Web sites and use the power of the Linux source code to improve the performance of your Beowulf.

4.4.2 Hardware Performance Counters

Most modern CPUs have built-in performance counters. Each CPU design measures and counts metrics corresponding to its architecture. Several research groups have attempted to make portable interfaces for the hardware performance counters across the wide range of CPU architectures. One of the best known is PAPI: A Portable Interface to Hardware Performance Counters [23]. Another interface, Rabbit [16], is available for Intel or AMD CPUs. Both provide access to performance counter data from the CPU. Such low-level packages require interaction with the kernel; they are extensions to its basic functionality. In order to use any of the C library interfaces, either support must be compiled directly into the kernel, or a special hardware performance counter module must be built and loaded. Beowulf builders are encouraged to immediately extend their operating system with support for hardware performance counters. Users find this low-level CPU information, especially with respect to cache behavior, invaluable in their quest for better node-OS utilization. Three components will be required: the kernel extensions (either compiled in or built as a module), a compatible version of the Linux kernel, and the library interfaces that connect the user's code to the kernel interfaces for the performance counters.

4.5 Final Tuning with /proc

As mentioned earlier, the /proc file system is not really a file system at all, but a window on the running kernel. It contains handles that can be used to extract information from the kernel or, in some cases, change parameters deep inside the kernel. In this section, we discuss several of the most important parameters for Beowulfs. A multitude of Linux Web pages are dedicated to tuning the kernel and important daemons, with the goal of serving a few more Web pages per second. A good place to get started is `linuxperf.nl.linux.org`. Many Linux users take it as a personal challenge to tune the kernel sufficiently so their machine is faster than every other operating system in the world.

However, before diving in, some perspective is in order. Remember that in a properly configured Beowulf node, nearly all of the available CPU cycles and memory are devoted to the scientific application. As mentioned earlier, the Linux operating system will perform admirably with absolutely no changes. Trimming down the kernel and removing unneeded daemons and processes provides slightly more room for the host application. Tuning up the remaining very small kernel can further refine the results. Occasionally, a performance bottleneck can be dislodged with some simple kernel tuning. However, unless performance is awry, tinkering with parameters in `/proc` will more likely yield a little extra performance and a fascinating look at the interaction between Linux and the scientific application than incredible speed increases.

Now for a look at the Ethernet device:

```
% cat /proc/net/dev
Inter-| Receive | Transmit
face |bytes packets errs drop fifo frame compressed multicast|bytes
packets errs drop fifo colls carrier compressed
lo:363880104 559348 0 0 0 0 0 363880104 559348 0 0 0 0 0 0
eth0:1709724751 195793854 0 0 357 0 0 0 4105118568 202431445
0 0 0 0 481 0
brg0: 0 0 0 0 0 0 0 0 0 0 0 0 0 0 0 0
```

It is a bit hard to read, but the output is raw columnar data. A better formatting can be seen with `/sbin/ifconfig`. One set of important values is the total bytes and the total packets sent or received on an interface. Sometimes a little basic scientific observation and data gathering can go a long way. Are the numbers reasonable? Is application traffic using the correct interface? You may need to tune the default route to use a high-speed interface in favor of a 10-baseT Ethernet. Is something flooding your network? What is the size of the average packet? Another key set of values is for the collisions (colls), errs, drop, and frame. All of those values represent some degree of inefficiency in the Ethernet. Ideally, they will all be zero. A couple of dropped packets is usually nothing to fret about. But should those values grow at the rate of several per second, some serious problems are likely. The "collisions" count will naturally be nonzero if traffic goes through an Ethernet hub rather than an Ethernet switch. High collision rates for hubs are expected; that's why they are less expensive.

Tunable kernel parameters are in /proc/sys. Network parameters are generally in /proc/sys/net. Many parameters can be changed. Some administrators tweak a Beowulf kernel by modifying parameters such as tcp_sack, tcp_timestamps, tcp_window_scaling, rmem_default, rmem_max, wmem_default, or wmem_max. The exact changes and values depend on the kernel version and networking configuration, such as private network, protected from denial of service attacks or a public network where each node must guard against SYN flooding and the like. You are encouraged to peruse the documentation available at www.linuxhq.com and other places where kernel documentation or source is freely distributed, to learn all the details pertaining to their system.

With regard to memory, the meminfo handle provides many useful data points:

```
% cat /proc/meminfo
total:    used:    free:    shared: buffers: cached:
Mem: 263380992 152883200 110497792 64057344 12832768 44445696
Swap: 271392768 17141760 254251008
MemTotal:  257208 kB
MemFree:   107908 kB
MemShared:  62556 kB
Buffers:    12532 kB
Cached:     43404 kB
SwapTotal: 265032 kB
SwapFree:  248292 kB}
```

In the example output, the system has 256 megabytes of RAM, about 12.5 megabytes allocated for buffers and 108 megabytes of free memory.

The tunable virtual memory parameters are in /proc/sys/vm. Some Beowulf administrators may wish to tune the amount of memory used for buffering.

```
% cat /proc/sys/vm/buffermem
2 10 60
```

The first value represents, as a percentage, the amount of the total system memory used for buffering on the Beowulf node. For a 256-megabyte node, no less than about 5 megabytes will be used for buffering. To change the value is simple:

```
% echo 4 10 60 > /proc/sys/vm/buffermem
```

Like networking and virtual memory, there are many **/proc** handles for tuning or probing the file system. A node spawning many tasks can use many file handles. A standard ssh to a remote machine, where the connection is maintained, and not dropped, requires four file handles. The number of file handles permitted can be displayed with the command

```
% cat /proc/sys/fs/file-max
4096
```

The command for a quick look at the current system is

```
% cat /proc/sys/fs/file-nr
1157 728 4096
```

This shows the high-water mark (in this case, we have nothing to worry about), the current number of handles in use, and the max.

Once again, a simple echo command can increase the limit:

```
% echo 8192 > /proc/sys/fs/file-max
```

The utility **/sbin/hdparm** is especially handy at querying, testing, and even setting hard disk parameters:

```
% /sbin/hdparm -I /dev/hda

/dev/hda:

 Model=DW CDW01A0 A , FwRev=500.B550, SerialNo=DWW-AMC1211431 9
 Config={ HardSect NotMFM HdSw>15uSec SpinMotCtl Fixed DTR>5Mbs FmtGapReq }
 RawCHS=16383/16/63, TrkSize=57600, SectSize=600, ECCbytes=40
 BuffType=3(DualPortCache), BuffSize=2048kB, MaxMultSect=16, MultSect=8
 DblWordIO=no, maxPIO=2(fast), DMA=yes, maxDMA=0(slow)
 CurCHS=17475/15/63, CurSects=16513875, LBA=yes
 LBA CHS=512/511/63 Remapping, LBA=yes, LBAsects=19541088
 tDMA={min:120,rec:120}, DMA modes: mword0 mword1 mword2
 IORDY=on/off, tPIO={min:120,w/IORDY:120}, PIO modes: mode3 mode4
 UDMA modes: mode0 mode1 *mode2 }
```

Using a Beowulf builder and a simple disk test,

```
% /sbin/hdparm -t /dev/hda1

/dev/hda1:
Timing buffered disk reads: 64 MB in 20.05 seconds = 3.19 MB/sec
```

you can understand whether your disk is performing as it should, and as you expect.

Finally, some basic parameters of that kernel can be displayed or modified. `/proc/sys/kernel` contains structures. For some message-passing codes, the key may be `/proc/sys/kernel/shmmax`. It can be used to get or set the maximum size of shared-memory segments. For example,

```
% cat /proc/sys/kernel/shmmax
33554432
```

shows that the largest shared-memory segment available is 32 megabytes. Especially on an SMP, some messaging layers may use shared-memory segments to pass messages within a node, and for some systems and applications 32 megabytes may be too small.

All of these examples are merely quick forays into the world of `/proc`. Naturally, there are many, many more statistics and handles in `/proc` than can be viewed in this quick overview. You are encouraged to look on the Web for more complete documentation and to explore the Linux source—the definitive answer to the question "What will happen if I change this?" A caveat is warranted: You can make your Beowulf node perform worse as a result of tampering with kernel parameters. Good science demands data collection and repeatability. Both will go a long way toward ensuring that kernel performance increases, rather than decreases.

4.6   Conclusions

Linux is a flexible, robust node operating system for Beowulf computational clusters. Stability and adaptability set it apart from the legacy operating systems that dominate desktop environments. While not a "cancer" like some detractors have labeled Linux, it has spread quickly from its humble beginnings as a student's hobby project to a full-featured server operating system with advanced features and legendary stability. And while almost any Linux distribution will perform adequately as a Beowulf node operating system, a little tuning and trimming will skinny down the already lean Linux kernel, leaving more compute resources for scientific applications. If this chapter seems a little overwhelming, we note that there are companies that will completely configure and deliver Beowulf systems, including all the aforementioned tweaks and modifications to the kernel. There are also revolutionary systems such as the Beowulf software from Scyld Computing Corporation (`www.sycld.com`). The software from Scyld combines a custom Linux kernel and distribution with a complete environment for submitting jobs and administering the cluster. With its extremely simple single-system image approach to management, the Scyld software can make Beowulfs very easy indeed.

One final reminder is in order. Many Beowulf builders became acquainted with Linux purely out of necessity. They started constructing their Beowulf saying, "Every OS is pretty much like every other, and Linux is free... free is good, right?". On the back of restaurant napkins, they sketched out their improved price/performance ratios. After the hardware arrived, the obligatory LINPACK report was sent to the Top500 list, and the real scientific application ran endlessly on the new Beowulf. Then it happened. Scientists using Linux purely as a tool stopped and peered inquisitively at the tool. They read the source code for the kernel. Suddenly, the simulation of the impending collision of the Andromeda galaxy with our own Milky Way seemed less interesting. Even though the two galaxies are closing at a rate of 300,000 miles per hour and we have only 5 billion years to wait, the simulation simply seemed less exciting than improving the virtual memory paging algorithm in the kernel source, sending Linus Torvalds the patch, and reading all the kernel mailing list traffic. Beware. Even the shortest of peeks down the rabbit's hole can sometimes lead to a wonderland much more interesting than your own.

5 Network Hardware

Thomas Sterling

Networking converts a shelf full of PCs into a single system. Networking also allows a system to be accessed remotely and to provide services to remote clients. The incredible growth of both the Internet and enterprise-specific intranets has resulted in the availability of high-performance, low-cost networking hardware that Beowulf systems use to create a single system from a collection of nodes. This chapter reviews networking hardware, with a particular emphasis on Fast Ethernet because of its superb price/performance ratio.

For Beowulf systems, the most demanding communication requirements are not with the external environment but with the other nodes on the system area network. In a Beowulf system, every Beowulf node may need to interact with every other node, independently or together, to move a wide range of data types between processors. Such data may be large blocks of contiguous information representing subpartitions of very large global data sets, small packets containing single values, or synchronization signals in support of collective operation. In the former case, a high bandwidth communication path may be required. In the latter case, low latency communication is required to expedite execution. Requirements in both cases are highly sensitive to the characteristics of the parallel program being executed. In any case, communications capability will determine the generality of the Beowulf-class system and the degree of difficulty in constructing efficient programs. The choice of network hardware and software dictates the nature of this capability.

Section 5.1 introduces some of the most popular networking technologies for Beowulf clusters. In Section 5.2, we take a detailed look at the most popular networking choice, Fast Ethernet (and Gigabit Ethernet). We conclude in Section 5.3 with comments on interconnect technology choice and some other practical issues

5.1 Interconnect Technologies

In spite of its popular use in existing Beowulfs, Ethernet-based networking is not the only technology choice for enabling internode communication. Other solutions exist that can deliver equal or better performance depending on the application. Fast Ethernet is a popular choice because of its ubiquity and consequent low price. A Fast Ethernet card costs only about 2 percent of the price of today's $1,000 Beowulf nodes. Only the network switches have a significant impact on the overall price of the system. With other networking technologies, each network interface card can cost as much as a 16-port Fast Ethernet switch. So you have to think carefully before committing to an alternative network. If the kinds of applications you intend to run require specific properties, such as low latency, which are not provided by Fast Ethernet, then it is likely worth the additional cost. For example, real-time image processing, parallel video streaming, and real-time transaction processing all require low latencies and do not work well with Fast Ethernet. We will briefly discuss the most common networking technologies used by Beowulf systems. Not enough data has been collected on application performance in systems using these technologies for us to comment on when each should be used.

5.1.1   The Ethernets

The most popular and inexpensive networking choice for Beowulfs is Ethernet, particularly Fast Ethernet. Ethernet, first developed at Xerox PARC in the early 1970s and standardized by the IEEE in the early 1980s, is the most widely used technology for local area networks. Ethernet continues to be an evolving technology: 10 Gigabit Ethernet (10 Gbps) has entered vendor field testing and should be available in quantity by early 2002. With the very low cost of Fast Ethernet and the rapid emergence of Gigabit and 10 Gigabit Ethernet, Ethernet will continue to play a critical role in Beowulf-class computing for some time to come.

Fast Ethernet.   Beowulf was enabled by the availability of a low-cost, moderate-bandwidth networking technology. Ethernet, operating initially at 10 megabits per second (Mbps) for early Beowulfs and shortly thereafter at 100 Mbps peak bandwidth, provided a cost-effective means of interconnecting PCs to form an integrated cluster. Used primarily for commercial local area network technology, Ethernet supplied the means of implementing a system area network at about 20 percent of the cost of the total system, even when employing low-cost personal computers. Fast Ethernet with TCP/IP provides 90–95 Mbps to applications with latencies in the hundreds of microseconds. Drivers for Fast Ethernet and TCP/IP have been integrated into the mainline Linux kernel sources for quite some time and are well tested, with a large user base. Cost of Fast Ethernet interfaces has dropped to the point that many motherboard vendors have begun to integrate single- or dual-port interfaces into their products. While other networking continues to be available (and used in some Beowulfs), Fast Ethernet will continue to be a mainstay of many Beowulf implementations because of its extremely low cost.

Gigabit Ethernet.   The success of 100 base-T Fast Ethernet and the growing demands imposed on networks by high-resolution image data, real-time data browsing, and Beowulf-class distributed applications have driven the industry to establish a new set of standards for Ethernet technology capable of 1 Gbps. Referred to as "Gigabit Ethernet," a backward-compatible network infrastructure has been devised, and products are available from various vendors. A number of changes were required to Fast Ethernet, including the physical layer and a large part of the data exchange protocols. However, to maintain compatibility with Fast Ethernet, or 100-baseT systems, means for mixed-mode operation has been provided. Currently, Gigabit Ethernet is not quite cost effective for Beowulf-class computing. The early product offerings for Gigabit Ethernet, as the early offerings for 10 Gigabit Ethernet will be, were for backbone service and traffic aggregation rather than for direct host connections; hence, the demand for NICs was assumed to be low, and a large market has not yet emerged to amortize development costs. Both switches and NICs are substantially more expensive than their Fast Ethernet equivalents.

Several factors will motivate the migration of next-generation Gigabit Ethernet into the role of system area networks for Beowulf-class systems. While Fast Ethernet served well for 200 MHz Intel Pentium Pro processor-based Beowulf nodes, current Pentium 4 processors are available at speeds of 1.7 GHz. The PCI bus now supports a data path twice as wide and twice the clock rate, permitting high-bandwidth data transfers to peripheral devices including Gigabit NICs. A broader range of Beowulf applications can be supported with higher bandwidth. Unfortunately, Gigabit Ethernet with TCP/IP does not provide substantially better latencies than does Fast Ethernet. Some Beowulf installations have already experimented with Gigabit Ethernet, and the Beowulf project has already delivered drivers to the Linux operating system for several Gigabit Ethernet cards. Some vendors have even begun to supply high-performance, open source gigabit drivers for their NICs. The experience with Fast Ethernet demonstrated that a rapid and dramatic drop in price can be expected once the technology is adopted by the mass market. With the introduction of inexpensive combination ethernet/Fast Ethernet/Gigabit Ethernet ASICs, motherboard integration and low-cost gigabit adapters are beginning to appear. Gigabit switch prices have also begun to fall. The 1 Gbps technology is in place, and experience by manufacturers is leading to rapid improvements and cost cutting. With these advances, we expect that Gigabit Ethernet will become a leader in interconnect price/performance in the next one to two years.

5.1.2 Myrinet

Myrinet is a system area network (SAN) designed by Myricom, Inc. On November 2, 1998, it was approved as American National Standard ANSI/VITA 26-1998. It is designed around simple low-latency blocking switches. The path through these switches is implemented with "header-stripping" source routing, where the sending node prepends the route through the network, and each switch removes the first byte of the message and uses it as the output port. Packets can be of arbitrary length.

The bandwidth of the adapter and switch is hidden from the application and has regularly increased over time from the original 640 Mbps to the current 2.4 Gbps. Myrinet delivers between 10 and 7 microseconds, depending on the generation of adapter and switch. A limitation of Myrinet is that the switches are incrementally blocking. If a destination port is busy in a multistage network, the packet is stalled, and that stalled packet potentially blocks other packets traveling the network, even to unrelated source and destination nodes. This problem is mitigated, however, by the network's high speed and the ability to construct topologies with rich interconnects. Blocking is minimized by higher-density switches that reduce the number of a stages traversed by a typical message in a network of fixed size.

While Myrinet is the strongest provider of high-bandwidth SANs, it has the limitation of being provided by a single vendor. The price of the network adapters and per port costs of switches has remained high, typically exceeding the price of the entire computing node. Myrinet's big advantage is its customized protocols. These protocols are designed to yield high performance and low latency by offloading as much work as possible to the NIC itself and bypassing the operating system whenever possible. Myrinet NICs effectively provide a second processor that can do much of the protocol work and avoid interrupting the host CPU during communication. This advantage could also be obtained for less money by adding a second primary processor. This advantage is most significant with active messages, where the on-board processor can handle the message and generate a reply without and interrupting the host CPU. In order for the hardware to be used in this way, Myricom provides a substantial amount of open source software, both drivers and a tuned version of MPICH. Using customized protocols also encourages user-level access to the hardware. This strategy has also been pursued with commodity hardware (see Section 5.3.3 for a brief discussion of MVIA, an implementation for commodity hardware by the Virtual Interface Architecture, VIA). Unfortunately, user-level access protocols have the disadvantage of precluding clusters from transparently scaling from standard TCP and Ethernet on small-scale machines to alternative hardware such as Myrinet on big clusters.

5.1.3   cLAN

The cLAN high-performance cluster switches provide a native implementation of the VIA (see `www.viarch.org`). Eight port and thirty port switches are available, offering 1.25 Gbps per port (2.5 Gbps bidirectional). Because these implement the

VIA directly in hardware, latencies are low (around 0.5 microsecond) and bandwidths are high (comparable to the other high-end networking solutions). The developer of cLAN was Giganet, which was acquired by Emulex in March 2001.

While VIA is defined by a consortium and is not a single-vendor design, the VIA standard specifies only a set of concepts and operations. There is no specification of the signals (they can be electrical, optical, or anything else) or the interfaces to individual computers. There is also no standard programmer interface, although most VIA efforts (including cLAN) use the sample application programming interface provided in the VIA specification. However, because the VIA standard does not specify the hardware over which VIA is used, there is no possibility of interoperable VIA solutions. Infiniband, discussed below, addresses this issue.

5.1.4 Scalable Coherent Interface

The Scalable Coherent Interface is an IEEE standard originally designed to provide an interconnect for cache-coherent shared-memory systems. One of the first major deployments of SCI was on the Convex Exemplar SPP-1000 in 1994. SCI has not been able to gain ground in traditional networking markets, despite its ability to serve as a general-purpose interconnect. The main reason Beowulf designers choose to use SCI is for its low latency of well under 10 μs. Current PC motherboard chip sets do not support the coherency mechanisms required to construct an SCI-based shared-memory Beowulf. But if that functionality is ever added to commodity motherboards, we may see an increase in the popularity of SCI as researchers experiment with shared-memory Beowulf systems. Seven years ago, SCI delivered many clear advantages, but today commodity network technology has caught up, although SCI still delivers significantly lower latency. Dolphin Interconnect offers an SCI-based interconnect for Beowulf systems along with closed-source binary drivers and an implementation of MPI tuned for the SCI network.

5.1.5 QsNet

Another high-performance network, called QsNet, is produced by Quadrics. This network provides a bandwidth of 340 Mbps and an MPI latency of around 5 μs. While this network is one the costliest, it has been chosen by some of the largest clusters, including Compaq SC systems for the ASCI Q system and the NSF teraflops system at the Pittsburg Supercomputing Center. To provide high performance, Quadrics uses many techniques similar to those mentioned above for Myrinet.

Preamble 1010.....1010	SYNCH 11	DESTINATION ADDRESS	SOURCE ADDRESS	TYPE	DATA	FRAME CHECK SEQUENCE
62 BITS	2 BITS	6 BYTES	6 BYTES	2 BYTES	16-1500 BYTES	4 BYTES

Figure 5.1
Ethernet packet format.

5.1.6   Infiniband

Infiniband (`www.infinibandta.org`) combines many of the concepts of VIA with a detailed electrical and interface specification that will allow vendors to produce interoperable components. This addresses the major limitation of the VIA specification. One goal of the Infiniband trade organization (with over two hundred members) is to increase the rate at which networking performance improves.

As of early 2001, no Infiniband products were available. Many are under development, however, and by 2002 Infiniband may become an important alternative to the other networks described here. Intel has committed to delivering integrated Infiniband interfaces on its motherboards in the next one to two years. This should provide another high-bandwidth, low-latency interconnect at a relatively low price point.

5.2   A Detailed Look at Ethernet

Ethernet was originally developed as a packet-based, serial multidrop network requiring no centralized control. All network access and arbitration control is performed by distributed mechanisms. Variable-length message packets comprise a sequence of bits including a header, data, and error-detecting nodes. A fixed-topology (no switched line routing) network passes packets from the source to destination through intermediate elements known as hubs or switches. The next step through the network is determined by addressing information in the packet header. The topology can be a shared multidrop passive cable to which many Ethernet controllers are attached, a tree structure of hubs or switches, or some more complicated switching technology for high bandwidths and low latency under heavy loads.

5.2.1   Packet Format

The Ethernet message packet comprises a sequence of seven multibit fields, one of which is variable length. The fields include a combination of network control information and data payload. The structure of the Ethernet packet is shown in

Figure 5.1 and is described below. The packet's variable length allows improved overall network performance across a wide range of payload requirements. Thus, a transfer of only a few words between nodes does not impose the full burden of the longest possible packet. However, even with this capability, sustained data transfer throughput is sensitive to packet length and can vary by more than an order of magnitude depending on payload size, even in the absence of network contention.

Preamble. Arrival of a message packet at a receiving node (whether or not the message is addressed for that node) is asynchronous. Prior to data assimilation, the node and the incident packet must first synchronize. The preamble field is a 62-bit sequence of alternating 1s and 0s that allows the phase lock loop circuitry of the node receiver to lock on to the incoming signal and synchronize with the bit stream.

Synch. The synch field is a 2-bit sequence of 1s (11) that breaks the sequence of alternating 1s and 0s provided by the preamble and indicates where the remaining information in the packet begins. If the preamble provides carrier-level synchronization, the synch field provides bit field registration.

Destination Address. The destination address field is 6 bytes (or 48 bits) in length and specifies the network designation of the network node intended to receive the packet. A message packet may be intended for an individual node or a group of nodes. If the first bit of the destination address field is 0, then the message is intended for a single receiving node. If the first bit is 1, then the message is multicast, intended for some or all network nodes. In the case of multicast communications, a group address is employed providing a logical association among some subset of all receiving nodes. Any node that is a member of a group specified by the message destination address field (with the first bit equal to 1) must accept the message. In the case of a multicast transmitted packet, a destination address field of all 1s indicates that the packet is a broadcast message intended for all nodes on the network. Ethernet node receivers must be capable of receiving, detecting, and accepting broadcast messages.

In addition to distinguishing among single destination and multicast transmission, the destination address also determines whether the specified address is a globally or locally administered address. A globally administered address is unique and is provided by an industrywide assignment process. The address is built into the network adaptor (interface card) by the manufacturer. A locally administered address is provided by the local systems administrator and can be changed by the organization managing the network. The second bit of the destination address field

is a 0 if globally administered and a 1 if the address designation is locally administered. The sequence of bits of the destination address field is sent least significant
bit first.

Source Address. The source address is a 48-bit field that indicates the address
of the transmitting node. The format of the source address is the same as that of
the destination address. The source address is always the individual address and
never a group address of the node sending a packet. Therefore, the least significant
bit is always 0. Likewise, the broadcast address is never used in this field.

Type. The type field is 16 bits in length and designates the message protocol
type. This information is used at higher levels of message-handling software and
does not affect the actual exchange of data bits across the network. The most
significant of the two bytes is sent first, with the least significant bit of each byte
of the type field being sent first.

Data. The message payload of the packet is included in the data field. The data
field is variable length. It may have as few as 46 bytes and as many as 1,500 bytes.
Thus, a packet may be as small as 72 bytes or as long as 1,526 bytes. The contents
of the data field are passed to higher-level software and do no affect the network
transfer control. Data is transferred least significant bit first.

Frame Check Sequence. Error detection for message corruption in transmission
is provided by computing a cyclic redundancy check (CRC) for the destination
address, source address, type, and data fields. The four-byte CRC value is provided
as the last field of the message packet. It is computed by both the transmitting and
receiving nodes and compared by the receiving node to determine that the integrity
of the packet has been retained in transmission.

5.2.2   NIC Architecture

The Network Interface Controller accepts message data from the host node processor and presents an encapsulated and encoded version of the data to the physical
network medium for transmission. While there have been many different implementations of the Ethernet NIC hardware, with some enhancements, their basic
architecture is the same. Figure 5.2 shows a block diagram of the typical Ethernet
NIC architecture. The Data Link Layer of the architecture is responsible for constructing the message packet and controlling the logical network interface functions.
The Physical Layer is responsible for encoding the message packet in a form that
can actually be applied to the transmission medium.

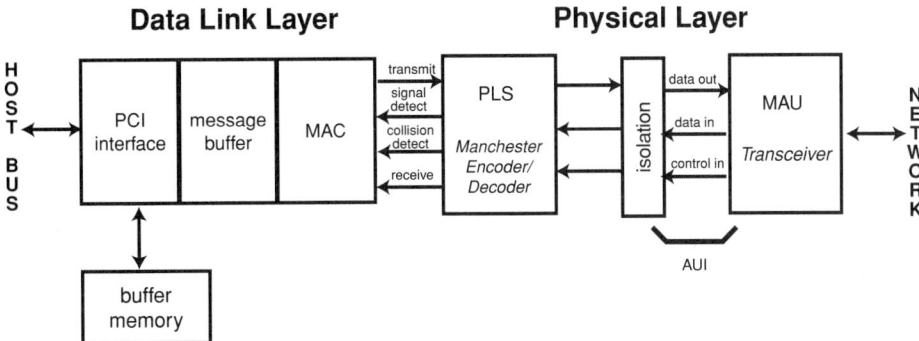

Figure 5.2
Ethernet NIC architecture.

Data Link Layer. The Data Link Layer provides the logical interface between the host processor and the Physical Layer of the Ethernet. When a message is to be transmitted, the Data Link Layer accepts, temporarily stores, and encapsulates the message and controls the transmission process of the Physical Layer. When a message is being received, it accepts the packet from the Physical Layer, determines whether the node is the correct destination, verifies bit integrity, unpacks the data into byte sequence, temporarily buffers the data, and passes it on to the processor. The Data Link Layer is made up of the Logical Link Control sublayer and the Media Access Control sublayer.

For most current-generation Beowulf nodes, the Logical Link Control sublayer incorporates an interface to the PCI bus. This element of the Ethernet controller provides all logical control required to accept commands from the host processor and to provide direct memory access to the node main memory for rapid data transfers between memory and the network. Usually included is some form of FIFO buffering within the Data Link Layer to hold one or more incoming or outgoing messages in the node. The Logical Link Control sublayer presents variable-length byte sequences to the Media Access Control sublayer and accepts data byte sequences from it. The exact form and operation of the Logical Link Control sublayer is not standardized, and manufacturer differences are a source of headaches for device driver writers.

The Media Access Controller (MAC) is largely responsible for conducting the Ethernet protocol for both transmitted and received messages. Its two principal tasks are message encapsulation and packet collision handling. To transmit a message, the MAC accepts the byte sequence of the data to be sent, as well as the destination address, from the Logical Link Controller. It formats the message packet including the preamble, synch bits, destination address, its own address in the source address field, and the protocol type provided by the logical link controller as well as the data field. It then computes the CRC value and appends it to the message packet. When receiving an Ethernet packet from the Physical Layer, the MAC strips away the preamble and synch bits and determines if the destination address is that of its host node. If not, the rest of the message is discarded and the receive process terminates. If the Destination Address field matches the local address, the MAC accepts the data, reformatting it into the correctly ordered byte sequence for the Logical Link Controller. The MAC computes the cyclic redundancy check and compares it with the value included in the message to verify transmission integrity.

The MAC is also responsible for handling the CSMA/CD (Carrier Sense Multiple Access/Collision Detect) arbitration protocol. The Physical Layer provides signals to the MAC indicating whether there is packet transmission on the data link and whether there is a collision among two or more packets on the link. When a signal is available, the MAC operates as above to determine whether the message is for the host node and, if so, acquires the data. In the case of a collision, the MAC simply discards any partial incoming messages and waits for new packet data. When transmitting, the MAC is responsible for handling collision avoidance and resolution. As described above, the MAC waits for access to the data link and supplies the packet to the physical layer that begins transmission. If in the process of packet transmission the MAC receives a collision signal from the Physical Layer, after briefly continuing transmission (to overcome the network propagation delay) it terminates the message and begins its random roll-back sequence to determine a new time when it will again attempt to transmit the message.

Physical Layer. The Physical Layer encodes the message packet provided by the Data Link Layer and converts it to electrical signals appropriate for the physical transmission medium. Upon receiving messages transmitted by other nodes, the Physical Layer acquires the electrical signals from the transmission medium, converts them to digital signals, and decodes them into the message's binary bit sequence. The Physical Layer includes two major stages: the transceiver and the Physical Line Signaling (PLS) sublayer. The transceiver, also referred to as the Medium Attachment Unit (MAU), performs the electrical conversion from transmission media signals to logical signal levels.

The interface between the PLS sublayer of the Physical Layer and the MAC sublayer of the Data Link Layer exchanges data with bits represented as discrete voltage levels. This form of information representation is inadequate for Ethernet for two reasons. First, in a highly noisy (in the electrical sense) environment such as presented by a local area network, signal levels can be significantly attenuated and distorted. Second, in a single bit-serial communication protocol such as that employed by the Ethernet interconnect, both data and timing information need to be incorporated in the signal. For this reason, Manchester encoding is used to convey the information with the value of a bit specified by the sense (direction) of the signal transition rather than a specific range of values. With data fixed at the point of signal transition, the timing information is provided simultaneously.

The actual Ethernet signal is differential; that is, one line is high when the other is low and vice versa. The PLS sublayer converts the message packet provided by the MAC first into its Manchester encoded representation and then into differential form. The PLS layer performs the decoding task for incoming signals from the transceiver, converting Manchester sequences into regular bit strings. The PLS layer also provides the collision detect signal to the MAC.

5.2.3   Hubs and Switches

The Network Interface Controllers provide the connection between the processor node and the system area network. The effectiveness of the SAN and its scalability depend on the means by which the nodes are interconnected. These include passive multidrop coaxial cable, active repeaters, and intelligent routing switches, as well as more complicated through-the-node store and forward techniques.

Repeaters and Hubs. An early advantage of Ethernet was that the medium of communication was a passive multidrop coaxial cable. Over a limited distance and number of nodes, such a cable located all expensive logic and electronics in the NICs. As technology costs dropped and demands on network performance increased, other approaches could compete. Ironically, the coax cables that had helped keep costs down became the dominant cost driver. Twisted-pair connections using inexpensive repeaters or hubs have now replaced coaxial cables in all but the oldest installations. Logically, hubs provide the same NIC interface. All nodes are visible from all other nodes, and the CSMA/CD arbitration protocol is still employed. A repeater is an active unit that accepts signals from the distributed nodes on separate twisted pair wires, actively cleans up the signals, amplifies them to desired levels, and then redistributes them to all of the attached nodes.

Switches. The demand for higher sustained bandwidths and the need to include larger number of nodes on a single network spurred development of more sophisticated means of exchanging messages among nodes. Switches, like hubs or repeaters, accept packets on twisted-pair wires from the nodes. Unlike repeaters, however, these signals are not broadcast to all connected nodes. Instead, the destination address fields of the message packets are interpreted and the packet is sent only to the target node or nodes. This functionality is much more complicated than that of a simple repeater, requiring buffer space and logic not required by a hub. At the time of the earliest Beowulfs, the cost of switches was prohibitive. By the third generation of Beowulf systems (based on Intel Pentium Pro processors), however, the cost of switches was sufficiently low that they became standard Beowulf components.

Today, 16-way switches have dropped in price another factor of four or more, and they are the backbone of many moderate-sized systems. Moderate-cost switches with up to 48 connections are widely available. For greater connectivity, multiple switches can be interconnected. There is a catch, however. The network must be a tree; it may not contain any cycles.

A problem occurs with the tree topology. The bisection bandwidth of the root or top level switch becomes a communication bottleneck. All the traffic might have to go through this channel. A typical bandwidth for low-cost, 16-way Fast Ethernet switches is near or at 1.6 Gbps. Backplane saturation with Fast Ethernet switches is not a serious problem at this point. Current generation of gigabit switches provides much higher backplane bisection bandwidth and therefore the possibility of many more network ports without contention. With a properly sized core gigabit switch, the network core can be easily (with money) scaled to 192 Gbps or more. With these, use of Fast Ethernet switches with dual or quad gigabit uplinks scale properly, without serious contention in the network to a scale easily upwards of 1,000 nodes.

5.3   Network Practicalities: Interconnect Choice

Network choice for a system area network can be a difficult process. In this section we consider various factors and present two examples illustrating how different choices can affect performance.

5.3.1   Importance of the Interconnect

The cost for the NIC and switch complex can equal or exceed the cost of node hardware on a large cluster: it is not a factor that should be taken lightly.

In the absence of financial considerations, however, the most important factor when choosing an interconnect technology is the communication patterns of the intended workload for the cluster. While the peak CPU performance of the processors in a cluster tends to add up rather quickly, a given application may or may not be able to effectively utilize it without a high bandwidth and/or low latency interconnect. This can account for up to a 95% penalty when comparing theoretical speed with achieved performance. Because of this fact, and the high cost of interconnect hardware, it is important to build a properly sized system area network for a given workload.

If a cluster is being built for a small number of applications, thorough application benchmarking is in order. The spectrum of communication patterns exhibited by applications ranges from occasional communication from one node to another to consistent communication from all nodes to all other nodes. At one extreme are applications that behave like Seti@Home, wherein compute nodes infrequently query a master node for a work unit to process for hours or days. At the other extreme are applications like MILC (MIMD Lattice Computation), where nodes are in constant communication with one or more other nodes and the speed of the computation is limited by the performance of the slowest node. As is obvious from the communication pattern description, basically any interconnect would perform admirably in the first case, while the fastest interconnect possible is desirable in the second case.

5.3.2   Differences between the Interconnect Choices

As seen in the preceding descriptions, interconnects vary wildly with respect to bandwidth, latency, scalability, and cost. Available interconnect bandwidth can range from a shared 10 Mbps network segment for the entire cluster to upwards to 340 Mbps available to all nodes simultaneously. Latency delivered to applications can range from in the hundreds of microseconds down to half a microsecond. This is near the latency cost of using the PCI bus. Various interconnects scale to different levels. Switched Ethernet-based interconnects, for example, basically work for any number of nodes on a network segment, as reliable packet delivery is provided by the TCP/IP layer. For this reason, Ethernet switch complexes deal well with congestion. Interconnect networks do not universally possess these characteristics, however; various interconnect types have topology scalability issues, and others basically require a full bisectional bandwidth switch complex to be built to minimize switch congestion. The cost of these technologies ranges from practically free to into the thousands of dollars per node of up-front cost. This does not take into consideration the substantial, recurring effort of integration, software, and hardware debugging. Variance in the types of drivers provided can also affect difficulty in integration. Some vendors provide binary drivers only for particular versions of the Linux kernel. These cause clusters using these interconnects to become kernel "version locked." In many cases, the kernel bugs that cluster administrators are likely to encounter are fixed by subsequent releases of the kernel. Hence, version-locked machines are harder to support.

5.3.3 Strategies to Improve Performance over Ethernet

Realistically, financial considerations are fairly important while designing a cluster. This is clearly indicated by the high frequency of clusters with Ethernet as an interconnect. As this is the slowest interconnect on the above list, performance optimization is of the utmost importance. The simplest approach is to tune the system's Ethernet and TCP/IP stacks; these changes are fairly nonintrusive and straightforward to implement, and there is a fairly good document detailing this tuning process at `www.psc.edu/networking/perf_tune.html`. Other approaches can be more intrusive. These fall into three categories: hardware choice, software features, and other network topologies.

Ethernet card performance will be heavily influenced by the characteristics of the NIC chosen. Higher-quality Ethernet NICs will deliver better throughput and latency at a lower host CPU utilization. This better performance is achieved through a number of techniques. Use of jumbo frames is one way to reduce host CPU utilization. By using a large MTU setting of 9,000 bytes as opposed to the usual 1,500 bytes, the NIC has to package up a considerably smaller number of Ethernet frames. Jumbo frames are supported only in Gigabit networks, but their use can significantly increase network throughput. Some NICs support TCP checksum calculation in hardware on the NIC itself. This removes one of the most expensive tasks from the host CPU. Some NICs also support interrupt coalescing. This means that the NIC has some quantity of local memory into which received packets can be stored temporarily, to reduce the interrupt load of NIC use. Without interrupt coalescing, heavy network use can induce enough context switching for interrupt servicing that computational throughput of the host CPU drops substantially. This feature is also really used only on Gigabit networks. Substantial differences in the feature set are supported by Gigabit network adapters.

On the other hand, Fast Ethernet NICs have a basically comparable hardware feature set and depend on drivers to deliver outstanding performance. There is a large variation in the quality of Gigabit drivers as well. All of the hardware features mentioned above need to be supported in software as well as in hardware in order to be used. Alternatively, TCP/IP may not be used at all. All of the properties a network protocol provides, such as reliable delivery and out-of-order packet reassembly, come at the cost of latency and bandwidth penalties. Some of these properties are important, some not. The VIA specification (`www.viarch.org`) describes an architecture that implements only those properties that are required in cluster communication. This provides a protocol with far less overhead than Ethernet's CSMA/CD and TCP/IP have. By using the MVIA implementation (`www.nersc.gov/research/FTG/via/`) of the VIA specification and its drivers for Fast Ethernet or Gigabit Ethernet NICs, more bandwidth is delivered to applications with less latency using commodity hardware. (This is the same protocol mentioned in Section 5.1.3.)

The final approach taken to maximize Ethernet performance is to use a different network topology. One of these topologies is to use EtherChannel, or Ethernet bonding. This software makes multiple physical Ethernet interfaces negotiate a virtual aggregated connection from the switch (there is no benefit to doing this in a shared network segment) to the client. This can increase the amount of bandwidth available to applications by integer multiples based on the number of physical interfaces available. Unfortunately, this has no positive effect on latency, as the logical path that a message takes from end to end has bonding routines to go through as well. Another topology designed to improve bisectional bandwidth and latency is FNN (`www.aggregate.org/FNN`), or Flat Network Neighborhoods. In this topology, hosts have multiple network interfaces that each home on a different switch. In a properly setup network, each host will have a NIC on the same switch as an interface on any given other host in the network. This technique attempts to leverage the large performance difference between backplanes and uplinks in a cost-effective manner.

5.3.4 Cluster Network Pitfalls

Linux gigabit support doesn't interact well with switch autonegotiation and time-sensitive protocols such as DHCP. We have had several problems with gigabit switch port initialization time. These long initialization times cause DHCP requests to time out. We have tracked this problem to a number of factors on the switch, all of which had to do with autonegotiation. Gigabit switches try to autonegotiate a number of settings when link comes up. The list of settings that are autonegotiated by default includes flow control, port negotiation, etherchannel (bonding), and 802.1q trunking. Then a spanning tree check is run to determine whether any switching loops exist in the network. All said, this process can take up to a minute to complete. This is certainly longer than the default DHCP request timeout. On Fast Ethernet networks, a number of these same settings are autonegotiated. While this list is shorter, and the port setup time is considerably less than on Gigabit Ethernet, problems can still result if many hosts are brought up in parallel.

To this end, disabling autonegotiation whenever possible will immensely simplify the network itself and reduce the number of problems encountered.

As Fast Ethernet is the most common interconnect, and Ethernet is the most common sort of Linux host networking, internode communication and cluster administrative processes may compete with one another for resources. This event should be avoided if at all possible. With the heavy usage of transparent network-based services like NFS, it is possible to unintentionally use large quantities of network bandwidth with fairly innocuous operations. Extraneous processes, even administrative tasks, should be avoided if possible while user jobs are running.

The nature of cluster administrative operations, whether synchronous, like `pdsh`, or asynchronous, like cron jobs, is that they run in a loosely parallel fashion. While these jobs are not synchronized internally, their methods of invocation cause them to be started in very small time windows. When these administrative operations are performed in parallel, the load pattern on servers is more bursty than normal Unix servers. In these cases, peak capacity is important more often than sustained throughput.

5.3.5   An Example of an Ethernet Interconnected Beowulf

The Clemson Mini-grid Beowulf employs four switches. The processor pool utilizes a Foundry Networks FastIron III with a backplane throughput of 480 Gbps and supports up to 336 Fast Ethernet ports or up to 120 Gigabit Ethernet ports. The configuration used in the Clemson machine includes 16 Gigabit Ethernet ports and 264 Fast Ethernet ports. The Mini-grid processor pool includes 130 nodes each with two Fast Ethernet NICs connected to this switch. In addition, the processor pool's switch is connected to three primary clusters one of which employs a Foundry Networks FastIron II Plus with a backplane throughput of 256 Gbps connected to 66 dual-NIC nodes, and two of which employ a Foundry Networks FastIron II with a backplane throughput of 128 Gbps connected to 34 dual-NIC nodes. The switches in the Mini-grid are connected by multiple trunked Gigabit Ethernet links. There are four trunked links between the pool and the larger cluster and two trunked links each between the pool and the two smaller clusters. The dual-NIC nodes in the pool and the clusters use Linux channel bonding to double the throughput of a normal Fast Ethernet NIC. The Foundry Networks switches use a similar technique to trunk up to eight Gigabit Ethernet links between any two switches. Using this approach one could build a Fast Ethernet switching system with up to 1080 ports with no bottlenecks. In practice, considerably larger networks can be built, though not with full bisection bandwidth. For many applications somewhat less bandwidth may be adequate. Other vendors with large Fast Ethernet switches include Hewlett Packard, Cisco, and Extreme.

5.3.6 An Example of a Myrinet Interconnected Cluster

The Chiba City cluster at Argonne National Laboratory (discussed in more detail in Chapter 18) has two discrete networks: (1) a Myrinet network consisting of 5 Clos switches, 4 Spine switches, and 320 host ports, and (2) a Fast/Gigabit Ethernet network consisting of 10 Cisco Catalyst 4000s and a Catalyst C6509 with 480 Fast Ethernet ports and 102 Gigabit Ethernet ports. The Myrinet network is used primarily as the system interconnect; however, if need be, Ethernet can be used as well. The Myrinet topology is symmetric, as is the Ethernet topology. Each spine switch has 128 network ports, with connections to all of the Clos switches in the network, but no connections to other spines. Each Myrinet Clos switch has 64 host ports and 64 network (switch interconnect) ports. Each Clos has its network ports distributed across all four spine switches. This yields 4096 potential routes from any given node to any other node in the network. This is required to guarantee full bisectional bandwidth for all possible workloads.

The Ethernet network is also fairly symmetric. Each group of 32 nodes and their management node are connected to a Catalyst 4000. Each of the 32 nodes is connected with Fast Ethernet, and the manager is connected with Gigabit Ethernet. Each of these switches has dual gigabit uplinks to the core Catalyst C6509. Because of the oversubscription of uplinks between each Catalyst 4000 and the core C6509, this network does not have full bisectional bandwidth. If this were primarily an interconnect network, and full bisectional bandwidth were important, this could be remedied by upgrading all switch uplinks from dual to quad gigabit connections.

6 Network Software

Thomas Sterling

In this chapter, we turn to the networking software options available to the Beowulf programmer, administrator, and user. Networking software is usually described as a stack, made up of different protocol layers that interoperate with one another. We survey a few of the layers in the networking stack, focusing on those services and tools that are used extensively on Beowulf systems.

6.1 TCP/IP

Parallel computers have traditionally used special high-performance interprocessor communication networks that use custom protocols to transmit data between processing elements. In contrast, Beowulf clusters rely on commodity networks whose original design goals did not include serving as the interconnect for a commodity supercomputer. The use of commodity networks implies the use of commodity protocols when costs must be kept down. Thanks to the tremendous growth of the Internet during the last decade of the twentieth century, TCP/IP has become the de facto standard network communication protocol. Network software vendors have been forced to abandon their proprietary networking protocols in favor of this once obscure but now ubiquitous protocol. Beowulfs naturally default to communicating with this protocol.

The IP protocol is conceptually divided into different logical layers that combine to form a protocol stack. The IP layer is a routable datagram layer. Data to be transferred is fragmented into datagrams—individual packets of data. Packet length is limited by the physical transport layer, and the IP layer contains the logic to fragment requests that are too large into multiple IP packets that are reassembled at the destination. Each datagram is individually routable and contains a four-byte IP address that specifies the destination host. This version of IP is called IPv4. A new version, called IPv6, will increase the address space available to IP applications. The four-byte addresses used in IPv4 are too small for the total number of computers currently connected to the world's networks. This address depletion will be remedied by IPv6, which uses 16 bytes to represent host addresses. Currently, however, IPv4 remains dominant, particularly in the United States.

The IP stack commonly supports two services: TCP (Transmission Control Protocol) and UDP (User Datagram Protocol). TCP, the most common IP service, provides a reliable, sequenced byte stream service. While the underlying physical transport layer usually provides error checking, TCP provides its own final data integrity checking. Most multiple-hop physical transports provide only a best-effort delivery promise. TCP incorporates a positive-acknowledgment sliding-window retransmission mechanism that recovers from packet loss. It also tolerates latency while maintaining high performance in the normal case of no packet loss. Moreover, TCP provides its own data stream packetization, avoiding fragmentation in the IP layer.

The drawbacks of TCP come from its ability to handle wide area networks. New TCP streams use "slow start" to detect the bandwidth limit of the network gradually. Congestion is detected by recording dropped packets. Any corrupted or dropped packet immediately drops the offered load. The Nagel algorithm used by TCP can cause problems for message-passing libraries. In order to minimize "tinygrams" (short packets), Nagel's algorithm delays the sending of small messages until the acknowledgment for an initial small message is returned. You can avoid this behavior either by compiling the Linux kernel with an option not to use Nagel's algorithm or by constructing your programs to use large messages. You can also turn off the algorithm in an application by using the `TCP_NODELAY` socket option, although some early versions of Linux did not properly implement this feature. See `www.icase.edu/coral/LinuxTCP.html` and `www.icase.edu/coral/LinuxTCP2.html` for a discussion of TCP performance issues in Linux.

The other IP service, UDP, provides unsequenced, unreliable datagram transport. The advantages of UDP are that it has a relatively low latency because it incurs no startup delay. Its primary disadvantage is that you typically have to provide retransmission services similar to those of TCP when you use UDP.

6.1.1   IP Addresses

The destination of an Internet Protocol packet is specified by a 32-bit IP address (or 128 bits) for IPv6) that uniquely identifies the destination host. IP addresses are usually written in "dotted decimal notation," with the bytes of the address written as a decimal numbers separated by decimal points. The IP address range is divided into networks along an address bit boundary. The portion of the address that remains fixed within a network is called the network address, and the remainder is the host address. The division between these two parts is specified by the netmask. A typical netmask is 255.255.255.0, which specifies 24 bits of network address and 8 bits of host addresses.

Three IP address ranges have been reserved for private networks:

- 10.0.0.0 - 10.255.255.255
- 172.16.0.0 - 172.31.255.255

- 192.168.0.0 - 192.168.255.255

These address ranges are permanently unassigned and will not be forwarded by Internet backbone routers or conflict with publicly accessible IP addresses. We will use IP addresses from the range 192.168.1.0–192.168.1.255 in the following examples.

In the past only a few netmasks were permitted. The netmasks were split on byte boundaries. These boundaries were given the names Class A (255.0.0.0 with about 16 million host addresses), Class B (255.255.0.0 with about 64,000 host addresses) and Class C (255.255.255.0 with 254 host addresses). Netmasks may now fall on any bit boundary but are split on byte boundaries where possible. The class names are still used when this occurs. We will use the Class C network 192.168.1.0.

Two addresses in the host address range are reserved: the addresses with all host bits 0 or 1. The host address with all bits set (e.g., 192.168.1.255) is the network broadcast address. Packets sent to this address will be forwarded to every host on the network. The address with all bits unset is not a host address at all—it is the network address. Similarly when a larger network is divided into subnets the highest and lowest address ranges are best avoided. While the Class C network 192.168.0.0 is valid, starting at 192.168.1.0 is recommended. It is syntactically possible to specify an invalid netmask—one with noncontiguous set bits. A "slash" notation is sometimes used to avoid this; for example, 192.168.1.0/24 specifies our network of 192.168.1.0 with a netmask of 255.255.255.0.

An alternative to assigning specific IP addresses to each node is to use the Dynamic Host Configuration Protocol (DHCP).

6.1.2   Zero-Copy Protocols

One way to improve network performance, especially for high-performance networks, is to eliminate unnecessary copying of data between buffers in the kernel or between the kernel and user space. So-called zero-copy protocols give applications nearly direct access to the network hardware, which copies data directly to and from buffers in the application program.

Implementing true zero-copy TCP from user-level applications is difficult. On the transmit side the kernel must wire down the pages, so that they are not moved during the network operation, and set copy-on-write in the virtual memory system, so that there isn't a race condition with an application writing the data while it is being transferred. Transmit buffers are often quickly reused, so the copy-on-write results in page copies rather than data buffer copies. If many small writes are done to socket, all of the data pages must be wired down until the ACK is received.

After all of this kernel overhead, not much work has been saved. Protocol layers must still construct the protocol headers and do the TCP checksums over the data to be transmitted.

When a frame arrives, the kernel has to decide where to put it. While it is possible to only read the variable-length IP header and defer handling the data, if the user-level process isn't already waiting in a `read()` call with a large enough buffer, the system has to perform a copy. The kernel also still has to process the TCP checksum. Some of this work can be handled by a smart adapter, which moves part of the protocol stack onto a coprocessor. When the protocol stack must function with all types of network adapters, zero-copy becomes impossible because of details such as byte alignment. The Ethernet header is 14 bytes, which always misaligns the IP header fields. Several research projects have developed methods for direct user-level-program access to the network because modifying the existing socket interface to use a zero-copy mechanism is very difficult. The most notable projects are the Virtual Interface Architecture (VIA) and U-Net, but neither is yet in widespread use.

6.2   Sockets

Sockets are the low-level interface between user-level programs and the operating system and hardware layers of a communication network. They provide a reasonably portable mechanism for two (or more) applications to communicate, and they support a variety of addressing formats, semantics, and underlying protocols. Sockets were introduced in the BSD 4.2 release of Unix and are being formally codified by the POSIX 1003.1g draft standard. Since its introduction, the sockets API has been widely adopted and is available on all modern Unix variants, including Linux. On Linux, the socket API is supported directly by the operating system, but (as noted above) research projects have proposed lower-level zero-copy protocols that would allow applications more direct access to the kernel.

The socket API is powerful but not particularly elegant. Many programmers avoid working with sockets directly, opting instead to hide the socket interface behind one or more additional layers of abstraction (e.g., remote procedure calls or a library like MPI). Nevertheless, our survey of networking would not be complete without a brief introduction to sockets. If you intend to program with sockets, you should consult both on-line (e.g., `man socket`) and printed documentation. The excellent book by Stevens [31] has many examples and thoroughly covers the finer points of sockets programming.

The basic idea behind the socket abstraction is that network communication resembles file I/O sufficiently closely that the same system calls can be used for both. Once a network connection is established between two processes, the transmission and receipt of data are performed with `read` and `write`, just as one sends data to a file, a tape, or any other device. The socket API is primarily concerned with naming and locating communication endpoints (i.e., sockets) and assigning them to file descriptors suitable for use by `read` and `write`.

A socket is created by invoking the `socket` system call with arguments specifying an address family, a socket type, and a protocol. Theoretically, an enormous number of combinations are possible, but in practice only two make up the vast majority of socket applications.

The first type is *unreliable, connectionless, datagram sockets.* The Internet address family `AF_INET`, the stream socket type `SOCK_DGRAM`, and the Unreliable Datagram Protocol `IPPROTO_UDP` allow one to create connectionless datagram sockets. These sockets allow for the transmission of a single message or datagram at a time. Neither the integrity nor the delivery of the data is guaranteed by the underlying protocol layers, so error-correcting codes, sequencing, and acknowledgment/retry are up to the application. A UDP socket is analogous to a conventional postal service mailbox. Many-to-one communication is the norm; that is, one UDP socket (mailbox) can receive datagrams (letters) from multiple senders, and one-to-many communication is possible simply by addressing datagrams (letters) to different recipients. Bidirectional communication is possible if two parties regularly reply to one another's messages, but the correspondents must be aware that messages can occasionally be lost, damaged, or delivered out of order. Return addresses are always available for UDP datagrams. `SOCK_DGRAM` sockets are very lightweight, consuming only one file descriptor and demanding minimal processing in the lower levels of the protocol stack. They are small and fast and are appropriate for tasks that can tolerate the lack of reliability and for which resource consumption may be an issue. One must carefully weigh the costs, however. If reliability is established at the application layer by means of acknowledgments, error correcting codes, and the like, the speed and size advantage may disappear. Many implementations of NFS use UDP datagram sockets as the underlying transport mechanism.

The second type of socket application is *reliable, connection-oriented, stream-type sockets.* Sockets in the Internet address family `AF_INET`, of type `SOCK_STREAM` generally use the Transmission Control Protocol `IPPROTO_TCP` and provide reliable, connection-oriented virtual circuits. TCP provides a connection-oriented channel like a conventional two-party telephone circuit. Once established, bidirectional communication flows between two endpoints until one of them is closed. The channel is stream oriented: individual messages are merged seamlessly into a continuous stream of data. The receiver gets no information about the individual `write` requests made by the sender. Data is returned to `read` requests in sequence, but without message boundary markers of any kind. `Reads` do not correspond to whole `write`s and it is very common for the operating system to deliver only part of the data requested in a `read` or to accept only part of the data requested by a `write`.

`SOCK_STREAM` sockets are very reliable. Failure usually means that there is some kind of misconfiguration or that the remote server has crashed, although failure can also occur if the network is congested (even temporarily). Thus, the burden on the programmer is greatly reduced. Occasionally, the lack of message boundaries means that the application must insert markers of some kind into the data stream, but this task is far easier than overcoming the unreliability of `SOCK_DGRAM` sockets. The greatest shortcoming of `SOCK_STREAM` sockets is their resource consumption. Each open circuit requires its own file descriptor, of which only a finite number are available, as well as kernel resources to maintain the state of the connection. Maintaining thousands of simultaneously active stream sockets would impose a significant burden on a system.

Server vs. Client Programming. Frequently in network programs there is a clear distinction between servers and clients. Servers are programs that run more or less indefinitely, waiting for requests or connections that are initiated by clients. This distinction is not always so clearcut, however, and the sockets API actually allows considerable flexibility in cases where the roles are blurred.

Client tasks: The client has four basic tasks:

1. create a local socket with an otherwise unused address,
2. determine the address of the server,
3. establish a connection (TCP only), and
4. send and receive data.

Clients create sockets using the `socket` function discussed above. Since the client is usually content to let the operating system choose an unused address, there is no need to call `bind` (see below). Sending and receiving data are done with the conventional `read` and `write` system calls (for `SOCK_DGRAM` sockets, however, the `sendto`, `sendmsg`, `recvfrom` and `recvmsg` functions may be more convenient). The only task of any complexity is identifying the address of the server. Once the server's address is known, the `connect` system call is used to establish a `SOCK_-STREAM` channel.

Socket addresses: Addresses in the `AF_INET` family are represented by a `struct sockaddr_in`, found in the header file `<netinet/in.h>`. Internet family addresses consist of two numbers: an IP address and a port number. The IP address contains enough information to locate the host computer on the Internet using IP. It is usually written in the familiar "dotted" notation (i.e., 131.215.145.137). In a program it is represented as a four-byte integer in network (i.e., big-endian) byte order. Obtaining the Internet address of a foreign server usually involves recourse to one or more library functions such as `gethostbyname`, `inet_aton`, or the constants `INADDR_ANY`, `INADDR_LOOPBACK` defined in the the include file '`<netinet/in.h>`'.

The port number is a 16-bit integer that is unique for each socket endpoint on a single Internet host. Servers usually "advertise" their services so that their port numbers are "well known." There is a registry of officially recognized port numbers,[1] and the file '`/etc/services`' contains a partial listing of that registry, which can be searched by the library utility `getservbyname`. However, for new, private, or experimental services it is more common for servers and clients to simply agree on a port number in advance, for example, by referring to a macro in a shared header file. Conventional wisdom is that such a port should be greater than 5,000, less than 49,152 and different from any registered port.

One other subtlety is that the `sin_port` and `sin_addr` fields in the `sockaddr_-in` structure must be stored in network byte order. The functions `htonl`, `htons`, `ntohl`, and `ntohs` can be used to convert long and short integers between host and network byte order. On big-endian machines (e.g., the IBM PowerPC family of processors) these are no-ops, but on little-endian machines (e.g., the Intel x86 family of processors) they perform byte swapping.

Server tasks: Servers are more complicated than clients. There are a number of different design choices for servers, with various tradeoffs between response time, scalability (how many clients can be supported), resource consumption, programming style, and robustness. Popular choices include a multithreaded server, a server that forks a new process for every connection, or a server that is invoked by the Internet daemon `inetd`. A few tasks are common to all these design choices:

1. create a local socket,
2. select a port number,
3. bind the port number to the socket,
4. make the port number known to clients,
5. listen for connections (TCP only),

---

[1] `ftp://ftp.isi.in-notes/iana/assignments/port-numbers`

6. accept connections (TCP only), and

7. send and receive data.

Creating a local server socket is no different from creating a local client socket. The process of selecting a port number and making it known to clients is discussed above. Once a port number is selected, the server must call `bind` to associate the address with the socket. The caller must specify a complete address, including both the port number and IP address in the `sockaddr_in` structure. Usually, the IP address is set to the constant `htonl(INADDR_ANY)`, which indicates that the socket should accept any connections (or datagrams for `SOCK_DGRAM` sockets) destined for any IP address associated with the host. (Recall that machines may have several IP addresses.) Other possibilities are `htonl(INADDR_LOOPBACK)` or a value obtained from `gethostname`, `gethostbyname`, and the like.

Communication with `recvfrom` and `sendto`: Once a `SOCK_DGRAM` socket is bound to an address, it is ready to send and receive datagrams. `Read` and `write` may be used to communicate with clients. The `recvfrom` call is particularly useful for servers because in addition to the contents of the datagram, it also supplies the caller with a return address, suitable for use in a subsequent call to `sendto`.

Listening for and accepting connections: `SOCK_STREAM` sockets, on the other hand, must take a few more steps before they are ready for use. First, they must call `listen` to inform the operating system of their intention to accept connections. The `accept` system call allocates a new file descriptor that can be used with `read` and `write` to communicate with the foreign entity. In addition, `accept` supplies the caller with the address of the connecting entity.

Many of the design choices for server software architecture are concerned with the detailed behavior of `accept`. It can be made blocking or nonblocking, and upon acceptance of a connection, a new thread or process may or may not be created. Signals (including timer signals) may be used to force a premature return, and `select` can be used to learn about status changes. The large number of possibilities tends to make servers much more complex than clients.

6.3   Higher-Level Protocols

Sockets form the lowest layer of user-level network programming. If you go any lower, you enter the realm of driver-writing and operating system internals. Most Beowulf users don't write applications using sockets. Sockets are usually reserved for the systems programming arena, where basic client/server functions are implemented. Beowulf users depend on higher-level programming abstractions to develop applications. MPI (Message Passing Interface), discussed in Chapters 9 and 10, and PVM (Parallel Virtual Machine), discussed in Chapters 11 and 12, are the workhorses of scientific computing on Beowulfs, providing not only platform-independent message passing semantics, but also frequently used parallel programming constructs. These APIs are not familiar to the enterprise systems programmer first entering the world of parallel computing. Enterprise network applications are distributed systems in the truest sense of the term and are developed by using higher-level protocols that do not require meddling with sockets. Remote procedure calls and distributed objects are the two most common programming interfaces applied in this vein; and they are equally suitable to parallel application development. If you come from a corporate computing or distributed applications development background, you will be happy to find that you can apply the same familiar software technologies to develop Beowulf applications.

6.3.1   Remote Procedure Calls

Programming with sockets is part of the client/server programming model, where all data exchange is explicitly performed with sends and receives. This model exposes the underlying transport mechanisms to the programmer and is sometimes compared with programming in assembly language. A remote procedure call (RPC) follows a different paradigm of distributed computation, removing the programmer from explicit message passing. The idea behind an RPC is to make distributed programs look like sequential programs. A procedure is called inside a program; rather than executing on the local machine, however, the local program suspends while the procedure executes on a remote machine. When the procedure returns, the local program wakes up and receives any results that may have been produced by the procedure.

RPC was designed not so much for parallel programming as for distributed programming. Parallel programming is a more tightly coupled concept where a single program (conceptually) works on a problem, concurrently executing on multiple processors. Distributed programming is a looser concept where two or more programs may require services from one another and therefore need to communicate, but they are not necessarily working on the same problem. Web browsers and Web servers are examples of distributed programs. Nevertheless, RPC can be used effectively on Beowulf systems, especially for porting applications that are already designed to use it.

In principle, the remote procedure call is a simple idea that should eliminate all the complexity of explicit message passing. As always, some difficulties exist. By invoking a remote procedure, you cause an action to be executed in a disjoint address space. This requires the caller to marshal procedure parameters, converting them to some platform-independent representation to allow for a heterogeneous environment. When marshaling parameters, if the native data representation format differs significantly from the platform-independent representation, buffer allocation and type conversion can be costly. In addition, procedures need to be exported through a naming service so that they may be located and invoked. All of this additional overhead can adversely impact performance.

Two different RPC implementations are commonly found on Unix systems. The first is ONC RPC, originally known as Sun RPC, but later renamed ONC, for Open Network Computing. This is the RPC standard used by Linux and Beowulf systems. The second implementation is DCE RPC, which is the standard remote procedure call interface for the Open Group's Distributed Computing Environment. The two systems are incompatible and offer different features. The advantages of the DCE version are that it permits asynchronous procedure calls and provides a more efficient parameter conversion protocol, which bypasses network-encoding when two communicating machines share the same binary data representation format. ONC RPC permits only synchronous procedure calls and requires parameter conversion regardless of homogeneity. This makes it a less attractive candidate for writing distributed programs on Beowulf clusters, even though it is standard software.

Writing RPC programs is not without difficulty. Although they provide a conceptually familiar mechanism, the data-encoding process introduces additional complexity. Rather than simply call a procedure in your program, you must generate support code that performs data encoding and the actual network communication. ONC RPC provides a tool called `rpcgen` and a data representation format called XDR, for extended data representation, that automates this code generation. XDR provides a language specification to describe data, which you use to specify the types of parameters passed to a procedure. The `rpcgen` program then compiles your procedure definition, generating code that will encode and decode parameters. It also produces a header file that you include in your C program to reference the remote procedure. Using pregenerated procedures is rather painless because it is quite like calling normal library routines. Actually creating a remote procedure can be an involved process, requiring an understanding of XDR and `rpcgen`.

The synchronous nature of ONC RPC calls makes it unsuitable for writing general parallel programs. Synchronous calls effectively serialize your program because the calling node stops doing all work while the called node executes a procedure. Asynchronous RPC allows you to initiate independent actions on a remote node without waiting for them to complete. This maps better to parallel programming on a Beowulf, because you can tell processors to perform arbitrary work without blocking, and interprocessor coordination can be relegated to synchronous calls.

6.3.2 Distributed Objects: CORBA and Java RMI

As the software development advantages of object-oriented programming languages became more evident during the late 1980s and early 1990s, programmers saw that they could extend the concept of a remote procedure call to that of a remote object allowing remote method invocations. You could represent network services as objects distributed across a network and use method invocations to perform transactions, rather than esoteric socket-based protocols or unwieldy collections of remote procedure calls. Again, the idea was to simplify the programming model by making distributed programs appear like sequential programs—you should be able to reference objects and invoke their methods independent of their location on the network.

Distributed objects are used mostly to build corporate enterprise applications that require access to data spread out in different locations across the network. Sometimes this process actually requires coordinating computation with machines in different parts of the world. A common use is to simplify the implementation of application-specific network databases that can become difficult to implement using a client/server approach and queries in the Structured Query Language (SQL). It is much easier for a programmer to write something like the following than to pass an embedded SQL query to a vendor-specific client API.

```
EmployeeBenefits myBenefits;
EmployeeRetirementPlan myRetirement;
EmployeeID myID;
SSN mySSN;

mySSN = getSSN(); // Get my social security number from some input source
myID = employeeIDs.getID(mySSN);              // Lookup my employee ID
myBenefits   = employeeBenefits.getBenefits(myID); // Lookup my benefits
myRetirement = myBenefits.getRetirementPlan();   // Lookup my retirement plan
```

Here the program may be accessing anywhere from one to three databases in different parts of the network, but the programmer doesn't have to be aware of that fact. In a client/server program, the programmer would have to specifically set up connections to network databases, issue queries in SQL or some other query language, and convert results into a usable form. With distributed objects, a programmer can access network resources in a transparent manner. To the programmer, `employeeIDs` is just another object to be used through its public methods. In reality, `employeeIDs` may represent a directory service on another machine. The `employeeBenefits` object may be a database located in yet another part of the network, and the result of the `getBenefits()` call may be a reference to an additional database. Alternatively, all of the objects may actually reside in one location as one database. The point is that the programmer doesn't have to know.

Several distributed object systems have been designed over the years, but the most promising ones for Beowulf application development are CORBA and Java RMI. Microsoft's DCOM is also a viable alternative for Windows-based clusters. The Object Management Group (OMG), established in 1989, saw the need to establish a vendor-independent standard for programming with distributed objects in heterogeneous systems. Their work has produced the Common Object Request Broker Architecture specification, or CORBA for short.

The foundation of CORBA programming is tied to the CORBA Interface Definition Language (IDL), with which object interfaces are defined. Even though programmers manipulate CORBA objects as native language structures, IDL defines them in a language and operating-system-independent manner. An IDL definition specifies the relationships between objects and their attributes. IDL definitions must be compiled with a preprocessor to generate native language code stubs with which objects are actually implemented.

The other half of the CORBA system is the Object Request Broker (ORB), of which the programmer does not have to be explicitly aware. An ORB is a server process that provides the plumbing for distributed object communication. It provides services for locating objects, translating remote method invocations into local invocations, and converting parameters to and from platform independent representations. As you can probably guess, going through an intervening daemon to perform object instantiation and method invocation sacrifices performance. However, ORBs have proven effective in providing the middleware necessary for heterogeneous distributed application development. Many free CORBA implementations, as well as several commercial ones, are suitable for deployment on a Beowulf, but the fastest and most preferred appears to be OmniORB, freely available from Olivetti & Oracle Research Laboratory (`www.orl.co.uk/omniORB/omniORB.html`).

In 1995, Sun Microsystems introduced the Java programming language and runtime environment. Since then, Java has gained enormous popularity and support in both industry and academia. Java's promise of platform-independent "write once, run everywhere" programming has made many programmers willing to put up with its growing pains and performance deficiencies. Java has been touted as an ideal Internet programming language because of its platform independence, dynamic binding, mobile code properties, and built-in security model. To achieve all of this, however, Java requires significant runtime support.

Unlike programming languages such as C and Pascal, Java is normally not compiled to an assembly language that is native to the CPU's instruction set. Rather, it is compiled to a platform-independent byte-code that is interpreted by the Java Virtual Machine (JVM).[2] A JVM will often be implemented with a just-in-time (JIT) compiler that will compile the byte-code into native code on the fly at runtime to improve performance. Even with this enhancement, Java has yet to match the performance of C or C++. Nevertheless, there is a good deal of interest in using Java to program computing clusters.

Java has been used to write parallel programs from the very beginning since it has a built-in platform-independent thread API. This makes it much easier to write scalable multithreaded applications on symmetric multiprocessors. The Java thread model allows parallel programming only in shared-memory environments. Java threads cannot interact between disjoint address spaces, such as nodes in a Beowulf cluster. That is why Java includes its own distributed object API, called Remote Method Invocation (RMI).

Like CORBA, Java RMI allows the invocation of methods on remote objects. Unlike CORBA, RMI is a language-intrinsic facility, built entirely in Java, and it does not require an interface definition language. RMI does require an additional server, called the Java Remote Object Registry. You can think of the RMI registry as a lightweight ORB. It allows objects to register themselves with names and for RMI programs to locate those objects. Java RMI programs are easy to write because once you obtain a reference to a named object, it operates exactly as though the object were local to your program. Some Beowulf users have already started using Java RMI to simulate molecular dynamics and future processor architectures. Using Java for these compute-intensive tasks is ill advised at this time, however, because the performance of the Java runtimes available for Linux, and therefore most Beowulfs, at this stage trails that of other platforms.

Using distributed objects for parallel programming on Beowulf is a natural way to write nonperformance-oriented applications where the emphasis is placed on ease of development and code maintainability. Distributed object technologies have been designed with heterogeneous networks in mind. Beowulf clusters are largely homogeneous in terms of the operating system, data representation, and executable program format. Therefore, distributed object systems often contain additional overheads that are not necessary on Beowulf clusters. In the future, we may see dis-

---

[2]For more information about the JVM, see the "Java Virtual Machine Specification" at `java.sun.com/docs`.

tributed objects tailor their implementations for high performance on Beowulf-like systems as the use of PC clusters becomes more common in corporate computing.

6.4 Distributed File Systems

Every node in a Beowulf cluster equipped with a hard drive has a local file system that processes running on other nodes may want to access. Even diskless internal nodes require access to the worldly node's file system so that they may boot and execute programs. The need for internode file system access requires Beowulf clusters to adopt one or more distributed file systems. Most distributed file systems possess the following set of characteristics that make them appear indistinguishable from the local file system.

- *Network transparency:* Remote files can be accessed using the same operations or system calls that are used to access local files.
- *Location transparency:* The name of a file is not bound to its network location. The location of the file server host is not an intrinsic part of the file path.
- *Location independence:* When the physical location of a file changes, its name is not forced to change. The name of the file server host is not an intrinsic part of the file path.

6.4.1 NFS

Beowulf clusters almost always use the Network File System protocol to provide distributed file system services. NFS started its steady climb in popularity in 1985, after Sun Microsystems published the protocol specification for adoption as an open standard. This version of the protocol, NFS version 2 (NFSv2), has been widely adopted by every major version of the Unix operating system. A revision of the protocol, NFSv3, was published in 1993 and has been implemented by most vendors, including Linux.

NFS is structured as a client/server architecture, using RPC calls to communicate between clients and servers. The server exports files to clients, which access the files as though they were local files. Unlike other protocols, an NFS server is stateless: it doesn't save any information about a client between requests. In other words, all client requests are considered independently and must therefore contain all the information necessary for execution. All NFS read and write requests must include file offsets, unlike local file reads and writes that proceed from where the last one left off. The stateless nature of the NFS server causes messages to be larger, potentially consuming network bandwidth. The advantage of statelessness is that the server is not affected when a client crashes. The best way to configure NFS on a Beowulf system is to minimize the number of mount points, set the read and write buffer sizes to the maximum allowable values (8,192 bytes), and use the `autofs` daemon discussed later in this section. You can set the buffer sizes using the `rsize` and `wsize` options for the NFS file systems listed `/etc/fstab`. A typical `fstab` entry for mounting '`/home`' may look like the following:

```
b001:/home  /home nfs  rw,hard,intr,bg,rsize=8192,wsize=8192 0 0
```

The original Linux NFS implementation allowed only a single NFS server to run at a time. This presented severe scaling problems for Beowulf clusters, where many internal nodes would mount home directories and other file systems from the worldly node. A single NFS server would serialize all network file system accesses, creating a severe bottleneck for disk writes. Disk reads were not as adversely impacted because the clients would cache files locally. More recent versions of the Linux NFS implementation allowed multiple servers operating in read-only mode. While this was useful for certain local area network applications, where workstations might mount read-only '`/usr/`' partitions, it was not of such great benefit to Beowulf clusters, where internal nodes frequently require NFS for performing disk writes. The versions of the Linux NFS code released in 1998, starting with version 2.2beta32, have added support for multiple servers in read/write mode, though scaling remains an issue.

While the stateless nature of the NFS approach provides a relatively simple way to achieve reliability in the presence of occasional failures, it introduces significant performance penalties because each operation must "start from scratch." To address the performance issues, NFS is normally operated in a mode that caches information at both the server (the system directly attached to the disk) and the client (the node that is accessing the NFS-mounted file). The mechanisms provided by NFS are usually sufficient when only one client is accessing a file; this is the usual situation encounter by users. Even in NFSv3, however, the mechanisms are not sufficient to maintain cache consistency *between* clients. Hence, problems can arise for parallel applications that attempt to write to a single NFS-mounted file.

6.4.2   AFS

The Andrew File System (AFS) was originally developed at Carnegie Mellon University as a joint venture with IBM in the mid-1980s. Its purpose was to overcome the scaling problems of other network file systems such as NFS. AFS proved to be able to reduce CPU usage and network traffic while still delivering efficient file system access for larger numbers of clients. In 1989, development of AFS was transferred to Transarc Corporation, which evolved AFS into the Distributed File System (DFS) included as part of the Distributed Computing Environment (DCE). AFS effectively became a proprietary technology before Linux was developed, so AFS never played much of a role in the design of Beowulf systems. Recently, however, AFS-based file systems have become available for Linux, and a new interest in this network file system has emerged in the Beowulf community. The inability of NFS to effectively scale to systems containing on the order of 100 processors has motivated this experimentation with more scalable file system architectures. However, improvements have been made in the Linux NFS code that may obviate the need to explore other network file systems.

6.4.3   Autofs: The Automounter

As more nodes are added to a Beowulf, the startup time of the system can increase dramatically because of contention for the NFS server on the worldly node that exports home directories to the rest of the system. NFS is implemented using ONC RPC, which supports only synchronous RPC calls. Therefore the NFS server becomes a single bottleneck through which the other systems must pass, one at a time. This phenomenon was a problem on local area networks until Sun Microsystems developed an automounting mechanism for NFS. The Linux version of this mechanism is the `autofs` service. `Autofs` mounts NFS partitions only when they are first accessed, rather than automatically at startup. If the NFS partition is not accessed for a configurable period of time (typically five minutes), `autofs` will unmount it. Using `autofs` can reduce system startup times as well as reduce overall system load.

6.5   Remote Command Execution

In the course of administering or using a Beowulf cluster, it is often necessary to execute commands on nodes without explicitly logging into them and typing on the command line. For example, the commands may be executed from within a shell script or by a cron job.

6.5.1   BSD R Commands

The BSD R commands are a set of programs that first appeared in 4.2BSD to execute commands and copy files on remote machines. The major commands are as follows:

- rsh: The remote shell allows you to execute shell commands on remote nodes and also initiate interactive login sessions. Interactive login sessions are initiated by invoking **rlogin**.
- rlogin: The remote login command allows you to start a terminal session by logging in to a remote node.
- rcp: The remote copy command llows you to copy files from one node to the other.

The **rsh** command is the standard way of executing commands and starting parallel applications on other nodes. A considerable amount of system software, including the PVM and some implementations of the MPI libraries, relies heavily on **rsh** for remote command execution. The **rsh** command requires that an **rsh** server ('**/usr/sbin/in.rshd**' on most Linux systems) run on the remote node. The **rsh** program connects to the server, which then checks that the client's originating port is a privileged port before taking any further action. On Unix systems, only processes with root privileges may open privileged ports between 1 and 1024. The **rsh** check is a historical artifact dating from the days when a connection originating from a privileged port could be trusted on that basis alone. After performing the check, the server compares the client's host address with a file called '**/etc/hosts.equiv**', which contains a list of trusted hosts. Connections originating from trusted hosts do not require a password to be granted system access. If the host is not in '**/etc/hosts.equiv**', the server checks the home directory of the user with the same user id as the user originating the connection for a file called '**.rhosts**'. The '**.rhosts**' file can contain a list of hosts from which a user can connect without entering a password. It is like '**hosts.equiv**', but checked on a user basis rather than a global basis. If the host is not found in '**.rhosts**', then the user is challenged for a password in order to execute the remote command. The **rsh** command is extremely useful for performing system administration tasks and launching parallel applications. However, it allows the execution of a command only on one other node. Many times you will want to execute a command on multiple nodes at a time. Typically, Beowulf users will write shell scripts that spawn multiple copies of **rsh** to do this work. More comprehensive sets of parallel remote shell commands, designed to be more robust in the presence of failures and scalable to large numbers of nodes, have been described in [10] and implemented by several groups. In fact, the need to execute commands in parallel is so great that many groups have independently invented variations of the parallel remote shell command.

6.5.2   SSH—The Secure Shell

The secure shell, SSH, is a set of security-conscious drop-in replacements for the BSD `rsh`, `rlogin`, and `rcp` commands. The SSH counterparts are `ssh`, `slogin`, and `scp`. The main problem with the BSD R commands is that they transmit passwords across the network in plain text, which makes it extremely easy to steal passwords. In addition, the use of '`.rhosts`' files tends be a weak point in system security. Another problem is that the R commands have to be installed as `suid` root because they must open privileged ports on the client node. The R commands are more than adequate to use in an ostensibly secure environment, such as the internal nodes of a guarded Beowulf system (see Section 7.1.3), which are normally configured with their own private network. Nodes exposed to the external world, however, should be allowed access only via a secure mechanism such as SSH.

SSH is a commercial product developed by SSH Communications Security, Ltd., which offers both Win32 and Unix versions. The Unix version is available as open source software and can be downloaded from `www.ssh.fi`, with precompiled binaries available at many sites. SSH encrypts all network communication, including passwords, and uses a public key-based authentication system to verify host and user identities. Many Beowulf systems install SSH as standard system software, a practice we strongly recommend. Eventually, the use of `rsh` will have to be discarded because of its reliance on a fundamentally insecure authentication model. Also, `rsh` makes poor use of the limited number of privileged ports between 512 and 1024, using two of them for every connection that maintains a standard error stream. Thus, the worldly node of a Beowulf with 32 internal nodes and only four users executing commands on all nodes would have its allowable `rsh` connections maxed out. Even if the additional security is unnecessary, SSH should be used to keep from running out of privileged ports.

7 Setting Up Clusters: Installation and Configuration

Thomas Sterling and Daniel Savarese

If building a Beowulf only involved assembling nodes, installing software on each one, and connecting the nodes to each other with a network, this book would end right here. But as you may have guessed, there is more to building a Beowulf than just those tasks. Once you have assembled a Beowulf, you have to keep it running, maintain software, add and remove user accounts, organize the file system layout, and perform countless other tasks that fall under the heading of system management. Some of these management tasks are very similar to those of traditional LAN administration, about which entire books have been written. But the rules have not yet been fully established for Beowulf system administration. It is still something of a black art, requiring not only familiarity with traditional LAN management concepts, but also some parallel programming skills and a creative ability to adapt workstation and LAN software to the Beowulf environment. This chapter describes some of the more common approaches applied by practitioners of this evolving craft and presents some other procedures that have not yet become common practice.

Even though both corporate LANs and Beowulf systems comprise collections of networked PCs, they differ significantly in terms of their installation, use, maintenance, and overall management. A LAN is usually formed from a loosely coupled heterogeneous collection of computers that share disk and printing resources, in addition to some network services, such as Web and database servers. A Beowulf cluster is a more tightly coupled collection of computers where the majority of components are identically configured and collectively operate as a single machine.

This chapter begins by discussing the choices available for connecting your Beowulf to the outside world. We then discuss the steps needed to set up the Beowulf nodes. The remaining sections cover the rudiments of system administration for a Beowulf.

7.1 System Access Models

Before assigning IP addresses to Beowulf nodes, designing the network topology, and booting the machine, you need to decide how the system will be accessed. System access literally refers to how a user can log in to a system and use the machine. Allowable system access modes relate directly to how you configure your system both logically and physically. There are three principal schemes for permitting user access to Beowulf machines, the first of which is seldom used.

7.1.1 The Standalone System

The most basic way of configuring a Beowulf is to set it up as a standalone system unattached to any external networks. This design requires a user to be in the same room as the Beowulf, sitting at its front-end keyboard and monitor to write and execute programs. Usually this is done only when first assembling the system and when upgrading or debugging the system. Certain high-security environments may require that a system be configured in this manner, but the utility of the system becomes limited when the system cannot be accessed over an external network. Institutions that decide to configure a Beowulf in this manner should include multiple front-end nodes, so that multiple users may simultaneously use the machine. When a system is configured in this manner, it is not necessary to pay any special attention to the IP addresses used. Any valid set of network addresses will do, but it is advisable to use the reserved address ranges mentioned in Section 6.1.1.

7.1.2 The Universally Accessible Machine

At the opposite end of the spectrum from the standalone configuration lies the universally accessible machine. In this configuration, each system node draws its IP address from the pool of addresses assigned to an organization. This allows internal nodes to be directly accessible by outside connection requests. In other words, every node is accessible from the entire Internet. The primary negative aspect of this configuration is that it greatly increases management tasks associated with security. It also unnecessarily consumes a large quantity of IP addresses that could otherwise be used by the organization's local area network. If your local area network already sits behind a firewall and uses a reserved address range, then this may be an appropriate configuration, allowing access to any node from any machine on your LAN. Also, some applications, such as Web and database load-balancing servers, may require exposing all nodes to the external network. However, you will have to take care in arranging your network switches and associated connections so as to prevent LAN traffic congestion from interfering with Beowulf system traffic. In addition, if you choose to add multiple network interfaces to each node, you should probably not attach them to the external network.

7.1.3 The Guarded Beowulf

Somewhere in between the first two configurations stands the guarded Beowulf, which is probably the most commonly used configuration. The guarded Beowulf assigns reserved IP addresses to all of its internal nodes, even when using multiple networks. To communicate with the outside world, a single front-end, called the worldly node, is given an extra network interface with an IP address from the organization's local area network. Sometimes more than one worldly node is provided. But in all cases, to access the rest of the system, a user must first log in to a worldly node. The benefits of this approach are that you don't consume precious organizational IP addresses and you constrain system access to a limited number of controllable access points, facilitating overall system management and security policy implementation. The disadvantage is that internal nodes cannot access the external network. But that feature can be remedied by using IP masquerading (discussed later). For increased security, it is often desirable to place the worldly nodes behind a firewall. In the rest of this chapter, we will use the Guarded Beowulf as the canonical example system unless explicitly stated otherwise.

7.2 Assigning Names

Beowulf system components need to communicate with each other. For intercomponent communication to be possible, each component, or node, requires a unique name. For the purposes of this chapter, node naming refers to the assignment of both IP addresses and hostnames. Naming workstations on a LAN can often be quite arbitrary, except that sometimes segmentation of the network restricts the IP addresses available to a set of workstations located on a particular segment. Naming Beowulf nodes requires a bit more thought and care.

7.2.1 Statistically Assigned Addresses

Beowulf clusters communicate internally over one or more private system area networks. One (or perhaps more, for redundancy and performance) of the nodes has an additional network connection to the outside. These nodes are referred to as worldly nodes to distinguish them from internal nodes, which are connected only to the private cluster network. Because the internal nodes are not directly connected to the outside, they can use the reserved IP addresses discussed in Chapter 6. Specifically, most clusters assign their worldly node to address 192.168.1.1, and assign internal nodes sequentially to addresses in the range 192.168.1.2 to 192.168.1.253. The worldly node will always have a second network interface, possessing a routable IP address that provides connectivity to the organizational LAN.

From long experience, we have found that internal hostnames should be trivial. Most Beowulf clusters have assigned very simple internal hostnames of the format <cluster-letter><node-number>. For instance, the first Beowulf named its nodes using simply the letter b as a prefix, but made the mistake of calling its first node b0. While it is natural for those steeped in the long-standing computer science tradition of starting indices at zero, it is better to map the numbers contained in hostnames directly to the last octet of the node IP address. For example, 198.168.1.1 becomes node b1, and 198.168.1.2 becomes b2. As you can see, there can be no b0 node, because 198.168.1.0 is a network number, and not a host address. Directly mapping the numbers starting from 1 facilitates the writing of custom system utilities, diagnostic tools, and other short programs usually implemented as shell scripts. If you plan to have more than 9 nodes in your system, it might be desirable to name all of your nodes using two digits. For example, b1 becomes b01 and b2 becomes b02. Similarly, for systems with more than 99 nodes, b1 should become b001 and b10 should become b010.

When physically administrating a cluster, you often need to know the MAC addresses of the network cards in nodes, as well as their names and IP addresses. The simplest reason is that when something goes wrong with a node, you have to walk into the machine room and diagnose the problem, often simply rebooting the culprit node. For this reason, you should label each node with its hostname, IP address, and the MAC addresses of the network interface cards. If you use a consistent IP address to hostname mapping, you can get by with labeling the nodes with their names and MAC addresses. MAC addresses go in the 'bootptab' (see Section 7.3.3), so you will want to record them when you install the NICs into their cases. If you forgot to do this, the ifconfig command will report the MAC address of configured controllers. For small systems, labeling of nodes is superfluous, but for larger numbers of nodes, this simple measure could save you many hours.

7.2.2 Dynamically Assigned Addresses

So far we have discussed naming nodes with statically assigned addresses. Every time a node is booted, it obtains its hostname and IP address from its local configuration files. You need not always configure your system this way. If all of your internal nodes have identical software images, there is no reason why they necessarily require fixed IP addresses and hostnames. It is possible to configure a system so that every time an internal node boots, it receives an IP address from a pool of available addresses. Worldly nodes, however, need to continue using fixed IP addresses because they provide resources to internal nodes that must be accessed through a known host address. The advantage of using dynamically assigned addresses is that internal nodes become completely interchangeable, facilitating certain system maintenance procedures. If you decide to convert your universally accessible machine to a guarded Beowulf, all you have to do is change the IP addresses in the DHCP (Dynamic Host Configuration Protocol) or BOOTP server's configuration files, rather than update config files on every single node. The downside of dynamic addressing is that unless you take proper precautions, it can become difficult to determine what physical box in the machine room corresponds to a specific IP address. This is where the suggested labeling of nodes with MAC addresses comes in handy. If you know the MAC address of a misbehaving node, you can find it by visually scanning the labels. All in all, it is easier if the mapping between MAC addresses, hostnames, and IP addresses changes as infrequently as possible.

7.3 Installing Node Software

After choosing a configuration scheme, the next step in turning your mass of machines into a Beowulf is to install an operating system and standard software on all of the nodes.

The internal nodes of a Beowulf cluster are almost always identically configured.[1] The hardware can be slightly different, incorporating different generation processors, disks, and network interface cards. But the file system layout, kernel version, and installed software are the same. Only the worldly node exhibits differences, since it generally serves as the repository of user home directories and centralized software installations exported via NFS.

In general, you will install the operating system and extra support software on the worldly node first. Once this is complete, you can begin to install software on the remainder of the nodes.

Years ago this was a daunting task involving the installation of nodes one at a time by hand, building custom boot disks and installing over the network, or copying entire disks. Today, a number of packages automate a great deal of the process for most systems. Three examples of cluster installation packages are

- NPACI Rocks Clustering Toolkit, `rocks.npaci.edu`
- OSCAR Packaged Cluster Software Stack, `www.csm.ornl.gov/oscar/software.html`
- Scalable Cluster Environment, `smile.cpe.ku.ac.th/research/sce`

All of these packages work in a similar manner. The desired configuration is described via either text files or a GUI. This includes how the disk will be organized into partitions and file systems, what packages should be installed, and what network addresses should be used. Defaults for these are available as a starting point. A boot floppy image for use in installation is provided. The nodes are booted and

---

[1]Management and use of a Beowulf are greatly simplified when all nodes are nearly identical.

discovered by the server using DHCP or BOOTP and IP addresses are matched to MAC addresses. Finally, the package configures the nodes as specified.

To provide a clearer picture of what goes on during this process, we will walk through the necessary steps, most of which are now handled by the above-mentioned software. You can skip to Section 7.4 if you do not need or want to know how this works. The approach is simple. First, a single internal node is configured. Once this is done, all other nodes are "cloned" from this installation. This way, only two systems are configured by hand. Aside from saving time up front, cloning also facilitates major system upgrades. Changes to the software configuration of internal nodes that require an update to all of the nodes may be performed by modifying a single node and pushing changes out to the remainder of the nodes. In addition, cloning makes it easier to recover from certain unexpected events such as disk failures or accidental file system corruption. Installing a new disk (in the case of a disk failure), then recloning the node, returns it to working order.

Node cloning relies on the BOOTP protocol to provide a node with an IP address and a root file system for the duration of the cloning procedure. In brief, the following steps are involved:

1. Manually configure a single internal node.
2. Create tar files for each partition.
3. Set up a clone root directory on the worldly node.
4. Configure BOOTP on the worldly node.
5. Install a special init script in the clone root directory on the worldly node.
6. Create a boot disk with an NFSROOT kernel.

The basic premise behind our example cloning procedure is for the new node to mount a root file system over NFS, which contains the cloning support programs, configuration files, and partition archives. When the Linux kernel finishes loading, it looks for a program called '/sbin/init', which executes system initialization scripts and puts the system into multiuser mode. The cloning procedure replaces the standard '/sbin/init' with a program that partitions the hard drives, untars partition archives, and executes any custom cloning configuration scripts before rebooting the newly cloned system.

7.3.1   Creating Tar Images

After configuring the internal node, an archive of each disk partition is made, omitting '/proc' because it is not a physical disk partition. The normal procedure is to change the current working directory to the partition mount point and use a tar command such as

```
tar zlcf /worldly/nfsroot/partition-name.tgz .
```

The l option tells the `tar` command to archive files only in directories stored on the local partition, avoiding files in directories that serve as mount points for other partitions. A potential pitfall of this archiving method is that there may not be enough room on the local disk to store the partitions. Rather than creating them locally, one should store the tar file on an NFS partition on the worldly node. Ultimately, the files must be moved to the worldly node, so it makes sense to store them there in the first place.

7.3.2 Setting Up a Clone Root Partition

Next we create a root directory on the worldly node for use in the cloning process. This directory is exported via NFS to the internal node network. The directory contains the following subdirectories: 'bin', 'dev', 'etc', 'lib', 'mnt', 'proc', 'sbin', 'tmp'. The 'proc' and 'mnt' directories are empty, as they will be used as mount points during the cloning process. The 'dev' directory contains all the standard Linux device files. Device files are special, and cannot be copied normally. The easiest way to create this directory is by letting tar do the work by executing the following command as root:

```
tar -C / -c -f - dev | tar xf -
```

This will create a 'dev' directory containing all the device files found on the worldly node. All the remaining directories are copied normally, except for 'tmp' and 'etc', which are left empty. The 'usr' directory tree should not be needed. An 'fstab' file should also be created in 'etc' containing only the following line, so that the '/proc' file system may be mounted properly:

```
none    /proc    proc    default    0 0
```

You also may need to include a 'hosts' file.

Once the NFS root file system is built, the partition archives are moved into the file system as well. We place these in a separate directory which will be accessed by our init script. We replace the 'sbin/init' executable with our cloning init script. This script will be invoked by the clone node's kernel to perform the cloning process. Tasks performed by the script include drive partitioning, archive extraction, and configuration file tweaking. Some configuration files in the NFS root file system must be tweaked if nodes aren't set up to configure themselves through DHCP or BOOTP. The primary configuration files are ones dependent on the node IP address, such as '/etc/sysconfig/network' and '/etc/sysconfig/network-scripts/ifcfg-eth0' on Red Hat–based systems.

```
.default:\
        :sm=255.255.255.0:\
        :ht=ether:\
        :gw=192.168.1.1:\
        :rp=/export/nfsroot/:
b002:ip=192.168.1.2:ha=0080c8638a2c:tc=.default
b003:ip=192.168.1.3:ha=0080c86359d9:tc=.default
b004:ip=192.168.1.4:ha=0080c86795c8:tc=.default
```

Figure 7.1
Sample bootptab for a system with three nodes: b002, b003, and b004.

7.3.3 Setting Up BOOTP

BOOTP[2] was originally devised to allow the booting of diskless clients over a network. BOOTP provides a mapping between a hardware address and an IP address. A BOOTP client needs to fetch an IP address before making use of any additional information so that it may speak to NFS or other servers referenced by the configuration information. The BOOTP daemon further makes available the name of a directory on the BOOTP server containing a boot kernel, the name of the kernel file, and the name of a root directory structure exported via NFS that the diskless client can mount. We will utilize this facility in our install process in order to assign IP addresses to nodes as they are booted and to provide the location of our NFS root file system.

The 'bootptab' file tells the bootpd daemon how to map hardware addresses to IP addresses and hostnames. It also describes a root path entry for our NFS exported root directory. The 'bootptab' file will look something like the example shown in Figure 7.1.

The .default entry is a macro defining a set of options common to all of the entries. Each entry includes these default options by including tc=.default. The other entries are simply hostnames followed by IP addresses and hardware addresses. The rp option specifies our NFS root partition.

IP addresses to be used during the installation process are defined in this file. It is convenient to define the permanent mapping of IP addresses to nodes at this point and use these same addresses during the installation.

The BOOTP software distributed with Linux is well documented, so we won't describe it in length. To activate the BOOTP daemon, create the '/etc/bootptab'

---

[2] "Bootstrap Protocol (BOOTP)," Internet Engineering Task Force RFC 951, info.internet. isi.edu/in-notes/rfc/files/rfc951.txt.

configuration file, uncomment the line in '/etc/inetd.conf' (see Section 4.3.1) that invokes bootpd, and restart the inetd server on the BOOTP server (i.e., the worldly node). At this point the worldly node is prepared to assign IP addresses and serve files during the installation process.

On the client side, the diskless client boot sequence involves obtaining an IP address using BOOTP, establishing a TFTP connection to the boot server and fetching a kernel, loading the kernel, and mounting an NFS exported directory as a root file system. In general this process is initiated either by a ROM-based facility for operation without a drive or by a bootable floppy disk or CD-ROM. We will assume that a hardware facility is not available, so next we must create the boot floppy that will be used to initiate the cloning process on the client nodes.

7.3.4   Building a Clone Boot Floppy

The purpose of our boot disk is simply to bootstrap the cloning procedure by obtaining an IP address and NFS file system location from the BOOTP server and mounting this file system, over the network, as root. Unfortunately, it is not likely that the kernel installed on the worldly node has these capabilities built in, so it is necessary to build one. A kernel with these capabilities is commonly called an NFSROOT kernel. Compiling the Linux kernel is relatively easy, as discussed in Section 4.2.1.

The configuration of this kernel must include NFS root file system support as well as support for the network interface cards. Once compiled, the kernel will be stored in a file called 'zImage' or 'bzImage' depending on the compression option used. This kernel must be further modified in order to force it to boot, using the NFS directory obtained via BOOTP. The root device used by a kernel is stored in the kernel image and can be altered with the rdev program, usually located in '/usr/sbin'. The root device must be the NFS file system, but no device file exists for this purpose by default, so you must create one. This is accomplished with mknod:

```
mknod /dev/nfsroot b 0 255
```

This creates a dummy block device with special major and minor device numbers that have special meaning to the Linux kernel. Once this device file is available, you should instruct the Linux kernel to use this as the root device with

```
rdev zImage /dev/nfsroot
```

Following this, write the kernel to a floppy with the dd command

```
dd if=zImage of=/dev/fd0 bs=512
```

After creating your first clone disk, test it on a node to make sure everything works. After this test, you can duplicate the floppy to clone multiple nodes at once. Once the system is up and running, it is no longer necessary to use floppies for cloning. Instead, you can clone nodes that already have an active operating system by installing a clone kernel and rebooting; this can even be done remotely.

7.4 Basic System Administration

Simply getting a cluster up and running can be a challenging endeavor; but once you've done it, it won't seem so difficult anymore. For your first cluster, it will probably be a lot easier to skip the cloning process. You can go ahead and install identical software from scratch on all of your nodes, including your worldly node. After you get a feel for how you are using the system, you can fine tune it by removing nonessential software from internal nodes and setting up a node cloning system.

7.4.1 Booting and Shutting Down

Perhaps one of the most inelegant features of a Beowulf cluster is how you turn it on and off. There is no master switch you can flip to turn on the entire system. This facility would be of limited usefulness in any case because Beowulfs usually consist of many parts some of which depend on others to boot properly. A robust and usable power management system is required, which also provides fine-grained control over each piece of the machine. The least expensive solution is to walk from machine to machine turning on or off individual nodes. While this method works out fairly well for small to medium sized clusters, however, it is not acceptable for any sizable cluster.

For large machines, remote control over the power state of each node is required. Although some vendors are starting to support power management via special on-board hardware, most node hardware is not equipped with remote power management logic. When on-board support is unavailable, a network-accessible power strip can provide a useful alternative. Multiple vendors offer network-accessible power strips that allow you to control individual power ports over the network. While these provide complete control over the power supplied to each node, a few remaining details must be considered before deployment. One important issue when choosing a power management system is the "statefulness" of your node's power switch. Some motherboards do not automatically reboot on restoration of power;

if this is the case with your hardware, then a network-enabled power strip is not a viable solution. Finally, it is important when using this configuration to ensure that your kernel does not power off the machine on shutdown. Otherwise extra trips to the machine room will be in order.

An example of a large cluster using remote power management can be found in Chapter 18.

7.4.2 The Node File System

The Linux operating system follows a convention called the Linux File system Hierarchy Standard.[3] Beowulf nodes by default follow the same convention with one or two twists. The main consideration in deciding how to set up node file systems isn't so much how to organize the directory structure, but rather how to partition the disks and what mount points to use for each partition. The primary partitions usually correspond to the following directories:

/ The root partition, containing system configuration and log files

/boot An optional partition for storing kernel images, often just a regular directory in the root partition

/home A partition containing all user directories

/opt An optional partition for additional software

/usr A partition containing all standard system software

/scratch A partition used as scratch space for large temporary data files (for nodes with a very large disk or multiple disks, it is common to have several scratch partitions, named 'scratch1', 'scratch2', and so on)

The real issue with regard to file systems on the cluster is the availability of user home directories across the cluster. Typically, user data is stored in '/home' on the worldly node. Users log in to this node and perform any number of interactive tasks before spawning a parallel job on the cluster. Ideally, you would like the same file system space seen on the worldly node to be seen on the nodes by allowing networked access to the files. In practice, this is problematic, for two reasons. First, this introduces additional nonapplication traffic on the internal network, which leads to poorer and less predictable application communication

---

[3]The Linux FHS was formerly known as the Linux File System Standard (FSSTND). The latest version of the Linux FHS, as well as the older FSSTND, is published at www.pathname.com/fhs/.

performance. Second, the most popular mechanism for providing this functionality, NFS, has been shown to scale poorly to large clusters. This said, the convenience of globally accessible home directories leads many cluster administrators to provide this functionality, and one must hope that in the future an adequate "global file system" will become available.

The most common alternative is to provide users with separate directory space on each node and to provide utilities for aiding in application and data migration onto the cluster. The advantages and disadvantages of this approach in the context of a large cluster are discussed in Chapter 18.

Other less common file system configurations include "crossmounting" of file systems, which makes the file systems of each node available on every other node via NFS or some other network file system, and shared '/usr' partitions. Crossmounting helps take advantage of unused disk space on nodes by making this space available across the cluster; however, this comes at the expense of some network performance due to the file system traffic. Shared '/usr' partitions helps save space on node disks. The drop in cost of storage space for commodity clusters has virtually eliminated the use of shared shared partitions such as this, however, since nodes tend to have more than adequate free space.

7.4.3 Account Management

User account management generally is handled in one of two ways. The first is to assign an account to a user on the worldly node and then copy the '/etc/passwd' file to every node. The second is to configure the internal nodes to use Network Information System, either NIS or NIS+, for user authentication. This approach requires that accounts be configured on the worldly node, which should be the home of the NIS server. Each method has advantages and disadvantages, which we will mention shortly. In both cases, setting up the account on the worldly node works the same way. You can use either the useradd command, which supersedes the older adduser command (this may be a symbolic link to useradd on some systems), or one of the emerging Linux system administration tools such as linuxconf. These commands will create a home directory for the new user containing system default config files and will create an entry in '/etc/passwd' storing the user's encrypted password, home directory location, and shell.

After a new user has an account on the worldly node, the internal nodes must have some mechanism for accessing this data for authentication purposes. The most commonly implemented method is to simply copy the '/etc/passwd' file to all the internal nodes, usually using one of rdist, rcp, or pdsh. The '/etc/group' file is often modified in the process of adding a user, so it should be copied as well.

When multiple administrators are granting or modifying accounts, care must be taken that these configurations files remain identical on all the nodes. The use of utilities such as `userdel` (or `deluser`) and `groupdel` helps to ensure that the worldly node files are not simultaneously updated, which is a good first step in maintaining consistency.

The alternative method of managing user accounts is to use a directory service, such as NIS, to store user account information. NIS stores all directory data in a central server, which is contacted by clients (the nodes) to perform authentication. This eases system administration considerably, since only one point of control exists for account management. However, this has the side effect of generating extra network traffic. For example, every time a user logs into a node, the node must contact the server to verify the user exists and check the supplied password. The latency involved in this process can greatly slow parallel application launching as well. For these reasons, many Beowulf sites forego NIS for distributing account information.

7.4.4 Running Unix Commands in Parallel

Managing a Beowulf cluster involves an almost endless number of tasks that require execution of a command on multiple nodes at a time. Common operations include copying files to every node of a Beowulf (such as user applications, libraries, or configuration files) or checking for and killing runaway processes. Many groups have developed a command or suite of commands to run a program on every node (or a subset of nodes) in a Beowulf. One set, called the Scalable Unix Tools and defined in 1994 [10], was originally developed for massively parallel computers but is equally appropriate for Beowulf clusters. Several implementations of these tools are available at `www.mcs.anl.gov/sut` [25] and `smile.cpe.ku.ac.th`. For example, `ptexec` may be used to execute the same command on any collection of nodes:

```
ptexec -M "node1 node2" /sbin/shutdown -h now
```

The command

```
ptexec -all killall amok
```

kills all versions of the process named `amok` on the cluster. The Scalable Unix Tools follow the Unix philosophy of tool building; it is easy to build tools by piping the output from one tool into the input of another. For example,

```
ptpred -all '-f /home/me/myapp' | ptdisp
```

presents a graphical display showing which nodes have the file '/home/me/myapp'.

7.5   Avoiding Security Compromises

After the number of computers connected to the Internet exploded in the mid-1990s, it became impossible to attach a computer to a network without paying some attention to preventive security measures. The situation is no different with Beowulf clusters and is even more important because making a Beowulf accessible via the Internet is like setting up one or more new departmental LANs. We have already made some minor references to security but will discuss it now in more detail.

Linux workstations and Beowulf clusters are not inherently more insecure than other computers. Any computer attached to a network has the potential to be broken into. Even if one takes measures to restrict access to a computer as tightly as possible, software running on it may have exploitable bugs that can grant unauthorized access to the system. The only way to maintain a secure network is to keep abreast of the latest CERT advisories[4] and take basic preventive measures. Several Beowulf systems have been victimized by crackers[5] in ways that could have been prevented by paying a little bit of attention to security issues.

7.5.1   System Configuration

How you defend your Beowulf from attack will depend on the choice of system access model. The universally accessible machine is the most vulnerable, while the standalone machine is the most secure, since it is not attached to an external network. The guarded Beowulf is the most practical configuration to defend, because its only entry points are its worldly nodes. It is possible to focus on implementing security measures for only the worldly nodes and allow the internal nodes to trust each other completely. Even though it is possible for an intruder to gain access to the internal nodes once a worldly node is compromised, it is not necessary to completely secure the internal nodes. These nodes can easily be recreated through cloning and generally do not store sensitive persistent data. Despite the security advantages presented by the guarded Beowulf access model, however, other needs may demand the implementation of a universally accessible machine. For such a

---

[4]CERT is the Computer Emergency Response Team, run by Carnegie Mellon's Software Engineering Institute. CERT posts regular bulletins reporting the latest Internet security vulnerabilities at `www.cert.org/`.

[5]Cracker is the accepted term among computer programmers for a rogue hacker who tries to gain unauthorized access to computer systems. The term hacker is restricted to those computer programmers not seduced by the Dark Side of the Force.

configuration, each individual node must be secured, since each one constitutes an external access point.

7.5.2 Restricting Host Access

The primary way crackers force access to a machine is by exploiting known bugs in commonly run server software. The easiest way to avoid compromises, then, is to carefully control the ways in which the machine may be accessed. The first step in controlling access is disabling unused services. This process has the side benefit of freeing up additional resources on your machine, which can lead to better performance. Chapter 4 thoroughly covers this process.

Some services must be left so that users can access the machine remotely. For these remaining services it makes sense to limit who can connect to them; however, many servers permit universal access without authentication. Two mechanisms are commonly used to limit the hosts that can access these services: TCP wrappers and IP filtering (i.e., using a firewall). The TCP wrappers package, distributed as standard Linux software, acts as a intermediary between server daemons and potential clients, performing additional authentication and host-based access checks before allowing the client to communicate with the server. The TCP wrappers package requires that a daemon be able to treat its standard input and output as a socket connection. By requiring this, the TCP wrappers daemon, `tcpd`, can accept connections for another daemon, check for authorization, and then invoke the other daemon, turning the socket file descriptor into the daemon's standard input and output. The `tcpd` daemon is normally invoked by `inetd` and listed in '`/etc/inetd.conf`' in front of each daemon. This is because all daemons that support `inetd` launching are TCP wrappers compatible. The TCP wrappers package uses the '`/etc/hosts.deny`' and '`/etc/hosts.allow`' files to decide whether or not to allow a server connection to proceed.

Rather than protecting every single one of the system daemons with TCP wrappers, one can shield the entire system behind a firewall. This is becoming an increasingly popular measure as security attacks become more common. Firewalls come in many shapes and sizes, including dedicated hardware running custom ROMs. An inexpensive option is to use the Linux operating system and a spare PC equipped with two network interface cards. The Linux Documentation Project[6] provides information on how to do this in its Firewall HOWTO document. Firewalls have two advantages over the use of TCP wrappers. First, firewalls allow control of access at

---

[6]The Linux Documentation Project pages are mirrored at many Web sites across the world, but the master page is located at `www.linuxdoc.org`.

both the packet and protocol levels, which can provide protection from a larger variety of attacks, including some denial-of-service attacks. Second, security policies may be implemented at a single administrative point, simplifying the maintenance of the system.

7.5.3   Secure Shell

The easiest way to break into a system is to steal someone's password. Programs for capturing the traffic across networks and extracting password information are readily available on the Internet. While administrators have little control over the quality of passwords users choose, eliminating access to the system via services that transmit passwords in plaintext reduces the chances of passwords being "sniffed" off the network.

Traditional host access protocols such as FTP, Telnet, and RSH require passwords to be transmitted over the network in the clear (in unencrypted plain text). Although the local network may be secure, once packets leave this safe area they travel through many other systems before reaching their ultimate destination. One of those systems may have had its security compromised. When a user logs into a Beowulf from across the country using such a service, all of his keystrokes might be actively monitored by some sniffer in an intervening network. For this reason, it is highly recommended not to allow Telnet, FTP, or RSH access to your Beowulf. A universally accessible machine should disable these services on all of the nodes, while a guarded Beowulf might disable the services only on the worldly node.

The best alternative to these services for remote access to a Beowulf is SSH, which is now the standard remote login and remote execution method used on Unix machines on the Internet. SSH encrypts all communications between two endpoints, including the X-Window display protocol, eliminating the chance that passwords or other sensitive bits of information are discovered by intermediate eavesdroppers. Many SSH implementations are available, including implementations for the Windows platform. OpenSSH[7] is becoming the most widely used implementation for Unix systems, since it is well supported and current (it is also open source and released under an unrestrictive license). Since OpenSSH is easy to install and very portable, Beowulf machines have also started using it as an `rsh` replacement. Most SSH packages also include a program called 'scp' as a replacement for 'rcp', thus allowing secure file transfer as well as interactive login sessions.

---

[7]OpenSSH is available from www.openssh.com

7.5.4   IP Masquerading

If a guarded configuration is implemented and it is necessary for nodes to contact the outside world, network address translation is the best option. Network Address Translation,[8] commonly referred to as NAT, is a technique devised for reusing IP addresses as a stopgap measure to slow the depletion of the IPv4 address space. NAT permits IP address reuse by allowing multiple networks to use the same addresses but having them communicate between each other through a pair of nonshared IP address. IP masquerading is a type of NAT performed by the worldly node of a Beowulf cluster that makes external network connections appear to originate from the single worldly node. This feature allows the internal nodes to originate network connections to external Internet hosts but provides security by not having a mechanism for an external host to set up a connection to an internal node.

A nice feature about IP masquerading is that it doesn't involve too many steps to set up. Only the node performing the masquerading requires any amount of reconfiguration. The internal nodes simply require their default route to be set to the internal network address of the worldly node, usually 192.168.1.1. You can do this with the route command as follows:

```
route add default gw 192.168.1.1
```

However, most Linux distributions perform gateway assignment at boot time based on a configuration file. Red Hat Linux stores gateway configuration information in the file '/etc/sysconfig/network', which contains two variables: GATEWAY and GATEWAYDEV. These should be set to the IP address of the worldly node and the primary internal network interface name of the internal node. A typical network configuration file for an internal node might look something like the following:

```
NETWORKING=yes
FORWARD_IPV4=false
HOSTNAME=b001
DOMAINNAME=beowulf.org
GATEWAY=192.168.1.1
GATEWAYDEV=eth0
```

Configuring the worldly node to perform the IP masquerading requires a little more work, but nothing particularly difficult. The first requirement is to compile

---

[8]"The IP Network Address Translator (NAT)," Internet Engineering Task Force RFC 1631, info.internet.isi.edu/in-notes/rfc/files/rfc1631.txt.

your kernel with support for network firewalls, IP forwarding/gatewaying, and IP masquerading. There are also some additional options you may wish to include, but these are the essential ones. More information about the particulars of each option can be found in the Linux kernel source tree in the 'masquerading.txt' documentation file and also in the IP Masquerade HOWTO.[9]

After installing a kernel capable of IP masquerading, you need to enable IP forwarding. You can do this on Red Hat Linux systems by setting the `FORWARD_-IPV4` variable to `true` in '`/etc/sysconfig/network`'. IP forwarding is the process by which a host will forward to its destination a packet it receives for which it is not itself the destination. This allows internal node packets to be forwarded to external hosts.

The last step is to configure IP masquerading rules. You don't want your worldly node to forward packets coming from just anywhere, so you have to tell it specifically what packets to forward. Currently, you can do this by using the `iptables` utility with 2.4.x Linux kernels; this is the evolution of the pre-2.4.x `ipfwadm` and `ipchains` utilities.

The program `iptables` configures firewall packet filtering and forwarding rules. It can specify rules based on the source and destination of a packet, the network interfaces on which a packet is received or transmitted, the network protocol used, destination and source ports, and quite a bit of other information. For the purposes of setting up a worldly node, you can use `iptables` to tell the kernel to masquerade only for packets originating from an internal node. Use a command like the following:

```
iptables -t nat -P PREROUTING DROP
iptables -t nat --source 192.168.1.0/24 -j ACCEPT
iptables -t nat -P PREROUTING -j LOG
```

The first command sets the default forwarding policy to *DROP* for the nat (network address translation) table. This is a safety measure to make sure your worldly node doesn't forward packets not originating from internal nodes. The second command asks the kernel to masquerade only for packets originating from within the internal network (192.168.1.0) and destined for any location. `iptables` works on a system of routing chains, such as `POSTROUTING` and `PREROUTING` that have lists of rules to determine where packets matching given characteristics go. The `-j` switches specify the destination policy for any packet matching that rule. Packets move down the

---

[9]The IP Masquerade HOWTO can be found online at the Linux Documentation Project `www.linuxdoc.org`. Additional IP masquerading information is also stored at the Linux IP Masquerade Resource, `ipmasq.cjb.net/`.

chain of rules until they find a matching one; a common and helpful debugging measure involves defining the last rule in a chain to have no constraints and send packets to the policy LOG. These are handled by `iptables`, which sends them to `syslogd` so that they can be examined. Ideally no packets should fall into this category. Typically, these commands are placed at the end of '`/etc/rc.d/rc.local`', so that they will be executed at boot time, but you can also create a script suitable for use in the '`/etc/rc.d/init.d`' startup system. The meanings of the various `iptables` options can be garnered from the `iptables` man page (`iptables` is a very complex utility, and a thorough perusal of the manual is highly recommended), but a quick summary is in order for the options necessary to configure a worldly node:

-P sets the policy for a given chain.

-A appends rules to the end of a selected chain.

-D deletes a rule from the selected chain.

-j target specifies the target of a rule.

-s address/mask indicates that a rule applies only to packets originating from the given source address range.

-d address/mask indicates that a rule applies only to packets destined for an address in the indicated range.

   While there is much more to system security than we have presented, these tips should get you started. Beowulf systems can easily be made as secure as the policies of your institution require. See Appendixes B and C for pointers to more specific guides to system administation and security.

7.6   Job Scheduling

Many Beowulf administrators are interested in better job scheduling functions. Beowulfs usually start out with only a few users in a single department, but as news about the system spreads to neighboring departments, more users are added to the system. Once that happens, it becomes important to keep user-developed applications from interfering with each other. This is usually done by funneling all user programs through a job scheduler, which decides in what order and on what processors to execute the programs. Part III of this book describes scheduling systems that are often used with Beowulf systems (as well as other kinds of parallel computers).

7.7   Some Advice on Upgrading Your Software

The world of Beowulf software development is about to start moving at the same rapid pace as general Linux development. To avoid playing the constant game of catchup, you will have to be prepared to decide when you have a satisfactory and stable software environment. It will help if you separate out one or two experimental nodes for software evaluation and testing. Before upgrading to a new kernel, make sure you've stressed it on a single node for a week or two. Before installing a fancy new scheduler, test it extensively. The last thing you want is for your entire Beowulf to grind to a halt because a scheduler has a bug that swamps the entire system with more processes than it can handle. If your users demand a new compiler, install it in such a way that they still have access to the old compiler, in case the new one doesn't always do quite the right thing. If your production system is humming along just fine, don't mess with it. Users don't like system down time. If they can already do all the work they want, then you should think very carefully before perturbing the system configuration. These are recommendations, not hard and fast rules, but they tend to be useful guides in the course of managing a system. The future of Beowulf system software promises to be very exciting. If you pick and choose only those tools that do what you need, you will likely minimize problems and increase the productivity of your system.

8 How Fast Is My Beowulf?

David Bailey

One of the first questions that a user of a new Beowulf-type system asks is "How fast does my system run?" Performance is more than just a curiosity for cluster systems. It is arguably the central motivation for building a clustered system in the first place—a single node is not sufficient for the task at hand. Thus the measurement of performance, as well as comparisons of performance between various available system designs and constructions, is of paramount importance.

8.1 Metrics

Many different metrics for system performance exist, varying greatly in their meaningfulness and ease of measurement. We discuss here some of the more widely used metrics.

1. **Theoretical peak performance**. This statistic is merely the maximum aggregate performance of the system. For scientific users, theoretical peak performance means the maximum aggregate floating-point operations per second, usually calculated as

$$P = N * C * F * R,$$

where P is the performance, N is the number of nodes, C is the number of CPUs per node, F is the number of floating-point operations per clock period, and R is the clock rate, measured in cycles per second. P is typically given in Mflops or Gflops. For nonscientific applications, integer operations are counted instead of floating-point operations per second, and rates are typically measured in Mops and Gops, variantly given as Mips and Gips. For nonhomogeneous systems, P is calculated as the total of the theoretical peak performance figures for each homogeneous subsystem.

The advantage of this metric is that is very easy to calculate. What's more, there is little disputing the result: the relevant data is in many cases publicly available. The disadvantage of this metric is that by definition it is unattainable by ordinary application programs. Indeed, a growing concern of scientific users—in particular, users of parallel and distributed systems—is that the typical gap between peak and sustained performance seems to be increasing, not decreasing.

2. **Application performance.** This statistic is the number of operations performed while executing an application program, divided by the total run time. As with theoretical peak performance, it is typically given in Mflops, Gflops, Mops, or Gops. This metric, if calculated for an application program that reasonably closely

resembles the program that the user ultimately intends to run on the system, is obviously a much more meaningful metric than theoretical peak performance. The metric is correspondingly harder to use, however, because you must first port the benchmark program to the cluster system, often a laborious and time-consuming task. Moreover, you must determine fairly accurately the number of floating-point (or integer) operations actually performed by the code. Along this line, you should ascertain that the algorithms used in the code are really the most efficient available for this task, or you should use a floating-point operation count that corresponds to that of an efficient algorithm implementation; otherwise, the results can be questioned. One key difficulty with this metric is the extent to which the source code has been "tuned" for optimal performance on the given system: comparing results that on one system are based on a highly tuned implementation to those on another system where the application has not be highly tuned can be misleading. Nonetheless, if used properly, this metric can be very useful.

3. **Application run time.** This statistic simply means the total wall-clock run time for performing a given application. One advantage of this statistic is that it frees you from having to count operations performed. Also, it avoids the potential distortion of using a code to assess performance whose operation count is larger than it needs be. In many regards, this is the ultimate metric, in the sense that it is precisely the ultimate figure of merit for an application running on a system. The disadvantage of this metric is that unless you are comparing two systems both of which have run exactly the same application, it is hard to meaningfully compare systems based solely on comparisons of runtime performance. Further, the issue of tuning also is present here: In comparing performance between systems, you have to ensure that both implementations have been comparably tuned.

4. **Scalability.** Users often cite scalability statistics when describing the performance of their system. Scalability is usually computed as

$$S = \frac{T(1)}{T(N)},$$

where $T(1)$ is the wall clock run time for a particular program on a single processor and $T(N)$ is the run time on N processors. A scalability figure close to N means that the program scales well. That is, the parallel implementation is very efficient, and the parallel overhead very low, so that nearly a linear speedup has been achieved. Scalability statistics can often provide useful information. For example, they can help you determine an optimal number of processors for a given application. But they can also be misleading, particularly if cited in the absence of application performance statistics. For example, an impressive speedup statistic may be due to a very low value of $T(N)$, which appears in the denominator, but it may also be due to a large value of $T(1)$—in other words, an inefficient one-processor implementation. Indeed, researchers working with parallel systems commonly note that their speedup statistic worsens when they accelerate their parallel program by clever tuning. Also, it is often simply impossible to compute this statistic because, while a benchmark test program may run on all or most of the processors in a system, it may require too much memory to run on a single node.

5. **Parallel efficiency.** A variant of the scalability metric is parallel efficiency, which is usually defined to be $P(N)/N$. Parallel efficiency statistics near one are ideal. This metric suffers from the same potential difficulties as the scalability metric.

6. **Percentage of peak.** Sometimes application performance statistics are given in terms of the percentage of theoretical peak performance. Such statistics are useful in highlighting the extent to which an application is using the full computational power of the system. For example, a low percentage of peak may indicate a mismatch of the architecture and the application, deserving further study to determine the source of the difficulty. However, a percentage-of-peak figure by itself is not too informative. An embarrassingly parallel application can achieve a high percentage of peak, but this is not a notable achievement. In general, percentage-of-peak figures beg the question "What percentage of peak is a realistic target for a given type of application?"

7. **Latency and bandwidth.** Many users are interested in the latency (time delay) and bandwidth (transfer rate) of the interprocessor communications network, since the network is one of the key elements of the system design. These metrics have the advantage of being fairly easy to determine. The disadvantage is that the network often performs differently under highly loaded situations from what the latency and bandwidth figures by themselves reveal. And, needless to say, these metrics characterize only the network and give no information on the computational speed of individual processors.

8. **System utilization.** One common weakness of the cited metrics is that they tend to ignore system-level effects. These effects include competition between two different tasks running in the system, competition between I/O-intensive tasks and non-I/O-intensive tasks, inefficiencies in job schedulers, and job startup delays. To address this issue, some Beowulf system users have measured the performance of

a system on a long-term throughput basis, as a contrast to conventional benchmark performance testing.

Clearly, no single type of performance measurement—much less a single figure of merit—is simultaneously easy to determine and completely informative. In one sense, only one figure of merit matters, as emphasized above: the wall clock run time for your particular application on your particular system. But this is not easy to determine before a purchase or upgrade decision has been made. And even if you can make such a measurement, it is not clear how to compare your results with the thousands of other Beowulf system users around the world, not to mention other types of systems and clusters.

These considerations have led many users of parallel and cluster systems to compare performance based on a few standard benchmark programs. In this way, you can determine whether your particular system design is as effective (as measured by a handful of benchmarks) as another. Such comparisons might not be entirely relevant to your particular application, but with some experience you can find one or more well-known benchmarks that give performance figures that are well correlated with your particular needs.

8.2 Ping-Pong Test

One of the most widely used measurements performed on cluster systems is the Ping-Pong test, one of several test programs that measure the latency and bandwidth of the interprocessor communications network. There are a number of tools for testing TCP performance, including `netperf` and `netpipe` (see `www.netperf.org` and `www.scl.ameslab.gov/netpipe`). Ping-Pong tests that are appropriate for application developers measure the performance of the user API and are typically written in C and assume that the MPI communications library is installed on the system. More details on downloading and running these are given in Section 10.10.

8.3 The LINPACK Benchmark

The LINPACK benchmark dates back to the early 1980s, when Jack Dongarra (then at Argonne National Laboratory) began collecting performance results of systems, based on their speed in solving a 100×100 linear system using Fortran routines from the LINPACK library. While a problem of this size is no longer a supercomputer-class exercise, it is still useful for assessing the computational performance of a single-processor system. In particular, it is a reasonable way to measure the performance of a single node of a Beowulf-type system. One can obtain the LINPACK source code, plus instructions for running the LINPACK benchmark, from the `www.netlib.org/benchmark`.

More recently, Dongarra has released the "highly parallel computing" benchmark. This benchmark was developed for medium-to-large parallel and distributed systems and has been tabulated on hundreds of computer systems [8, Table 3]. Unlike the basic LINPACK benchmark, the scalable version does not specify a matrix size. Instead, the user is invited to solve the largest problem that can reasonably be run on the available system, given limitations of memory. Further, the user is not restricted to running a fixed source code, as with the single-processor version. Instead, almost any reasonable programming language and parallel computation library can be run, including assembly-coded library routines if desired.

A portable implementation of the highly parallel LINPACK benchmark, called the High Performance LINPACK (HPL) benchmark, is available. More details on downloading and running the HPL benchmark are given in Section 10.10.3.

During the past ten years, Dongarra and Strohmaier have compiled a running list of the world's so-called Top500 computers, based on the scalable LINPACK benchmark. The current listing is available from the `www.top500.org`. One of the top-ranking systems is the ASCI Red system at Sandia National Laboratories in Albuquerque, New Mexico. The ASCI Red system is a Pentium-based cluster system, although not truly a "Beowulf" system because it has a custom-designed interprocessor network. With an Rmax rating of 2.379 Tflops, it currently ranks third in the Top500 list (based on the June 2001 listing).

The LINPACK benchmarks are fairly easy to download and run. Once a timing figure is obtained, the calculation of performance is very easy. Most significant, there is a huge collection of results for comparison: it is very easy to determine how your system stacks up against other similar systems.

The principal disadvantage of the LINPACK benchmarks, both single processor and parallel, is that they tend to overestimate the performance that real-world scientific applications can expect to achieve on a given system. This is because the LINPACK codes are "dense matrix" calculations, which have very favorable data locality characteristics. It is not uncommon for the scalable LINPACK benchmark, for example, to achieve 30 percent or more of the theoretical peak performance potential of a system. Real scientific application codes, in contrast, seldom achieve more than 10 percent of the peak figure on modern distributed-memory parallel systems such as Beowulf systems.

8.4   The NAS Parallel Benchmark Suite

The NAS Parallel Benchmark (NPB) suite was designed at NASA Ames Research Center in 1990 to typify high-end aeroscience computations. This suite consists of eight individual benchmarks, including five general computational kernels and three simulated computational fluid dynamics applications:

EP: An "embarrassingly parallel" calculation, it requires almost no interprocessor communication.

MG: A multigrid calculation, it tests both short- and long-distance communication.

CG: A conjugate gradient calculation, it tests irregular communication.

FT: A three-dimensional fast Fourier transform calculation, it tests massive all-to-all communication.

IS: An integer sort, it involves integer data and irregular communication.

LU: A simulated fluid dynamics application, it uses the LU approach.

SP: A simulated fluid dynamics application, it uses the SP approach.

BT: A simulated fluid dynamics application, it uses the BT approach.

The original NPB suite was a "paper-and-pencil" specification—the specific calculations to be performed for each benchmark were specified in a technical document, even down to the detail of how to generate the initial data. Some straightforward one-processor sample program codes were provided in the original release, but it was intended that those implementing this suite would use one of several vendor-specific parallel programming models available at the time (1990). The original NPB problem set was deemed Class A size. Subsequently some larger problem sets were defined: Class B, which are about four times as large as the Class A problems, and Class C, which are about four times as large as Class B problems. The small single-processor sample codes are sometimes referred to as the Class W size.

Since the original NPB release, implementations of the NPB using MPI and also OpenMP have been provided by the NASA team. These are available at `www.nas.nasa.gov/Software/NPB/`.

As with the LINPACK benchmark, the NPB suite can be used to measure the performance of either a single node of a Beowulf system or the entire system. In particular, the Class W problems can easily be run on a single-processor system. For a Beowulf system with, say, 32 processors, the Class A problems are an appropriate test. The Class B problems are appropriate for systems with roughly 32–128 processors. The Class C problems can be used for systems with up to 256 CPUs.

Unfortunately, almost the entire NASA research team that designed and championed the NPB suite has now left NASA. As a result, NASA is no longer actively supporting and promoting the benchmarks. Thus, there probably will not be any larger problem sets developed. Further, NASA is no longer actively collecting results.

The NPB suite does, however, continue to attract attention from the parallel computing research community. This is because the suite reflects real-world parallel scientific computation to a significantly greater degree than do most other available benchmarks.

We recommend that users of Beowulf-type systems use the MPI version of the NPB suite. Instructions for downloading, installing, and running the suite are given at the NPB Web site.

II PARALLEL PROGRAMMING

9 Parallel Programming with MPI

William Gropp and Ewing Lusk

Parallel computation on a Beowulf is accomplished by dividing a computation into parts and making use of multiple processes, each executing on a separate processor, to carry out these parts. Sometimes an ordinary program can be used by all the processes, but with distinct input files or parameters. In such a situation, no communication occurs among the separate tasks. When the power of a parallel computer is needed to attack a large problem with a more complex structure, however, such communication is necessary.

One of the most straightforward approaches to communication is to have the processes coordinate their activities by sending and receiving messages, much as a group of people might cooperate to perform a complex task. This approach to achieving parallelism is called *message passing*.

In this chapter and the next, we show how to write parallel programs using MPI, the Message Passing Interface. MPI is a message-passing library specification. All three parts of this description are significant.

- MPI addresses the message-passing model of parallel computation, in which processes with separate address spaces synchronize with one another and move data from the address space of one process to that of another by sending and receiving messages.[1]
- MPI specifies a library interface, that is, a collection of subroutines and their arguments. It is not a language; rather, MPI routines are called from programs written in conventional languages such as Fortran, C, and C++.
- MPI is a specification, not a particular implementation. The specification was created by the MPI Forum, a group of parallel computer vendors, computer scientists, and users who came together to cooperatively work out a community standard. The first phase of meetings resulted in a release of the standard in 1994 that is sometimes referred to as MPI-1. Once the standard was implemented and in wide use a second series of meetings resulted in a set of extensions, referred to as MPI-2. MPI refers to both MPI-1 and MPI-2.

As a specification, MPI is defined by a standards document, the way C, Fortran, or POSIX are defined. The MPI standards documents are available at `www.mpi-forum.org` and may be freely downloaded. The MPI-1 and MPI-2 standards are also available as journal issues [21, 22] and in annotated form as books

---

[1]Processes may be single threaded, with one program counter, or multithreaded, with multiple program counters. MPI is for communication among processes rather than threads. Signal handlers can be thought of as executing in a separate thread.

in this series [29, 11]. Implementations of MPI are available for almost all parallel computers, from clusters to the largest and most powerful parallel computers in the world. In Section 9.8 we provide a summary of the most popular cluster implementations.

A goal of the MPI Forum was to create a powerful, flexible library that could be implemented efficiently on the largest computers and provide a tool to attack the most difficult problems in parallel computing. It does not always do the simplest things in the simplest way but comes into its own as more complex functionality is needed. In this chapter and the next we work through a set of examples, starting with the simplest.

9.1 Hello World in MPI

To see what an MPI program looks like, we start with the classic "hello world" program. MPI specifies only the library calls to be used in a C, Fortran, or C++ program; consequently, all of the capabilities of the language are available. The simplest "Hello World" program is shown in Figure 9.1.

```
#include "mpi.h"
#include <stdio.h>

int main( int argc, char *argv[] )
{
    MPI_Init( &argc, &argv );
    printf( "Hello World\n" );
    MPI_Finalize();
    return 0;
}
```

Figure 9.1
Simple "Hello World" program in MPI.

All MPI programs must contain one call to MPI_Init and one to MPI_Finalize. All other[2] MPI routines must be called after MPI_Init and before MPI_Finalize. All C and C++ programs must also include the file 'mpi.h'; Fortran programs must either use the MPI module or include mpif.h.

The simple program in Figure 9.1 is not very interesting. In particular, all processes print the same text. A more interesting version has each process identify

---

[2]There are a few exceptions, including MPI_Initialized.

```
#include "mpi.h"
#include <stdio.h>

int main( int argc, char *argv[] )
{
    int rank, size;

    MPI_Init( &argc, &argv );
    MPI_Comm_rank( MPI_COMM_WORLD, &rank );
    MPI_Comm_size( MPI_COMM_WORLD, &size );
    printf( "Hello World from process %d of %d\n", rank, size );
    MPI_Finalize();
    return 0;
}
```

Figure 9.2
A more interesting version of "Hello World".

itself. This version, shown in Figure 9.2, illustrates several important points. Of particular note are the variables `rank` and `size`. Because MPI programs are made up of communicating processes, each process has its own set of variables. In this case, each process has its own address space containing its own variables `rank` and `size` (and `argc`, `argv`, etc.). The routine `MPI_Comm_size` returns the number of processes in the MPI job in the second argument. Each of the MPI processes is identified by a number, called the *rank*, ranging from zero to the value of `size` minus one. The routine `MPI_Comm_rank` returns in the second argument the rank of the process. The output of this program might look something like the following:

```
Hello World from process 0 of 4
Hello World from process 2 of 4
Hello World from process 3 of 4
Hello World from process 1 of 4
```

Note that the output is not ordered from processes 0 to 3. MPI does not specify the behavior of other routines or language statements such as `printf`; in particular, it does not specify the order of output from print statements.

9.1.1 Compiling and Running MPI Programs

The MPI standard does not specify how to compile and link programs (neither do C or Fortran). However, most MPI implementations provide tools to compile and link programs.

For example, one popular implementation, MPICH, provides scripts to ensure that the correct include directories are specified and that the correct libraries are linked. The script `mpicc` can be used just like `cc` to compile and link C programs. Similarly, the scripts `mpif77`, `mpif90`, and `mpiCC` may be used to compile and link Fortran 77, Fortran, and C++ programs.

If you prefer not to use these scripts, you need only ensure that the correct paths and libraries are provided. The MPICH implementation provides the switch `-show` for `mpicc` that shows the command lines used with the C compiler and is an easy way to find the paths. Note that the name of the MPI library may be `libmpich.a`, `libmpi.a`, or something similar and that additional libraries, such as `libsocket.a` or `libgm.a`, may be required. The include path may refer to a specific installation of MPI, such as `/usr/include/local/mpich-1.2.2/include`.

Running an MPI program (in most implementations) also requires a special program, particularly when parallel programs are started by a batch system as described in Chapter 13. Many implementations provide a program `mpirun` that can be used to start MPI programs. For example, the command

```
mpirun -np 4 helloworld
```

runs the program `helloworld` using four processes. Most MPI implementations will attempt to run each process on a different processor; most MPI implementations provide a way to select particular processors for each MPI process.

The name and command-line arguments of the program that starts MPI programs were not specified by the original MPI standard, just as the C standard does not specify how to start C programs. However, the MPI Forum did recommend, as part of the MPI-2 standard, an `mpiexec` command and standard command-line arguments to be used in starting MPI programs. By 2002, most MPI implementations should provide `mpiexec`. This name was selected because no MPI implementation was using it (many are using `mpirun`, but with incompatible arguments). The syntax is almost the same as for the MPICH version of `mpirun`; instead of using `-np` to specify the number of processes, the switch `-n` is used:

```
mpiexec -n 4 helloworld
```

The MPI standard defines additional switches for `mpiexec`; for more details, see Section 4.1, "Portable MPI Process Startup", in the MPI-2 standard.

9.1.2 Adding Communication to Hello World

The code in Figure 9.2 does not guarantee that the output will be printed in any particular order. To force a particular order for the output, and to illustrate how data is communicated between processes, we add communication to the "Hello World" program. The revised program implements the following algorithm:

```
Find the name of the processor that is running the process
If the process has rank > 0, then
    send the name of the processor to the process with rank 0
Else
    print the name of this processor
    for each rank,
        receive the name of the processor and print it
Endif
```

This program is shown in Figure 9.3. The new MPI calls are to `MPI_Send` and `MPI_Recv` and to `MPI_Get_processor_name`. The latter is a convenient way to get the name of the processor on which a process is running. `MPI_Send` and `MPI_Recv` can be understood by stepping back and considering the two requirements that must be satisfied to communicate data between two processes:

1. Describe the data to be sent or the location in which to receive the data

2. Describe the destination (for a send) or the source (for a receive) of the data.

In addition, MPI provides a way to tag messages and to discover information about the size and source of the message. We will discuss each of these in turn.

Describing the Data Buffer. A data buffer typically is described by an address and a length, such as "a,100," where a is a pointer to 100 bytes of data. For example, the Unix `write` call describes the data to be written with an address and length (along with a file descriptor). MPI generalizes this to provide two additional capabilities: describing noncontiguous regions of data and describing data so that it can be communicated between processors with different data representations. To do this, MPI uses three values to describe a data buffer: the address, the (MPI) datatype, and the number or *count* of the items of that datatype. For example, a buffer containing four C `ints` is described by the triple "a, 4, MPI_INT." There are predefined MPI datatypes for all of the basic datatypes defined in C, Fortran, and C++. The most common datatypes are shown in Table 9.1.

```
#include "mpi.h"
#include <stdio.h>

int main( int argc, char *argv[] )
{
    int  numprocs, myrank, namelen, i;
    char processor_name[MPI_MAX_PROCESSOR_NAME];
    char greeting[MPI_MAX_PROCESSOR_NAME + 80];
    MPI_Status status;

    MPI_Init( &argc, &argv );
    MPI_Comm_size( MPI_COMM_WORLD, &numprocs );
    MPI_Comm_rank( MPI_COMM_WORLD, &myrank );
    MPI_Get_processor_name( processor_name, &namelen );

    sprintf( greeting, "Hello, world, from process %d of %d on %s",
             myrank, numprocs, processor_name );

    if ( myrank == 0 ) {
        printf( "%s\n", greeting );
        for ( i = 1; i < numprocs; i++ ) {
            MPI_Recv( greeting, sizeof( greeting ), MPI_CHAR,
                      i, 1, MPI_COMM_WORLD, &status );
            printf( "%s\n", greeting );
        }
    }
    else {
        MPI_Send( greeting, strlen( greeting ) + 1, MPI_CHAR,
                  0, 1, MPI_COMM_WORLD );
    }

    MPI_Finalize( );
    return( 0 );
}
```

Figure 9.3
A more complex "Hello World" program in MPI. Only process 0 writes to stdout; each process sends a message to process 0.

	C		Fortran	
	MPI type			MPI type
int	MPI_INT	INTEGER		MPI_INTEGER
double	MPI_DOUBLE	DOUBLE PRECISION		MPI_DOUBLE_PRECISION
float	MPI_FLOAT	REAL		MPI_REAL
long	MPI_LONG			
char	MPI_CHAR	CHARACTER		MPI_CHARACTER
		LOGICAL		MPI_LOGICAL
—	MPI_BYTE	—		MPI_BYTE

Table 9.1
The most common MPI datatypes. C and Fortran types on the same row are often but not always the same type. The type MPI_BYTE is used for raw data bytes and does not coorespond to any particular datatype. The C++ MPI datatypes have the same name as the C datatype, but without the MPI_ prefix, for example, MPI::INT.

Describing the Destination or Source. The destination or source is specified by using the rank of the process. MPI generalizes the notion of destination and source rank by making the rank relative to a group of processes. This group may be a subset of the original group of processes. Allowing subsets of processes and using relative ranks make it easier to use MPI to write component-oriented software (more on this in Section 10.4). The MPI object that defines a group of processes (and a special communication context that will be discussed in Section 10.4) is called a *communicator*. Thus, sources and destinations are given by two parameters: a rank and a communicator. The communicator MPI_COMM_WORLD is predefined and contains all of the processes started by mpirun or mpiexec. As a source, the special value MPI_ANY_SOURCE may be used to indicate that the message may be received from any rank of the MPI processes in this MPI program.

Selecting among Messages. The "extra" argument for MPI_Send is a nonnegative integer *tag* value. This tag allows a program to send one extra number with the data. MPI_Recv can use this value either to select which message to receive (by specifying a specific tag value) or to use the tag to convey extra data (by specifying the *wild card* value MPI_ANY_TAG). In the latter case, the tag value of the received message is stored in the status argument (this is the last parameter to MPI_Recv in the C binding). This is a structure in C, an integer array in Fortran, and a class in C++. The tag and rank of the sending process can be accessed by referring to the appropriate element of status as shown in Table 9.2.

C	Fortran	C++
status.MPI_SOURCE	status(MPI_SOURCE)	status.Get_source()
status.MPI_TAG	status(MPI_TAG)	status.Get_tag()

Table 9.2
Accessing the source and tag after an MPI_Recv.

Determining the Amount of Data Received.   The amount of data received can be found by using the routine MPI_Get_count. For example,

    MPI_Get_count(&status, MPI_CHAR, &num_chars);

returns in num_chars the number of characters sent. The second argument should be the same MPI datatype that was used to receive the message. (Since many applications do not need this information, the use of a routine allows the implementation to avoid computing num_chars unless the user needs the value.)

Our example provides a maximum-sized buffer in the receive. It is also possible to find the amount of memory needed to receive a message by using MPI_Probe, as shown in Figure 9.4.

```
char *greeting;
int num_chars, src;
MPI_Status status;
...
MPI_Probe( MPI_ANY_SOURCE, 1, MPI_COMM_WORLD, &status );
MPI_Get_count( &status, MPI_CHAR, &num_chars );
greeting = (char *)malloc( num_chars );
src      = status.MPI_SOURCE;
MPI_Recv( greeting, num_chars, MPI_CHAR,
          src, 1, MPI_COMM_WORLD, &status );
```

Figure 9.4
Using MPI_Probe to find the size of a message before receiving it.

MPI guarantees that messages are ordered and that an MPI_Recv after an MPI_-Probe will receive the message that the probe returned information on as long as the same message selection criteria (source rank, communicator, and message tag) are used. Note that in this example, the source for the MPI_Recv is specified as status.MPI_SOURCE, not MPI_ANY_SOURCE, to ensure that the message received is the same as the one about which MPI_Probe returned information.

9.2 Manager/Worker Example

We now begin a series of examples illustrating approaches to parallel computations that accomplish useful work. While each parallel application is unique, a number of paradigms have emerged as widely applicable, and many parallel algorithms are variations on these patterns.

One of the most universal is the "manager/worker" or "task parallelism" approach. The idea is that the work that needs to be done can be divided by a "manager" into separate pieces and the pieces can be assigned to individual "worker" processes. Thus the manager executes a different algorithm from that of the workers, but all of the workers execute the same algorithm. Most implementations of MPI (including MPICH) allow MPI processes to be running different programs (executable files), but it is often convenient (and in some cases required) to combine the manager and worker code into a single program with the structure shown in Figure 9.5.

```
#include "mpi.h"

int main( int argc, char *argv[] )
{
    int numprocs, myrank;

    MPI_Init( &argc, &argv );
    MPI_Comm_size( MPI_COMM_WORLD, &numprocs );
    MPI_Comm_rank( MPI_COMM_WORLD, &myrank );

    if ( myrank == 0 )              /* manager process */
        manager_code ( numprocs );
    else                            /* worker process */
        worker_code ( );
    MPI_Finalize( );
    return 0;
}
```

Figure 9.5
Framework of the matrix-vector multiply program.

Sometimes the work can be evenly divided into exactly as many pieces as there are workers, but a more flexible approach is to have the manager keep a pool of units of work larger than the number of workers, and assign new work dynamically to workers as they complete their tasks and send their results back to the manager. This approach, called *self-scheduling*, works well in the presence of tasks of varying sizes and/or workers of varying speeds.

We illustrate this technique with a parallel program to multiply a matrix by a vector. (A Fortran version of this same program can be found in [13].) This program is not a particularly good way to carry out this operation, but it illustrates the approach and is simple enough to be shown in its entirety. The program multiplies a square matrix a by a vector b and stores the result in c. The units of work are the individual dot products of the rows of a with the vector b. Thus the manager, code for which is shown in Figure 9.6, starts by initializing a. The manager then sends out initial units of work, one row to each worker. We use the MPI tag on each such message to encode the row number we are sending. Since row numbers start at 0 but we wish to reserve 0 as a tag with the special meaning of "no more work to do", we set the tag to one greater than the row number. When a worker sends back a dot product, we store it in the appropriate place in c and send that worker another row to work on. Once all the rows have been assigned, workers completing a task are sent a "no more work" message, indicated by a message with tag 0.

The code for the worker part of the program is shown in Figure 9.7. A worker initializes b, receives a row of a in a message, computes the dot product of that row and the vector b, and then returns the answer to the manager, again using the tag to identify the row. A worker repeats this until it receives the "no more work" message, identified by its tag of 0.

This program requires at least two processes to run: one manager and one worker. Unfortunately, adding more workers is unlikely to make the job go faster. We can analyze the cost of computation and communication mathematically and see what happens as we increase the number of workers. Increasing the number of workers will decrease the amount of computation done by each worker, and since they work in parallel, this should decrease total elapsed time. On the other hand, more workers mean more communication, and the cost of communicating a number is usually much greater than the cost of an arithmetical operation on it. The study of how the total time for a parallel algorithm is affected by changes in the number of processes, the problem size, and the speed of the processor and communication network is called *scalability analysis*. We analyze the matrix-vector program as a simple example.

First, let us compute the number of floating-point operations. For a matrix of size n, we have to compute n dot products, each of which requires n multiplications and $n-1$ additions. Thus the number of floating-point operations is $n \times (n + (n-1)) = n \times (2n-1) = 2n^2 - n$. If T_{calc} is the time it takes a processor to do one floating-point

```
#define SIZE 1000
#define MIN( x, y ) ((x) < (y) ? x : y)

void manager_code( int numprocs )
{
    double a[SIZE][SIZE], c[SIZE];

    int i, j, sender, row, numsent = 0;
    double dotp;
    MPI_Status status;

    /* (arbitrary) initialization of a */
    for (i = 0; i < SIZE; i++ )
        for ( j = 0; j < SIZE; j++ )
            a[i][j] = ( double ) j;

    for ( i = 1; i < MIN( numprocs, SIZE ); i++ ) {
        MPI_Send( a[i-1], SIZE, MPI_DOUBLE, i, i, MPI_COMM_WORLD );
        numsent++;
    }
    /* receive dot products back from workers */
    for ( i = 0; i < SIZE; i++ ) {
        MPI_Recv( &dotp, 1, MPI_DOUBLE, MPI_ANY_SOURCE, MPI_ANY_TAG,
                  MPI_COMM_WORLD, &status );
        sender = status.MPI_SOURCE;
        row    = status.MPI_TAG - 1;
        c[row] = dotp;
        /* send another row back to this worker if there is one */
        if ( numsent < SIZE ) {
            MPI_Send( a[numsent], SIZE, MPI_DOUBLE, sender,
                      numsent + 1, MPI_COMM_WORLD );
            numsent++;
        }
        else                            /* no more work */
            MPI_Send( MPI_BOTTOM, 0, MPI_DOUBLE, sender, 0,
                      MPI_COMM_WORLD );
    }
}
```

Figure 9.6
The matrix-vector multiply program, manager code.

```
void worker_code( void )
{
    double b[SIZE], c[SIZE];
    int i, row, myrank;
    double dotp;
    MPI_Status status;

    for ( i = 0; i < SIZE; i++ ) /* (arbitrary) b initialization */
        b[i] = 1.0;

    MPI_Comm_rank( MPI_COMM_WORLD, &myrank );
    if ( myrank <= SIZE ) {
        MPI_Recv( c, SIZE, MPI_DOUBLE, 0, MPI_ANY_TAG,
                    MPI_COMM_WORLD, &status );
        while ( status.MPI_TAG > 0 ) {
            row = status.MPI_TAG - 1;
            dotp = 0.0;
            for ( i = 0; i < SIZE; i++ )
                dotp += c[i] * b[i];
            MPI_Send( &dotp, 1, MPI_DOUBLE, 0, row + 1,
                        MPI_COMM_WORLD );
            MPI_Recv( c, SIZE, MPI_DOUBLE, 0, MPI_ANY_TAG,
                        MPI_COMM_WORLD, &status );
        }
    }
}
```

Figure 9.7
The matrix-vector multiply program, worker code.

operation, then the total computation time is $(2n^2 - n) \times T_{calc}$. Next, we compute the number of communications, defined as sending one floating-point number. (We ignore for this simple analysis the effect of message lengths.) Leaving aside the cost of communicating b (perhaps it is computed locally in a preceding step), we have to send each row of a and receive back one dot product answer. So the number of floating-point numbers communicated is $(n \times n) + n = n^2 + n$. If T_{comm} is the time to communicate one number, we get $(n^2 + n) \times T_{comm}$ for the total communication time. Thus the ratio of communication time to computation time is

$$\left(\frac{n^2 + n}{2n^2 - n} \right) \times \left(\frac{T_{comm}}{T_{calc}} \right).$$

In many computations the ratio of communication to computation can be reduced almost to 0 by making the problem size larger. Our analysis shows that this is not the case here. As n gets larger, the term on the left approaches $\frac{1}{2}$. Thus we can expect communication costs to prevent this algorithm from showing good speedups, even on large problem sizes.

The situation is better in the case of matrix-*matrix* multiplication, which could be carried out by a similar algorithm. We would replace the vectors b and c by matrices, send the entire matrix b to the workers at the beginning of the computation, and then hand out the rows of a as work units, just as before. The workers would compute an entire row of the product, consisting of the dot products of the row of a with all of the column of b, and then return a row of c to the manager.

Let us now do the scalability analysis for the matrix-matrix multiplication. Again we ignore the initial communication of b. The number of operations for one dot product is $n + (n + 1)$ as before, and the total number of dot products calculated is n^2. Thus the total number of operations is $n^2 \times (2n - 1) = 2n^3 - n^2$. The number of numbers communicated has gone up to $(n \times n) + (n \times n) = 2n^2$. So the ratio of communication time to computation time has become

$$\left(\frac{2n^2}{2n^3 - n^2} \right) \times \left(\frac{T_{comm}}{T_{calc}} \right),$$

which does tend to 0 as n gets larger. Thus, for large matrices the communication costs play less of a role.

Two other difficulties with this algorithm might occur as we increase the size of the problem and the number of workers. The first is that as messages get longer, the workers waste more time waiting for the next row to arrive. A solution to this problem is to "double buffer" the distribution of work, having the manager send two rows to each worker to begin with, so that a worker always has some work to do while waiting for the next row to arrive.

Another difficulty for larger numbers of processes can be that the manager can become overloaded so that it cannot assign work in a timely manner. This problem can most easily be addressed by increasing the size of the work unit, but in some cases it is necessary to parallelize the manager task itself, with multiple managers handling subpools of work units.

A more subtle problem has to do with *fairness*: ensuring that all worker processes are fairly serviced by the manager. MPI provides several ways to ensure fairness; see [13, Section 7.1.4].

9.3   Two-Dimensional Jacobi Example with One-Dimensional Decomposition

A common use of parallel computers in scientific computation is to approximate the solution of a partial differential equation (PDE). One of the most common PDEs, at least in textbooks, is the Poisson equation (here shown in two dimensions):

$$\frac{\partial^2 u}{\partial x^2} + \frac{\partial^2 u}{\partial y^2} = f(x, y) \text{ in } \Gamma \tag{9.3.1}$$

$$u = g(x, y) \text{ on } \partial\Gamma \tag{9.3.2}$$

This equation is used to describe many physical phenomena, including fluid flow and electrostatics. The equation has two parts: a differential equation applied everywhere within a domain Γ (9.3.1) and a specification of the value of the unknown u along the boundary of Γ (the notation $\partial\Gamma$ means "the boundary of Γ"). For example, if this equation is used to model the equilibrium distribution of temperature inside a region, the boundary condition $g(x, y)$ specifies the applied temperature along the boundary, $f(x, y)$ is zero, and $u(x, y)$ is the temperature within the region. To simplify the rest of this example, we will consider only a simple domain Γ consisting of a square (see Figure 9.8).

To compute an approximation to $u(x, y)$, we must first reduce the problem to finite size. We cannot determine the value of u everywhere; instead, we will approximate u at a finite number of points (x_i, y_j) in the domain, where $x_i = i \times h$ and $y_j = j \times h$. (Of course, we can define a value for u at other points in the domain by interpolating from these values that we determine, but the approximation is defined by the value of u at the points (x_i, y_j).) These points are shown as black disks in Figure 9.8. Because of this regular spacing, the points are said to make up a *regular mesh*. At each of these points, we approximate the partial derivatives with finite differences. For example,

$$\frac{\partial^2 u}{\partial x^2}(x_i, y_j) \approx \frac{u(x_{i+1}, y_j) - 2u(x_i, y_j) + u(x_{i-1}, y_j)}{h^2}.$$

If we now let $u_{i,j}$ stand for our approximation to solution of Equation 9.3.1 at the point (x_i, y_j), we have the following set of simultaneous linear equations for the values of u:

$$\frac{u_{i+1,j} - 2u_{i,j} + u_{i-1,j}}{h^2} +$$
$$\frac{u_{i,j+1} - 2u_{i,j} + u_{i,j-1}}{h^2} = f(x_i, y_j). \tag{9.3.3}$$

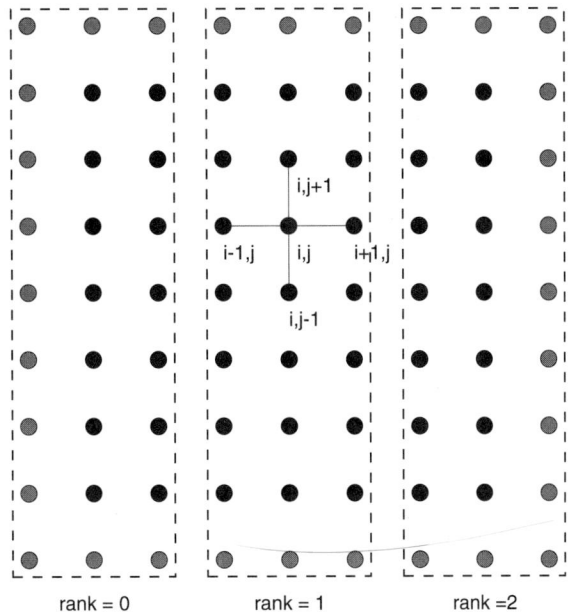

rank = 0   rank = 1   rank =2

Figure 9.8
Domain and 9×9 computational mesh for approximating the solution to the Poisson problem.

For values of u along the boundary (e.g., at $x = 0$ or $y = 1$), the value of the boundary condition g is used. If $h = 1/(n + 1)$ (so there are $n \times n$ points in the interior of the mesh), this gives us n^2 simultaneous linear equations to solve.

Many methods can be used to solve these equations. In fact, if you have this particular problem, you should use one of the numerical libraries described in Table 10.1. In this section, we describe a very simple (and inefficient) algorithm because, from a parallel computing perspective, it illustrates how to program more effective and general methods. The method that we use is called the *Jacobi* method for solving systems of linear equations. The Jacobi method computes successive approximations to the solution of Equation 9.3.3 by rewriting the equation as follows:

$$u_{i+1,j} \quad - \quad 2u_{i,j} + u_{i-1,j} + u_{i,j+1} - 2u_{i,j} + u_{i,j-1} = h^2 f(x_i, y_j)$$
$$u_{i,j} = \frac{1}{4}(u_{i+1,j} + u_{i-1,j} + u_{i,j+1} + u_{i,j-1} - h^2 f_{i,j}). \tag{9.3.4}$$

Each step in the Jacobi iteration computes a new approximation to $u_{i,j}^{N+1}$ in terms of the surrounding values of u^N:

$$u_{i,j}^{N+1} = \frac{1}{4}(u_{i+1,j}^N + u_{i-1,j}^N + u_{i,j+1}^N + u_{i,j-1}^N - h^2 f_{i,j}). \tag{9.3.5}$$

This is our algorithm for computing the approximation to the solution of the Poisson problem. We emphasize that the Jacobi method is a poor numerical method but that the same communication patterns apply to many finite difference, volume, or element discretizations solved by iterative techniques.

In the uniprocessor version of this algorithm, the solution u is represented by a two-dimensional array u[max_n][max_n], and the iteration is written as follows:

```
double u[NX+2][NY+2], u_new[NX+2][NY+2], f[NX+2][NY+2];
int    i, j;
...
for (i=1;i<=NX;i++)
   for (j=1;j<=NY;j++)
      u_new[i][j] = 0.25 * (u[i+1][j] + u[i-1][j] +
                            u[i][j+1] + u[i][j-1] - h*h*f[i][j]);
```

Here, we let u[0][j], u[n+1][j], u[i][0], and u[i][n+1] hold the values of the boundary conditions g (these correspond to $u(0, y)$, $u(1, y)$, $u(x, 0)$, and $u(x, 1)$ in Equation 9.3.1). To parallelize this method, we must first decide how to decompose the data structure u and u_new across the processes. Many possible decompositions exist. One of the simplest is to divide the domain into strips as shown in Figure 9.8.

Let the local representation of the array u be ulocal; that is, each process declares an array ulocal that contains the part of u held by that process. No process has all of u; the data structure representing u is *decomposed* among all of the processes. The code that is used on each process to implement the Jacobi method is

```
for (i=i_start;i<=i_end;i++)
  for (j=1;j<=NY;j++)
    ulocal_new[i-i_start][j] =
        0.25 * (ulocal[i-i_start+1][j] + ulocal[i-i_start-1][j] +
                ulocal[i-i_start][j+1] + ulocal[i-i_start][j-1] -
                h*h*flocal[i-i_start][j]);
```

where i_start and i_end describe the strip on this process (in practice, the loop would be from zero to i_end-i_start; we use this formulation to maintain the correspondence with the uniprocessor code). We have defined ulocal so that ulocal[0][j] corresponds to u[i_start][j] in the uniprocessor version of this code. Using variable names such as ulocal that make it obvious which variables are part of a distributed data structure is often a good idea.

From this code, we can see what data we need to communicate. For `i=i_start` we need the values of `u[i_start-1][j]`, and for `i=i_end` we need `u[i_end+1][j]`. These values belong to the adjacent processes and must be communicated. In addition, we need a location in which to store these values. We could use a separate array, but for regular meshes the most common approach is to use *ghost* or *halo* cells, where extra space is set aside in the `ulocal` array to hold the values from neighboring processes. In this case, we need only a single column of neighboring data, so we will let `u_local[1][j]` correspond to `u[i_start][j]`. This changes the code for a single iteration of the loop to

```
exchange_nbrs( ulocal, i_start, i_end, left, right );
for (i_local=1; i_local<=i_end-i_start+1; i_local++)
  for (j=1; j<=NY; j++)
    ulocal_new[i_local][j] =
        0.25 * (ulocal[i_local+1][j] + ulocal[i_local-1][j] +
                ulocal[i_local][j+1] + ulocal[i_local][j-1] -
                h*h*flocal[i_local][j]);
```

where we have converted the `i` index to be relative to the start of `ulocal` rather than `u`. All that is left is to describe the routine `exchange_nbrs` that exchanges data between the neighboring processes. A very simple routine is shown in Figure 9.9.

We note that ISO/ANSI C (unlike Fortran) does not allow runtime dimensioning of multidimensional arrays. To keep these examples simple in C, we use compile-time dimensioning of the arrays. An alternative in C is to pass the arrays a one-dimensional arrays and compute the appropriate offsets.

The values `left` and `right` are used for the ranks of the left and right neighbors, respectively. These can be computed simply by using the following:

```
int rank, size, left, right;
...
MPI_Comm_rank( MPI_COMM_WORLD, &rank );
MPI_Comm_size( MPI_COMM_WORLD, &size );
left  = rank - 1;
right = rank + 1;
if (left < 0)     left  = MPI_PROC_NULL;
if (right >= size) right = MPI_PROC_NULL;
```

The special rank `MPI_PROC_NULL` indicates the edges of the mesh. If `MPI_PROC_-NULL` is used as the source or destination rank in an MPI communication call, the

```
void exchange_nbrs( double ulocal[][NY+2], int i_start, int i_end,
                    int left, int right )
{
    MPI_Status status;
    int c;

    /* Send and receive from the left neighbor */
    MPI_Send( &ulocal[1][1], NY, MPI_DOUBLE, left, 0,
              MPI_COMM_WORLD );
    MPI_Recv( &ulocal[0][1], NY, MPI_DOUBLE, left, 0,
              MPI_COMM_WORLD, &status );

    /* Send and receive from the right neighbor */
    c = i_end - i_start + 1;
    MPI_Send( &ulocal[c][1], NY, MPI_DOUBLE, right, 0,
              MPI_COMM_WORLD );
    MPI_Recv( &ulocal[c+1][1], NY, MPI_DOUBLE, right, 0,
              MPI_COMM_WORLD, &status );
}
```

Figure 9.9
A simple version of the neighbor exchange code. See the text for a discussion of the limitations
of this routine.

operation is ignored. MPI also provides routines to compute the neighbors in a regular mesh of arbitrary dimension and to help an application choose a decomposition that is efficient for the parallel computer.

The code in `exchange_nbrs` will work with most MPI implementations for small values of **n** but, as described in Section 10.3, is not good practice (and will fail for values of NY greater than an implementation-defined threshold). A better approach in MPI is to use the `MPI_Sendrecv` routine when exchanging data between two processes, as shown in Figure 9.10.

In Sections 10.3 and 10.7, we discuss other implementations of the exchange routine that can provide higher performance. MPI support for more scalable decompositions of the data is described in Section 10.3.2.

9.4   Collective Operations

A *collective* operation is an MPI function that is called by all processes belonging to a communicator. (If the communicator is `MPI_COMM_WORLD`, this means all

```
/* Better exchange code.   */
void exchange_nbrs( double ulocal[][NY+2], int i_start, int i_end,
                    int left, int right )
{
    MPI_Status status;
    int c;

    /* Send and receive from the left neighbor */
    MPI_Sendrecv( &ulocal[1][1], NY, MPI_DOUBLE, left, 0,
                  &ulocal[0][1], NY, MPI_DOUBLE, left, 0,
                  MPI_COMM_WORLD, &status );

    /* Send and receive from the right neighbor */
    c = i_end - i_start + 1;
    MPI_Sendrecv( &ulocal[c][1], NY, MPI_DOUBLE, right, 0,
                  &ulocal[c+1][1], NY, MPI_DOUBLE, right, 0,
                  MPI_COMM_WORLD, &status );
}
```

Figure 9.10
A better version of the neighbor exchange code.

processes, but MPI allows collective operations on other sets of processes as well.)
Collective operations involve communication and also sometimes computation, but
since they describe particular patterns of communication and computation, the
MPI implementation may be able to optimize them beyond what is possible by
expressing them in terms of MPI point-to-point operations such as MPI_Send and
MPI_Recv. The patterns are also easier to express with collective operations.

Here we introduce two of the most commonly used collective operations and show
how the communication in a parallel program can be expressed entirely in terms
of collective operations with no individual MPI_Sends or MPI_Recvs at all. The
program shown in Figure 9.11 computes the value of π by numerical integration.
Since

$$\int_0^1 \frac{1}{1+x^2} dx = \arctan(x)\big|_0^1 = \arctan(1) - \arctan(0) = \arctan(1) = \frac{\pi}{4},$$

we can compute π by integrating the function $f(x) = 4/(1+x^2)$ from 0 to 1.
We compute an approximation by dividing the interval [0,1] into some number of
subintervals and then computing the total area of these rectangles by having each
process compute the areas of some subset. We could do this with a manager/worker

algorithm, but here we preassign the work. In fact, each worker can compute its set of tasks, and so the "manager" can be a worker, too, instead of just managing the pool of work. The more rectangles there are, the more work there is to do and the more accurate the resulting approximation of π is. To experiment, let us make the number of subintervals a command-line argument. (Although the MPI standard does not guarantee that any process receives command-line arguments, in most implementations, especially for Beowulf clusters, one can assume that at least the process with rank 0 can use `argc` and `argv`, although they may not be meaningful until after `MPI_Init` is called.) In our example, process 0 sets n, the number of subintervals, to `argv[1]`. Once a process knows n, it can claim approximately $\frac{1}{n}$ of the work by claiming every nth rectangle, starting with the one numbered by its own rank. Thus process j computes the areas of rectangles j , $j + n$, $j + 2n$, and so on.

Not all MPI implementations make the command-line arguments available to *all* processes, however, so we start by having process 0 send n to each of the other processes. We could have a simple loop, sending n to each of the other processes one at a time, but this is inefficient. If we know that the same message is to be delivered to all the other processes, we can ask the MPI implementation to do this in a more efficient way than with a series of `MPI_Send`s and `MPI_Recv`s.

Broadcast (`MPI_Bcast`) is an example of an MPI *collective* operation. A collective operation must be called by all processes in a communicator. This allows an implementation to arrange the communication and computation specified by a collective operation in a special way. In the case of `MPI_Bcast`, an implementation is likely to use a tree of communication, sometimes called a spanning tree, in which process 0 sends its message to a second process, then both processes send to two more, and so forth. In this way most communication takes place in parallel, and all the messages have been delivered in $\log_2 n$ steps.

The precise semantics of `MPI_Bcast` is sometimes confusing. The first three arguments specify a message with (address, count, datatype) as usual. The fourth argument (called the *root* of the broadcast) specifies which of the processes owns the data that is being sent to the other processes. In our case it is process 0. `MPI_Bcast` acts like an `MPI_Send` on the root process and like an `MPI_Recv` on all the other processes, but the call itself looks the same on each process. The last argument is the communicator that the collective call is *over*. All processes in the communicator must make this same call. Before the call, n is valid only at the root; after `MPI_Bcast` has returned, all processes have a copy of the value of n.

Next, each process, including process 0, adds up the areas of its rectangles into the local variable `mypi`. Instead of sending these values to one process and having

```
#include "mpi.h"
#include <stdio.h>
#include <math.h>
double f(double a) { return (4.0 / (1.0 + a*a)); }

int main(int argc,char *argv[])
{
  int   n, myid, numprocs, i;
  double PI25DT = 3.141592653589793238462643;
  double mypi, pi, h, sum, x;
  double startwtime = 0.0, endwtime;

  MPI_Init(&argc,&argv);
  MPI_Comm_size(MPI_COMM_WORLD,&numprocs);
  MPI_Comm_rank(MPI_COMM_WORLD,&myid);
  if (myid == 0) {
      startwtime = MPI_Wtime();
      n = atoi(argv[1]);
  }
  MPI_Bcast(&n, 1, MPI_INT, 0, MPI_COMM_WORLD);
  h   = 1.0 / (double) n;
  sum = 0.0;
  for (i = myid + 1; i <= n; i += numprocs) {
      x = h * ((double)i - 0.5);
      sum += f(x);
  }
  mypi = h * sum;
  MPI_Reduce(&mypi, &pi, 1, MPI_DOUBLE, MPI_SUM, 0, MPI_COMM_WORLD);
  if (myid == 0) {
      endwtime = MPI_Wtime();
      printf("pi is approximately %.16f, Error is %.16f\n",
             pi, fabs(pi - PI25DT));
      printf("wall clock time = %f\n", endwtime-startwtime);
  }
  MPI_Finalize();
  return 0;
}
```

Figure 9.11
Computing π using collective operations.

that process add them up, however, we use another collective operation, `MPI_-Reduce`. `MPI_Reduce` performs not only collective communication but also collective computation. In the call

```
MPI_Reduce( &mypi, &pi, 1, MPI_DOUBLE, MPI_SUM, 0,
            MPI_COMM_WORLD);
```

the sixth argument is again the root. All processes call `MPI_Reduce`, and the root process gets back a result in the second argument. The result comes from performing an arithmetic operation, in this case summation (specified by the fifth argument), on the data items on all processes specified by the first, third, and fourth arguments.

Process 0 concludes by printing out the answer, the difference between this approximation and a previously computed accurate value of π, and the time it took to compute it. This illustrates the use of `MPI_Wtime`.

`MPI_Wtime` returns a double-precision floating-point number of seconds. This value has no meaning in itself, but the *difference* between two such values is the wall-clock time between the two calls. Note that calls on two different processes are not guaranteed to have any relationship to one another, unless the MPI implementation promises that the clocks on different processes are synchronized (see `MPI_WTIME_-IS_GLOBAL` in any of the MPI books).

The routine `MPI_Allreduce` computes the same result as `MPI_Reduce` but returns the result to all processes, not just the root process. For example, in the Jacobi iteration, it is common to use the two-norm of the difference between two successive iterations as a measure of the convergence of the solution.

```
    ...
norm2local = 0.0;
for (ii=1; ii<i_end-i_start+1; ii++)
    for (jj=1; jj<NY; jj++)
        norm2local += ulocal[ii][jj] * ulocal[ii][jj];
MPI_Allreduce( &norm2local, &norm2, 1, MPI_DOUBLE,
               MPI_COMM_WORLD, MPI_SUM );
norm2 = sqrt( norm2 );
```

Note that `MPI_Allreduce` is not a routine for computing the norm of a vector. It merely combines values contributed from each process in the communicator.

9.5   Parallel Monte Carlo Computation

One of the types of computation that is easiest to parallelize is the *Monte Carlo* family of algorithms. In such computations, a random number generator is used to create a number of independent trials. Statistics done with the outcomes of the trials provide a solution to the problem.

We illustrate this technique with another computation of the value of π. If we select points at random in the unit square $[0, 1] \times [0, 1]$ and compute the percentage of them that lies inside the quarter circle of radius 1, then we will be approximating $\frac{\pi}{4}$. (See [13] for a more detailed discussion together with an approach that does not use a parallel random number generator.) We use the SPRNG parallel random number generator (sprng.cs.fsu.edu). The code is shown in Figure 9.12.

The defaults in SPRNG make it extremely easy to use. Calls to the sprng function return a random number between 0.0 and 1.0, and the stream of random numbers on the different processes is independent. We control the *grain size* of the parallelism by the constant BATCHSIZE, which determines how much computation is done before the processes communicate. Here a million points are generated, tested, and counted before we collect the results to print them. We use MPI_-Bcast to distribute the command-line argument specifying the number of batches, and we use MPI_Reduce to collect at the end of each batch the number of points that fell inside the quarter circle, so that we can print the increasingly accurate approximations to π.

9.6   Installing MPICH under Linux

The MPICH implementation of MPI [12] is one of the most popular versions of MPI. In this section we describe how to obtain, build, and install MPICH on a Beowulf cluster. We then describe how to set up an MPICH environment in which MPI programs can be compiled, executed, and debugged.

9.6.1   Obtaining and Installing MPICH

The current version of MPICH is available at www.mcs.anl.gov/mpi/mpich.[3] From there one can download a gzipped tar file containing the complete MPICH distribution, which contains

- all source code for MPICH,

---

[3]As this chapter is being written, the current version is version 1.2.2.

```
#include "mpi.h"
#include <stdio.h>
#define SIMPLE_SPRNG           /* simple interface  */
#define USE_MPI                /* use MPI           */
#include "sprng.h"             /* SPRNG header file */
#define BATCHSIZE 1000000

int main( int argc, char *argv[] )
{
    int i, j, numin = 0, totalin, total, numbatches, rank, numprocs;
    double x, y, approx, pi = 3.141592653589793238462643;

    MPI_Init( &argc, &argv );
    MPI_Comm_size( MPI_COMM_WORLD, &numprocs );
    MPI_Comm_rank( MPI_COMM_WORLD, &rank );
    if ( rank == 0 ) {
        numbatches = atoi( argv[1] );
    }
    MPI_Bcast( &numbatches, 1, MPI_INT, 0, MPI_COMM_WORLD );
    for ( i = 0; i < numbatches; i++ ) {
        for ( j = 0; j < BATCHSIZE; j++ ) {
            x = sprng( ); y = sprng( );
            if ( x * x + y * y  < 1.0 )
                numin++;
        }
        MPI_Reduce( &numin, &totalin, 1, MPI_INT, MPI_SUM, 0,
                    MPI_COMM_WORLD );
        if ( rank == 0 ) {
            total = BATCHSIZE * ( i + 1 ) * numprocs;
            approx = 4.0 * ( (double) totalin / total );
            printf( "pi = %.16f; error = %.16f, points = %d\n",
                    approx, pi - approx, total );
        }
    }
    MPI_Finalize( );
}
```

Figure 9.12
Computing π using the Monte Carlo method.

- configure scripts for building MPICH on a wide variety of environments, including Linux clusters,
- simple example programs like the ones in this chapter,
- MPI compliance test programs,
- performance benchmarking programs,
- several MPI profiling libraries,
- the MPE library of MPI extensions for event logging and X graphics,
- some more elaborate examples, using the MPE library for graphic output,
- the Jumpshot performance visualization system, and
- the MPD parallel process management system.

MPICH is architected so that a number of communication infrastructures can be used. These are called "devices." The devices most relevant for the Beowulf environment are the `ch_p4` and `ch_p4mpd` devices. The `ch_p4` device has a few more features, including the ability to exploit shared-memory communication and to have different processes execute different binaries. The `ch_p4mpd` device, on the other hand, provides much faster startup via the MPD process manager (see Section 9.6.3) and supports debugging via `gdb` (see Section 9.6.5). To run your first MPI program, carry out the following steps:

1. Download `mpich.tar.gz` from `www.mcs.anl.gov/mpi/mpich` or from `ftp://ftp.mcs.anl.gov/pub/mpi/mpich.tar.gz`

2. `tar xvfz mpich.tar.gz; cd mpich`

3. `configure <configure options> > configure.log`. Most users will want to specify a `prefix` for the installation path when configuring:

    `configure --prefix=/usr/local/mpich-1.2.2 >& configure.log`

By default, this creates the `ch_p4` device.

4. `make >& make.log`

5. `make install >& install.log`

6. Add the '`<prefix>/bin`' directory to your path; for example, for `tcsh`, do

    ```
    setenv PATH <prefix>/bin:$PATH
    rehash
    ```

7. `cd examples/basic`

8. `make cpi`

9. If you configured using the **ch_p4mpd** device, start the **mpds** (see Section 9.6.3).

10. `mpirun -np 4 cpi`

9.6.2   Running MPICH Jobs with the ch_p4 Device

By default, on Beowulf systems MPICH is built to use the **ch_p4** device for process startup and communication. This device can be used in multiple ways. The **mpirun** command starts process 0 on the local machine (the one where **mpirun** is executed). The first process reads a file (called the *procgroup* file) and uses **rsh** (or **ssh**) to start the other processes. The procgroup file contains lines specifying the processes that are to be started on remote machines. For example,

```
mpirun -p4pg cpi.pg cpi 1000
```

executed on the machine **donner**, where 'cpi.pg' contains

```
local  0
mentat 1 /home/lusk/progs/cpi
flute  1 /home/lusk/progs/cpi rusty
```

will run **cpi** with an `MPI_COMM_WORLD` containing three processes. The first runs on **donner**, the second runs on **mentat**, and the third on **flute**. Note that this mechanism allows different executables to be run on different machines, and indeed the **ch_p4** device in MPICH is "heterogeneous"; that is, the machines do not even have to be of the same hardware architecture. The "**rusty**" in the third line of the file specifies an alternate user id on that machine.

If all the executables and user ids are the same, one can use a shorthand form:

```
mpirun -np 3 cpi 1000
```

This will use a machine's file specified at installation time to select the hosts to run on.

Finally, process startup time can be improved by using the p4 *secure server*. This program is assumed to be running on each target machine ahead of time. See the MPICH documentation for how to use the p4 secure server.

The **ch_p4** device supports communication through shared memory when that is possible. To allow for this case, MPICH must be configured with the options

```
--with-device=ch_p4 comm=shared
```

Then processes specified to share memory will use it for MPI communication, which is more efficient that using TCP. The number of processes that should share memory is specified in the 'machines' file For more detailed control of which processes should use shared memory, you should use the "procgroup" method of starting processes. Thus

```
mpirun -p4pg cpi.pg cpi 1000
```

where the file cpi.pg contains

```
local 1
castenet 2 /home/lusk/mpich/examples/basic/cpi
```

starts four processes, two of them sharing memory on the local machine and two sharing memory on the machine castenet.

9.6.3 Starting and Managing MPD

Running MPI programs with the ch_p4mpd device assumes that the mpd daemon is running on each machine in your cluster. In this section we describe how to start and manage these daemons. The mpd and related executables are built when you build and install MPICH after configuring with

```
--with-device=ch_p4mpd -prefix=<prefix directory> <other options>
```

and are found in <prefix-directory>/bin, which you should ensure is in your path. A set of MPD daemons can be started with the command

```
mpichboot <file> <num>
```

where file is the name of a file containing the host names of your cluster and num is the number of daemons you want to start. The startup script uses rsh to start the daemons, but if it is more convenient, they can be started in other ways. The first one can be started with mpd -t. The first daemon, started in this way, will print out the port it is listening on for new mpds to connect to it. Each subsequent mpd is given a host and port to connect to. The mpichboot script automates this process. At any time you can see what mpds are running by using mpdtrace.

An mpd is identified by its host and a port. A number of commands are used to manage the ring of mpds:

mpdhelp prints this information

`mpdcleanup` deletes Unix socket files '`/tmp/mpd.*`' if necessary.

`mpdtrace` causes each `mpd` in the ring to respond with a message identifying itself and its neighbors.

`mpdshutdown mpd_id` shuts down the specified `mpd`; `mpd_id` is specified as `host_-portnum`.

`mpdallexit` causes all `mpds` to exit gracefully.

`mpdlistjobs` lists active jobs managed by `mpds` in ring.

`mpdkilljob job_id` aborts the specified job.

Several options control the behavior of the daemons, allowing them to be run either by individual users or by `root` without conflicts. The current set of command-line options comprises the following:

`-h <host to connect to>`

`-p <port to connect to>`

`-c` allow console (the default)

`-n` don't allow console

`-d <debug (0 or 1)>`

`-w <working directory>`

`-l <listener port>`

`-b` background; daemonize

`-e` don't let this `mpd` start processes, unless root

`-t` echo listener port at startup

The `-n` option allows multiple `mpds` to be run on a single host by disabling the console on the second and subsequent daemons.

9.6.4 Running MPICH Jobs under MPD

Because the MPD daemons are already in communication with one another before the job starts, job startup is much faster than with the `ch_p4` device. The `mpirun` command for the `ch_p4mpd` device has a number of special command-line arguments. If you type `mpirun` with no arguments, they are displayed:

```
% mpirun
Usage: mpirun <args> executable <args_to_executable>
Arguments are:
    -np num_processes_to_run  (required as first two args)
    [-s]  (close stdin; can run in bkgd w/o tty input problems)
    [-g group_size]  (start group_size processes per mpd)
    [-m machine_file]  (filename for allowed machines)
    [-l]  (line labels; unique id for each process' output
    [-1]  (do NOT start first process locally)
    [-y]  (run as Myrinet job)
```

The `-1` option allows you, for example, to run `mpirun` on a "login" or "development" node on your cluster but to start all the application processes on "computation" nodes.

The program `mpirun` runs in a separate (non-MPI) process that starts the MPI processes running the specified executable. It serves as a single-process representative of the parallel MPI processes in that signals sent to it, such as ^Z and ^C are conveyed by the MPD system to all the processes. The output streams `stdout` and `stderr` from the MPI processes are routed back to the `stdout` and `stderr` of `mpirun`. As in most MPI implementations, `mpirun`'s `stdin` is routed to the `stdin` of the MPI process with rank 0.

9.6.5 Debugging MPI Programs

Debugging parallel programs is notoriously difficult. Parallel programs are subject not only to the usual kinds of bugs but also to new kinds having to do with timing and synchronization errors. Often, the program "hangs," for example when a process is waiting for a message to arrive that is never sent or is sent with the wrong tag. Parallel bugs often disappear precisely when you adds code to try to identify the bug, which is particularly frustrating. In this section we discuss three approaches to parallel debugging.

The `printf` Approach.   Just as in sequential debugging, you often wish to trace interesting events in the program by printing trace messages. Usually you wish to identify a message by the rank of the process emitting it. This can be done explicitly by putting the rank in the trace message. As noted above, using the "line labels" option (-1) with mpirun in the ch_p4mpd device in MPICH adds the rank automatically.

Using a Commercial Debugger. The TotalView© debugger from Etnus, Ltd. [36] runs on a variety of platforms and interacts with many vendor implementations of MPI, including MPICH on Linux clusters. For the ch_p4 device you invoke TotalView with

```
mpirun -tv <other arguments>
```

and with the ch_p4mpd device you use

```
totalview mpirun <other arguments>
```

That is, again mpirun represents the parallel job as a whole. TotalView has special commands to display the message queues of an MPI process. It is possible to attach TotalView to a collection of processes that are already running in parallel; it is also possible to attach to just one of those processes.

Using mpigdb. The ch_p4mpd device version of MPICH features a "parallel debugger" that consists simply of multiple copies of the gdb debugger, together with a mechanism for redirecting stdin. The mpigdb command is a version of mpirun that runs each user process under the control of gdb and also takes control of stdin for gdb. The 'z' command allows you to direct terminal input to any specified process or to broadcast it to all processes. We demonstrate this by running the π example under this simple debugger.

```
donner% mpigdb -np 5 cpi              # default is stdin bcast
(mpigdb) b 29                         # set breakpoint for all
0-4: Breakpoint 1 at 0x8049e93: file cpi.c, line 29.
(mpigdb) r                            # run all
0-4: Starting program: /home/lusk/mpich/examples/basic/cpi
0: Breakpoint 1, main (argc=1, argv=0xbffffa84) at cpi.c:29
1-4: Breakpoint 1, main (argc=1, argv=0xbffffa74) at cpi.c:29
0-4: 29     n = 0;                    # all reach breakpoint
(mpigdb) n                            # single step all
0: 38             if (n==0) n=100; else n=0;
1-4: 42           MPI_Bcast(&n, 1, MPI_INT, 0, MPI_COMM_WORLD);
(mpigdb) z 0                          # limit stdin to rank 0
```

```
(mpigdb) n                                    # single step process 0
0: 40                      startwtime = MPI_Wtime();
(mpigdb) n                                    # until  caught up
0: 42                MPI_Bcast(&n, 1, MPI_INT, 0, MPI_COMM_WORLD);
(mpigdb) z                                    # go back to bcast stdin
(mpigdb) n                                    # single step all
          ...                                 # until interesting spot
(mpigdb) n
0-4: 52                      x = h * ((double)i - 0.5);
(mpigdb) p x                                  # bcast print command
0: $1 = 0.0050000000000000001                 # 0's value of x
1: $1 = 0.014999999999999999                  # 1's value of x
2: $1 = 0.025000000000000001                  # 2's value of x
3: $1 = 0.035000000000000003                  # 3's value of x
4: $1 = 0.044999999999999998                  # 4's value of x
(mpigdb) c                                    # continue all
0: pi is approximately 3.141600986923, Error is 0.000008333333
0-4: Program exited normally.
(mpigdb) q                                    # quit
donner%
```

If the debugging process hangs (no `mpigdb` prompt) because the current process is waiting for action by another process, `ctl-C` will bring up a menu that allows you to switch processes. The `mpigdb` is not nearly as advanced as TotalView, but it is often useful, and it is freely distributed with MPICH.

9.6.6   Other Compilers

MPI implementations are usually configured and built by using a particular set of compilers. For example, the `configure` script in the MPICH implementation determines many of the characteristics of the compiler and the associated runtime libraries. As a result, it can be difficult to use a different C or Fortran compiler with a particular MPI implementation. This can be a problem for Beowulf clusters because it is common for several different compilers to be used.

The compilation scripts (e.g., `mpicc`) accept an argument to select a different compiler. For example, if MPICH is configured with `gcc` but you want to use `pgcc` to compile and build an MPI program, you can use

```
mpicc -cc=pgcc -o hellow hellow.c
mpif77 -fc=pgf77 -o hellowf hellowf.f
```

This works as long as both compilers have similar capabilities and properties. For example, they must use the same lengths for the basic datatypes, and their runtime libraries must provide the functions that the MPI implementation requires. If the compilers are similar in nature but require slightly different libraries or compiler options, then a *configuration file* can be provided with the `-config=name` option:

```
mpicc -config=pgcc -o hellow hellow.c
```

Details on the format of the configuration files can be found in the MPICH installation manual.

The same approach can be used with Fortran as for C. If, however, the Fortran compilers are not compatible (for example, they use different values for Fortran `.true.` and `.false.`), then you must build new libraries. MPICH provides a way to build just the necessary Fortran support. See the MPICH installation manual for details.

9.7 Tools

A number of tools are available for developing, testing, and tuning MPI programs. Although they are distributed with MPICH, they can be used with other MPI implementations as well.

9.7.1 Profiling Libraries

The MPI Forum decided not to standardize any particular tool but rather to provide a general mechanism for intercepting calls to MPI functions, which is the sort of capability that tools need. The MPI standard requires that any MPI implementation provide two entry points for each MPI function: its normal `MPI_` name and a corresponding `PMPI` version. This strategy allows a user to write a custom version of `MPI_Send`, for example, that carries out whatever extra functions might be desired, calling `PMPI_Send` to perform the usual operations of `MPI_Send`. When the user's custom versions of MPI functions are placed in a library and the library precedes the usual MPI library in the link path, the user's custom code will be invoked around all MPI functions that have been replaced.

MPICH provides three such "profiling libraries" and some tools for creating more. These libraries are easily used by passing an extra argument to MPICH's `mpicc` command for compiling and linking.

`-mpilog` causes a file to be written containing timestamped events. The log file can be examined with tools such as Jumpshot (see below).

`-mpitrace` causes a trace of MPI calls, tagged with process rank in `MPI_COMM_-WORLD` to be written to `stdout`.

`-mpianim` shows a simple animation of message traffic while the program is running.

The profiling libraries are part of the MPE subsystem of MPICH, which is separately distributable and works with any MPI implementation.

9.7.2 Visualizing Parallel Program Behavior

The detailed behavior of a parallel program is surprisingly difficult to predict. It is often useful to examine a graphical display that shows the exact sequence of states that each process went through and what messages were exchanged at what times and in what order. The data for such a tool can be collected by means of a profiling library. One tool for looking at such log files is Jumpshot [39]. A screenshot of Jumpshot in action is shown in Figure 9.13.

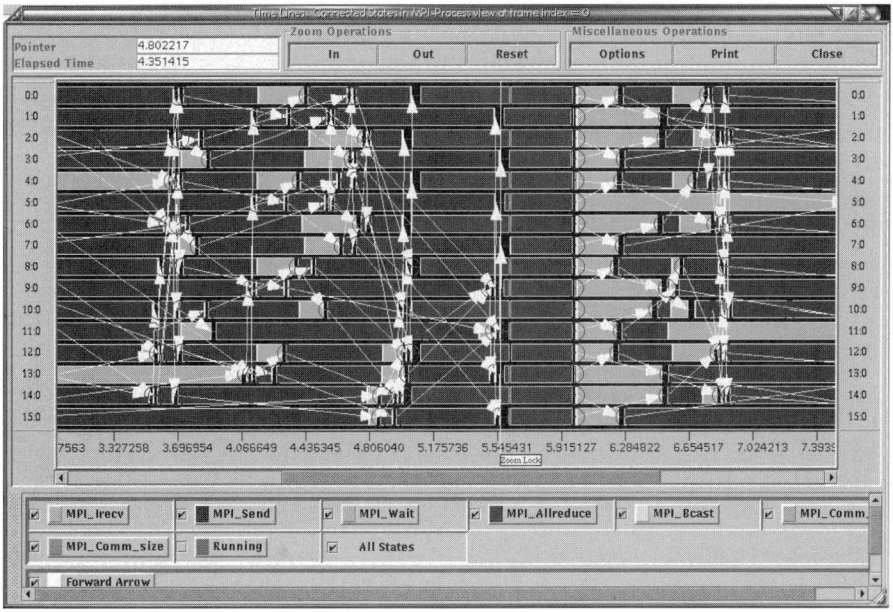

Figure 9.13
Jumpshot displaying message traffic

The horizontal axis represents time, and there is a horizontal line for each process. The states that processes are in during a particular time interval are represented by colored rectangles. Messages are represented by arrows. It is possible to zoom in for microsecond-level resolution in time.

9.8   MPI Implementations for Clusters

Many implementations of MPI are available for clusters; Table 9.3 lists some of the available implementations. These range from commercially supported software to supported, freely available software to distributed research project software.

Name	URL
BeoMPI	`www.scyld.com`
LAM	`www.lam-mpi.org`
MPICH	`www.mcs.anl.gov/mpi/mpich`
MPICH-GM	`www.myricom.com`
MPICH-G2	`www.niu.edu/mpi`
MPICH-Madeleine	`www.ens-lyon.fr/~mercierg/mpi.html`
MPI/GAMMA	`www.disi.unige.it/project/gamma/mpigamma/`
MPI/Pro	`www.mpi-softtech.com`
MPI-BIP	`lhpca.univ-lyon1.fr/mpibip.html`
MP-MPICH	`www.lfbs.rwth-aachen.de/users/joachim/MP-MPICH/`
MVICH	`www.nersc.gov/research/ftg/mvich/`
ScaMPI	`www.scali.com`

Table 9.3
Some MPI implementations for Linux.

9.9   MPI Routine Summary

This section provide a quick summary of the MPI routines used in this chapter for C, Fortran, and C++. Although these are only a small fraction of the routines available in MPI, they are sufficient for many applications.

C Routines.
int **MPI_Init**(int *argc, char ***argv)

int **MPI_Comm_size**(MPI_Comm comm, int *size)

int **MPI_Comm_rank**(MPI_Comm comm, int *rank)

int **MPI_Bcast**(void *buf, int count, MPI_Datatype datatype, int root,
                MPI_Comm comm)

int **MPI_Reduce**(void *sendbuf, void *recvbuf, int count, MPI_Datatype datatype,
                   MPI_Op op, int root, MPI_Comm comm)

int **MPI_Finalize**()

double **MPI_Wtime**()

int **MPI_Send**(void *buf, int count, MPI_Datatype datatype, int dest, int tag,
                 MPI_Comm comm)

int **MPI_Recv**(void *buf, int count, MPI_Datatype datatype, int source, int tag,
                 MPI_Comm comm, MPI_Status *status)

int **MPI_Probe**(int source, int tag, MPI_Comm comm, MPI_Status *status)

int **MPI_Sendrecv**(void *sendbuf, int sendcount,MPI_Datatype sendtype, int dest,
                     int sendtag, void *recvbuf, int recvcount, MPI_Datatype recvtype,
                     int source, MPI_Datatype recvtag, MPI_Comm comm,
                     MPI_Status *status)

int **MPI_Allreduce**(void *sendbuf, void *recvbuf, int count, MPI_Datatype datatype,
                      MPI_Op op, MPI_Comm comm)

Fortran routines.
MPI_INIT(ierror)
              integer ierror

MPI_COMM_SIZE(comm, size, ierror)
              integer comm, size, ierror

MPI_COMM_RANK(comm, rank, ierror)
              integer comm, rank, ierror

MPI_BCAST(buffer, count, datatype, root, comm, ierror)
              <type> buffer(*)
              integer count, datatype, root, comm, ierror

MPI_REDUCE(sendbuf, recvbuf, count, datatype, op, root, comm, ierror)
              <type> sendbuf(*), recvbuf(*)
              integer count, datatype, op, root, comm, ierror

MPI_FINALIZE(ierror)
              integer ierror

double precision **MPI_WTIME**()

MPI_SEND(buf, count, datatype, dest, tag, comm, ierror)
        <type> buf(*)
        integer count, datatype, dest, tag, comm, ierror

MPI_RECV(buf, count, datatype, source, tag, comm, status, ierror)
        <type> buf(*)
        integer count, datatype, source, tag, comm,
            status(MPI_STATUS_SIZE), ierror

MPI_PROBE(source, tag, comm, status, ierror)
        logical flag
        integer source, tag, comm, status(MPI_STATUS_SIZE), ierror

MPI_SENDRECV(sendbuf, sendcount, sendtype, dest, sendtag, recvbuf,recvcount,
        recvtype, source, recvtag, comm, status, ierror)
        <type> sendbuf(*), recvbuf(*)
        integer sendcount, sendtype, dest, sendtag, recvcount, recvtype,
            source, recvtag, comm, status(MPI_STATUS_SIZE), ierror

MPI_ALLREDUCE(sendbuf, recvbuf, count, datatype, op, comm, ierror)
        <type> sendbuf(*), recvbuf(*)
        integer count, datatype, op, comm, ierror

C++ routines.
void MPI::Init(int& argc, char**& argv)

void MPI::Init()

int MPI::Comm::Get_rank() const

int MPI::Comm::Get_size() const

void MPI::Intracomm::Bcast(void* buffer, int count, const Datatype& datatype,
            int root) const

void MPI::Intracomm::Reduce(const void* sendbuf, void* recvbuf, int count,
            const Datatype& datatype, const Op& op, int root) const

void MPI::Finalize()

double MPI::Wtime()

int MPI::Status::Get_source() const

int MPI::Status::Get_tag() const

void MPI::Comm::Recv(void* buf, int count, const Datatype& datatype,
                int source, int tag, Status& status) const

void MPI::Comm::Recv(void* buf, int count, const Datatype& datatype,
                int source, int tag) const

void MPI::Comm::Send(const void* buf, int count, const Datatype& datatype,
                int dest, int tag) const

void MPI::Comm::Probe(int source,int tag, Status& status) const

void MPI::Comm::Sendrecv(const void *sendbuf, int sendcount,
                const Datatype& sendtype, int dest, int sendtag, void *recvbuf,
                int recvcount, const Datatype& recvtype, int source, int recvtag,
                Status& status) const

void MPI::Intracomm::Allreduce(const void* sendbuf, void* recvbuf, int count,
                const Datatype& datatype, const Op& op) const

10 Advanced Topics in MPI Programming

William Gropp and Ewing Lusk

In this chapter we continue our exploration of parallel programming with MPI. We describe capabilities that are more specific to MPI rather than part of the message-passing programming model in general. We cover the more advanced features of MPI sometimes called MPI-2, such as dynamic process management, parallel I/O, and remote memory access.

10.1 Dynamic Process Management in MPI

A new aspect of the MPI-2 standard is the ability of an MPI program to create new MPI processes and communicate with them. (In the original MPI specification, the number of processes was fixed at startup.) MPI calls this capability (together with related capabilities such as connecting two independently started MPI jobs) *dynamic process management*. Three main issues are introduced by this collection of features:

- maintaining simplicity and flexibility;
- interacting with the operating system, a parallel process manager, and perhaps a job scheduler; and
- avoiding race conditions that could compromise correctness.

The key to avoiding race conditions is to make creation of new processes a collective operation, over both the processes creating the new processes and the new processes being created.

10.1.1 Intercommunicators

Recall that an MPI communicator consists of a group of processes together with a communication context. Strictly speaking, the communicators we have dealt with so far are *intracommunicators*. There is another kind of communicator, called an *intercommunicator*. An intercommunicator binds together a communication context and *two* groups of processes, called (from the point of view of a particular process) the *local* group and the *remote* group. Processes are identified by rank in group, but ranks in an intercommunicator always refer to the processes in the remote group. That is, an MPI_Send using an intercommunicator sends a message to the process with the destination rank in the *remote* group of the intercommunicator. Collective operations are also defined for intercommunicators; see [14, Chapter 7] for details.

10.1.2   Spawning New MPI Processes

We are now in a position to explain exactly how new MPI processes are created by an already running MPI program. The MPI function that does this is `MPI_Comm_-spawn`. Its key features are the following.

- It is collective over the communicator of processes initiating the operation (called the *parents*) and also collective with the calls to `MPI_Init` in the processes being created (called the *children*). That is, the `MPI_Comm_spawn` does not return in the parents until it has been called in all the parents and `MPI_Init` has been called in all the children.
- It returns an intercommunicator in which the local group contains the parents and the remote group contains the children.
- The new processes, which must call `MPI_Init`, have their own `MPI_COMM_WORLD`, consisting of all the processes created by this one collective call to `MPI_Comm_spawn`.
- The function `MPI_Comm_get_parent`, called by the children, returns an intercommunicator with the children in the local group and the parents in the remote group.
- The collective function `MPI_Intercomm_merge` may be called by parents and children to create a normal (intra)communicator containing all the processes, both old and new, but for many communication patterns this is not necessary.

10.1.3   Revisiting Matrix-Vector Multiplication

Here we illustrate the use of `MPI_Comm_spawn` by redoing the matrix-vector multiply program of Section 9.2. Instead of starting with a fixed number of processes, we compile separate executables for the manager and worker programs, start the manager with

```
mpiexec -n 1 manager <number-of-workers>
```

and then let the manager create the worker processes dynamically. The program for the manager is shown in Figure 10.1, and the code for the workers is shown in Figure 10.2. Here we assume that only the manager has the matrix **a** and the vector **b** and broadcasts them to the workers after the workers have been created.

Let us consider in detail the call in the manager that creates the worker processes.

```
MPI_Spawn( "worker", MPI_ARGV_NULL, numworkers, MPI_INFO_NULL,
           0, MPI_COMM_SELF, &workercomm, MPI_ERRCODES_IGNORE );
```

It has eight arguments. The first is the name of the executable to be run by the new processes. The second is the null-terminated argument vector to be passed to

```
#include "mpi.h"
#include <stdio.h>
#define SIZE 10000

int main( int argc, char *argv[] )
{
    double a[SIZE][SIZE], b[SIZE], c[SIZE];
    int i, j, row, numworkers;
    MPI_Status status;
    MPI_Comm workercomm;

    MPI_Init( &argc, &argv );
    if ( argc != 2 || !isnumeric( argv[1] ))
        printf( "usage: %s <number of workers>\n", argv[0] );
    else
        numworkers = atoi( argv[1] );

    MPI_Spawn( "worker", MPI_ARGV_NULL, numworkers, MPI_INFO_NULL,
               0, MPI_COMM_SELF, &workercomm, MPI_ERRCODES_IGNORE );
    ...
    /* initialize a and b */
    ...
    /* send b to each worker */
    MPI_Bcast( b, SIZE, MPI_DOUBLE, MPI_ROOT, workercomm );
    ...
    /* then normal manager code as before*/
    ...
    MPI_Finalize();
    return 0;
}
```

Figure 10.1
Dynamic process matrix-vector multiply program, manager part.

all of the new processes; here we are passing no arguments at all, so we specify
the special value `MPI_ARGV_NULL`. Next is the number of new processes to create.
The fourth argument is an MPI "Info" object, which can be used to specify special
environment- and/or implementation-dependent parameters, such as the names of
the nodes to start the new processes on. In our case we leave this decision to
the MPI implementation or local process manager, and we pass the special value

MPI_INFO_NULL. The next argument is the "root" process for this call to MPI_-Comm_spawn; it specifies which process in the communicator given in the following argument is supplying the valid arguments for this call. The communicator we are using consists here of just the one manager process, so we pass MPI_COMM_SELF. Next is the address of the new intercommunicator to be filled in, and finally an array of error codes for examining possible problems in starting the new processes. Here we use MPI_ERRCODES_IGNORE to indicate that we will not be looking at these error codes.

Code for the worker processes that are spawned is shown in Figure 10.2. It is essentially the same as the worker subroutine in the preceding chapter but is an MPI program in itself. Note the use of intercommunicator broadcast in order to receive the vector b from the parents. We free the parent intercommunicator with MPI_Comm_free before exiting.

10.1.4   More on Dynamic Process Management

For more complex examples of the use of MPI_Comm_spawn, including how to start processes with different executables or different argument lists, see [14, Chapter 7]. MPI_Comm_spawn is only the most basic of the functions provided in MPI for dealing with a dynamic MPI environment. By querying the attribute MPI_UNIVERSE_SIZE, you can find out how many processes can be usefully created. Separately started MPI computations can find each other and connect with MPI_Comm_connect and MPI_Comm_accept. Processes can exploit non-MPI connections to "bootstrap" MPI communication. These features are explained in detail in [14].

10.2   Fault Tolerance

Communicators are a fundamental concept in MPI. Their sizes are fixed at the time they are created, and the efficiency and correctness of collective operations rely on this fact. Users sometimes conclude from the fixed size of communicators that MPI provides no mechanism for writing fault-tolerant programs. Now that we have introduced intercommunicators, however, we are in a position to discuss how this topic might be addressed and how you might write a manager-worker program with MPI in such a way that it would be fault tolerant. In this context we mean that if one of the worker processes terminates abnormally, instead of terminating the job you will be able to carry on the computation with fewer workers, or perhaps dynamically replace the lost worker.

The key idea is to create a separate (inter)communicator for each worker and

```
#include "mpi.h"

int main( int argc, char *argv[] )
{
    int numprocs, myrank;
    double b[SIZE], c[SIZE];
    int i, row, myrank;
    double dotp;
    MPI_Status status;
    MPI_Comm parentcomm;

    MPI_Init( &argc, &argv );
    MPI_Comm_size( MPI_COMM_WORLD, &numprocs );
    MPI_Comm_rank( MPI_COMM_WORLD, &myrank );

    MPI_Comm_get_Parentp &parentcomm );

    MPI_Bcast( b, SIZE, MPI_DOUBLE, 0, parentcomm );

    ...
    /* same as worker code from original matrix-vector multiply */
    ...

    MPI_Comm_free(parentcomm );
    MPI_Finalize( );
    return 0;
}
```

Figure 10.2
Dynamic process matrix-vector multiply program, worker part.

use it for communications with that worker rather than use a communicator that contains all of the workers. If an implementation returns "invalid communicator" from an MPI_Send or MPI_Recv call, then the manager has lost contact only with one worker and can still communicate with the other workers through the other, still-intact communicators. Since the manager will be using separate communicators rather than separate ranks in a larger communicator to send and receive message from the workers, it might be convenient to maintain an array of communicators and a parallel array to remember which row has been last sent to a worker, so that if that worker disappears, the same row can be assigned to a different worker.

Figure 10.3 shows these arrays and how they might be used. What we are doing

```
/* highly incomplete */

MPI_Comm worker_comms[MAX_WORKERS];
int last_row_sent[MAX_WORKERS];

rc = MPI_Send( a[numsent], SIZE, MPI_DOUBLE, 0, numsent+1,
               worker_comms[sender] );
if ( rc != MPI_SUCCESS ) {
    /* Check that error class is one we can recover from */
    ...
    MPI_Comm_spawn( "worker" , ... );
```

Figure 10.3
Fault-tolerant manager.

with this approach is recognizing that two-party communication can be made fault tolerant, since one party can recognize the failure of the other and take appropriate action. A normal MPI communicator is not a two-party system and cannot be made fault tolerant without changing the semantics of MPI communication. If, however, the communication in an MPI program can be expressed in terms of intercommunicators, which are inherently two-party (the local group and the remote group), then fault tolerance can be achieved.

Note that while the MPI standard, through the use of intercommunicators, makes it possible to write an implementation of MPI that encourages fault-tolerant programming, the MPI standard itself does not require MPI implementations to continue past an error. This is a "quality of implementation" issue and allows the MPI implementor to trade performance for the ability to continue after a fault. As this section makes clear, however, there is nothing in the MPI standard that stands in the way of fault tolerance, and the two primary MPI implementations for Beowulf clusters, MPICH and LAM/MPI, both endeavor to support some style of fault tolerance for applications.

10.3 Revisiting Mesh Exchanges

The discussion of the mesh exchanges for the Jacobi problem in Section 9.3 concentrated on the algorithm and data structures, particularly the ghost-cell exchange. In this section, we return to that example and cover two other important issues: the use of blocking and nonblocking communications and communicating noncontiguous data.

10.3.1 Blocking and Nonblocking Communication

Consider the following simple code (note that this is similar to the simple version of `exchange_nbrs` in Section 9.3):

```
if (rank == 0) {
    MPI_Send( sbuf, n, MPI_INT, 1, 0, MPI_COMM_WORLD );
    MPI_Recv( rbuf, n, MPI_INT, 1, 0, MPI_COMM_WORLD, &status );
}
else if (rank == 1) {
    MPI_Send( sbuf, n, MPI_INT, 0, 0, MPI_COMM_WORLD );
    MPI_Recv( rbuf, n, MPI_INT, 0, 0, MPI_COMM_WORLD, &status );
}
```

What happens with this code? It looks like process 0 is sending a message to process 1 and that process 1 is sending a message to process 0. But more is going on here. Consider the steps that the MPI implementation must take to make this code work:

1. Copy the data from the `MPI_Send` into a temporary, system-managed buffer.

2. Once the `MPI_Send` completes (on each process), start the `MPI_Recv`. The data that was previously copied into a system buffer by the `MPI_Send` operation can now be delivered into the user's buffer (`rbuf` in this case).

This approach presents two problems, both related to the fact that data must be copied into a system buffer to allow the `MPI_Send` to complete. The first problem is obvious: any data motion takes time and reduces the performance of the code. The second problem is more subtle and important: the amount of available system buffer space always has a limit. For values of **n** in the above example that exceed the available buffer space, the above code will *hang*: neither `MPI_Send` will complete, and the code will wait forever for the other process to start an `MPI_Recv`. This is true for *any* message-passing system, not just MPI. The amount of buffer space available for buffering a message varies among MPI implementations, ranging from many megabytes to as little as 128 bytes.

How can we write code that sends data among several processes and that does not rely on the availability of system buffers? One approach is to carefully order the send and receive operations so that each send is guaranteed to have a matching

receive. For example, we can swap the order of the `MPI_Send` and `MPI_Recv` in the
code for process 1:

```
if (rank == 0) {
    MPI_Send( sbuf, n, MPI_INT, 1, 0, MPI_COMM_WORLD );
    MPI_Recv( rbuf, n, MPI_INT, 1, 0, MPI_COMM_WORLD, &status );
}
else if (rank == 1) {
    MPI_Recv( rbuf, n, MPI_INT, 0, 0, MPI_COMM_WORLD, &status );
    MPI_Send( sbuf, n, MPI_INT, 0, 0, MPI_COMM_WORLD );
}
```

However, this can be awkward to implement, particularly for more complex communication patterns; in addition, it does not address the extra copy that may be performed by `MPI_Send`.

The approach used by MPI, following earlier message-passing systems as well as nonblocking sockets (see [13, Chapter 9]), is to split the send and receive operations into two steps: one to initiate the operation and one to complete the operation. Other operations, including other communication operations, can be issued between the two steps. For example, an MPI receive operation can be initiated by a call to `MPI_Irecv` and completed with a call to `MPI_Wait`. Because the routines that initiate these operations do not wait for them to complete, they are called *nonblocking* operations. The "I" in the routine name stands for "immediate"; this indicates that the routine may return immediately without completing the operation. The arguments to `MPI_Irecv` are the same as for `MPI_Recv` except for the last (`status`) argument. This is replaced by an `MPI_Request` value; it is a *handle* that is used to identify an initiated operation. To complete a nonblocking operation, the request is given to `MPI_Wait`, along with a `status` argument; the `status` argument serves the same purpose as `status` for an `MPI_Recv`. Similarly, the nonblocking counterpart to `MPI_Send` is `MPI_Isend`; this has the same arguments as `MPI_Send` with the addition of an `MPI_Request` as the last argument (in C). Using these routines, our example becomes the following:

```
if (rank == 0) {
    MPI_Request req1, req2;
    MPI_Isend( sbuf, n, MPI_INT, 1, 0, MPI_COMM_WORLD, &req1 );
    MPI_Irecv( rbuf, n, MPI_INT, 1, 0, MPI_COMM_WORLD, &req2 );
    MPI_Wait( &req1, &status );
    MPI_Wait( &req2, &status );
```

```
    }
    else if (rank == 1) {
        MPI_Request req1, req2;
        MPI_Irecv( rbuf, n, MPI_INT, 0, 0, MPI_COMM_WORLD, &req1 );
        MPI_Isend( sbuf, n, MPI_INT, 0, 0, MPI_COMM_WORLD, &req2 );
        MPI_Wait( &req1, &status );
        MPI_Wait( &req2, &status );
    }
```

The buffer sbuf provided to MPI_Isend must not be modified until the operation is completed with MPI_Wait. Similarly, the buffer rbuf provided to MPI_Irecv must not be modified or read until the MPI_Irecv is completed.

The nonblocking communication routines allow the MPI implementation to wait until the message can be sent directly from one user buffer to another (e.g., from sbuf to rbuf) without requiring any copy or using any system buffer space.

Because it is common to start multiple nonblocking operations, MPI provides routines to test or wait for completion of any one, all, or some of the requests. For example, MPI_Waitall waits for all requests in an array of requests to complete. Figure 10.4 shows the use of nonblocking communication routines for the Jacobi example.[1]

MPI nonblocking operations are not the same as asynchronous operations. The MPI standard does not require that the data transfers overlap computation with communication. MPI specifies only the semantics of the operations, not the details of the implementation choices. The MPI nonblocking routines are provided primarily for correctness (avoiding the limitations of system buffers) and performance (avoidance of copies).

10.3.2 Communicating Noncontiguous Data in MPI

The one-dimensional decomposition used in the Jacobi example (Section 9.3) is simple but does not scale well and can lead to performance problems. We can analyze the performance of the Jacobi following the discussion in Section 9.2. Let the time to communicate n bytes be

$$T_{comm} = s + rn,$$

where s is the *latency* and r is the (additional) time to communicate one byte. The time to compute one step of the Jacobi method, using the one-dimensional decomposition in Section 9.3, is

---

[1] On many systems, calling MPI_Isend before MPI_Irecv will improve performance.

```
void exchange_nbrs( double ulocal[][NY+2], int i_start, int i_end,
                    int left, int right )
{
    MPI_Status  statuses[4];
    MPI_Request requests[4];
    int c;

    /* Begin send and receive from the left neighbor */
    MPI_Isend( &ulocal[1][1], NY, MPI_DOUBLE, left, 0,
               MPI_COMM_WORLD, &requests[0] );
    MPI_Irecv( &ulocal[0][1], NY, MPI_DOUBLE, left, 0,
               MPI_COMM_WORLD, &requests[1] );

    /* Begin send and receive from the right neighbor */
    c = i_end - i_start + 1;
    MPI_Isend( &ulocal[c][1], NY, MPI_DOUBLE, right, 0,
               MPI_COMM_WORLD, &requests[2] );
    MPI_Irecv( &ulocal[c+1][1], NY, MPI_DOUBLE, right, 0,
               MPI_COMM_WORLD, &requests[3] );

    /* Wait for all communications to complete */
    MPI_Waitall( 4, requests, statuses );
}
```

Figure 10.4
Nonblocking exchange code for the Jacobi example.

$$\frac{5n}{p}f + 2(s + rn),$$

where f is the time to perform a floating-point operation and p is the number of processes. Note that the cost of communication is independent of the number of processes; eventually, this cost will dominate the calculation. Hence, a better approach is to use a two-dimensional decomposition, as shown in Figure 10.5.

The time for one step of the Jacobi method with a two-dimensional decomposition is just

$$\frac{5n}{p}f + 4\left(s + r\frac{n}{\sqrt{p}}\right).$$

This is faster than the one-dimensional decomposition as long as

$$n > \frac{2}{1 - 4/\sqrt{p}}\frac{s}{r}$$

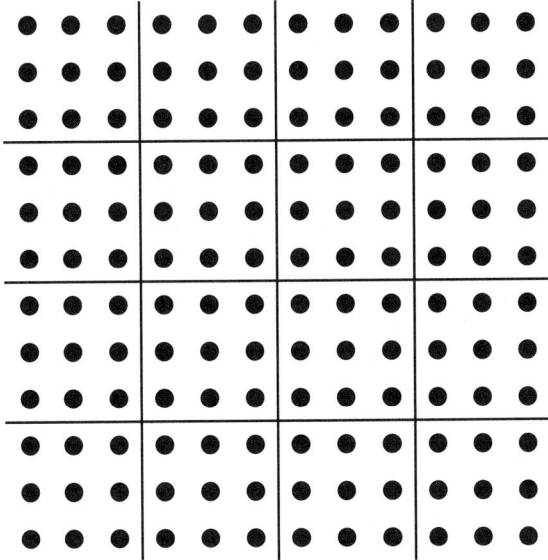

Figure 10.5
Domain and 9 × 9 computational mesh for approximating the solution to the Poisson problem
using a two-dimensional decomposition.

(assuming $p \geq 16$). To implement this decomposition, we need to communicate
data to four neighbors, as shown in Figure 10.6.

The left and right edges can be sent and received by using the same code as
for the one-dimensional case. The top and bottom edges have noncontiguous data.
For example, the top edge needs to send the tenth, sixteenth, and twenty-second
element. There are four ways to move this data:

1.   Each value can be sent separately. Because of the high latency of message
passing, this approach is inefficient and normally should not be used.

2.   The data can be copied into a temporary buffer using a simple loop, for
example,

```
for (i=0; i<3; i++) {
    tmp[i] = u_local[i][6];
}
MPI_Send( tmp, 3, MPI_DOUBLE, .. );
```

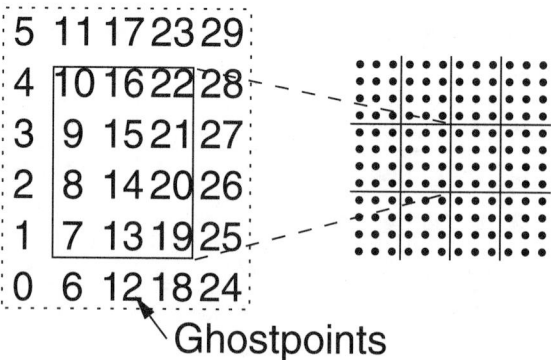

Figure 10.6
Locations of mesh points in `ulocal` for a two-dimensional decomposition.

This is a common approach and, for some systems and MPI implementations, may be the most efficient.

3. MPI provides two routines to pack and unpack a buffer. These routines are `MPI_Pack` and `MPI_Unpack`. A buffer created with these routines should be sent and received with MPI datatype `MPI_PACKED`. We note, however, that these routines are most useful for complex data layouts that change frequently within a program.

4. MPI provides a way to construct new datatypes representing any data layout. These routines can be optimized by the MPI implementation, in principle providing better performance than the user can achieve using a simple loop [37]. In addition, using these datatypes is crucial to achieving high performance with parallel I/O.

MPI provides several routines to create datatypes representing common patterns of memory. These new datatypes are called *derived* datatypes. For this case, `MPI_-Type_vector` is what is needed to create a new MPI datatype representing data values separated by a constant *stride*. In this case, the stride is `NY+2`, and the number of elements is `i_end-i_start+1`.

```
MPI_Type_vector( i_end - i_start + 1, 1, NY+2,
                 MPI_DOUBLE, &vectype );
MPI_Type_commit( &vectype );
```

The second argument is a *block count* and is the number of the basic datatype items (`MPI_DOUBLE` in this case); this is useful particularly in multicomponent PDE problems. The routine `MPI_Type_commit` must be called to *commit* the MPI datatype;

this call allows the MPI implementation to optimize the datatype (the optimization is not included as part of the routines that create MPI datatypes because some complex datatypes are created recursively from other derived datatypes).

Using an MPI derived datatype representing a strided data pattern, we can write a version of `exchange_nbr` for a two-dimensional decomposition of the mesh; the code is shown in Figure 10.7. Note that we use the same derived datatype `vectype` for the sends and receives at the top and bottom by specifying the first element into which data is moved in the array `u_local` in the MPI calls.

When a derived datatype is no longer needed, it should be freed with `MPI_Type_-free`. Many other routines are available for creating datatypes; for example, `MPI_-Type_indexed` is useful for scatter-gather patterns, and `MPI_Type_create_struct` can be used for an arbitrary collection of memory locations.

10.4 Motivation for Communicators

Communicators in MPI serve two purposes. The most obvious purpose is to describe a collection of processes. This feature allows collective routines, such as `MPI_Bcast` or `MPI_Allreduce`, to be used with any collection of processes. This capability is particularly important for hierarchical algorithms, and also facilitates dividing a computation into subtasks, each of which has its own collection of processes. For example, in the manager-worker example in Section 9.2, it may be appropriate to divide each task among a small collection of processes, particularly if this causes the problem description to reside only in the fast memory cache. MPI communicators are perfect for this; the MPI routine `MPI_Comm_split` is the only routine needed when creating new communicators. Using ranks relative to a communicator for specifying the source and destination of messages also facilitates dividing parallel tasks among smaller but still parallel subtasks, each with its own communicator.

A more subtle but equally important purpose of the MPI communicator involves the *communication context* that each communicator contains. This context is essential for writing software libraries that can be safely and robustly combined with other code, both other libraries and user-specific application code, to build complete applications. Used properly, the communication context guarantees that messages are received by appropriate routines *even if other routines are not as careful*. Consider the example in Figure 10.8 (taken from [13, Section 6.1.2]). In this example, there are two routines, provided by separate libraries or software modules. One, `SendRight`, sends a message to the right neighbor and receives from the left. The other, `SendEnd`, sends a message from process 0 (the leftmost) to the last process

```
void exchange_nbrs2d( double ulocal[][NY+2],
                      int i_start, int i_end, int j_start, int j_end,
                      int left, int right, int top, int bottom,
                      MPI_Datatype vectype )
{
    MPI_Status   statuses[8];
    MPI_Request requests[8];
    int c;

    /* Begin send and receive from the left neighbor */
    MPI_Isend( &ulocal[1][1], NY, MPI_DOUBLE, left, 0,
               MPI_COMM_WORLD, &requests[0] );
    MPI_Irecv( &ulocal[0][1], NY, MPI_DOUBLE, left, 0,
               MPI_COMM_WORLD, &requests[1] );

    /* Begin send and receive from the right neighbor */
    c = i_end - i_start + 1;
    MPI_Isend( &ulocal[c][1], NY, MPI_DOUBLE, right, 0,
               MPI_COMM_WORLD, &requests[2] );
    MPI_Irecv( &ulocal[c+1][1], NY, MPI_DOUBLE, right, 0,
               MPI_COMM_WORLD, &requests[3] );

    /* Begin send and receive from the top neighbor */
    MPI_Isend( &ulocal[1][NY], 1, vectype, top, 0,
               MPI_COMM_WORLD, &requests[4] );
    MPI_Irecv( &ulocal[1][NY+1], 1, vectype, top, 0,
               MPI_COMM_WORLD, &requests[5] );

    /* Begin send and receive from the bottom neighbor */
    MPI_Isend( &ulocal[1][1], 1, vectype, bottom, 0,
               MPI_COMM_WORLD, &requests[6] );
    MPI_Irecv( &ulocal[1][0], 1, vectype, bottom, 0,
               MPI_COMM_WORLD, &requests[7] );

    /* Wait for all communications to complete */
    MPI_Waitall( 8, requests, statuses );
}
```

Figure 10.7
Nonblocking exchange code for the Jacobi problem for a two-dimensional decomposition of the mesh.

(the rightmost). Both of these routines use `MPI_ANY_SOURCE` instead of a particular source in the `MPI_Recv` call. As Figure 10.8 shows, the messages can be confused, causing the program to receive the wrong data. How can we prevent this situation? Several approaches will *not* work. One is to avoid the use of `MPI_ANY_SOURCE`. This fixes this example, but only if both `SendRight` and `SendEnd` follow this rule. The approach may be adequate (though fragile) for code written by a single person or team, but it isn't adequate for libraries. For example, if `SendEnd` was written by a commercial vendor and did not use `MPI_ANY_SOURCE`, but `SendRight`, written by a different vendor or an inexperienced programmer, did use `MPI_ANY_SOURCE`, then the program would still fail, and it would look like `SendEnd` was at fault (because the message from `SendEnd` was received first).

Another approach that does not work is to use message tags to separate messages. Again, this can work if one group writes all of the code and is very careful about allocating message tags to different software modules. However, using `MPI_ANY_-TAG` in an MPI receive call can still bypass this approach. Further, as shown in Figure 6.5 in [13], even if `MPI_ANY_SOURCE` and `MPI_ANY_TAG` are not used, it is still possible for separate code modules to receive the wrong message.

The communication context in an MPI communicator provides a solution to these problems. The routine `MPI_Comm_dup` creates a new communicator from an input communicator that contains the same processes (in the same rank order) but with a new communication context. MPI messages sent in one communication context can be received only in that context. Thus, any software module or library that wants to ensure that all of its messages will be seen only within that library needs only to call `MPI_Comm_dup` at the beginning to get a new communicator. All well-written libraries that use MPI create a private communicator used only within that library.

Enabling the development of libraries was one of the design goals of MPI. In that respect MPI has been very successful. Many libraries and applications now use MPI, and, because of MPI's portability, most of these run on Beowulf clusters. Table 10.1 provides a partial list of libraries that use MPI to provide parallelism. More complete descriptions and lists are available at `www.mcs.anl.gov/mpi/libraries` and at `sal.kachinatech.com/C/3`.

10.5   More on Collective Operations

One of the strengths of MPI is its collection of scalable collective communication and computation routines. Figure 10.9 shows the capabilities of some of the most important collective communication routines. As an example of their utility, we

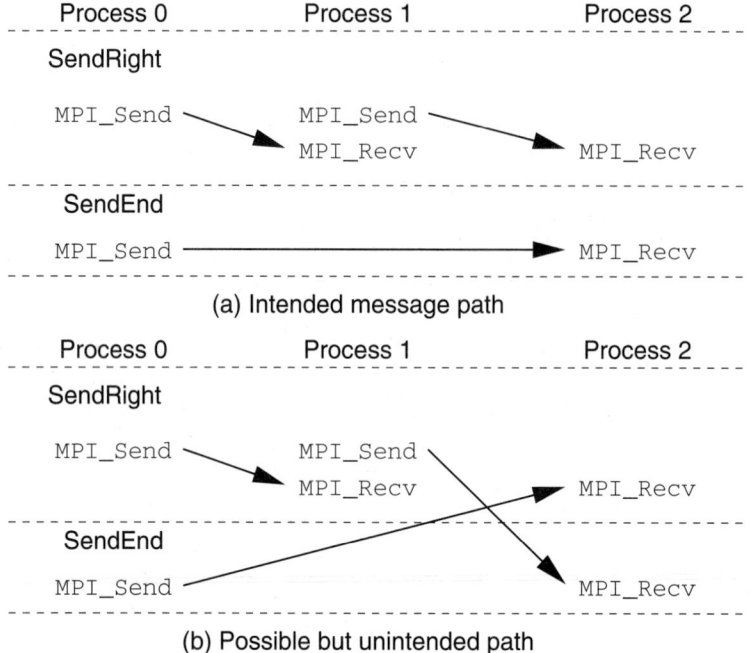

Figure 10.8
Two possible message-matching patterns when `MPI_ANY_SOURCE` is used in the `MPI_Recv` calls (from [13]).

consider a simple example.

Suppose we want to gather the names of all of the nodes that our program is running on, and we want all MPI processes to have this list of names. This is an easy task using `MPI_Allgather`:

```
char my_hostname[MAX_LEN], all_names[MAX_PROCS][MAX_LEN];
MPI_Allgather( my_hostname, MAX_LEN, MPI_CHAR,
               all_names, MAX_LEN, MPI_CHAR, MPI_COMM_WORLD );
```

This code assumes that no hostname is longer than `MAX_LEN` characters (including the trailing null). A better code would check this:

```
char my_hostname[MAX_LEN], all_names[MAX_PROCS][MAX_LEN];
MPI_Allreduce( &my_name_len, &max_name_len, 1, MPI_INT, MPI_MAX,
               MPI_COMM_WORLD );
if (max_name_len > MAX_LEN) {
```

Library	Description	URL
PETSc	Linear and nonlinear solvers for PDEs	www.mcs.anl.gov/petsc
Aztec	Parallel iterative solution of sparse linear systems	www.cs.sandia.gov/CRF/ aztec1.html
Cactus	Framework for PDE solutions	www.cactuscode.org
FFTW	Parallel FFT	www.fftw.org
PPFPrint	Parallel print	www.llnl.gov/sccd/lc/ ptcprint
HDF	Parallel I/O for Hierarchical Data Format (HDF) files	hdf.ncsa.uiuc.edu/Parallel_ HDF
NAG	Numerical library	www.nag.co.uk/numeric/fd/ FDdescription.asp
ScaLAPACK	Parallel linear algebra	www.netlib.org/scalapack
SPRNG	Scalable pseudorandom number generator	sprng.cs.fsu.edu

Table 10.1
A sampling of libraries that use MPI.

```
    printf( "Error: names too long (%d)", max_name_len );
}
MPI_Allgather( my_hostname, MAX_LEN, MPI_CHAR,
               all_names, MAX_LEN, MPI_CHAR, MPI_COMM_WORLD );
```

Both of these approaches move more data than necessary, however. An even better approach is to first gather the size of each processor's name and then gather exactly the number of characters needed from each processor. This uses the "v" (for vector) version of the allgather routine, MPI_Allgatherv, as shown in Figure 10.10.

This example provides a different way to accomplish the action of the example in Section 9.3. Many parallel codes can be written with MPI collective routines instead of MPI point-to-point communication; such codes often have a simpler logical structure and can benefit from scalable implementations of the collective communications routines.

10.6   Parallel I/O

MPI-2 provides a wide variety of parallel I/O operations, more than we have space to cover here. See [14, Chapter 3] for a more thorough discussion of I/O in MPI.

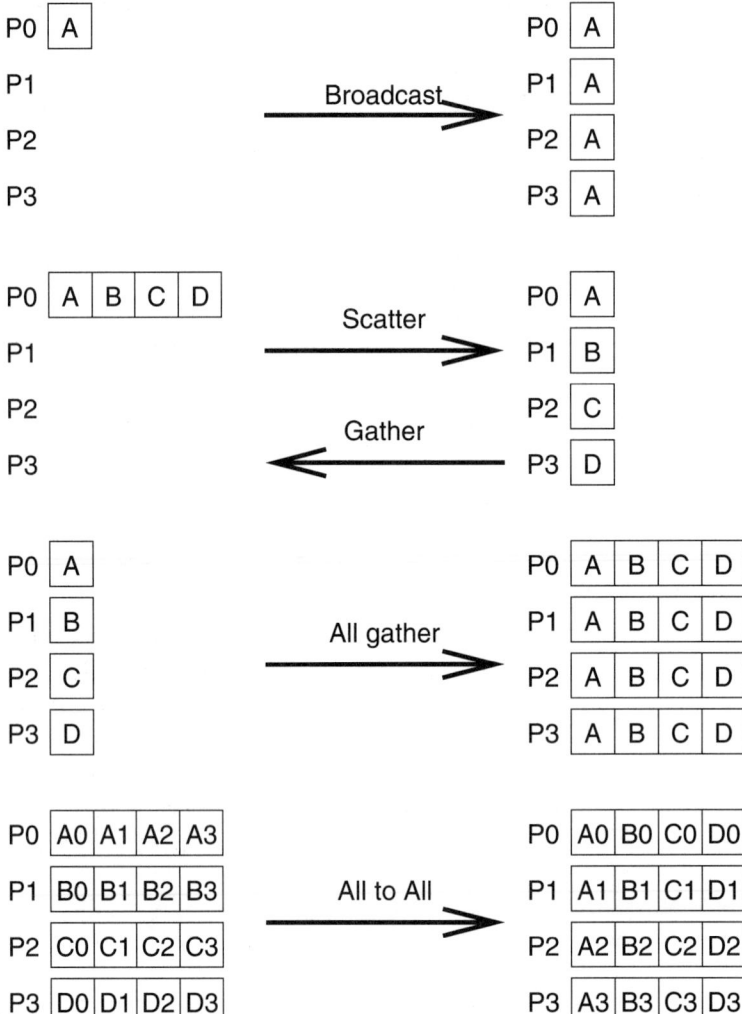

Figure 10.9
Schematic representation of collective data movement in MPI.

The fundamental idea in MPI's approach to parallel I/O is that a file is opened collectively by a set of processes that are all given access to the same file. MPI thus associates a communicator with the file, allowing a flexible set of both individual and collective operations on the file.

```
mylen = strlen(my_hostname) + 1;  /* Include the trailing null */
MPI_Allgather( &mylen, 1, MPI_INT, all_lens, 1, MPI_INT,
               MPI_COMM_WORLD );
totlen = all_lens[size-1];
for (i=0; i<size-1; i++) {
    displs[i+1] = displs[i] + all_lens[i];
    totlen      += all_lens[i];
}
all_names = (char *)malloc( totlen );
if (!all_names) MPI_Abort( MPI_COMM_WORLD, 1 );
MPI_Allgatherv( my_hostname, mylen, MPI_CHAR,
                all_names, all_lens, displs, MPI_CHAR,
                MPI_COMM_WORLD );
/* Hostname for the jth process is &all_names[displs[j]] */
```

Figure 10.10
Using MPI_Allgather and MPI_Allgatherv.

10.6.1   A Simple Example

We first provide a simple example of how processes write contiguous blocks of data into the same file in parallel. Then we give a more complex example, in which the data in each process is not contiguous but can be described by an MPI datatype.

For our first example, let us suppose that after solving the Poisson equation as we did in Section 9.3, we wish to write the solution to a file. We do not need the values of the ghost cells, and in the one-dimensional decomposition the set of rows in each process makes up a contiguous area in memory, which greatly simplifies the program. The I/O part of the program is shown in Figure 10.11.

Recall that the data to be written from each process, not counting ghost cells but including the boundary data, is in the array ulocal[i][j] for i=i_start to i_end and j=0 to NY+1.

Note that the type of an MPI file object is MPI_File. Such file objects are opened and closed much the way normal files are opened and closed. The most significant difference is that opening a file is a collective operation over a group of processes specified by the communicator in the first argument of MPI_File_open. A single process can open a file by specifying the single-process communicator MPI_COMM_SELF. Here we want all of the processes to share the file, and so we use MPI_COMM_WORLD.

In our discussion of dynamic process management, we mentioned MPI_Info ob-

```
MPI_File outfile;
size = NX * (NY + 2);
MPI_File_open( MPI_COMM_WORLD, "solutionfile",
               MPI_MODE_CREATE | MPI_MODE_WRONLY,
               MPI_INFO_NULL, &outfile );
MPI_File_set_view( outfile,
               rank * (NY+2) * (i_end - i_start) * sizeof(double),
               MPI_DOUBLE, MPI_DOUBLE, "native", MPI_INFO_NULL );
MPI_File_write( outfile, &ulocal[1][0], size, MPI_DOUBLE,
               MPI_STATUS_IGNORE );
MPI_File_close( &outfile );
```

Figure 10.11
Parallel I/O of Jacobi solution. Note that this choice of file view works only for a single output step; if output of multiple steps of the Jacobi method are needed, the arguments to MPI_File_set_view must be modified.

jects. An MPI info object is a collection of `key=value` pairs that can be used to encapsulate a variety of special-purpose information that may not be applicable to all MPI implementations. In this section we will use `MPI_INFO_NULL` whenever this type of argument is required, since we have no special information to convey. For details about `MPI_Info`, see [14, Chapter 2].

The part of the file that will be seen by each process is called the file *view* and is set for each process by a call to `MPI_File_set_view`. In our example the call is

```
MPI_File_set_view( outfile, rank * (NY+2) * ( ... ),
               MPI_DOUBLE, MPI_DOUBLE, "native", MPI_INFO_NULL )
```

The first argument identifies the file; the second is the displacement (in bytes) into the file of where the process's view of the file is to start. Here we simply multiply the size of the data to be written by the process's rank, so that each process's view starts at the appropriate place in the file. The type of this argument is `MPI_Offset`, which can be expected to be a 64-bit integer on systems that support large files.

The next argument is called the *etype* of the view; it specifies the unit of data in the file. Here it is just `MPI_DOUBLE`, since we will be writing some number of doubles. The next argument is called the *filetype*; it is a flexible way of describing noncontiguous views in the file. In our case, with no noncontiguous units to be written, we can just use the etype, `MPI_DOUBLE`. In general, any MPI predefined or derived datatype can be used for both etypes and filetypes. We explore this use in more detail in the next example.

The next argument is a string defining the *data representation* to be used. The native representation says to represent data on disk exactly as it is in memory, which provides the fastest I/O performance, at the possible expense of portability. We specify that we have no extra information by providing `MPI_INFO_NULL` for the final argument.

The call to `MPI_File_write` is then straightforward. The data to be written is a contiguous array of doubles, even though it consists of several rows of the (distributed) matrix. On each process it starts at `&ulocal[0][1]` so the data is described in (address, count, datatype) form, just as it would be for an MPI message. We ignore the status by passing `MPI_STATUS_IGNORE`. Finally we (collectively) close the file with `MPI_File_close`.

10.6.2   A More Complex Example

Parallel I/O requires more than just calling `MPI_File_write` instead of write. The key idea is to identify the object (across processes), rather than the contribution from each process. We illustrate this with an example of a regular distributed array.

The code in Figure 10.12 writes out an array that is distributed among processes with a two-dimensional decomposition. To illustrate the expressiveness of the MPI interface, we show a complex case where, as in the Jacobi example, the distributed array is surrounded by ghost cells. This example is covered in more depth in Chapter 3 of *Using MPI 2* [14], including the simpler case of a distributed array without ghost cells.

This example may look complex, but each step is relatively simple.

1.   Set up a communicator that represents a virtual array of processes that matches the way that the distributed array is distributed. This approach uses the `MPI_Cart_create` routine and uses `MPI_Cart_coords` to find the coordinates of the calling process in this array of processes. This particular choice of process ordering is important because it matches the ordering required by `MPI_Type_create_subarray`.

2.   Create a *file view* that describes the part of the file that this process will write to. The MPI routine `MPI_Type_create_subarray` makes it easy to construct the MPI datatype that describes this region of the file. The arguments to this routine specify the dimensionality of the array (two in our case), the global size of the array, the local size (that is, the size of the part of the array on the calling process), the location of the local part (`start_indices`), the ordering of indices (column major is `MPI_ORDER_FORTRAN` and row major is `MPI_ORDER_C`), and the basic datatype.

```
/* no. of processes in vertical and horizontal dimensions
   of process grid */
dims[0] = 2;    dims[1] = 3;
periods[0] = periods[1] = 1;
MPI_Cart_create(MPI_COMM_WORLD, 2, dims, periods, 0, &comm);
MPI_Comm_rank(comm, &rank);
MPI_Cart_coords(comm, rank, 2, coords);
/* global indices of the first element of the local array */

/* no. of rows and columns in global array*/
gsizes[0] = m;    gsizes[1] = n;

lsizes[0] = m/dims[0];   /* no. of rows in local array */
lsizes[1] = n/dims[1];   /* no. of columns in local array */

start_indices[0] = coords[0] * lsizes[0];
start_indices[1] = coords[1] * lsizes[1];
MPI_Type_create_subarray(2, gsizes, lsizes, start_indices,
                         MPI_ORDER_C, MPI_FLOAT, &filetype);
MPI_Type_commit(&filetype);

MPI_File_open(comm, "/pfs/datafile",
              MPI_MODE_CREATE | MPI_MODE_WRONLY,
              MPI_INFO_NULL, &fh);
MPI_File_set_view(fh, 0, MPI_FLOAT, filetype, "native",
                  MPI_INFO_NULL);

/* create a derived datatype that describes the layout of the local
   array in the memory buffer that includes the ghost area. This is
   another subarray datatype! */
memsizes[0] = lsizes[0] + 8; /* no. of rows in allocated array */
memsizes[1] = lsizes[1] + 8; /* no. of columns in allocated array */
start_indices[0] = start_indices[1] = 4;
/* indices of the first element of the local array in the
   allocated array */
MPI_Type_create_subarray(2, memsizes, lsizes, start_indices,
                         MPI_ORDER_C, MPI_FLOAT, &memtype);
MPI_Type_commit(&memtype);
MPI_File_write_all(fh, local_array, 1, memtype, &status);
MPI_File_close(&fh);
```

Figure 10.12
C program for writing a distributed array that is also noncontiguous in memory because of a
ghost area (derived from an example in [14]).

3. Open the file for writing (`MPI_MODE_WRONLY`), and set the file view with the datatype we have just constructed.

4. Create a datatype that describes the data to be written. We can use `MPI_-Type_create_subarray` here as well to define the part of the local array that does *not* include the ghost points. If there were no ghost points, we could instead use `MPI_FLOAT` as the datatype with a count of `lsizes[0]*lsizes[1]` in the call to `MPI_File_write_all`.

5. Perform a collective write to the file with `MPI_File_write_all`, and close the file.

By using MPI datatypes to describe both the data to be written and the destination of the data in the file with a collective file write operation, the MPI implementation can make the best use of the I/O system. The result is that file I/O operations performed with MPI I/O can achieve hundredfold improvements in performance over using individual Unix I/O operations [35].

10.7   Remote Memory Access

The message-passing programming model requires that both the sender and the receiver (or all members of a communicator in a collective operation) participate in moving data between two processes. An alternative model where one process controls the communication, called one-sided communication, can offer better performance and in some cases a simpler programming model. MPI-2 provides support for this one-sided approach. The MPI-2 model was inspired by the work on the bulk synchronous programming (BSP) model [17] and the Cray SHMEM library used on the massively parallel Cray T3D and T3E computers [6].

In one-sided communication, one process may *put* data directly into the memory of another process, without that process using an explicit receive call. For this reason, this also called *remote memory access* (RMA).

Using RMA involves four steps:

1. Describe the memory into which data may be put.

2. Allow access to the memory.

3. Begin put operations (e.g., with `MPI_Put`).

4. Complete all pending RMA operations.

The first step is to describe the region of memory into which data may be placed by an `MPI_Put` operation (also accessed by `MPI_Get` or updated by `MPI_-Accumulate`). This is done with the routine `MPI_Win_create`:

```
MPI_Win win;
double ulocal[MAX_NX][NY+2];

MPI_Win_create( ulocal, (NY+2)*(i_end-i_start+3)*sizeof(double),
            sizeof(double), MPI_INFO_NULL, MPI_COMM_WORLD, &win );
```

The input arguments are, in order, the array `ulocal`, the size of the array in bytes, the size of a basic unit of the array (`sizeof(double)` in this case), a "hint" object, and the communicator that specifies which processes may use RMA to access the array. `MPI_Win_create` is a collective call over the communicator. The output is an MPI *window object* `win`. When a window object is no longer needed, it should be freed with `MPI_Win_free`.

RMA operations take place between two sentinels. One begins a period where access is allowed to a window object, and one ends that period. These periods are called *epochs*.[2] The easiest routine to use to begin and end epochs is `MPI_Win_-fence`. This routine is collective over the processes that created the window object and both ends the previous epoch and starts a new one. The routine is called a "fence" because all RMA operations before the fence complete before the fence returns, and any RMA operation initiated by another process (in the epoch begun by the matching fence on that process) does not start until the fence returns. This may seem complex, but it is easy to use. In practice, `MPI_Win_fence` is needed only to separate RMA operations into groups. This model closely follows the BSP and Cray SHMEM models, though with the added ability to work with any subset of processes.

Three routines are available for initiating the transfer of data in RMA. These are `MPI_Put`, `MPI_Get`, and `MPI_Accumulate`. All are nonblocking in the same sense MPI point-to-point communication is nonblocking (Section 10.3.1). They complete at the end of the epoch that they start in, for example, at the closing `MPI_Win_-fence`. Because these routines specify both the source and destination of data, they have more arguments than do the point-to-point communication routines. The arguments can be easily understood by taking them a few at a time.

---

[2]MPI has two kinds of epochs for RMA: an *access epoch* and an *exposure epoch*. For the example used here, the epochs occur together, and we refer to both of them as just epochs.

1.   The first three arguments describe the *origin* data; that is, the data on the calling process. These are the usual "buffer, count, datatype" arguments.

2.   The next argument is the rank of the *target* process. This serves the same function as the destination of an `MPI_Send`. The rank is relative to the communicator used when creating the MPI window object.

3.   The next three arguments describe the destination buffer. The `count` and `datatype` arguments have the same meaning as for an `MPI_Recv`, but the buffer location is specified as an offset from the beginning of the memory specified to `MPI_Win_create` on the target process. This offset is in units of the displacement argument of the `MPI_Win_create` and is usually the size of the basic datatype.

4.   The last argument is the MPI window object.

Note that there are no MPI requests; the `MPI_Win_fence` completes all preceding RMA operations. `MPI_Win_fence` provides a collective synchronization model for RMA operations in which all processes participate. This is called *active target* synchronization.

With these routines, we can create a version of the mesh exchange that uses RMA instead of point-to-point communication. Figure 10.13 shows one possible implementation.

Another form of access requires no MPI calls (not even a fence) at the target process. This is called *passive target* synchronization. The origin process uses `MPI_-Win_lock` to begin an access epoch and `MPI_Win_unlock` to end the access epoch.[3] Because of the passive nature of this type of RMA, the local memory (passed as the first argument to `MPI_Win_create`) should be allocated with `MPI_Alloc_mem` and freed with `MPI_Free_mem`. For more information on passive target RMA operations, see [14, Chapter 6]. Also note that as of 2001, few MPI implementations support passive target RMA operation. More implementations are expected to support these operations in 2002.

A more complete discussion of remote memory access can be found in [14, Chapters 5 and 6]. Note that MPI implementations are just beginning to provide the RMA routines described in this section. Most current RMA implementations emphasize functionality over performance. As implementations mature, however, the performance of RMA operations will also improve.

---

[3]The names `MPI_Win_lock` and `MPI_Win_unlock` are really misnomers; think of them as begin-RMA and end-RMA.

```
void exchang_nbrs( double u_local[][NY+2], int i_start, int i_end,
                   int left, int right, MPI_Win win )
{
    MPI_Aint left_ghost_disp, right_ghost_disp;
    int      c;

    MPI_Win_fence( 0, win );
    /* Put the left edge into the left neighbors rightmost
       ghost cells.  See text about right_ghost_disp */
    right_ghost_disp = 1 + (NY+2) * (i_end-i-start+2);
    MPI_Put( &u_local[1][1], NY, MPI_DOUBLE,
             left, right_ghost_disp, NY, MPI_DOUBLE, win );
    /* Put the right edge into the right neighbors leftmost ghost
       cells */
    left_ghost_disp = 1;
    c = i_end - i_start + 1;
    MPI_Put( &u_local[c][1], NY, MPI_DOUBLE,
             right, left_ghost_disp, NY, MPI_DOUBLE, win );

    MPI_Win_fence( 0, win )
}
```

Figure 10.13
Neighbor exchange using MPI remote memory access.

10.8   Using C++ and Fortran 90

MPI-1 defined bindings to C and Fortran 77. These bindings were very similar; the only major difference was the handling of the error code (returned in C, set through the last argument in Fortran 77). In MPI-2, a binding was added for C++, and an MPI module was defined for Fortran 90.

The C++ binding provides a lightweight model that is more than just a C++ version of the C binding but not a no-holds-barred object-oriented model. MPI objects are defined in the MPI namespace. Most MPI objects have corresponding classes, such as Datatype for MPI_Datatype. Communicators and requests are slightly different. There is an abstract base class Comm for general communicators with four derived classes: Intracomm, Intercomm, Graphcomm, and Cartcomm. Most communicators are Intracomms; GraphComm and CartComm are derived from Intracomm. Requests have two derived classes: Prequest for persistent requests and Grequest for generalized requests (new in MPI-2). Most MPI operations are

methods on the appropriate objects; for example, most point-to-point and collec-
tive communications are methods on the communicator. A few routines, such as
Init and Finalize, stand alone. A simple MPI program in C++ is shown in
Figure 10.14.

```cpp
#include "mpi.h"
#include <iostream.h>

int main( int argc, char *argv[] )
{
    int data;
    MPI::Init();

    if (MPI::COMM_WORLD.Get_rank() == 0) {
        // Broadcast data from process 0 to all others
        cout << "Enter an int" << endl;
        data << cin;
    }
    MPI::COMM_WORLD.Bcast( data, 1, MPI::INT, 0 );

    MPI::Finalize();
    return 0;
}
```

Figure 10.14
Simple MPI program in C++.

The C++ binding for MPI has a few quirks. One is that the multiple completion
operations such as MPI::Waitall are methods on requests, even though there is no
unique request to use for these methods. Another is the C++ analogue to MPI_-
Comm_dup. In the C++ binding, MPI::Comm is an abstract base class (ABC). Since
it is impossible to create an instance of an abstract base class, there can be no
general "dup" function that returns a new MPI::Comm. Since it is possible in C++
to create a reference to an ABC, however, MPI defines the routine (available only
in the C++ binding) MPI::Clone that returns a reference to a new communicator.

Two levels of Fortran 90 support are provided in MPI. The basic support provides an 'mpif.h' include file. The extended support provides an MPI module. The
module makes it easy to detect the two most common errors in Fortran MPI programs: forgetting to provide the variable for the error return value and forgetting
to declare status as an array of size MPI_STATUS_SIZE. There are a few drawbacks.

Fortran derived datatypes cannot be directly supported (the Fortran 90 language provides no way to handle an arbitrary type). Often, you can use the first element of the Fortran 90 derived type. Array sections should not be used in receive operations, particularly nonblocking communication (see Section 10.2.2 in the MPI-2 standard for more information). Another problem is that while Fortran 90 enables the user to define MPI interfaces in the MPI module, a different Fortran 90 interface file must be used for each combination of Fortran datatype and array dimension (scalars are different from arrays of dimension one, etc.). This leads to a Fortran 90 MPI module library that is often (depending on the Fortran 90 compiler) far larger than the entire MPI library. However, particularly during program development, the MPI module is very helpful.

10.9   MPI, OpenMP, and Threads

The MPI standard was carefully written to be a thread-safe specification. That means that the design of MPI doesn't include concepts such as "last message" or "current pack buffer" that are not well defined when multiple threads are present. MPI implementations can choose whether to provide thread-safe *implementations*. Allowing this choice is particularly important because thread safety usually comes at the price of performance due to the extra overhead required to ensure that internal data structures are not modified inconsistently by two different threads. Most early MPI implementations were not thread safe.

MPI-2 introduced four levels of thread safety that an MPI implementation could provide. The lowest level, `MPI_THREAD_SINGLE`, allows only single threaded programs. The next level, `MPI_THREAD_FUNNELED`, allows multiple threads provided that all MPI calls are made in a single thread; most MPI implementations provide `MPI_THREAD_FUNNELED`. The next level, `MPI_THREAD_SERIALIZED`, allows many user threads to make MPI calls, but only one thread at a time. The highest level of support, `MPI_THREAD_MULTIPLE`, allows any thread to call any MPI routine.

Understanding the level of thread support is important when combining MPI with approaches to thread-based parallelism. OpenMP [26] is a popular and powerful language for specifying thread-based parallelism. While OpenMP provides some tools for general threaded parallelism, one of the most common uses is to parallelize a loop. If the loop contains no MPI calls, then OpenMP may be combined with MPI. For example, in the Jacobi example, OpenMP can be used to parallelize the loop computation:

```
exchange_nbrs( u_local, i_start, i_end, left, right );
```

```
#pragma omp for
for (i_local=1; i<=i_end-i_start+1; i++)
  for (j=1; j<=NY; j++)
    ulocal_new[i_local][j] =
        0.25 * (ulocal[i_local+1][j] + ulocal[i_local-1][j] +
                ulocal[i_local][j+1] + ulocal[i_local][j-1] -
                h*h*flocal[i_local][j]);
```

This exploits the fact that MPI was designed to work well with other tools, leveraging improvements in compilers and threaded parallelism.

10.10 Measuring MPI Performance

Many tools have been developed for measuring performance. The best is always your own application, but a number of tests are available that can give a more general overview of the performance of MPI on a cluster. Measuring communication performance is actually quite tricky; see [15] for a discussion of some of the issues in making reproducible measurements of performance. That paper describes the methods used in the mpptest program for measuring MPI performance.

10.10.1 mpptest

The mpptest program allows you to measure many aspects of the performance of any MPI implementation. The most common MPI performance test is the Ping-Pong test (see Section 8.2). The mpptest program provides Ping-Pong tests for the different MPI communication modes, as well as providing a variety of tests for collective operations and for more realistic variations on point-to-point communication, such as halo communication (like that in Section 9.3) and communication that does not reuse the same memory locations (thus benefiting from using data that is already in memory cache). The mpptest program can also test the performance of some MPI-2 functions, including MPI_Put and MPI_Get.

Using mpptest. The mpptest program is distributed with MPICH in the directory 'examples/perftest'. You can also download it separately from www.mcs. anl.gov/mpi/perftest. Building and using mpptest is very simple:

```
% tar zxf perftest.tar.gz
% cd perftest-1.2.1
% ./configure --with-mpich
% make
```

```
% mpirun -np 2 ./mpptest -logscale
% mpirun -np 16 ./mpptest -bisect
% mpirun -np 2 ./mpptest -auto
```

To run with LAM/MPI, simply configure with the option `--with-lammpi`. The
'`README`' file contains instructions for building with other MPI implementations.

10.10.2 SKaMPI

The SKaMPI test suite [27] is a comprehensive test of MPI performance, covering
virtually all of the MPI-1 communication functions.

One interesting feature of the SKaMPI benchmarks is the online tables showing
the performance of MPI implementations on various parallel computers, ranging
from Beowulf clusters to parallel vector supercomputers.

10.10.3 High Performance LINPACK

Perhaps the best known benchmark in technical computing is the LINPACK Benchmark, discussed in Section 8.3. The version of this benchmark that is appropriate
for clusters is the High Performance LINPACK (HPL). Obtaining and running this
benchmark is relatively easy, though getting good performance can require a significant amount of effort. In addition, as pointed out in Section 8.3, while the
LINPACK benchmark is widely known, it tends to significantly overestimate the
achieveable performance for many applications.

The HPL benchmark depends on another library, the basic linear algebra subroutines (BLAS), for much of the computation. Thus, to get good performance on
the HPL benchmark, you must have a high-quality implementation of the BLAS.
Fortunately, several sources of these routines are available. You can often get
implementations of the BLAS from the CPU vendor directly, sometimes at no cost.

Another possibility is to use the ATLAS implementation of the BLAS.

ATLAS. ATLAS is available from `www.netlib.org/atlas`. If prebuilt binaries
fit your system, you should use those. Note that ATLAS is tuned for specific system
characteristics including clock speed and cache sizes; if you have any doubts about
whether your configuration matches that of a prebuilt version, you should build
ATLAS yourself.

To build ATLAS, first download ATLAS from the Web site and then extract it.
This will create an '`ATLAS`' directory into which the libraries will be built, so extract
this where you want the libraries to reside.

```
% tar zxf atlas3.2.1.tgz
```

```
% cd ATLAS
```

Check the 'errata.html' file at www.netlib.org/atlas/errata.html for updates. You may need to edit various files (no patches are supplied for ATLAS). Next, have ATLAS configure itself. Select a compiler; note that you should not use the Portland Group compiler here.

```
% make config CC=gcc
```

Answer **yes** to most questions, including threaded and express setup, and accept the suggested architecture name. Next, make ATLAS:

```
% make install arch=<thename> >&make.log
```

Note that this is not an "install" in the usual sense; the ATLAS libraries are not copied to '/usr/local/lib' and the like by the install. This step may take as long as several hours, unless ATLAS finds a precomputed set of parameters that fits your machine. At the end of this step, the BLAS are in 'ATLAS/lib/<archname>'. You are ready for the next step.

HPL.   Download the HPL package from www.netlib.org/benchmark/hpl:

```
% tar zxf hpl.tgz
% cd hpl
```

Create a 'Make.<archname>' in the 'hpl' directory. Consider an **archname** like **Linux_P4_CBLAS_p4** for a Linux system on Pentium 4 processors, using the C version of the BLAS constructed by ATLAS, and using the **ch_p4** device from the MPICH implementation of MPI. To create this file, look at the samples in the 'hpl/makes' directory, for example,

```
% cp makes/Make.Linux_PII_CBLAS_gm Make.Linux_P4_CBLAS_p4
```

Edit this file, changing ARCH to the name you selected (e.g., **Linux_P4_CBLAS_p4**), and set **LAdir** to the location of the ATLAS libraries. Then do the following:

```
% make arch=<thename>
% cd bin/<thename>
% mpirun -np 4 ./xhpl
```

Check the output to make sure that you have the right answer. The file 'HPL.dat' controls the actual test parameters. The version of 'HPL.dat' that comes with the **hpl** package is appropriate for testing **hpl**. To run **hpl** for performance requires modifying 'HPL.dat'. The file 'hpl/TUNING' contains some hints on setting the values in this file for performance. Here are a few of the most important:

1.   Change the problem size to a large value. Don't make it too large, however, since the total computational work grows as the cube of the problem size (doubling the problem size increases the amount of work by a factor of eight). Problem sizes of around 5,000–10,000 are reasonable.

2.   Change the block size to a modest size. A block size of around 64 is a good place to start.

3.   Change the processor decomposition and number of nodes to match your configuration. In most cases, you should try to keep the decomposition close to square (e.g., P and Q should be about the same value), with $P \geq Q$.

4.   Experiment with different values for RFACT and PFACT. On some systems, these parameters can have a significant effect on performance. For one large cluster, setting both to right was preferable.

10.11   MPI-2 Status

MPI-2 is a significant extension of the MPI-1 standard. Unlike the MPI-1 standard, where complete implementations of the entire standard were available when the standard was released, complete implementations of all of MPI-2 have been slow in coming. As of June 2001, there are few complete implementations of MPI-2 and none for Beowulf clusters. Most MPI implementations include the MPI-IO routines, in large part because of the ROMIO implementation of these routines. Significant parts of MPI-2 are available, however, including the routines described in this book. Progress continues in both the completeness and performance of MPI-2 implementations, and we expect full MPI-2 implementations to appear in 2002.

10.12   MPI Routine Summary

This section provides a quick summary in C, Fortran, C++, and other MPI routines used in this chapter. Although these are only a small fraction of the routines available in MPI, they are sufficient for many applications.

C Routines.
int **MPI_Irecv**(void* buf, int count, MPI_Datatype datatype, int source, int tag,
                  MPI_Comm comm, MPI_Request *request)

int **MPI_Wait**(MPI_Request *request, MPI_Status *status)

int **MPI_Test**(MPI_Request *request, int *flag, MPI_Status *status)

int **MPI_Waitall**(int count, MPI_Request *array_of_requests,
                MPI_Status *array_of_statuses)

int **MPI_Win_create**(void *base, MPI_Aint size, int disp_unit, MPI_Info info,
                MPI_Comm comm, MPI_Win *win)

int **MPI_Win_free**(MPI_Win *win)

int **MPI_Put**(void *origin_addr, int origin_count, MPI_Datatype origin_datatype,
                int target_rank, MPI_Aint target_disp, int target_count,
                MPI_Datatype target_datatype, MPI_Win win)

int **MPI_Get**(void *origin_addr, int origin_count, MPI_Datatype origin_datatype,
                int target_rank, MPI_Aint target_disp, int target_count,
                MPI_Datatype target_datatype, MPI_Win win)

int **MPI_Win_fence**(int assert, MPI_Win win)

int **MPI_File_open**(MPI_Comm comm, char *filename, int amode, MPI_Info info,
                MPI_File *fh)

int **MPI_File_set_view**(MPI_File fh, MPI_Offset disp, MPI_Datatype etype,
                MPI_Datatype filetype, char *datarep, MPI_Info info)

int **MPI_File_read**(MPI_File fh, void *buf, int count, MPI_Datatype datatype,
                MPI_Status *status)

int **MPI_File_write**(MPI_File fh, void *buf, int count, MPI_Datatype datatype,
                MPI_Status *status)

int **MPI_File_read_all**(MPI_File fh, void *buf, int count, MPI_Datatype datatype,
                MPI_Status *status)

int **MPI_File_write_all**(MPI_File fh, void *buf, int count, MPI_Datatype datatype,
                MPI_Status *status)

int **MPI_File_close**(MPI_File *fh)

int **MPI_Comm_spawn**(char *command, char *argv[], int maxprocs, MPI_Info info,
              int root, MPI_Comm comm, MPI_Comm *intercomm,
              int array_of_errcodes[])

int **MPI_Comm_get_parent**(MPI_Comm *parent)

Fortran routines.

MPI_ISEND(buf, count, datatype, dest, tag, comm, request, ierror)
              <type> buf(*)
              integer count, datatype, dest, tag, comm, request, ierror

MPI_IRECV(buf, count, datatype, source, tag, comm, request,ierror)
              <type> buf(*)
              integer count, datatype, source, tag, comm, request, ierror

MPI_WAIT(request, status, ierror)
              integer request,status(MPI_STATUS_SIZE), ierror

MPI_TEST(request, flag, status, ierror)
              logical flag
              integer request, status(MPI_STATUS_SIZE), ierror

MPI_WAITALL(count, array_of_requests, array_of_statuses,ierror)
              integer count, array_of_requests(*),
                     array_of_statuses(MPI_STATUS_SIZE,*), ierror

MPI_WIN_CREATE(base, size, disp_unit, info, comm, win, ierror)
              <type> base(*)
              integer(kind=MPI_ADDRESS_KIND) size
              integer disp_unit, info, comm, win, ierror

MPI_WIN_FREE(win, ierror)
              integer win, ierror

MPI_PUT(origin_addr, origin_count, origin_datatype, target_rank, target_disp,
              target_count, target_datatype, win, ierror)
              <type> origin_addr(*)
              integer(kind=MPI_ADDRESS_KIND) target_disp
              integer origin_count, origin_datatype, target_rank, target_count,
                     target_datatype, win, ierror

MPI_GET(origin_addr, origin_count, origin_datatype,target_rank, target_disp,
        target_count, target_datatype, win, ierror)
        <type> origin_addr(*)
        integer(kind=MPI_ADDRESS_KIND) target_disp
        integer origin_count, origin_datatype, target_rank, target_count,
        target_datatype, win, ierror

MPI_WIN_FENCE(assert, win, ierror)
        integer assert, win, ierror

MPI_FILE_OPEN(comm, filename, amode, info, fh, ierror)
        character*(*) filename
        integer comm, amode, info, fh, ierror

MPI_FILE_SET_VIEW(fh, disp, etype, filetype, datarep, info, ierror)
        integer fh, etype, filetype, info, ierror
        character*(*) datarep
        integer(kind=MPI_OFFSET_KIND) disp

MPI_FILE_READ(fh, buf, count, datatype, status, ierror)
        <type> buf(*)
        integer fh, count, datatype, status(MPI_STATUS_SIZE), ierror

MPI_FILE_WRITE(fh, buf, count, datatype, status, ierror)
        <type> buf(*)
        integer fh, count, datatype, status(MPI_STATUS_SIZE), ierror

MPI_FILE_READ_ALL(fh, buf, count, datatype, status, ierror)
        <type> buf(*)
        integer fh, count, datatype, status(MPI_STATUS_SIZE), ierror

MPI_FILE_WRITE_ALL(fh, buf, count, datatype, status, ierror)
        <type> buf(*)
        integer fh, count, datatype, status(MPI_STATUS_SIZE), ierror

MPI_FILE_CLOSE(fh, ierror)
        integer fh, ierror

MPI_COMM_SPAWN(command, argv, maxprocs, info, root, comm, intercomm,
        array_of_errcodes, ierror)
        character*(*) command, argv(*)

        integer info, maxprocs, root, comm, intercomm, array_of_errcodes(**),
        ierror

MPI_COMM_GET_PARENT(parent, ierror)
        integer parent, ierror

C++ routines.

Request MPI::Comm::Isend(const void* buf, int count,
        const Datatype& datatype, int dest, int tag) const

Request MPI::Comm::Irecv(void* buf, int count, const Datatype& datatype,
        int source, int tag) const

void MPI::Request::Wait(Status& status)

void MPI::Request::Wait()

bool MPI::Request::Test(Status& status)

bool MPI::Request::Test()

void MPI::Request::Waitall(int count, Request array_of_requests[],
        Status array_of_statuses[])

void MPI::Request::Waitall(int count, Request array_of_requests[])

MPI::Win MPI::Win::Create(const void* base, Aint size, int disp_unit,
        const Info& info, const Intracomm& comm)

void MPI::Win::Free()

void MPI::Win::Put(const void* origin_addr, int
        origin_count, const Datatype& origin_datatype, int target_rank, Aint
        target_disp, int target_count, const Datatype& target_datatype) const

void MPI::Win::Get(void *origin_addr, int
        origin_count, const MPI::Datatype& origin_datatype, int target_rank,
        MPI::Aint target_disp, int target_count,
        const MPI::Datatype& target_datatype) const

void MPI::Win::Fence(int assert) const

MPI::File MPI::File::Open(const MPI::Intracomm& comm, const char* filename,
        int amode, const MPI::Info& info)

MPI::Offset MPI::File::Get_size const

void MPI::File::Set_view(MPI::Offset disp, const MPI::Datatype& etype,
        const MPI::Datatype& filetype, const char* datarep,
        const MPI::Info& info)

void MPI::File::Read(void* buf, int count, const MPI::Datatype& datatype,
        MPI::Status& status)

void MPI::File::Read(void* buf, int count, const MPI::Datatype& datatype)

void MPI::File::Write(void* buf, int count, const MPI::Datatype& datatype,
        MPI::Status& status)

void MPI::File::Write(void* buf, int count, const MPI::Datatype& datatype)

void MPI::File::Read_all(void* buf, int count, const MPI::Datatype& datatype,
        MPI::Status& status)

void MPI::File::Read_all(void* buf, int count, const MPI::Datatype& datatype)

void MPI::File::Write_all(const void* buf, int count,
        const MPI::Datatype& datatype, MPI::Status& status)

void MPI::File::Write_all(const void* buf, int count, const MPI::Datatype& datatype)

void MPI::File::Close

MPI::Intercomm MPI::Intracomm::Spawn(const char* command,
        const char* argv[], int maxprocs, const MPI::Info& info, int root,
        int array_of_errcodes[]) const

MPI::Intercomm MPI::Intracomm::Spawn(const char* command,
        const char* argv[], int maxprocs, const MPI::Info& info, int root) const

MPI::Intercomm MPI::Comm::Get_parent()

11 Parallel Programming with PVM

Al Geist and Stephen Scott

PVM (Parallel Virtual Machine) is an outgrowth of an ongoing computing research project involving Oak Ridge National Laboratory, the University of Tennessee, and Emory University. The general goals of this project are to investigate issues in, and develop solutions for, heterogeneous concurrent computing. PVM is an integrated set of software tools and libraries that emulates a general-purpose, flexible, heterogeneous parallel computing framework on interconnected computers of varied architecture. The overall objective of the PVM system is to enable such a collection of computers to be used cooperatively for a concurrent or parallel computation. This chapter provides detailed descriptions and discussions of the concepts, logistics, and methodologies involved in programming with PVM.

11.1 Overview

PVM is based on the following principles:

- **User-configured host pool:** The application's computational tasks execute on a set of machines that are selected by the user for a given run of the PVM program. Both single-CPU machines and hardware multiprocessors (including shared-memory and distributed-memory computers) may be part of the host pool. The host pool may be altered by adding and deleting machines during operation (an important feature for fault tolerance). When PVM is used on Beowulf clusters, the nodes make up the host pool.
- **Translucent access to hardware:** Application programs may view the hardware environment as an attributeless collection of virtual processing elements or may exploit the capabilities of specific machines in the host pool by positioning certain computational tasks on the most appropriate computers.
- **Process-based computation:** The unit of parallelism in PVM is a task, an independent sequential thread of control that has communication and computation capabilities. No process-to-processor mapping is implied or enforced by PVM; in particular, multiple tasks may execute on a single processor.
- **Explicit message-passing model:** Collections of computational tasks, each performing a part of an application's workload, cooperate by explicitly sending to and receiving messages from one another. PVM dynamically allocates space for message buffers so message size is limited only by the amount of available memory.
- **Heterogeneity support:** The PVM system supports heterogeneity in terms of machines, networks, and applications. With regard to message passing, PVM

permits messages containing more than one datatype to be exchanged between machines having different data representations.

- **Multiprocessor support:** PVM uses the native message-passing facilities on multiprocessors to take advantage of the underlying hardware. For example, on the IBM SP, PVM transparently uses IBM's MPI to move data. On the SGI Origin, PVM uses shared memory to move data.

The PVM system is composed of two parts. The first part is a daemon, called `pvmd3` and sometimes abbreviated `pvmd`, that resides on all the computers making up the virtual machine. (An example of a daemon program is the mail program that runs in the background and handles all the incoming and outgoing electronic mail on a computer.) The daemon `pvmd3` is designed so any user with a valid login can install this daemon on a machine. To run a PVM application, you first create a virtual machine by starting up PVM (Section 11.7.2 details how this is done). You can then start the PVM application on any of the hosts. Multiple users can configure virtual machines that overlap the same cluster nodes, and each user can execute several PVM applications simultaneously.

The second part of the system is a library of PVM interface routines. It contains a functionally complete repertoire of primitives that are needed for cooperation between tasks of an application. This library contains user-callable routines for message passing, spawning processes, coordinating tasks, and modifying the virtual machine.

The PVM computing model is based on the notion that an application consists of several tasks each responsible for a part of the application's computational workload. Sometimes an application is parallelized along its functions. That is, each task performs a different function, for example, input, problem setup, solution, output, or display. This is often called functional parallelism. A more common method of parallelizing an application is called data parallelism. In this method all the tasks are the same, but each one knows and solves only a small part of the data. This is also referred to as the SPMD (single program, multiple data) model of computing. PVM supports either or a mixture of both these methods. Depending on their functions, tasks may execute in parallel and may need to synchronize or exchange data.

The PVM system currently supports C, C++, and Fortran languages. These language interfaces have been included based on the observation that the predominant majority of target applications are written in C and Fortran, with an emerging trend in experimenting with object-based languages and methodologies. Third-party groups have created freely available Java, Perl, Python, and IDL interfaces to PVM.

The C and C++ language bindings for the PVM user interface library are implemented as functions, following the general conventions used by most C systems. To elaborate, function arguments are a combination of value parameters and pointers as appropriate, and function result values indicate the outcome of the call. In addition, macro definitions are used for system constants, and global variables such as `errno` and `pvm_errno` are the mechanism for discriminating between multiple possible outcomes. Application programs written in C and C++ access PVM library functions by linking against an archival library (`libpvm3.a`) that is part of the standard distribution.

Fortran language bindings are implemented as subroutines rather than as functions. This approach was taken because some compilers on the supported architectures would not reliably interface Fortran functions with C functions. One immediate implication of this is that an additional argument is introduced into each PVM library call for status results to be returned to the invoking program. Another difference is that library routines for the placement and retrieval of typed data in message buffers are unified, with an additional parameter indicating the datatype. Apart from these differences (and the standard naming prefixes *pvm_* for C, and *pvmf* for Fortran), a one-to-one correspondence exists between the two language bindings. Fortran interfaces to PVM are implemented as library stubs that in turn invoke the corresponding C routines, after casting and/or dereferencing arguments as appropriate. Thus, Fortran applications are required to link against the stubs library (`libfpvm3.a`) as well as the C library.

All PVM tasks are identified by an integer task identifier *tid*. Messages are sent to tids and received from tids. Since tids must be unique across the entire virtual machine, they are supplied by the local pvmd and are not user chosen. Although PVM encodes information into each tid, the user is expected to treat the tids as opaque integer identifiers. PVM contains several routines that return tid values so that the user application can identify other tasks in the system.

In some applications it is natural to think of a *group* of tasks. And there are cases where you would like to identify your tasks by the numbers 0 to $(p - 1)$, where p is the number of tasks. PVM includes the concept of user-named groups. When a task joins a group, it is assigned a unique "instance" number in that group. Instance numbers start at 0 and count up. In keeping with the PVM philosophy, the group functions are designed to be very general and transparent to the user. For example, any PVM task can join or leave any group at any time without having to inform any other task in the affected groups, groups can overlap, and tasks can broadcast messages to groups of which they are not a member. To use any of the group functions, a program must be linked with libgpvm3.a.

The general paradigm for application programming with PVM is as follows. You write one or more sequential programs in C, C++, or Fortran 77 that contain embedded calls to the PVM library. Each program corresponds to a task making up the application. These programs are compiled for each architecture in the host pool, and the resulting object files are placed at a location accessible from machines in the host pool. To execute an application, you typically start one copy of one task (typically the "manager" or "initiating" task) by hand from a machine within the host pool. This process subsequently starts other PVM tasks eventually resulting in a collection of active tasks that then compute locally and exchange messages with each other to solve the problem.

Note that while this scenario is typical, as many tasks as appropriate may be started manually. As mentioned earlier, tasks interact through explicit message passing, identifying each other with a system-assigned, opaque tid.

```c
#include "pvm3.h"

main()
{
        int cc, tid, msgtag;
        char buf[100];

        printf("i'm t%x\n", pvm_mytid());

        cc = pvm_spawn("hello_other", (char**)0, 0, "", 1, &tid);

        if (cc == 1) {
                msgtag = 1;
                pvm_recv(tid, msgtag);
                pvm_upkstr(buf);
                printf("from t%x: %s\n", tid, buf);
        } else
                printf("can't start hello_other\n");

        pvm_exit();
}
```

Figure 11.1
PVM program 'hello.c'.

Shown in Figure 11.1 is the body of the PVM program 'hello.c', a simple example that illustrates the basic concepts of PVM programming. This program is intended to be invoked manually; after printing its task id (obtained with pvm_mytid()), it initiates a copy of another program called 'hello_other.c' using the pvm_spawn() function. A successful spawn causes the program to execute a blocking receive using pvm_recv. After receiving the message, the program prints the message sent by its counterpart, as well its task id; the buffer is extracted from the message using pvm_upkstr. The final pvm_exit call dissociates the program from the PVM system.

```c
#include "pvm3.h"

main()
{
        int ptid, msgtag;
        char buf[100];

        ptid = pvm_parent();

        strcpy(buf, "hello, world from ");
        gethostname(buf + strlen(buf), 64);
        msgtag = 1;
        pvm_initsend(PvmDataDefault);
        pvm_pkstr(buf);
        pvm_send(ptid, msgtag);

        pvm_exit();
}
```

Figure 11.2
PVM program 'hello_other.c'.

Figure 11.2 is a listing of the "slave," or spawned program; its first PVM action is to obtain the task id of the "master" using the pvm_parent call. This program then obtains its hostname and transmits it to the master using the three-call sequence: pvm_initsend to initialize the (transparent) send buffer; pvm_pkstr to place a string in a strongly typed and architecture independent manner into the send buffer; and pvm_send to transmit it to the destination process specified by *ptid*, "tagging" the message with the number 1.

11.2   Program Examples

In this section we discuss several complete PVM programs in detail. The first example, `forkjoin.c`, shows how to spawn off processes and synchronize with them. We then discuss a Fortran dot product program PSDOT.F and a matrix multiply example. Lastly, we show how PVM can be used to compute heat diffusion through a wire.

11.3   Fork/Join

The fork/join example demonstrates how to spawn off PVM tasks and synchronize with them. The program spawns several tasks, three by default. The children then synchronize by sending a message to their parent task. The parent receives a message from each of the spawned tasks and prints out information about the message from the child tasks.

This program contains the code for both the parent and the child tasks. Let's examine it in more detail. The very first thing the program does is call `pvm_mytid()`. In fork/join we check the value of `mytid`; if it is negative, indicating an error, we call `pvm_perror()` and exit the program. The `pvm_perror()` call will print a message indicating what went wrong with the last PVM call. In this case the last call was `pvm_mytid()`, so `pvm_perror()` might print a message indicating that PVM hasn't been started on this machine. The argument to `pvm_perror()` is a string that will be prepended to any error message printed by `pvm_perror()`. In this case we pass `argv[0]`, which is the name of the program as it was typed on the command-line. The `pvm_perror()` function is modeled after the Unix `perror()` function.

Assuming we obtained a valid result for `mytid`, we now call `pvm_parent()`. The `pvm_parent()` function will return the tid of the task that spawned the calling task. Since we run the initial `forkjoin` program from a command prompt, this initial task will not have a parent; it will not have been spawned by some other PVM task but will have been started manually by the user. For the initial fork/join task the result of `pvm_parent()` will not be any particular task id but an error code, `PvmNoParent`. Thus we can distinguish the parent fork/join task from the children by checking whether the result of the `pvm_parent()` call is equal to `PvmNoParent`. If this task is the parent, then it must spawn the children. If it is not the parent, then it must send a message to the parent.

Let's examine the code executed by the parent task. The number of tasks is taken from the command-line as `argv[1]`. If the number of tasks is not legal then we exit the program, calling `pvm_exit()` and then returning. The call to `pvm_exit()` is important because it tells PVM this program will no longer be using any of the PVM facilities. (In this case the task exits and PVM will deduce that the dead task no longer needs its services. Regardless, it is good style to exit cleanly.) Assuming the number of tasks is valid, fork/join will then attempt to spawn the children.

The `pvm_spawn()` call tells PVM to start `ntask` tasks named `argv[0]`. The second parameter is the argument list given to the spawned tasks. In this case we don't care to give the children any particular command-line arguments, so this value is null. The third parameter to spawn, `PvmTaskDefault`, is a flag telling PVM to spawn the tasks in the default location. Had we been interested in placing the children on a specific machine or a machine of a particular architecture, we would have used `PvmTaskHost` or `PvmTaskArch` for this flag and specified the host or architecture as the fourth parameter. Since we don't care where the tasks execute, we use `PvmTaskDefault` for the flag and `null` for the fourth parameter. Finally, `ntask` tells `spawn` how many tasks to start, and the integer array `child` will hold the task ids of the newly spawned children. The return value of `pvm_spawn()` indicates how many tasks were successfully spawned. If `info` is not equal to `ntask`, then some error occurred during the spawn. In case of an error, the error code is placed in the task id array, child, instead of the actual task id; `forkjoin` loops over this array and prints the task ids or any error codes. If no tasks were successfully spawned, then the program exits.

For each child task, the parent receives a message and prints out information about that message. The `pvm_recv()` call receives a message from any task as long as the tag for that message is `JOINTAG`. The return value of `pvm_recv()` is an integer indicating a message buffer. This integer can be used to find out information about message buffers. The subsequent call to `pvm_bufinfo()` does just this; it gets the length, tag, and task id of the sending process for the message indicated by `buf`. In `forkjoin` the messages sent by the children contain a single integer value, the task id of the child task. The `pvm_upkint()` call unpacks the integer from the message into the `mydata` variable. As a sanity check, `forkjoin` tests the value of `mydata` and the task id returned by `pvm_bufinfo()`. If the values differ, the program has a bug, and an error message is printed. Finally, the information about the message is printed, and the parent program exits.

The last segment of code in `forkjoin` will be executed by the child tasks. Before data is placed in a message buffer, the buffer must be initialized by calling `pvm_initsend()`. The parameter `PvmDataDefault` indicates that PVM should do whatever data conversion is needed to assure that the data arrives in the correct format on the destination processor. In some cases this may result in unnecessary data conversions. If you are sure no data conversion will be needed since the destination machine uses the same data format, then you can use `PvmDataRaw` as a parameter to `pvm_initsend()`. The `pvm_pkint()` call places a single integer, `mytid`, into the message buffer. It is important to make sure the corresponding unpack call exactly matches the pack call. Packing an integer and unpacking it as a float will not work correctly. There should be a one-to-one correspondence between pack and unpack calls. Finally, the message is sent to the parent task using a message tag of `JOINTAG`.

```
/*
    Fork Join Example
    Demonstrates how to spawn processes and exchange messages
*/

/* defines and prototypes for the PVM library */
#include <pvm3.h>

/* Maximum number of children this program will spawn */
#define MAXNCHILD    20
/* Tag to use for the joing message */
#define JOINTAG      11

int
main(int argc, char* argv[])
{

    /* number of tasks to spawn, use 3 as the default */
    int ntask = 3;
    /* return code from pvm calls */
    int info;
    /* my task id */
    int mytid;
    /* my parents task id */
    int myparent;
    /* children task id array */
    int child[MAXNCHILD];
    int i, mydata, buf, len, tag, tid;

    /* find out my task id number */
    mytid = pvm_mytid();

    /* check for error */
    if (mytid < 0) {
        /* print out the error */
```

```
        pvm_perror(argv[0]);
        /* exit the program */
        return -1;
        }
/* find my parent's task id number */
myparent = pvm_parent();

/* exit if there is some error other than PvmNoParent */
if ((myparent < 0) && (myparent != PvmNoParent)
    && (myparent != PvmParentNotSet)) {
    pvm_perror(argv[0]);
    pvm_exit();
    return -1;
    }

/* if i don't have a parent then i am the parent */
if (myparent == PvmNoParent || myparent == PvmParentNotSet) {
    /* find out how many tasks to spawn */
    if (argc == 2) ntask = atoi(argv[1]);

    /* make sure ntask is legal */
    if ((ntask < 1) || (ntask > MAXNCHILD)) { pvm_exit(); return 0; }

    /* spawn the child tasks */
    info = pvm_spawn(argv[0], (char**)0, PvmTaskDefault, (char*)0,
        ntask, child);
    /* print out the task ids */
    for (i = 0; i < ntask; i++)
        if (child[i] < 0) /* print the error code in decimal*/
            printf(" %d", child[i]);
        else  /* print the task id in hex */
            printf("t%x\t", child[i]);
    putchar('\n');

    /* make sure spawn succeeded */
    if (info == 0) { pvm_exit(); return -1; }

    /* only expect responses from those spawned correctly */
    ntask = info;

    for (i = 0; i < ntask; i++) {
        /* recv a message from any child process */
        buf = pvm_recv(-1, JOINTAG);
        if (buf < 0) pvm_perror("calling recv");
```

```
            info = pvm_bufinfo(buf, &len, &tag, &tid);
            if (info < 0) pvm_perror("calling pvm_bufinfo");
            info = pvm_upkint(&mydata, 1, 1);
            if (info < 0) pvm_perror("calling pvm_upkint");
            if (mydata != tid) printf("This should not happen!\n");
            printf("Length %d, Tag %d, Tid t%x\n", len, tag, tid);
            }
        pvm_exit();
        return 0;
        }

    /* i'm a child */
    info = pvm_initsend(PvmDataDefault);
    if (info < 0) {
        pvm_perror("calling pvm_initsend"); pvm_exit(); return -1;
        }
    info = pvm_pkint(&mytid, 1, 1);
    if (info < 0) {
        pvm_perror("calling pvm_pkint"); pvm_exit(); return -1;
        }
    info = pvm_send(myparent, JOINTAG);
    if (info < 0) {
        pvm_perror("calling pvm_send"); pvm_exit(); return -1;
        }
    pvm_exit();
    return 0;
}
```

Figure 11.3 shows the output of running fork/join. Notice that the order the messages were received is nondeterministic. Since the main loop of the parent processes messages on a first-come first-served basis, the order of the prints are determined simply by the time it takes messages to travel from the child tasks to the parent.

11.4   Dot Product

Here we show a simple Fortran program, PSDOT, for computing a dot product. The program computes the dot product of two arrays, X and Y. First PSDOT calls PVMFMYTID() and PVMFPARENT(). The PVMFPARENT call will return PVMNOPARENT if the task wasn't spawned by another PVM task. If this is the case, then PSDOT task is the master and must spawn the other worker copies of PSDOT. PSDOT then asks the user for the number of processes to use and the

```
% forkjoin
t10001c t40149  tc0037
Length 4, Tag 11, Tid t40149
Length 4, Tag 11, Tid tc0037
Length 4, Tag 11, Tid t10001c
% forkjoin 4
t10001e t10001d t4014b  tc0038
Length 4, Tag 11, Tid t4014b
Length 4, Tag 11, Tid tc0038
Length 4, Tag 11, Tid t10001d
Length 4, Tag 11, Tid t10001e
```

Figure 11.3
Output of fork/join program.

length of vectors to compute. Each spawned process will receive $n/nproc$ elements
of X and Y, where n is the length of the vectors and $nproc$ is the number of processes
being used in the computation. If $nproc$ does not divide n evenly, then the master
will compute the dot product on extra the elements. The subroutine SGENMAT
randomly generates values for X and Y. PSDOT then spawns $nproc - 1$ copies of
itself and sends each new task a part of the X and Y arrays. The message contains
the length of the subarrays in the message and the subarrays themselves. After
the master spawns the worker processes and sends out the subvectors, the master
then computes the dot-product on its portion of X and Y. The master process then
receives the other local dot products from the worker processes. Notice that the
PVMFRECV call uses a wild card (-1) for the task id parameter. This indicates
that a message from *any* task will satisfy the receive. Using the wild card in this
manner results in a race condition. In this case the race condition does not cause a
problem since addition is commutative. In other words, it doesn't matter in which
order we add up the partial sums from the workers. Unless one is certain that the
race will not affect the program adversely, race conditions should be avoided.

Once the master receives all the local dot products and sums them into a global
dot product, it then calculates the entire dot product locally. These two results
are then subtracted and the difference between the two values is printed. A small
difference can be expected due to the variation in floating-point roundoff errors.

If the PSDOT program is a worker, then it receives a message from the master
process containing subarrays of X and Y. It calculates the dot product of these
subarrays and sends the result back to the master process. In the interests of
brevity we do not include the SGENMAT and SDOT subroutines.

```
      PROGRAM PSDOT
*
*  PSDOT performs a parallel inner (or dot) product, where the vectors
*  X and Y start out on a master node, which then sets up the virtual
*  machine, farms out the data and work, and sums up the local pieces
*  to get a global inner product.
*
*        .. External Subroutines ..
         EXTERNAL PVMFMYTID, PVMFPARENT, PVMFSPAWN, PVMFEXIT, PVMFINITSEND
         EXTERNAL PVMFPACK, PVMFSEND, PVMFRECV, PVMFUNPACK, SGENMAT
*
*        .. External Functions ..
         INTEGER ISAMAX
         REAL SDOT
         EXTERNAL ISAMAX, SDOT
*
*        .. Intrinsic Functions ..
         INTRINSIC MOD
*
*        .. Parameters ..
         INTEGER MAXN
         PARAMETER ( MAXN = 8000 )
         INCLUDE 'fpvm3.h'
*
*        .. Scalars ..
         INTEGER N, LN, MYTID, NPROCS, IBUF, IERR
         INTEGER I, J, K
         REAL LDOT, GDOT
*
*        .. Arrays ..
         INTEGER TIDS(0:63)
         REAL X(MAXN), Y(MAXN)
*
*  Enroll in PVM and get my and the master process' task ID number
*
         CALL PVMFMYTID( MYTID )
         CALL PVMFPARENT( TIDS(0) )
*
*  If I need to spawn other processes (I am master process)
*
         IF ( TIDS(0) .EQ. PVMNOPARENT ) THEN
*
*        Get starting information
*
```

```
          WRITE(*,*) 'How many processes should participate (1-64)?'
          READ(*,*) NPROCS
          WRITE(*,2000) MAXN
          READ(*,*) N
          TIDS(0) = MYTID
          IF ( N .GT. MAXN ) THEN
             WRITE(*,*) 'N too large.  Increase parameter MAXN to run'//
     $                  'this case.'
             STOP
          END IF
*
*         LN is the number of elements of the dot product to do
*         locally.  Everyone has the same number, with the master
*         getting any left over elements.  J stores the number of
*         elements rest of procs do.
*
          J = N / NPROCS
          LN = J + MOD(N, NPROCS)
          I = LN + 1
*
*         Randomly generate X and Y
*         Note: SGENMAT() routine is not provided here
*
          CALL SGENMAT( N, 1, X, N, MYTID, NPROCS, MAXN, J )
          CALL SGENMAT( N, 1, Y, N, I, N, LN, NPROCS )
*
*         Loop over all worker processes
*
          DO 10 K = 1, NPROCS-1
*
*            Spawn process and check for error
*
             CALL PVMFSPAWN( 'psdot', 0, 'anywhere', 1, TIDS(K), IERR )
             IF (IERR .NE. 1) THEN
                WRITE(*,*) 'ERROR, could not spawn process #',K,
     $                     '. Dying . . .'
                CALL PVMFEXIT( IERR )
                STOP
             END IF
*
*            Send out startup info
*
             CALL PVMFINITSEND( PVMDEFAULT, IBUF )
             CALL PVMFPACK( INTEGER4, J, 1, 1, IERR )
```

```
            CALL PVMFPACK( REAL4, X(I), J, 1, IERR )
            CALL PVMFPACK( REAL4, Y(I), J, 1, IERR )
            CALL PVMFSEND( TIDS(K), 0, IERR )
            I = I + J
   10     CONTINUE
*
*         Figure master's part of dot product
*         SDOT() is part of the BLAS Library (compile with -lblas)
*
          GDOT = SDOT( LN, X, 1, Y, 1 )
*
*         Receive the local dot products, and
*         add to get the global dot product
*
          DO 20 K = 1, NPROCS-1
             CALL PVMFRECV( -1, 1, IBUF )
             CALL PVMFUNPACK( REAL4, LDOT, 1, 1, IERR )
             GDOT = GDOT + LDOT
   20     CONTINUE
*
*         Print out result
*
          WRITE(*,*) ' '
          WRITE(*,*) '<x,y> = ',GDOT
*
*         Do sequential dot product and subtract from
*         distributed dot product to get desired error estimate
*
          LDOT = SDOT( N, X, 1, Y, 1 )
          WRITE(*,*) '<x,y> : sequential dot product.  <x,y>^ : '//
     $               'distributed dot product.'
          WRITE(*,*) '| <x,y> - <x,y>^ | = ',ABS(GDOT - LDOT)
          WRITE(*,*) 'Run completed.'
*
*      If I am a worker process (i.e. spawned by master process)
*
        ELSE
*
*         Receive startup info
*
          CALL PVMFRECV( TIDS(0), 0, IBUF )
          CALL PVMFUNPACK( INTEGER4, LN, 1, 1, IERR )
          CALL PVMFUNPACK( REAL4, X, LN, 1, IERR )
          CALL PVMFUNPACK( REAL4, Y, LN, 1, IERR )
```

```
*
*       Figure local dot product and send it in to master
*
        LDOT = SDOT( LN, X, 1, Y, 1 )
        CALL PVMFINITSEND( PVMDEFAULT, IBUF )
        CALL PVMFPACK( REAL4, LDOT, 1, 1, IERR )
        CALL PVMFSEND( TIDS(0), 1, IERR )
      END IF
*
      CALL PVMFEXIT( 0 )
*
1000  FORMAT(I10,' Successfully spawned process #',I2,', TID =',I10)
2000  FORMAT('Enter the length of vectors to multiply (1 -',I7,'):')
      STOP
*
*     End program PSDOT
*
      END
```

11.5   Matrix Multiply

In this example we program a matrix multiply algorithm described by Fox et al. in [9]. The mmult program can be found at the end of this section. The mmult program will calculate $C = AB$ where C, A, and B are all square matrices. For simplicity we assume that $m \times m$ tasks are used to calculate the solution. Each task calculates a subblock of the resulting matrix C. The block size and the value of m are given as a command-line argument to the program. The matrices A and B are also stored as blocks distributed over the m^2 tasks. Before delving into the details of the program, let us first describe the algorithm at a high level.

In our grid of $m \times m$ tasks, each task (t_{ij}, where $0 \le i, j < m$), initially contains blocks C_{ij}, A_{ij}, and B_{ij}. In the first step of the algorithm the tasks on the diagonal (t_{ij} where $i = j$) send their block A_{ii} to all the other tasks in row i. After the transmission of A_{ii}, all tasks calculate $A_{ii} \times B_{ij}$ and add the result into C_{ij}. In the next step, the column blocks of B are rotated. That is, t_{ij} sends its block of B to $t_{(i-1)j}$. (Task t_{0j} sends its B block to $t_{(m-1)j}$). The tasks now return to the first step, $A_{i(i+1)}$ is multicast to all other tasks in row i, and the algorithm continues. After m iterations the C matrix contains $A \times B$, and the B matrix has been rotated back into place.

Let us now go over the matrix multiply as it is programmed in PVM. In PVM there is no restriction on which tasks may communicate with which other tasks.

However, for this program we would like to think of the tasks as a two-dimensional conceptual torus. In order to enumerate the tasks, each task joins the group `mmult`. Group ids are used to map tasks to our torus. The first task to join a group is given the group id of zero. In the `mmult` program, the task with group id zero spawns the other tasks and sends the parameters for the matrix multiply to those tasks. The parameters are m and *bklsize*, the square root of the number of blocks and the size of a block, respectively. After all the tasks have been spawned and the parameters transmitted, `pvm_barrier()` is called to make sure all the tasks have joined the group. If the barrier is not performed, later calls to `pvm_gettid()` might fail, since a task may not have yet joined the group.

After the barrier, the task ids for the other tasks are stored in the `row` in the array `myrow`. Specifically, the program calculates group ids for all the tasks in the row, and we ask PVM for the task id for the corresponding group id. Next the program allocates the blocks for the matrices using `malloc()`. (In an actual application program we would expect that the matrices would already be allocated.) Then the program calculates the row and column of the block of C it will be computing; this is based on the value of the group id. The group ids range from 0 to $m - 1$ inclusive. Thus, the integer division of $(mygid/m)$ will give the task's row and $(mygid \bmod m)$ will give the column if we assume a row major mapping of group ids to tasks. Using a similar mapping, we calculate the group id of the task directly *above* and *below* in the torus and store their task ids in `up` and `down`, respectively.

Next the blocks are initialized by calling `InitBlock()`. This function simply initializes A to random values, B to the identity matrix, and C to zeros. This will allow us to verify the computation at the end of the program by checking that $A = C$.

Finally we enter the main loop to calculate the matrix multiply. First the tasks on the diagonal multicast their block of A to the other tasks in their row. Note that the array `myrow` actually contains the task id of the task doing the multicast. Recall that `pvm_mcast()` will send to all the tasks in the tasks array except the calling task. This works well in the case of `mmult`, since we don't want to have to needlessly handle the extra message coming into the multicasting task with an extra `pvm_recv()`. Both the multicasting task and the tasks receiving the block calculate the AB for the diagonal block and the block of B residing in the task.

After the subblocks have been multiplied and added into the C block, we now shift the B blocks vertically. This is done by packing the block of B into a message and sending it to the `up` task id and then receiving a new B block from the `down` task id.

Note that we use different message tags for sending the A blocks and the B blocks as well as for different iterations of the loop. We also fully specify the task ids when doing a pvm_recv(). It's tempting to use wild cards for the fields of pvm_recv(); however, such use can be dangerous. For instance, had we incorrectly calculated the value for up and used a wild card for the pvm_recv() instead of down, it is possible that we would be sending messages to the wrong tasks without knowing it. In this example we fully specify messages, thereby reducing the possibility of receiving a message from the wrong task or the wrong phase of the algorithm.

Once the computation is complete, we check to see that $A = C$ just to verify that the matrix multiply correctly calculated the values of C. This step would not be done in a matrix multiply library routine, for example.

You do not have to call pvm_lvgroup() because PVM will realize that the task has exited and will remove it from the group. It is good form, however, to leave the group before calling pvm_exit(). The reset command from the PVM console will reset all the PVM groups. The pvm_gstat command will print the status of any groups that currently exist.

```
/*
   Matrix Multiply
*/

/* defines and prototypes for the PVM library */
#include <pvm3.h>
#include <stdio.h>

/* Maximum number of children this program will spawn */
#define MAXNTIDS    100
#define MAXROW      10

/* Message tags */
#define ATAG        2
#define BTAG        3
#define DIMTAG      5

void
InitBlock(float *a, float *b, float *c, int blk, int row, int col)
{
    int len, ind;
    int i,j;

    srand(pvm_mytid());
    len = blk*blk;
```

```
    for (ind = 0; ind < len; ind++)
        { a[ind] = (float)(rand()%1000)/100.0; c[ind] = 0.0; }
    for (i = 0; i < blk; i++) {
        for (j = 0; j < blk; j++) {
            if (row == col)
                b[j*blk+i] = (i==j)? 1.0 : 0.0;
            else
                b[j*blk+i] = 0.0;
            }
        }
}

void
BlockMult(float* c, float* a, float* b, int blk)
{
    int i,j,k;

    for (i = 0; i < blk; i++)
        for (j = 0; j < blk; j ++)
            for (k = 0; k < blk; k++)
                c[i*blk+j] += (a[i*blk+k] * b[k*blk+j]);
}

int
main(int argc, char* argv[])
{

    /* number of tasks to spawn, use 3 as the default */
    int ntask = 2;
    /* return code from pvm calls */
    int info;
    /* my task and group id */
    int mytid, mygid;
    /* children task id array */
    int child[MAXNTIDS-1];
    int i, m, blksize;
    /* array of the tids in my row */
    int myrow[MAXROW];
    float *a, *b, *c, *atmp;
    int row, col, up, down;

    /* find out my task id number */
    mytid = pvm_mytid();
    pvm_setopt(PvmRoute, PvmRouteDirect);
```

```
/* check for error */
if (mytid < 0) {
    /* print out the error */
    pvm_perror(argv[0]);
    /* exit the program */
    return -1;
    }

/* join the mmult group */
mygid = pvm_joingroup("mmult");
if (mygid < 0) {
    pvm_perror(argv[0]); pvm_exit(); return -1;
    }

/* if my group id is 0 then I must spawn the other tasks */
if (mygid == 0) {
    /* find out how many tasks to spawn */
    if (argc == 3) {
        m = atoi(argv[1]);
        blksize = atoi(argv[2]);
        }
    if (argc < 3) {
        fprintf(stderr, "usage: mmult m blk\n");
        pvm_lvgroup("mmult"); pvm_exit(); return -1;
        }

    /* make sure ntask is legal */
    ntask = m*m;
    if ((ntask < 1) || (ntask >= MAXNTIDS)) {
        fprintf(stderr, "ntask = %d not valid.\n", ntask);
        pvm_lvgroup("mmult"); pvm_exit(); return -1;
        }
    /* no need to spawn if there is only one task */
    if (ntask == 1) goto barrier;

    /* spawn the child tasks */
    info = pvm_spawn("mmult", (char**)0, PvmTaskDefault, (char*)0,
        ntask-1, child);

    /* make sure spawn succeeded */
    if (info != ntask-1) {
        pvm_lvgroup("mmult"); pvm_exit(); return -1;
        }
```

```
    /* send the matrix dimension */
    pvm_initsend(PvmDataDefault);
    pvm_pkint(&m, 1, 1);
    pvm_pkint(&blksize, 1, 1);
    pvm_mcast(child, ntask-1, DIMTAG);
    }
else {
    /* recv the matrix dimension */
    pvm_recv(pvm_gettid("mmult", 0), DIMTAG);
    pvm_upkint(&m, 1, 1);
    pvm_upkint(&blksize, 1, 1);
    ntask = m*m;
    }

/* make sure all tasks have joined the group */

info = pvm_barrier("mmult",ntask);
if (info < 0) pvm_perror(argv[0]);

/* find the tids in my row */
for (i = 0; i < m; i++)
    myrow[i] = pvm_gettid("mmult", (mygid/m)*m + i);

/* allocate the memory for the local blocks */
a = (float*)malloc(sizeof(float)*blksize*blksize);
b = (float*)malloc(sizeof(float)*blksize*blksize);
c = (float*)malloc(sizeof(float)*blksize*blksize);
atmp = (float*)malloc(sizeof(float)*blksize*blksize);
/* check for valid pointers */
if (!(a && b && c && atmp)) {
    fprintf(stderr, "%s: out of memory!\n", argv[0]);
    free(a); free(b); free(c); free(atmp);
    pvm_lvgroup("mmult"); pvm_exit(); return -1;
    }

/* find my block's row and column */
row = mygid/m; col = mygid % m;
/* calculate the neighbor's above and below */
up = pvm_gettid("mmult", ((row)?(row-1):(m-1))*m+col);
down = pvm_gettid("mmult", ((row == (m-1))?col:(row+1)*m+col));

/* initialize the blocks */
InitBlock(a, b, c, blksize, row, col);
```

```
/* do the matrix multiply */
for (i = 0; i < m; i++) {
    /* mcast the block of matrix A */
    if (col == (row + i)%m) {
        pvm_initsend(PvmDataDefault);
        pvm_pkfloat(a, blksize*blksize, 1);
        pvm_mcast(myrow, m, (i+1)*ATAG);
        BlockMult(c,a,b,blksize);
        }
    else {
        pvm_recv(pvm_gettid("mmult", row*m + (row +i)%m), (i+1)*ATAG);
        pvm_upkfloat(atmp, blksize*blksize, 1);
        BlockMult(c,atmp,b,blksize);
        }
    /* rotate the columns of B */
    pvm_initsend(PvmDataDefault);
    pvm_pkfloat(b, blksize*blksize, 1);
    pvm_send(up, (i+1)*BTAG);
    pvm_recv(down, (i+1)*BTAG);
    pvm_upkfloat(b, blksize*blksize, 1);
    }

/* check it */
for (i = 0 ; i < blksize*blksize; i++)
    if (a[i] != c[i])
        printf("Error a[%d] (%g) != c[%d] (%g) \n", i, a[i],i,c[i]);

printf("Done.\n");
free(a); free(b); free(c); free(atmp);
pvm_lvgroup("mmult");
pvm_exit();
return 0;
}
```

11.6   One-Dimensional Heat Equation

Here we present a PVM program that calculates heat diffusion through a substrate, in this case a wire. Consider the one-dimensional heat equation on a thin wire:

$$\frac{\partial A}{\partial t} = \frac{\partial^2 A}{\partial x^2} \tag{11.6.1}$$

and a discretization of the form

$$\frac{A_{i+1,j} - A_{i,j}}{\triangle t} = \frac{A_{i,j+1} - 2A_{i,j} + A_{i,j-1}}{\triangle x^2},$$ (11.6.2)

giving the explicit formula

$$A_{i+1,j} = A_{i,j} + \frac{\triangle t}{\triangle x^2}(A_{i,j+1} - 2A_{i,j} + A_{i,j-1}).$$ (11.6.3)

The initial and boundary conditions are

$A(t, 0) = 0$, $A(t, 1) = 0$ for all t
$A(0, x) = \sin(\pi x)$ for $0 \leq x \leq 1$.
The pseudocode for this computation is as follows:

```
for i = 1:tsteps-1;
    t = t+dt;
    a(i+1,1)=0;
    a(i+1,n+2)=0;
    for j = 2:n+1;
        a(i+1,j)=a(i,j) + mu*(a(i,j+1)-2*a(i,j)+a(i,j-1));
    end;
end
```

For this example we use a master/worker programming model. The master, heat.c, spawns five copies of the program heatslv. The workers compute the heat diffusion for subsections of the wire in parallel. At each time step the workers exchange boundary information, in this case the temperature of the wire at the boundaries between processors.

Let's take a closer look at the code. In heat.c the array solution will hold the solution for the heat diffusion equation at each time step. First the heatslv tasks are spawned. Next, the initial dataset is computed. Notice the ends of the wires are given initial temperature values of zero.

The main part of the program is then executed four times, each with a different value for $\triangle t$. A timer is used to compute the elapsed time of each compute phase. The initial datasets are sent to the heatslv tasks. The left and right neighbor task ids are sent along with the initial dataset. The heatslv tasks use these to communicate boundary information. Alternatively, we could have used the PVM group calls to map tasks to segments of the wire. By using this approach we would have avoided explicitly communicating the task ids to the slave processes.

After sending the initial data, the master process waits for results. When the results arrive, they are integrated into the solution matrix, the elapsed time is calculated, and the solution is written to the output file.

Once the data for all four phases have been computed and stored, the master program prints out the elapsed times and kills the slave processes.

```
/*
heat.c

    Use PVM to solve a simple heat diffusion differential equation,
    using 1 master program and 5 slaves.

    The master program sets up the data, communicates it to the slaves
    and waits for the results to be sent from the slaves.
    Produces xgraph ready files of the results.

*/

#include "pvm3.h"
#include <stdio.h>
#include <math.h>
#include <time.h>
#define SLAVENAME "heatslv"
#define NPROC 5
#define TIMESTEP 100
#define PLOTINC 10
#define SIZE 1000

int num_data = SIZE/NPROC;

main()
{   int mytid, task_ids[NPROC], i, j;
    int left, right, k, l;
    int step = TIMESTEP;
    int info;

    double init[SIZE], solution[TIMESTEP][SIZE];
    double result[TIMESTEP*SIZE/NPROC], deltax2;
    FILE *filenum;
    char *filename[4][7];
    double deltat[4];
    time_t t0;
    int etime[4];
```

```
        filename[0][0] = "graph1";
        filename[1][0] = "graph2";
        filename[2][0] = "graph3";
        filename[3][0] = "graph4";

        deltat[0] = 5.0e-1;
        deltat[1] = 5.0e-3;
        deltat[2] = 5.0e-6;
        deltat[3] = 5.0e-9;

/* enroll in pvm */
        mytid = pvm_mytid();

/* spawn the slave tasks */
        info = pvm_spawn(SLAVENAME,(char **)0,PvmTaskDefault,"",
            NPROC,task_ids);
/* create the initial data set */
        for (i = 0; i < SIZE; i++)
            init[i] = sin(M_PI * ( (double)i / (double)(SIZE-1) ));
        init[0] = 0.0;
        init[SIZE-1] = 0.0;

/* run the problem 4 times for different values of delta t */
        for (l = 0; l < 4; l++) {
            deltax2 = (deltat[l]/pow(1.0/(double)SIZE,2.0));
            /* start timing for this run */
            time(&t0);
            etime[l] = t0;
/* send the initial data to the slaves. */
/* include neighbor info for exchanging boundary data */
            for (i = 0; i < NPROC; i++) {
                pvm_initsend(PvmDataDefault);
                left = (i == 0) ? 0 : task_ids[i-1];
                pvm_pkint(&left, 1, 1);
                right = (i == (NPROC-1)) ? 0 : task_ids[i+1];
                pvm_pkint(&right, 1, 1);
                pvm_pkint(&step, 1, 1);
                pvm_pkdouble(&deltax2, 1, 1);
                pvm_pkint(&num_data, 1, 1);
                pvm_pkdouble(&init[num_data*i], num_data, 1);
                pvm_send(task_ids[i], 4);
                }

/* wait for the results */
```

```
        for (i = 0; i < NPROC; i++) {
            pvm_recv(task_ids[i], 7);
            pvm_upkdouble(&result[0], num_data*TIMESTEP, 1);
/* update the solution */
            for (j = 0; j < TIMESTEP; j++)
                for (k = 0; k < num_data; k++)
                    solution[j][num_data*i+k] = result[wh(j,k)];
        }

/* stop timing */
        time(&t0);
        etime[1] = t0 - etime[1];

/* produce the output */
        filenum = fopen(filename[1][0], "w");
        fprintf(filenum,"TitleText: Wire Heat over Delta Time: %e\n",
            deltat[1]);
        fprintf(filenum,"XUnitText: Distance\nYUnitText: Heat\n");
        for (i = 0; i < TIMESTEP; i = i + PLOTINC) {
            fprintf(filenum,"\"Time index: %d\n",i);
            for (j = 0; j < SIZE; j++)
                fprintf(filenum,"%d %e\n",j, solution[i][j]);
            fprintf(filenum,"\n");
            }
        fclose (filenum);
    }

/* print the timing information */
    printf("Problem size: %d\n",SIZE);
    for (i = 0; i < 4; i++)
        printf("Time for run %d: %d sec\n",i,etime[i]);

/* kill the slave processes */
    for (i = 0; i < NPROC; i++) pvm_kill(task_ids[i]);
    pvm_exit();
}

int wh(x, y)
int x, y;
{
    return(x*num_data+y);
}
```

The heatslv programs do the actual computation of the heat diffusion through the wire. The worker program consists of an infinite loop that receives an initial dataset, iteratively computes a solution based on this dataset (exchanging boundary information with neighbors on each iteration), and sends the resulting partial solution back to the master process. As an alternative to using an infinite loop in the worker tasks, we could send a special message to the slave ordering it to exit. Instead, we simply use the infinite loop in the worker tasks and kill them off from the master program. A third option would be to have the workers execute only once, exiting after processing a single dataset from the master. This would require placing the master's spawn call inside the main `for` loop of `heat.c`. While this option would work, it would needlessly add overhead to the overall computation.

For each time step and before each compute phase, the boundary values of the temperature matrix are exchanged. The left-hand boundary elements are first sent to the left neighbor task and received from the right neighbor task. Symmetrically, the right-hand boundary elements are sent to the right neighbor and then received from the left neighbor. The task ids for the neighbors are checked to make sure no attempt is made to send or receive messages to nonexistent tasks.

```
/*

heatslv.c

    The slaves receive the initial data from the host,
    exchange boundary information with neighbors,
    and calculate the heat change in the wire.
    This is done for a number of iterations, sent by the master.

*/

#include "pvm3.h"
#include <stdio.h>

int num_data;

main()
{
    int mytid, left, right, i, j, master;
    int timestep;

    double *init, *A;
    double leftdata, rightdata, delta, leftside, rightside;

/* enroll in pvm */
    mytid = pvm_mytid();
```

```
      master = pvm_parent();

/* receive my data from the master program */
  while(1) {
    pvm_recv(master, 4);
    pvm_upkint(&left, 1, 1);
    pvm_upkint(&right, 1, 1);
    pvm_upkint(&timestep, 1, 1);
    pvm_upkdouble(&delta, 1, 1);
    pvm_upkint(&num_data, 1, 1);
    init = (double *) malloc(num_data*sizeof(double));
    pvm_upkdouble(init, num_data, 1);

/* copy the initial data into my working array */

    A = (double *) malloc(num_data * timestep * sizeof(double));
    for (i = 0; i < num_data; i++) A[i] = init[i];

/* perform the calculation */

  for (i = 0; i < timestep-1; i++) {
    /* trade boundary info with my neighbors */
    /*  send left, receive right   */
    if (left != 0) {
        pvm_initsend(PvmDataDefault);
        pvm_pkdouble(&A[wh(i,0)],1,1);
        pvm_send(left, 5);
        }
    if (right != 0) {
        pvm_recv(right, 5);
        pvm_upkdouble(&rightdata, 1, 1);
    /* send right, receive left */
        pvm_initsend(PvmDataDefault);
        pvm_pkdouble(&A[wh(i,num_data-1)],1,1);
        pvm_send(right, 6);
        }
    if (left != 0) {
        pvm_recv(left, 6);
        pvm_upkdouble(&leftdata,1,1);
        }

/* do the calculations for this iteration */

    for (j = 0; j < num_data; j++) {
```

```
        leftside = (j == 0) ? leftdata : A[wh(i,j-1)];
        rightside = (j == (num_data-1)) ? rightdata : A[wh(i,j+1)];
        if ((j==0)&&(left==0))
            A[wh(i+1,j)] = 0.0;
        else if ((j==(num_data-1))&&(right==0))
            A[wh(i+1,j)] = 0.0;
        else
            A[wh(i+1,j)]=
                A[wh(i,j)]+delta*(rightside-2*A[wh(i,j)]+leftside);
        }
    }

/* send the results back to the master program */

    pvm_initsend(PvmDataDefault);
    pvm_pkdouble(&A[0],num_data*timestep,1);
    pvm_send(master,7);
    }

/* just for good measure */
    pvm_exit();
}

int wh(x, y)
int x, y;
{
    return(x*num_data+y);
}
```

In this section we have given a variety of example programs written in both Fortran and C. These examples demonstrate various ways of writing PVM programs. Some divide the application into two separate programs while others use a single program with conditionals to handle spawning and computing phases. These examples show different styles of communication, both among worker tasks and between worker and master tasks. In some cases messages are used for synchronization, and in others the master processes simply kill of the workers when they are no longer needed. We hope that these examples will help you understand how to write better PVM programs and to evaluate the design tradeoffs involved.

11.7   Using PVM

This section describes how to set up the PVM software package, how to configure a simple virtual machine, and how to compile and run the example programs supplied with PVM. The first part describes the straightforward use of PVM and the most common problems in setting up and running PVM. The latter part describes some of the more advanced options available for customizing your PVM environment.

11.7.1   Setting Up PVM

One of the reasons for PVM's popularity is that it is simple to set up and use. PVM does not require special privileges to be installed. Anyone with a valid login on the hosts can do so. In addition, only one person at an organization needs to get and install PVM for everyone at that organization to use it.

PVM uses two environment variables when starting and running. Each PVM user needs to set these two variables to use PVM. The first variable is PVM_ROOT, which is set to the location of the installed pvm3 directory. The second variable is PVM_ARCH, which tells PVM the architecture of this host and thus what executables to pick from the PVM_ROOT directory.

The easiest method is to set these two variables in your .cshrc file (this assumes you are using csh). Here is an example for setting PVM_ROOT:

```
setenv PVM_ROOT /home/hostnme/username/pvm3
```

The recommended method to set PVM_ARCH is to append the file PVM_ROOT/lib/ cshrc.stub onto your .cshrc file. The stub should be placed after PATH and PVM_ROOT are defined. This stub automatically determines the PVM_ARCH for this host and is particularly useful when the user shares a common file system (such as NFS) across several different architectures.

If PVM is already installed at your site, you can skip ahead to "Starting PVM." The PVM source comes with directories and makefiles for Linux and most architectures you are likely to have. Building for each architecture type is done automatically by logging on to a host, going into the PVM_ROOT directory, and typing make. The makefile will automatically determine which architecture it is being executed on, create appropriate subdirectories, and build pvmd3, libpvm3.a, and libfpvm3.a, pvmgs, and libgpvm3.a. It places all these files in PVM_ROOT/lib/PVM_ ARCH with the exception of pvmgs, which is placed in PVM_ROOT/bin/PVM_ARCH.

Setup Summary

- Set PVM_ROOT and PVM_ARCH in your .cshrc file.

- Build PVM for each architecture type.

- Create an `.rhosts` file on each host listing all the hosts.

- Create a `$HOME/.xpvm_hosts` file listing all the hosts prepended by an "&".

11.7.2   Starting PVM

Before we go over the steps to compile and run parallel PVM programs, you should be sure you can start up PVM and configure a virtual machine. On any host on which PVM has been installed you can type

```
% pvm
```

and you should get back a PVM console prompt signifying that PVM is now running on this host. You can add hosts to your virtual machine by typing at the console prompt

```
pvm> add hostname
```

You also can delete hosts (except the one you are on) from your virtual machine by typing

```
pvm> delete hostname
```

If you get the message "Can't Start `pvmd`," PVM will run autodiagnostics and report the reason found.

To see what the present virtual machine looks like, you can type

```
pvm> conf
```

To see what PVM tasks are running on the virtual machine, you type

```
pvm> ps -a
```

Of course, you don't have any tasks running yet. If you type "quit" at the console prompt, the console will quit, but your virtual machine and tasks will continue to run. At any command prompt on any host in the virtual machine you can type

```
% pvm
```

and you will get the message "pvm already running" and the console prompt. When you are finished with the virtual machine you should type

```
pvm> halt
```

This command kills any PVM tasks, shuts down the virtual machine, and exits the console. This is the recommended method to stop PVM because it makes sure that the virtual machine shuts down cleanly.

You should practice starting and stopping and adding hosts to PVM until you are comfortable with the PVM console. A full description of the PVM console and its many command options is given in Sections 11.8 and 11.9.

If you don't wish to type in a bunch of hostnames each time, there is a hostfile option. You can list the hostnames in a file one per line and then type

```
% pvm hostfile
```

PVM will then add all the listed hosts simultaneously before the console prompt appears. Several options can be specified on a per host basis in the hostfile; see Section 11.9 if you wish to customize your virtual machine for a particular application or environment.

PVM may also be started in other ways. The functions of the console and a performance monitor have been combined in a graphical user interface called XPVM, which is available from the PVM web site. If XPVM has been installed at your site, then it can be used to start PVM. To start PVM with this interface type:

```
% xpvm
```

The menu button labeled "hosts" will pull down a list of hosts you can add. By clicking on a hostname it is added and an icon of the machine appears in an animation of the virtual machine. A host is deleted if you click on a hostname that is already in the virtual machine. On startup XPVM reads the file $HOME/.xpvm_hosts, which is a list of hosts to display in this menu. Hosts without leading "&" are added all at once at start up.

The quit and halt buttons work just like the PVM console. If you quit XPVM and then restart it, XPVM will automatically display what the running virtual machine looks like. Practice starting and stopping and adding hosts with XPVM. If there are errors they should appear in the window where you started XPVM.

11.7.3 Running PVM Programs

In this section you will learn how to compile and run the example programs supplied with the PVM software. These example programs make useful templates on which to base your own PVM programs.

The first step is to copy the example programs into your own area:

```
% cp -r $PVM_ROOT/examples $HOME/pvm3/examples
% cd $HOME/pvm3/examples
```

The examples directory contains a `Makefile.aimk` and `Readme` file that describe how to build the examples. PVM supplies an architecture independent make, `aimk` that automatically determines `PVM_ARCH` and links any operating system specific libraries to your application. `aimk` was automatically added to your `$PATH` when you placed the `cshrc.stub` in your `.cshrc` file. Using `aimk` allows you to leave the source code and makefile unchanged as you compile across different architectures.

The master/worker programming model is the most popular model used in cluster computing. To compile the master/slave C example, type

```
% aimk master slave
```

If you prefer to work with Fortran, compile the Fortran version with

```
% aimk fmaster fslave
```

Depending on the location of `PVM_ROOT`, the `INCLUDE` statement at the top of the Fortran examples may need to be changed. If `PVM_ROOT` is not `HOME/pvm3`, then change the include to point to `$PVM_ROOT/include/fpvm3.h`. Note that `PVM_ROOT` is not expanded inside the Fortran, so you must insert the actual path.

The makefile moves the executables to `$HOME/pvm3/bin/PVM_ARCH` which is the default location PVM will look for them on all hosts. If your file system is not common across all your PVM hosts, then you will have to build or copy (depending on the architecture) these executables on all your PVM hosts.

From one window start up PVM and configure some hosts. These examples are designed to run on any number of hosts, including one. In another window, `cd` to the location of the PVM executables and type

```
% master
```

The program will ask about the number of tasks. This number does not have to match the number of hosts in these examples. Try several combinations.

The first example illustrates the ability to run a PVM program from a prompt on any host in the virtual machine. This is how you would run a serial `a.out` program on a workstation. Te next example, which is also a master/slave model called `hitc`, shows how to spawn PVM jobs from the PVM console and also from XPVM.

The model `hitc` illustrates dynamic load balancing using the pool of tasks paradigm. In this paradigm, the master program manages a large queue of tasks, always sending idle slave programs more work to do until the queue is empty. This paradigm is effective in situations where the hosts have very different computational powers because the least-loaded or more powerful hosts do more of the work and all the hosts stay busy until the end of the problem. To compile `hitc`, type

```
% aimk hitc hitc_slave
```

Since `hitc` does not require any user input, it can be spawned directly from the PVM console. Start the PVM console, and add a few hosts. At the PVM console prompt, type

```
pvm> spawn -> hitc
```

The "->" spawn option causes all the print statements in `hitc` and in the slaves to appear in the console window. This can be a useful feature when debugging your first few PVM programs. You may wish to experiment with this option by placing print statements in `hitc.f` and `hitc_slave.f` and recompiling.

To get an idea of XPVM's real-time animation capabilities, you again can use `hitc`. Start up XPVM, and build a virtual machine with four hosts. Click on the "tasks" button and select "spawn" from the menu. Type "hitc" where XPVM asks for the command, and click on "start". You will see the host icons light up as the machines become busy. You will see the `hitc_slave` tasks get spawned and see all the messages that travel between the tasks in the *Space Time* display. Several other views are selectable from the XPVM "views" menu. The "task output" view is equivalent to the "->" option in the PVM console. It causes the standard output from all tasks to appear in the window that pops up.

Programs that are spawned from XPVM (and the PVM console) are subject to one restriction: they must not contain any interactive input, such as asking for how many slaves to start up or how big a problem to solve. This type of information can be read from a file or put on the command-line as arguments, but there is nothing in place to get user input from the keyboard to a potentially remote task.

11.8   PVM Console Details

The PVM console, called `pvm`, is a standalone PVM task that allows you to interactively start, query, and modify the virtual machine. The console may be started and stopped multiple times on any of the hosts in the virtual machine without affecting PVM or any applications that may be running.

When the console is started, `pvm` determines whether PVM is already running and, if not, automatically executes `pvmd` on this host, passing `pvmd` the command-line options and hostfile. Thus, PVM need not be running to start the console.

```
pvm [-n<hostname>] [hostfile]
```

The $-n$ option is useful for specifying another name for the master `pvmd` (in case hostname doesn't match the IP address you want). This feature becomes very useful with Beowulf clusters because the nodes of the cluster sometime are on their own network. In this case the front-end node will have two hostnames: one for the cluster and one for the external network. The $-n$ option lets you specify the cluster name directly during PVM atartup.

Once started, the console prints the prompt

```
pvm>
```

and accepts commands from standard input. The available commands are as follows:

add followed by one or more hostnames, adds these hosts to the virtual machine.

alias defines or lists command aliases.

conf lists the configuration of the virtual machine including hostname, `pvmd` task ID, architecture type, and a relative speed rating.

delete followed by one or more hostnames, deletes these hosts from the virtual machine. PVM processes still running on these hosts are lost .

echo echoes arguments.

halt kills all PVM processes including console and then shuts down PVM. All daemons exit.

help can be used to get information about any of the interactive commands. The `help` command may be followed by a command name that will list options and flags available for this command.

id prints console task id.

jobs lists running jobs.

kill can be used to terminate any PVM process.

mstat shows status of specified hosts.

ps -a lists all processes currently on the virtual machine, their locations, their task IDs, and their parents' task IDs.

pstat shows status of a single PVM process.

quit exits the console, leaving daemons and PVM jobs running.

reset kills all PVM processes except consoles, and resets all the internal PVM tables and message queues. The daemons are left in an idle state.

setenv displays or sets environment variables.

sig followed by a signal number and tid, sends the signal to the task.

spawn starts a PVM application. Options include the following:

-count shows the number of tasks; default is 1

-(host) spawn on host; default is any

-(PVM_ARCH) spawn of hosts of type PVM_ARCH

-? enable debugging

-> redirect task output to console

->file redirect task output to file

->>file redirect task output append to file

- trace job; display output on console

-file trace job; output to file

unalias undefines command alias.

version prints version of PVM being used.

The console reads `$HOME/.pvmrc` before reading commands from the `tty`, so you can do things like

```
alias ? help
alias h help
alias j jobs
setenv PVM_EXPORT DISPLAY
# print my id
echo new pvm shell
id
```

PVM supports the use of multiple consoles. It is possible to run a console on any host in an existing virtual machine and even multiple consoles on the same machine. It is possible to start up a console in the middle of a PVM application and check on its progress.

11.9   Host File Options

As noted earlier, only one person at a site needs to install PVM, but each PVM user can have his own hostfile, which describes his personal virtual machine.

The hostfile defines the initial configuration of hosts that PVM combines into a virtual machine. It also contains information about hosts that you may wish to add to the configuration later.

The hostfile in its simplest form is just a list of hostnames one to a line. Blank lines are ignored, and lines that begin with a # are comment lines. This approach allows you to document the hostfile and also provides a handy way to modify the initial configuration by commenting out various hostnames.

```
# Configuration used for my PVM run
node4
node6
node9
node10
node11
```

Several options can be specified on each line after the hostname. The options are separated by white space.

lo= userid allows you to specify another login name for this host; otherwise, your login name on the startup machine is used.

so=pw causes PVM to prompt you for a password on this host. This is useful when you have a different userid and password on a remote system. PVM uses rsh by default to start up remote pvmds, but when pw is specified, PVM will use rexec() instead.

dx= location of pvmd allows you to specify a location other than the default for this host. This is useful if you wish to use your own copy of pvmd.

ep= paths to user executables allows you to specify a series of paths to search down to find the requested files to spawn on this host. Multiple paths are separated by a colon. If ep= is not specified, then PVM looks for the application tasks in $HOME/pvm3/bin/PVM_ARCH.

sp= value specifies the relative computational speed of the host compared with other hosts in the configuration. The range of possible values is 1 to 1,000,000, with 1,000 as the default.

bx= location of debugger specifies which debugger script to invoke on this host if debugging is requested in the spawn routine. Note that the environment variable PVM_DEBUGGER can also be set. The default debugger is pvm3/lib/debugger.

wd= working_directory specifies a working directory in which all spawned tasks on this host will execute. The default is $HOME.

so=ms specifies that a slave pvmd will be started manually on this host. This is useful if rsh and rexec network services are disabled but IP connectivity exists. When using this option you will see the following in the tty of the pvmd3:

```
[t80040000] ready   Fri Aug 27 18:47:47 1993
*** Manual startup ***
Login to "honk" and type:
pvm3/lib/pvmd -S -d0 -nhonk 1 80a9ca95:0cb6 4096 2 80a95c43:0000
Type response:
```

On honk, after typing the given line, you should see

```
ddpro<2312> arch<ALPHA> ip<80a95c43:0a8e> mtu<4096>
```

which you should relay back to the master pvmd. At that point, you will see

```
Thanks
```

and the two pvmds should be able to communicate.

If you wish to set any of the above options as defaults for a series of hosts, you can place these options on a single line with a * for the hostname field. The defaults will be in effect for all the following hosts until they are overridden by another set-defaults line.

Hosts that you don't want in the initial configuration but may add later can be specified in the hostfile by beginning those lines with an &. An example hostfile displaying most of these options is shown below.

```
# Comment lines start with a # (blank lines ignored)
gstws
ipsc dx=/usr/geist/pvm3/lib/I860/pvmd3
ibm1.scri.fsu.edu lo=gst so=pw
```

```
# set default options for following hosts with *
* ep=$sun/problem1:~/nla/mathlib
sparky
#azure.epm.ornl.gov
midnight.epm.ornl.gov

# replace default options with new values
* lo=gageist so=pw ep=problem1
thud.cs.utk.edu
speedy.cs.utk.edu

# machines for adding later are specified with &
# these only need listing if options are required
&sun4    ep=problem1
&castor dx=/usr/local/bin/pvmd3
&dasher.cs.utk.edu lo=gageist
&elvis   dx=~/pvm3/lib/SUN4/pvmd3
```

11.10   XPVM

It is often useful and always reassuring to be able to see the present configuration of the virtual machine and the status of the hosts. It would be even more useful if you could also see what your program is doing—what tasks are running, where messages are being sent, and the like. The PVM GUI called XPVM was developed to display this information and more.

XPVM combines the capabilities of the PVM console, a performance monitor, and a call-level debugger in single, easy-to-use graphical user interface. XPVM is available from Netlib (www.netlib.org) in the directory pvm3/xpvm. It is distributed as precompiled ready-to-run executables for SUN4, RS6K, ALPHA, SUN-SOL2, and SGI5. The XPVM source is also available for compiling on other machines.

XPVM is written entirely in C using the TCL/TK toolkit and runs as just another PVM task. If you want to build XPVM from the source, you must first obtain and install the TCL/TK software on your system. TCL and TK were developed by John Ousterhout and can be obtained from www.scriptics.com. The TCL and XPVM source distributions each contain a README file that describes the most up-to-date installation procedure for each package, respectively.

Figure 11.4 shows a snapshot of XPVM in use.

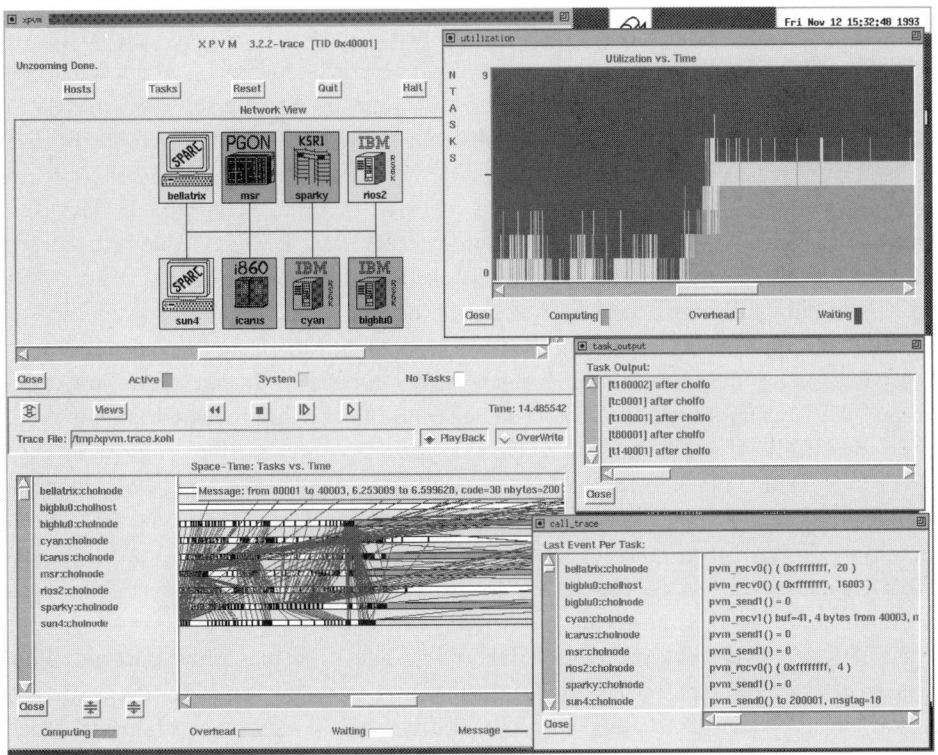

Figure 11.4
Snapshot of XPVM interface during use

Like the PVM console, XPVM will start PVM if it is not already running or just attach to the local **pvmd** if it is. The console can take an optional hostfile argument, whereas XPVM always reads **$HOME/.xpvm_hosts** as its hostfile. If this file does not exist, XPVM just starts PVM on the local host (or attaches to the existing PVM). In typical use, the hostfile **.xpvm_hosts** contains a list of hosts prepended with an &. These hostnames then get added to the *Hosts* menu for addition and deletion from the virtual machine by clicking on them.

The top row of buttons performs console-like functions. The *Hosts* button displays a menu of hosts. Clicking on a host toggles whether it is added or deleted from the virtual machine. At the bottom of the menu is an option for adding a host not listed. The *Tasks* button brings up a menu whose most used selection is *spawn.* Selecting spawn brings up a window where the executable name, spawn flags, starting place, number of copies to start, and so forth can be set. By default XPVM turns on tracing in all tasks (and their children) that are started inside XPVM. Clicking on *Start* in the spawn window starts the task, which will then appear in the Space-time view. The *Reset* button has a menu for resetting PVM (i.e., kill all PVM tasks) or resetting different parts of XPVM. The *Quit* button exits XPVM while leaving PVM running. If XPVM is being used to collect trace information, the information will not be collected if XPVM is stopped. The *Halt* button is to be used when you are through with PVM. Clicking on this button kills all running PVM tasks, shuts down PVM cleanly, and exits the XPVM interface. The *Help* button brings up a menu of topics for which information is available.

While an application is running, XPVM collects and displays the information in real time. Although XPVM updates the views as fast as it can, there are cases when XPVM cannot keep up with the events and falls behind the actual run time.

In the middle of the XPVM interface are tracefile controls. Here you can specify a tracefile; a default tracefile in '/tmp' is initially displayed. There are buttons to specify whether the specified tracefile is to be played back or overwritten by a new run. XPVM saves trace events in a file using the "self-defining data format" (SDDF) described in Dan Reed's Pablo trace displaying package (other packages such as Pablo can be used to analyze the PVM traces).

XPVM can play back its own SDDF files. The tape playerlike buttons allow you to rewind the tracefile, stop the display at any point, and step through the execution. A time display specifies the number of seconds from when the trace display began.

The *Views* button allows you to open or close any of several views presently supplied with XPVM. These views are described below.

During startup, XPVM joins a group called `xpvm`. This is done so tasks that are started outside the XPVM interface can get the tid of XPVM by doing `tid = pvm_gettid( xpvm, 0 )`. This tid would be needed if you wanted to manually turn on tracing inside such a task and pass the events back to XPVM for display. The expected TraceCode for these events is 666.

11.10.1 Network View

The *Network* view displays the present virtual machine configuration and the activity of the hosts. Each host is represented by an icon that includes the `PVM_ARCH` and hostname inside the icon. In the current release of XPVM, the icons are arranged arbitrarily on both sides of a bus network. In future releases the view will be extended to visualize network activity as well. At that time you will be able to specify the network topology to display.

These icons are illuminated in different colors to indicate their status in executing PVM tasks. Green implies that at least one task on that host is busy executing useful work. Yellow indicates that no tasks are executing user computation but at least one task is busy executing PVM system routines. When there are no tasks on a given host, its icon is left uncolored or white. The specific colors used in each case are user customizable.

You can tell at a glance how well the virtual machine is being utilized by your PVM application. If all the hosts are green most of the time, then machine utilization is good. The Network view does not display activity due to other users' PVM jobs or other processes that may be running on the hosts.

In future releases the view will allow you to click on a multiprocessor icon and get information about the number of processors, number of PVM tasks, and the like that are running on the host.

11.10.2 Space-Time View

The *Space-time* view displays the activities of individual PVM tasks that are running on the virtual machine. Listed on the left-hand side of the view are the executable names of the tasks preceded by the host they are running on. The task list is sorted by host so that it is easy to see whether tasks are being clumped on one host. This list also shows the task to host mappings (which are not available in the Network view).

The Space-time view combines three different displays. The first is like a Gantt chart. Beside each listed task is a horizontal bar stretching out in the "time" direction. The color of this bar at any time indicates the state of the task. Green indicates that user computations are being executed. Yellow marks the times when the task is executing PVM routines. White indicates when a task is waiting for messages. The bar begins at the time when the task starts executing and ends when the task exits normally. The specific colors used in each case are user customizable.

The second display overlays the first display with the communication activity among tasks. When a message is sent between two tasks, a red line is drawn starting at the sending task's bar at the time the message is sent and ending at the receiving task's bar when the message is received. Note that this is not the time the message arrived, but rather the time the task called pvm_recv(). Visually, the patterns and slopes of the red lines combined with white "waiting" regions reveal a lot about the communication efficiency of an application.

The third display appears only when you click on interesting features of the Space-time view with the left mouse button. A small "pop-up" window appears, giving detailed information regarding specific task states or messages. If a task bar is clicked on, the state begin and end times are displayed along with the last PVM system call information. If a message line is clicked on, the window displays the send and receive time as well as the number of bytes in the message and the message tag.

When the mouse is moved inside the Space-time view, a blue vertical line tracks the cursor, and the time corresponding to this vertical line is displayed as Query time at the bottom of the display. This vertical line also appears in the other "something vs. time" views so you can correlate a feature in one view with information given in another view.

You can zoom into any area of the Space-time view by dragging the vertical line with the middle mouse button. The view will unzoom back one level when the right mouse button is clicked. Often, very fine communication or waiting states are visible only when the view is magnified with the zoom feature. As with the Query time, the other views also zoom along with the Space-time view.

11.10.3   Other Views

XPVM is designed to be extensible. New views can be created and added to the *Views* menu. At present, there are three other views: Utilization, Call Trace, and Task Output. Unlike the Network and Space-time views, these views are closed by default. Since XPVM attempts to draw the views in real time, the fewer open views the faster XPVM can draw.

The Utilization view shows the number of tasks computing, in overhead, or waiting for each instant. It is a summary of the Space-time view for each instant. Since the number of tasks in a PVM application can change dynamically, the scale on the Utilization view will change dynamically when tasks are added, but not when they exit. When this happens, the displayed portion of the Utilization view is completely redrawn to the new scale.

The Call Trace view provides a textual record of the last PVM call made in each task. The list of tasks is the same as in the Space-time view. As an application runs, the text changes to reflect the most recent activity in each task. This view is useful as a call-level debugger to identify where a PVM program's execution hangs.

XPVM automatically tells all tasks it spawns to redirect their standard output back to XPVM when the Task Output view is opened. This view gives you the option of redirecting the output into a file. If you type a file name in the "Task Output" box, the output is printed in the window and into the file.

As with the trace events, a task started outside XPVM can be programmed to send standard output to XPVM for display by using the options in **pvm_setopt()**. XPVM expects the OutputCode to be set to 667.

12 Fault-Tolerant and Adaptive Programs with PVM

Al Geist and Jim Kohl

The use of Beowulf clusters has expanded rapidly in the past several years. Originally created by researchers to do scientific computing, today these clusters are being used in business and commercial settings where the requirements and expectations are quite different. For example, at a large Web hosting company the reliability and robustness of their applications are often more important than their raw performance.

A number of factors must be considered when you are developing applications for Beowulf clusters. In the preceding chapters the basic methods of message passing were illustrated so that you could create your own parallel programs. This chapter describes the issues and common methods for making parallel programs that are fault tolerant and adaptive.

Fault tolerance is the ability of an application to continue to run or make progress even if a hardware or software problem causes a node in the cluster to fail. It is also the ability to tolerate failures within the application itself. For example, one task inside a parallel application may get an error and abort. Because Beowulf clusters are built from commodity components that are designed for the desktop rather than heavy-duty computing, failures of components inside a cluster are higher than in a more expensive multiprocessor system that has an integrated RAS (Reliability, Availability, Serviceability) system.

While fault-tolerant programs can be thought of as adaptive, the term "adaptive programs" is used here more generally to mean parallel (or serial) programs that dynamically change their characteristics to better match the application's needs and the available resources. Examples include an application that adapts by adding or releasing nodes of the cluster according to its present computational needs and an application that creates and kills tasks based on what the computation needs.

In later chapters you will learn about Condor and other resource management tools that automatically provide some measure of fault tolerance and adaptability to jobs submitted to them. This chapter teaches the basics of how to write such tools yourself.

PVM is based on a dynamic computing model in which cluster nodes can be added and deleted from the computation on the fly and parallel tasks can be spawned or killed during the computation. PVM doesn't have nearly as rich a set of message-passing features as MPI; but, being a virtual machine model, PVM has a number of features that make it attractive for creating dynamic parallel programs. For this reason, PVM will be used to illustrate the concepts of fault tolerance and adaptability in this chapter.

12.1   Considerations for Fault Tolerance

A computational biologist at Oak Ridge National Laboratory wants to write an parallel application that runs 24/7 on his Beowulf cluster. The application involves calculations for the human genome and is driven by a constant stream of new data arriving from researchers all around the world. The data is not independent since new data helps refine and extend previously calculated sequences. How can he write such a program?

A company wants to write an application to process a constant stream of sales orders coming in from the Web. The program needs to be robust, since down time costs not only the lost revenue stream but also wages of workers who are idle. The company has recently purchased a Beowulf cluster to provide a reliable cost effective solution. But how do they write the fault-tolerant parallel program to run on the cluster?

When you are developing algorithms that must be reliable the first consideration is the hardware. The bad news is that your Beowulf cluster will have failures; it will need maintenance. It is not a matter of *whether* some node in the cluster will fail but *when*. Experience has shown that the more nodes the cluster has, the more likely one will fail within a given time. How often a hardware failure occurs varies widely between clusters. Some have failures every week; others run for months. It is not uncommon for several nodes to fail at about the same time with similar hardware problems. Evaluate your particular cluster under a simulated load for a couple of weeks to get data on expected mean time between failures (MTBF). If the MTBF is many times longer than your average application run time, then it may not make sense to restructure the application to be fault tolerant. In most cases it is more efficient simply to rerun a failed application if it has a short run time.

The second consideration is the fault tolerance of the underlying software environment. If the operating system is not stable, then the hardware is the least of your problems. The PVM system sits between the operating system and the application and, among other things, monitors the state of the virtual machine. The PVM system is designed to be fault tolerant and to reconfigure itself automatically when a failure is detected. It was discovered early in the PVM project that it doesn't help your fault-tolerant application if the underlying failure detection system crashes during a failure. The PVM failure detection system is responsible for detecting problems and notifying running applications about the problem. It makes no attempt to recover a parallel application automatically.

The third consideration is the application. Not every parallel application can recover from a failure; recovery depends on the design of the application and the nature of the failure. For example, in the manager/worker programs of the preceding chapters, if the node that fails was running a worker, then recovery is possible; but if the node was running the manager, then key data may be lost that can't be recovered.

At the least, any parallel program can be made fault tolerant by restarting it automatically from the beginning if a failure in detected.

Recovery of parallel programs is complicated because data in messages may be in flight when the recovery begins. There is a race condition. If the data did not arrive, then it will need to be resent as part of the recovery. But if the data managed to be received just before the recovery, then there isn't an outstanding receive call, and the data shouldn't be resent.

File I/O is another problem that complicates recovery. File pointers may need to be reset to the last checkpoint to avoid getting a repeated set of output data in the file.

Despite all these issues, a few common methods can be used to improve the fault tolerance of many parallel applications.

12.2   Building Fault-Tolerant Parallel Applications

From the application's view three steps must be performed for fault tolerance: notification, recovery, and continue.

The PVM system has a monitoring and notification feature built into it. Any or all tasks in an application can asked to be notified of specific events. These include the exiting of a task within the application. The requesting task can specify a particular task or set of tasks or can ask to be notified if any task within the application fails. In the last case the notification message contains the ID of the task that failed. There is no need for the notified task and the failed task ever to have communicated in order to detect the failure.

The failure or deletion of a node in the cluster is another notify event that can be specified. Again the requesting application task can specify a particular node, set of nodes, or all nodes. And, as before, the notification message returns the ID of the failed node(s).

The addition of one or more cluster nodes to the application's computational environment is also an event that PVM can notify an application about. In this case no ID can be specified, and the notification message returns the ID of the new node(s).

```
int info = pvm_notify( int EventType, int msgtag, int cnt, int *ids )
```

The EventType options are PvmTaskExit, PvmHostDelete, or PvmHostAdd. A separate notify call must be made for each event type that the application wishes to be notified about. The msgtag argument specifies what message tag the task will be using to listening for events. The cnt argument is the number task or node IDs in the ids list for which notification is requested.

Given the flexibility of the pvm_notify command, there are several options for how the application can be designed to receive notification from the PVM system. The first option is designing a separate watcher task. One or more of these watcher tasks are spawned across the cluster and often have the additional responsibility of managing the recovery phase of the application. The advantage of this approach is that the application code can remain cleaner. Note that in the manager/worker scheme the manager often assumes the additional duty as watcher.

A second option is for the application tasks to watch each other. A common method is to have each task watch its neighbor in a logical ring. Thus each task just watches one or two other tasks. Another common, but not particularly efficient, method is to have every task watch all the other tasks. Remember that the PVM system is doing the monitoring, not the application tasks. So the monitoring overhead is the same with all these options. The difference is the number of notification messages that get sent in the event of a failure.

Recovery is very dependent on the type of parallel algorithm used in the application. The most commonly used options are restart from the beginning, roll back to the last checkpoint, or reassign the work of a failed task.

The first option is the simplest to implement but the most expensive in the amount of calculation that must be redone. This option is used by many batch systems because it requires no knowledge of the application. It guarantees that the application will complete even if failures occur, although it does not guarantee how long this will take. On average the time is less than twice the normal run time. For short-running applications this is the best option.

For longer-running applications, checkpointing is a commonly used option. With this option you must understand the parallel application and modify it so that the application can restart from a input data file. You then have to modify the application to write out such a data file periodically. In the event of a failure, only computations from the last checkpoint are lost. The application restarts itself from the last successful data file written out. How often checkpoints are written out depends on the size of the restart file and how long the application is going to run. For large, scientific applications that run for days, checkpointing is typically done every few hours.

Note that if a failure is caused by the loss of a cluster node, then the application cannot be restarted until the node is repaired or is replaced by another node in the cluster. The restart file is almost always written out assuming that the same number of nodes are available during the restart.

In the special case where an application is based on a manager/worker scheme, it is often possible to reassign the job sent to the failed worker to another worker or to spawn a replacement worker to take its place. Manager/worker is a very popular parallel programming scheme for Beowulf clusters, so this special case arises often. Below is an example of a fault-tolerant manager/worker program.

```c
/* Fault Tolerant Manager / Worker Example
 * using notification and task spawning.
 * example1.c
 */

#include <stdio.h>
#include <math.h>
#include <pvm3.h>

#define NWORK      4
#define NPROB      10000
#define MSGTAG     123

int main()
{
    double sum = 0.0, result, input = 1.0;
    int tids[NWORK], numt, probs[NPROB], sent=0, recvd=0;
    int aok=0, cc, bufid, done=0, i, j, marker, next, src;

    /* If I am a Manager Task */
    if ( (cc = pvm_parent()) == PvmNoParent || cc == PvmParentNotSet ) {

        /* Spawn NWORK Worker Tasks */
        numt = pvm_spawn( "example1", (char **) NULL, PvmTaskDefault,
                (char *) NULL, NWORK, tids );

        /* Set Up Notify for Spawned Tasks */
        pvm_notify( PvmTaskExit, MSGTAG, numt, tids );

        /* Send Problem to Spawned Workers */
        for ( i=0 ; i < NPROB ; i++ ) probs[i] = -1;
        for ( i=0 ; i < numt ; i++ ) {
            pvm_initsend( PvmDataDefault );
```

```
        pvm_pkint( &aok, 1, 1 );   /* Valid Problem Marker */
        input = (double) (i + 1);
        pvm_pkdouble( &input, 1, 1 );
        pvm_send( tids[i], MSGTAG );
        probs[i] = i;  sent++;  /* Next Problem */
}

/* Collect Results / Handle Failures */
do {
    /* Receive Result */
    bufid = pvm_recv( -1, MSGTAG );
    pvm_upkint( &marker, 1, 1 );

    /* Handle Notify */
    if ( marker > 0 ) {
        /* Find Failed Task Index */
        for ( i=0, next = -1 ; i < numt ; i++ )
            if ( tids[i] == marker )
                /* Find Last Problem Sent to Task */
                for ( j=(sent-1) ; j > 0 ; j-- )
                    if ( probs[j] == i ) {
                        /* Spawn Replacement Task */
                        if ( pvm_spawn( "example1", (char **) NULL,
                                PvmTaskDefault, (char *) NULL, 1,
                                &(tids[i]) ) == 1 ) {
                            pvm_notify( PvmTaskExit, MSGTAG, 1,
                                    &(tids[i]) );
                            next = i;  sent--;
                        }
                        probs[j] = -1; /* Reinsert Prob */
                        break;
                    }
    } else {
        /* Get Source Task & Accumulate Solution */
        pvm_upkdouble( &result, 1, 1 );
        sum += result;
        recvd++;
        /* Get Task Index */
        pvm_bufinfo( bufid, (int *) NULL, (int *) NULL, &src );
        for ( i=0 ; i < numt ; i++ )
            if ( tids[i] == src ) next = i;
    }

    /* Send Another Problem */
```

```
            if ( next >= 0 ) {
                for ( i=0, input = -1.0 ; i < NPROB ; i++ )
                    if ( probs[i] < 0 ) {
                        input = (double) (i + 1);
                        probs[i] = next;  sent++;  /* Next Problem */
                        break;
                    }
                pvm_initsend( PvmDataDefault );
                pvm_pkint( &aok, 1, 1 );  /* Valid Problem Marker */
                pvm_pkdouble( &input, 1, 1 );
                pvm_send( tids[next], MSGTAG );
                if ( input < 0.0 ) tids[next] = -1;
            }

    } while ( recvd < sent );

    printf( "Sum = %lf\n", sum );
}

/* If I am a Worker Task */
else if ( cc > 0 ) {
    /* Notify Me If Manager Fails */
    pvm_notify( PvmTaskExit, MSGTAG, 1, &cc );
    /* Solve Problems Until Done */
    do {
        /* Get Problem from Master */
        pvm_recv( -1, MSGTAG );
        pvm_upkint( &aok, 1, 1 );
        if ( aok > 0 )  /* Master Died */
            break;
        pvm_upkdouble( &input, 1, 1 );
        if ( input > 0.0 ) {
            /* Compute Result */
            result = sqrt( ( 2.0 * input ) - 1.0 );
            /* Send Result to Master */
            pvm_initsend( PvmDataDefault );
            pvm_pkint( &aok, 1, 1 );    /* Ask for more... */
            pvm_pkdouble( &result, 1, 1 );
            pvm_send( cc, MSGTAG );
        } else
            done = 1;
    } while ( !done );
}
```

```
    pvm_exit();

    return( 0 );
}
```

This example illustrates another useful function: **pvm_spawn()**. The ability to spawn a replacement task is a powerful capability in fault tolerance. It is also a key function in adaptive programs, as we will see in the next section.

```
int numt = pvm_spawn( char *task, char **argv, int flag,
                      char *node, int ntasks, int *tids )
```

The routine **pvm_spawn()** starts up **ntasks** copies of an executable file **task** on the virtual machine. The PVM virtual machine is assumed to be running on the Beowulf cluster. Here **argv** is a pointer to an array of arguments to **task** with the end of the array specified by NULL. If task takes no arguments then **argv** is NULL. The **flag** argument is used to specify options and is a sum of the following options:

PvmTaskDefault: has PVM choose where to spawn processes

PvmTaskHost: uses a **where** argument to specify a particular host or cluster node to spawn on

PvmTaskArch: uses a **where** argument to specify an architecture class to spawn on

PvmTaskDebug: starts up these processes under debugger

PvmTaskTrace: uses PVM calls to generate trace data

PvmMppFront: starts process on MPP front-end/service node

PvmHostComp: starts process on complementary host set

For example, **flag = PvmTaskHost + PvmHostCompl** spawns tasks on every node but the specified node (which may be the manager, for instance).

On return, **numt** is set to the number of tasks successfully spawned or an error code if no tasks could be started. If tasks were started, then **pvm_spawn()** returns a vector of the spawned tasks' **tids**. If some tasks could not be started, the corresponding error codes are placed in the last $(ntask - numt)$ positions of the vector.

In the example above, **pvm_spawn()** is used by the manager to start all the worker tasks and also is used to replace workers who fail during the computation. This type of fault-tolerant method is useful for applications that run continuously with a steady stream of new work coming in, as was the case in our two initial examples. Both used a variation on the above PVM example code for their solution.

12.3   Adaptive Programs

In this section, we use some more of the PVM virtual machine functions to illustrate how cluster programs can be extended to adapt not only to faults but also to many other metrics and circumstances. The first example demonstrates a parallel application that dynamically adapts the size of the virtual machine through adding and releasing nodes based on the computational needs of the application. Such a feature is used every day on a 128-processor Beowulf cluster at Oak Ridge National Laboratory that is shared by three research groups.

```
int numh = pvm_addhosts( char **hosts, int nhost, int *infos)
int numh = pvm_delhosts( char **hosts, int nhost, int *infos)
```

The PVM addhosts and delhosts routines add or delete a set of hosts in the virtual machine. In a Beowulf cluster this corresponds to adding or deleting nodes from the computation; numh is returned as the number of nodes successfully added or deleted. The argument infos is an array of length nhost that contains the status code for each individual node being added or deleted. This allows you to check whether only one of a set of hosts caused a problem, rather than trying to add or delete the entire set of hosts again.

```
/*
 * Adaptive Host Allocation Example adds and removes cluster nodes
 * from computation on the fly for different computational phases
 */

#include <stdio.h>
#include <pvm3.h>

static char *host_set_A[] = { "msr", "nova", "sun4" };
static int nhosts_A = sizeof( host_set_A ) / sizeof( char ** );

static char *host_set_B[] = { "davinci", "nimbus" };
static int nhosts_B = sizeof( host_set_B ) / sizeof( char ** );

#define MAX_HOSTS    255
#define MSGTAG       123

double phase1( int prob ) {
    return( (prob == 1) ? 1 : ((double) prob * phase1( prob - 1 )) ); }

double phase2( int prob ) {
```

```
        return( (prob == 1) ? 1 : ((double) prob + phase2( prob - 1 )) ); }

int main( int argc, char **argv )
{
    double sum1 = 0.0, sum2 = 0.0, result;
    int status[MAX_HOSTS], prob, cc, i;
    char *args[3], input[16];

    /* If I am the Manager Task */
    if ( (cc = pvm_parent()) == PvmNoParent || cc == PvmParentNotSet ) {

        /* Phase #1 of computation - Use Host Set A */
        pvm_addhosts( host_set_A, nhosts_A, status );

        /* Spawn Worker Tasks - One Per Host */
        args[0] = "phase1";  args[1] = input;  args[2] = (char *) NULL;
        for ( i=0, prob=0 ; i < nhosts_A ; i++ )
            if ( status[i] > 0 ) { /* Successful Host Add */
                sprintf( input, "%d", prob++ );
                pvm_spawn( "example2", args, PvmTaskDefault | PvmTaskHost,
                        host_set_A[i], 1, (int *) NULL );
            }
        /* Collect Results */
        for ( i=0 ; i < prob ; i++ ) {
            pvm_recv( -1, MSGTAG );
            pvm_upkdouble( &result, 1, 1 );
            sum1 += result;
        }

        /* Remove Host Set A after Phase #1 */
        for ( i=0 ; i < nhosts_A ; i++ )
            if ( status[i] > 0 )  /* Only Delete Successful Hosts */
                pvm_delhosts( &(host_set_A[i]), 1, (int *) NULL );

        /* Phase #2 of Computation - Use Host Set B */
        pvm_addhosts( host_set_B, nhosts_B, status );

        /* Spawn Worker Tasks - One Per Host (None Locally) */
        args[0] = "phase2";
        for ( i=0, prob=0 ; i < nhosts_B ; i++ )
            if ( status[i] > 0 ) { /* Successful Host Add */
                sprintf( input, "%d", prob++ );
                pvm_spawn( "example2", args, PvmTaskDefault | PvmTaskHost,
                        host_set_B[i], 1, (int *) NULL );
```

```
        }
        /* Collect Results */
        for ( i=0 ; i < prob ; i++ ) {
            pvm_recv( -1, MSGTAG );
            pvm_upkdouble( &result, 1, 1 );
            sum2 += result;
        }

        /* Remove Host Set B from Phase #2 */
        for ( i=0 ; i < nhosts_B ; i++ )
            if ( status[i] > 0 )  /* Only Delete Successful Hosts */
                pvm_delhosts( &(host_set_B[i]), 1, (int *) NULL );

        /* Done */
        printf( "sum1 (%lf) / sum2 (%lf) = %lf\n", sum1, sum2, sum1/sum2 );
    }

    /* If I am a Worker Task */
    else if ( cc > 0 ) {
        /* Compute Result */
        prob = atoi( argv[2] );
        if ( !strcmp( argv[1], "phase1" ) )
            result = phase1( prob + 1 );
        else if ( !strcmp( argv[1], "phase2" ) )
            result = phase2( 100 * ( prob + 1 ) );
        /* Send Result to Master */
        pvm_initsend( PvmDataDefault );
        pvm_pkdouble( &result, 1, 1 );
        pvm_send( cc, MSGTAG );
    }

    pvm_exit();

    return( 0 );
}
```

One of the main difficulties of writing libraries for message-passing applications is that messages sent inside the application may get intercepted by the message-passing calls inside the library. The same problem occurs when two applications want to cooperate, for example, a performance monitor and a scientific application or an airframe stress application coupled with an aerodynamic flow application. Whenever two or more programmers are writing different parts of the overall message-passing application, there is the potential that a message will be inadvertently received by the wrong part of the application. The solution to this problem is communication context. As described earlier in the MPI chapters, communication context in MPI is handled cleanly through the MPI communicator.

In PVM 3.4, pvm_recv() requests a message from a particular source with a user-chosen message tag (either or both of these fields can be set to accept anything). In addition, communication context is a third field that a receive must match on before accepting a message; the context cannot be specified by a wild card. By default there is a base context that is a predefined and is similar to the default MPI_COMM_WORLD communicator in MPI.

PVM has four routines to manage communication contexts.

```
new_context = pvm_newcontext()
old_context = pvm_setcontext( new_context )
info        = pvm_freecontext( context )
context     = pvm_getcontext()
```

Pvm_newcontext() returns a systemwide unique context tag generated by the local daemon (in a way similar to the way the local daemon generates systemwide unique task IDs). Since it is a local operation, pvm_newcontext is very fast. The returned context can then be broadcast to all the tasks that are cooperating on this part of the application. Each of the tasks calls pvm_setcontext, which switches the active context and returns the old context tag so that it can be restored at the end of the module by another call to pvm_setcontext. Pvm_freecontext and pvm_getcontext are used to free memory associated with a context tag and to get the value of the active context tag, respectively.

Spawned tasks inherit the context of their parent. Thus, if you wish to add context to an existing parallel routine already written in PVM, you need to add only four lines to the source:

```
int mycxt, oldcxt;
/* near the beginning of the routine set a new context */
mycxt = pvm_newcontext();
oldcxt = pvm_setcontext( mycxt );

/* spawn slave tasks to help */
/* slave tasks require no source code change */
/* leave all the PVM calls in master unchanged */

/* just before exiting the routine restore previous context */
```

```
    mycxt = pvm_setcontext( oldcxt );
    pvm_freecontext( mycxt );

    return;
```

PVM has always had message handlers internally, which were used for controlling the virtual machine. In PVM 3.4 the ability to define and delete message handlers was raised to the user level so that parallel programs can be written that can add new features while the program is running.

The two new message handler functions are

```
    mhid = pvm_addmhf( src, tag, context, *function );
            pvm_delmhf( mhid );
```

Once a message handler has been added by a task, whenever a message arrives at this task with the specified source, message tag, and communication context, the specified function is executed. The function is passed the message so that it may unpack the message if desired. PVM places no restrictions on the complexity of the function, which is free to make system calls or other PVM calls. A message handler ID is returned by the add routine, which is used in the delete message handler routine.

There is no limit on the number of handlers you can set up, and handlers can be added and deleted dynamically by each application task independently.

By setting up message handlers, you can now write programs that can dynamically change the features of the underlying virtual machine. For example, message handlers could be added that implement active messages; the application then could use this form of communication rather than the typical send/receive. Similar opportunities exist for almost every feature of the virtual machine.

The ability of the application to adapt features of the virtual machine to meet its present needs is a powerful capability that has yet to be fully exploited in Beowulf clusters.

```
/* Adapting available Virtual Machine features with
 * user redefined message handlers.
 */
#include <stdio.h>
#include <pvm3.h>

#define NWORK          4
#define MAIN_MSGTAG    123
#define CNTR_MSGTAG    124
```

```
int counter = 0;

int handler( int mid ) {
    int ack, incr, src;

    /* Increment Counter */
    pvm_upkint( &incr, 1, 1 );
    counter += incr;
    printf( "counter = %d\n", counter );

    /* Acknowledge Counter Task */
    pvm_bufinfo( mid, (int *) NULL, (int *) NULL, &src );
    pvm_initsend( PvmDataDefault );
    ack = ( counter > 1000 ) ? -1 : 1;
    pvm_pkint( &ack, 1, 1 );
    pvm_send( src, CNTR_MSGTAG );

    return( 0 );
}

int main( int argc, char **argv )
{
    int ack, cc, ctx, bufid, incr=1, iter=1, max, numt, old, value=1, src;
    char *args[2];

    /* If I am a Manager Task */
    if ( (cc = pvm_parent()) == PvmNoParent || cc == PvmParentNotSet ) {

        /* Generate New Message Context for Counter Task messages */
        ctx = pvm_newcontext();

        /* Register Message Handler Function for Independent Counter */
        pvm_addmhf( -1, CNTR_MSGTAG, ctx, handler );

        /* Spawn 1 Counter Task */
        args[0] = "counter";  args[1] = (char *) NULL;
        old = pvm_setcontext( ctx );  /* Set Message Context for Task */
        if ( pvm_spawn( "example3", args, PvmTaskDefault,
                (char *) NULL, 1, (int *) NULL ) != 1 )
            counter = 1001;  /* Counter Failed to Spawn, Trigger Exit */
        pvm_setcontext( old );  /* Reset to Base Message Context */

        /* Spawn NWORK Worker Tasks */
```

```
        args[0] = "worker";
        numt = pvm_spawn( "example3", args, PvmTaskDefault,
                (char *) NULL, NWORK, (int *) NULL );

        /* Increment & Return Worker Values */
        do {
            /* Get Value */
            bufid = pvm_recv( -1, MAIN_MSGTAG );
            pvm_upkint( &value, 1, 1 );
            max = ( value > max ) ? value : max;
            printf( "recvd value = %d\n", value );

            /* Send Reply */
            pvm_bufinfo( bufid, (int *) NULL, (int *) NULL, &src );
            if ( counter <= 1000 ) value += iter++;
                else { value = -1; numt--; }  /* Tell Workers to Exit */
            pvm_initsend( PvmDataDefault );
            pvm_pkint( &value, 1, 1 );
            pvm_send( src, MAIN_MSGTAG );
        } while ( numt > 0 );

        printf( "Max Value = %d\n", max );
    }

    /* If I am a Worker Task */
    else if ( cc > 0 && !strcmp( argv[1], "worker" ) ) {
        /* Grow Values Until Done */
        do {
            /* Send Value to Master */
            value *= 2;
            pvm_initsend( PvmDataDefault );
            pvm_pkint( &value, 1, 1 );
            pvm_send( cc, MAIN_MSGTAG );
            /* Get Incremented Value from Master */
            pvm_recv( cc, MAIN_MSGTAG );
            pvm_upkint( &value, 1, 1 );
        } while ( value > 0 );
    }

    /* If I am a Counter Task */
    else if ( cc > 0 && !strcmp( argv[1], "counter" ) ) {
        /* Grow Values Until Done */
        do {
            /* Send Counter Increment to Master */
```

```
        pvm_initsend( PvmDataDefault );
        pvm_pkint( &incr, 1, 1 );
        pvm_send( cc, CNTR_MSGTAG );
        incr *= 2;
        /* Check Ack from Master */
        pvm_recv( cc, CNTR_MSGTAG );
        pvm_upkint( &ack, 1, 1 );
    } while ( ack > 0 );
}

pvm_exit();

return( 0 );
}
```

In a typical message-passing system, messages are transient, and the focus is on making their existence as brief as possible by decreasing latency and increasing bandwidth. But there are a growing number of situations in the parallel applications seen today in which programming would be much easier if there was a way to have persistent messages. This is the purpose of the *Message Box* feature in PVM. The Message Box is an internal tuple space in the virtual machine.

Four functions make up the Message Box:

```
index = pvm_putinfo( name, msgbuf, flag )
        pvm_recvinfo( name, index, flag )
        pvm_delinfo( name, index, flag )
        pvm_getmboxinfo( pattern, matching_names, info )
```

Tasks can use regular PVM pack routines to create an arbitrary message and then use pvm_putinfo() to place this message into the Message Box with an associated name. Copies of this message can be retrieved by any PVM task that knows the name. If the name is unknown or is changing dynamically, then pvm_getmboxinfo() can be used to find the list of names active in the Message Box. The flag defines the properties of the stored message, such as who is allowed to delete this message, whether this name allows multiple instances of messages, and whether a *put* to the same name can overwrite the message.

The Message Box has been used for many other purposes. For example, the PVM group server functionality has all been implemented in the new Message Box functions; the Cumulvs computational steering tool uses the Message Box to query for the instructions on how to attach to a remote distributed simulation; and performance monitors leave their findings in the Message Box for other tools to use.

The capability to have persistent messages in a parallel computing opens up many new application possibilities not only in high-performance computing but also in collaborative technologies.

```c
/* Example using persistent messages to adapt to change
 * Monitor tasks are created and killed as needed
 * Information is exchanged between these tasks using persistent messages
 */

#include <stdio.h>
#include <sys/time.h>
#include <pvm3.h>

#define MSGBOX          "load_stats"

int main()
{
    int cc, elapsed, i, index, load, num;
    struct timeval start, end;
    double value;

    /* If I am a Manager Task */
    if ( (cc = pvm_parent()) == PvmNoParent || cc == PvmParentNotSet ) {

        /* Periodically Spawn Load Monitor, Check Current System Load */
        do {
            /* Spawn Load Monitor Task */
            if ( pvm_spawn( "example4", (char **) NULL, PvmTaskDefault,
                    (char *) NULL, 1, (int *) NULL ) != 1 ) {
                perror( "spawning load monitor" );  break;
            }
            sleep( 1 );

            /* Check System Load (Microseconds Per Megaflop) */
            for ( i=0, load=0.0, num=0 ; i < 11 ; i++ )
                if ( pvm_recvinfo( MSGBOX, i, PvmMboxDefault ) >= 0 ) {
                    pvm_upkint( &elapsed, 1, 1 );
                    load += elapsed;  num++;
                }
            if ( num )
                printf( "Load Avg = %lf usec/Mflop\n",
                        (double) load / (double) num );
            sleep( 5 );
        } while ( 1 );
    }
```

```
/* If I am a Load Monitor Task */
else if ( cc > 0 ) {
    /* Time Simple Computation */
    gettimeofday( &start, (struct timezone *) NULL );
    for ( i=0, value=1.0 ; i < 1000000 ; i++ )
        value *= 1.2345678;
    gettimeofday( &end, (struct timezone *) NULL );
    elapsed = (end.tv_usec - start.tv_usec)
            + 1000000 * (end.tv_sec - start.tv_sec);

    /* Dump Into Next Available Message Mbox */
    pvm_initsend( PvmDataDefault );
    pvm_pkint( &elapsed, 1, 1 );
    index = pvm_putinfo( MSGBOX, pvm_getsbuf(),
            PvmMboxDefault | PvmMboxPersistent
                | PvmMboxMultiInstance | PvmMboxOverWritable );

    /* Free Next Mbox Index for Next Instance (Only Save 10) */
    pvm_delinfo( MSGBOX, (index + 1) % 11, PvmMboxDefault );
}

pvm_exit();

return( 0 );
}
```

III MANAGING CLUSTERS

13 Cluster Workload Management

James Patton Jones, David Lifka, Bill Nitzberg, and Todd Tannenbaum

A Beowulf cluster is a powerful (and attractive) tool. But managing the workload can present significant challenges. It is not uncommon to run hundreds or thousands of jobs or to share the cluster among many users. Some jobs may run only on certain nodes because not all the nodes in the cluster are identical; for instance, some nodes have more memory than others. Some nodes temporarily may not be functioning correctly. Certain users may require priority access to part or all of the cluster. Certain jobs may have to be run at certain times of the day or only after other jobs have completed. Even in the simplest environment, keeping track of all these activities and resource specifics while managing the ever-increasing web of priorities is a complex problem. Workload management software attacks this problem by providing a way to monitor and manage the flow of work through the system, allowing the *best* use of cluster resources as defined by a supplied policy.

Basically, workload management software maximizes the delivery of resources to jobs, given competing user requirements and local policy restrictions. Users package their work into sets of jobs, while the administrator (or system owner) describes local use policies (e.g., Tom's jobs always go first). The software monitors the state of the cluster, schedules work, enforces policy, and tracks usage.

A quick note on terminology: Many terms have been used to describe this area of management software. All of the following topics are related to workload management: distributed resource management, batch queuing, job scheduling, and, resource and task scheduling.

13.1 Goal of Workload Management Software

The goal of workload management software is to make certain the submitted jobs ultimately run to completion by utilizing cluster resources according to a supplied policy. But in order to achieve this goal, workload management systems usually must perform some or all of the following activities:

- Queuing
- Scheduling
- Monitoring
- Resource management
- Accounting

The typical relationship between users, resources, and these workload management activities is depicted in Figure 13.1. As shown in this figure, workload management software sits between the cluster users and the cluster resources. First, users submit jobs to a queue in order to specify the work to be performed. (Once a job has been submitted, the user can request status information about that job at any time.) The jobs then wait in the queue until they are scheduled to start on the cluster. The specifics of the scheduling process are defined by the policy rules. At this point, resource management mechanisms handle the details of properly launching the job and perhaps cleaning up any mess left behind after the job either completes or is aborted. While all this is going on, the workload management system is monitoring the status of system resources and accounting for which users are using what resources.

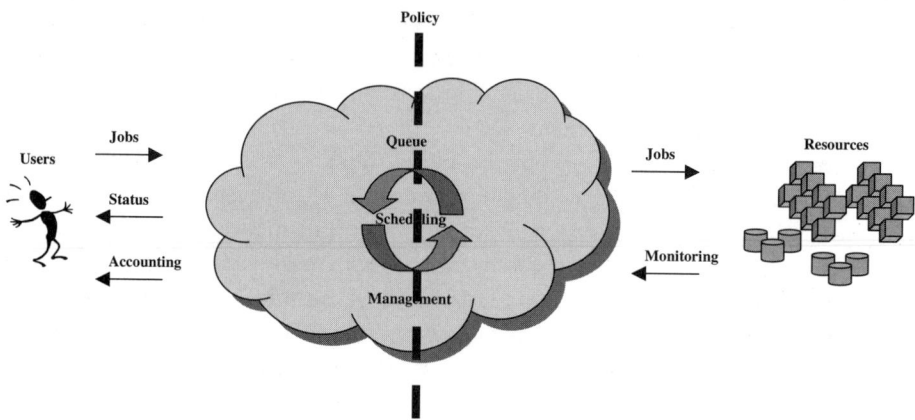

Figure 13.1
Activities performed by a workload management system.

13.2   Workload Management Activities

Now let us take a look in more detail at each of the major activities performed by a cluster workload management system.

13.2.1   Queueing

The first of the five aspects of workload management is *queuing*, or the process of collecting together "work" to be executed on a set of resources. This is also the portion most visible to the user.

The tasks the user wishes to have the computer perform, the work, is submitted to the workload management system in a container called a "batch job". The batch job consists of two primary parts: a set of resource directives (such as the amount of memory or number of CPUs needed) and a description of the task to be executed. This description contains all the information the workload management system needs in order to start a user's job when the time comes. For instance, the job description may contain information such as the name of the file to execute, a list of data files required by the job, and environment variables or command-line arguments to pass to the executable.

Once submitted to the workload management system, the batch jobs are held in a "queue" until the matching resources (e.g., the right kind of computers with the right amount of memory or number of CPUs) become available. Examples of real-life queues are lines at the bank or grocery store. Sometimes you get lucky and there's no wait, but usually you have to stand in line for a few minutes. And on days when the resources (clerks) are in high demand (like payday), the wait is substantially longer.

The same applies to computers and batch jobs. Sometimes the wait is very short, and the jobs run immediately. But more often (and thus the need for the workload management system) resources are oversubscribed, and so the jobs have to wait.

One important aspect of queues is that limits can be set that restrict access to the queue. This allows the cluster manager greater control over the usage policy of the cluster. For example, it may be desirable to have a queue that is available for short jobs only. This would be analogous to the "ten items or fewer express lane" at the grocery store, providing a shorter wait for "quick tasks."

Each of the different workload management systems discussed later in this volume offers a rich variety of queue limits and attributes.

13.2.2   Scheduling

The second area of workload management is scheduling, which is simply the process of choosing the *best* job to run. Unlike in our real-life examples of the bank and grocery store (which employ a simple first-come, first-served model of deciding who's next), workload management systems offer a variety of ways by which the *best* job is identified.

As we have discussed earlier, however, *best* can be a tricky goal, and depends on the usage policy set by local management, the available workload, the type and availability of cluster resources, and the types of application being run on the cluster. In general, however, scheduling can be broken into two primary activities: *policy enforcement* and *resource optimization.*

Policy encapsulates how the cluster resources are to be used, addressing such issues as priorities, traffic control, and capability vs. high throughput. Scheduling is then the act of enforcing the policy in the selection of jobs, ensuring the priorities are met and policy goals are achieved.

While implementing and enforcing the policy, the scheduler has a second set of goals. These are resource optimization goals, such as "pack jobs efficiently" or "exploit underused resources."

The difficult part of scheduling, then, is balancing policy enforcement with resource optimization in order to pick the *best* job to run.

Logically speaking, one could think of a scheduler as performing the following loop:

1. Select the best job to run, according to policy and available resources.

2. Start the job.

3. Stop the job and/or clean up after a completed job.

4. Repeat.

The nuts and bolts of scheduling is, of course, choosing and tuning the policy to meet your needs. Although different workload management systems each have their own idiosyncrasies, they typically all provide ways in which their scheduling policy can be customized. Subsequent chapters of this book will discuss the various scheduling policy mechanisms available in several popular workload management systems.

13.2.3 Monitoring

Resource monitoring is the third part of any cluster workload management system. It provides necessary information to administrators, users and the scheduling system itself on the status of jobs and resources. There are basically three critical times that resource monitoring comes into play:

1. When nodes are idle, to verify that they are in working order before starting another job on them.

2. When nodes are busy running a job. Users and administrators may want to check memory, CPU, network, I/O, and utilization of other system resources. Such checks often are useful in parallel programming when users wish to verify that they have balanced their workload correctly and are effectively using all the nodes they've been allocated.

3. When a job completes. Here, resource monitoring is used to ensure that there are no remaining processes from the completed job and that the node is still in working order before starting another job on it.

Workload management systems query the compute resources at these times and use the information to make informed decisions about running jobs. Much of the information is cached so that it can be reported quickly in answer to status requests. Some information is saved for historical analysis purposes. Still other bits of the information are used in the enforcement of local policy. The method of collection may differ between different workload management systems, but the general purposes are the same.

13.2.4   Resource Management

The fourth area, resource management, is essentially responsible for the starting, stopping, and cleaning up after jobs that are run on cluster nodes. In a batch system resource management involves running a job for a user, under the identity of the user, on the resources the user was allocated in such a way that the user need not be present at that time.

Many cluster workload management systems provide mechanisms to ensure the successful startup and cleanup of jobs and to maintain node status data internally, so that jobs are started only on nodes that are available and functioning correctly.

In addition, limits may need to be placed on the job and enforced by the workload management system. These limits are yet another aspect of policy enforcement, in addition to the limits on queues and those enacted by the scheduling component.

Another aspect of resource management is providing the ability to remove or add compute resources to the available pool of systems. Clusters are rarely static; systems go down, or new nodes are added. The "registration" of new nodes and the marking of nodes as unavailable are both additional aspects of resource management.

13.2.5   Accounting

The fifth aspect of workload management is accounting and reporting. Workload accounting is the process of collecting resource usage data for the batch jobs that run on the cluster. Such data includes the job owner, resources requested by the job, and total amount of resources consumed by the job. Other data about the job may also be available, depending on the specific workload managment system in use.

Cluster workload accounting data can used for a variety of purposes, such as

1. producing weekly system usage reports,

2. preparing monthly per user usage reports,

3. enforcing per project allocations,

4. tuning the scheduling policy,

5. calculating future resource allocations,

6. anticipating future computer component requirements, and

7. determining areas of improvement within the computer system.

The data for these purposes may be collected as part of the resource monitoring tasks or may be gathered separately. In either case, data is pulled from the available sources in order to meet the objectives of workload accounting. Details of using the workload accounting features of specific workload management systems are discussed in subsequent chapters of this book.

14 Condor: A Distributed Job Scheduler

Todd Tannenbaum, Derek Wright, Karen Miller, and Miron Livny

Condor is a sophisticated and unique distributed job scheduler developed by the Condor research project at the University of Wisconsin-Madison Department of Computer Sciences.

A public-domain version of the Condor software and complete documentation is freely available from the Condor project's Web site at `www.cs.wisc.edu/condor`. Organizations may purchase a commercial version of Condor with an accompanying support contract; for additional information see `www.condorcomputing.com`.

This chapter introduces all aspects of Condor, from its ability to satisfy the needs and desires of both submitters and resource owners, to the management of Condor on clusters. Following an overview of Condor and Condor's ClassAd mechanism is a description of Condor from the user's perspective. The architecture of the software is presented along with overviews of installation and management. The chapter ends with configuration scenarios specific to clusters.

14.1 Introduction to Condor

Condor is a specialized workload management system for compute-intensive jobs. Like other full-featured batch systems, Condor provides a job queuing mechanism, scheduling policy, priority scheme, resource monitoring, and resource management. Users submit their jobs to Condor, and Condor places them into a queue, chooses when and where to run them based upon a policy, monitors their progress, and ultimately informs the user upon completion.

While providing functionality similar to that of a more traditional batch queuing system, Condor's novel architecture allows it to succeed in areas where traditional scheduling systems fail. Condor can be used to manage a cluster of dedicated Beowulf nodes. In addition, several unique mechanisms enable Condor to effectively harness wasted CPU power from otherwise idle desktop workstations. Condor can be used to seemlessly combine all of your organization's computational power into one resource.

Condor is the product of the Condor Research Project at the University of Wisconsin-Madison (UW-Madison) and was first installed as a production system in the UW-Madison Department of Computer Sciences nearly ten years ago. This Condor installation has since served as a major source of computing cycles to UW-Madison faculty and students. Today, just in our department alone, Condor manages more than one thousand workstations, including the department's 500-CPU Linux Beowulf cluster. On a typical day, Condor delivers more than 650 CPU-*days* to UW researchers. Additional Condor installations have been established over the years across our campus and the world. Hundreds of organizations in industry, government, and academia have used Condor to establish compute environments ranging in size from a handful to hundreds of workstations.

14.1.1 Features of Condor

Condor's features are extensive. Condor provides great flexibility for both the user submitting jobs and for the owner of a machine that provides CPU time toward running jobs. The following list summarizes some of Condor's capabilities.

Distributed submission: There is no single, centralized submission machine. Instead, Condor allows jobs to be submitted from many machines, and each machine contains its own job queue. Users may submit to a cluster from their own desktop machines.

Job priorities: Users can assign priorities to their submitted jobs in order to control the execution order of the jobs. A "nice-user" mechanism requests the use of only those machines that would have otherwise been idle.

User priorities: Administrators may assign priorities to users using a flexible mechanism that enables a policy of fair share, strict ordering, fractional ordering, or a combination of policies.

Job dependency: Some sets of jobs require an ordering because of dependencies between jobs. "Start job X only after jobs Y and Z successfully complete" is an example of a dependency. Enforcing dependencies is easily handled.

Support for multiple job models: Condor handles both serial jobs and parallel jobs incorporating PVM, dynamic PVM, and MPI.

ClassAds: The ClassAd mechanism in Condor provides an extremely flexible and expressive framework for matching resource requests (jobs) with resource offers (machines). Jobs can easily state both job requirements and job preferences. Likewise, machines can specify requirements and preferences about the jobs they are willing to run. These requirements and preferences can be described in powerful expressions, resulting in Condor's adaptation to nearly any desired policy.

Job checkpoint and migration: With certain types of jobs, Condor can transparently take a checkpoint and subsequently resume the application. A checkpoint is a snapshot of a job's complete state. Given a checkpoint, the job can later continue its execution from where it left off at the time of the checkpoint. A checkpoint also enables the transparent migration of a job from one machine to another machine.

Periodic checkpoint: Condor can be configured to periodically produce a checkpoint for a job. This provides a form of fault tolerance and safeguards the accumulated computation time of a job. It reduces the loss in the event of a system failure such as the machine being shut down or hardware failure.

Job suspend and resume: Based on policy rules, Condor can ask the operating system to suspend and later resume a job.

Remote system calls: Despite running jobs on remote machines, Condor can often preserve the local execution environment via remote system calls. Users do not need to make data files available or even obtain a login account on remote workstations before Condor executes their programs there. The program behaves under Condor as if it were running as the user that submitted the job on the workstation where it was originally submitted, regardless of where it really executes.

Pools of machines working together: *Flocking* allows jobs to be scheduled across multiple Condor pools. It can be done across pools of machines owned by different organizations that impose their own policies.

Authentication and authorization: Administrators have fine-grained control of access permissions, and Condor can perform strong network authentication using a variety of mechanisms including Kerberos and X.509 public key certificates.

Heterogeneous platforms: In addition to Linux, Condor has been ported to most of the other primary flavors of Unix as well as Windows NT. A single pool can contain multiple platforms. Jobs to be executed under one platform may be submitted from a different platform. As an example, an executable that runs under Windows 2000 may be submitted from a machine running Linux.

Grid computing: Condor incorporates many of the emerging Grid-based computing methodologies and protocols. It can interact with resources managed by Globus.

14.1.2   Understanding Condor ClassAds

The ClassAd is a flexible representation of the characteristics and constraints of both machines and jobs in the Condor system. *Matchmaking* is the mechanism by which Condor matches an idle job with an available machine. Understanding this unique framework is the key to harness the full flexibility of the Condor system.

ClassAds are employed by users to specify which machines should service their jobs. Administrators use them to customize scheduling policy.

Conceptualizing Condor ClassAds: Just Like the Newspaper. Condor's ClassAds are analogous to the classified advertising section of the newspaper. Sellers advertise specifics about what they have to sell, hoping to attract a buyer. Buyers may advertise specifics about what they wish to purchase. Both buyers and sellers list constraints that must be satisfied. For instance, a buyer has a maximum spending limit, and a seller requires a minimum purchase price. Furthermore, both want to rank requests to their own advantage. Certainly a seller would rank one offer of $50 higher than a different offer of $25. In Condor, users submitting jobs can be thought of as buyers of compute resources and machine owners are sellers.

All machines in a Condor pool advertise their attributes, such as available RAM memory, CPU type and speed, virtual memory size, current load average, current time and date, and other static and dynamic properties. This machine ClassAd also advertises under what conditions it is willing to run a Condor job and what type of job it prefers. These policy attributes can reflect the individual terms and preferences by which the different owners have allowed their machines to participate in the Condor pool.

After a job is submitted to Condor, a job ClassAd is created. This ClassAd includes attributes about the job, such as the amount of memory the job uses, the name of the program to run, the user who submitted the job, and the time it was submitted. The job can also specify requirements and preferences (or *rank*) for the machine that will run the job. For instance, perhaps you are looking for the fastest floating-point performance available. You want Condor to rank available machines based on floating-point performance. Perhaps you care only that the machine has a minimum of 256 MBytes of RAM. Or, perhaps you will take any machine you can get! These job attributes and requirements are bundled up into a job ClassAd.

Condor plays the role of matchmaker by continuously reading all the job ClassAds and all the machine ClassAds, matching and ranking job ads with machine ads. Condor ensures that the requirements in both ClassAds are satisfied.

Structure of a ClassAd. A ClassAd is a set of uniquely named expressions. Each named expression is called an *attribute*. Each attribute has an *attribute name* and an *attribute value*. The attribute value can be a simple integer, string, or floating-point value, such as

```
Memory = 512
OpSys = "LINUX"
```

```
NetworkLatency = 7.5
```

An attribute value can also consist of a logical expression that will evaluate to TRUE, FALSE, or UNDEFINED. The syntax and operators allowed in these expressions are similar to those in C or Java, that is, == for equals, != for not equals, && for logical **and**, || for logical **or**, and so on. Furthermore, ClassAd expressions can incorporate attribute names to refer to other attribute values. For instance, consider the following small sample ClassAd:

```
MemoryInMegs = 512
MemoryInBytes = MemoryInMegs * 1024 * 1024
Cpus = 4
BigMachine = (MemoryInMegs > 256) && (Cpus >= 4)
VeryBigMachine = (MemoryInMegs > 512) && (Cpus >= 8)
FastMachine = BigMachine && SpeedRating
```

In this example, `BigMachine` evaluates to TRUE and `VeryBigMachine` evaluates to FALSE. But, because attribute `SpeedRating` is not specified, `FastMachine` would evaluate to UNDEFINED.

Condor provides *meta-operators* that allow you to explicitly compare with the UNDEFINED value by testing both the type and value of the operands. If both the types and values match, the two operands are considered *identical*; =?= is used for meta-equals (or, is-identical-to) and =!= is used for meta-not-equals (or, is-not-identical-to). These operators always return TRUE or FALSE and therefore enable Condor administrators to specify explicit policies given incomplete information.

A complete description of ClassAd semantics and syntax is documented in the Condor manual.

Matching ClassAds. ClassAds can be matched with one another. This is the fundamental mechanism by which Condor matches jobs with machines. Figure 14.1 displays a ClassAd from Condor representing a machine and another representing a queued job. Each ClassAd contains a `MyType` attribute, describing what type of resource the ad represents, and a `TargetType` attribute. The `TargetType` specifies the type of resource desired in a match. Job ads want to be matched with machine ads and vice versa.

Each ClassAd engaged in matchmaking specifies a `Requirements` and a `Rank` attribute. In order for two ClassAds to match, the `Requirements` expression in both ads must evaluate to TRUE. An important component of matchmaking is the `Requirements` and `Rank` expression can refer not only to attributes in their own ad but also to attributes in the candidate matching ad. For instance, the

Job ClassAd	Machine ClassAd
MyType = "Job"	**MyType** = "Machine"
TargetType = "Machine"	**TargetType** = "Job"
Requirements = ((Arch=="INTEL" && Op-Sys=="LINUX") && Disk > DiskUsage)	**Requirements** = Start
Rank = (Memory * 10000) + KFlops	**Rank** = TARGET.Department==MY.Department
Args = "-ini ./ies.ini"	**Activity** = "Idle"
ClusterId = 680	**Arch** = "INTEL"
Cmd = "/home/tannenba/bin/sim-exe"	**ClockDay** = 0
Department = "CompSci"	**ClockMin** = 614
DiskUsage = 465	**CondorLoadAvg** = 0.000000
StdErr = "sim.err"	**Cpus** = 1
ExitStatus = 0	**CurrentRank** = 0.000000
FileReadBytes = 0.000000	**Department** = "CompSci"
FileWriteBytes = 0.000000	**Disk** = 3076076
ImageSize = 465	**EnteredCurrentActivity** = 990371564
StdIn = "/dev/null"	**EnteredCurrentState** = 990330615
Iwd = "/home/tannenba/sim-m/run_55"	**FileSystemDomain** = "cs.wisc.edu"
JobPrio = 0	**IsInstructional** = FALSE
JobStartDate = 971403010	**KeyboardIdle** = 15
JobStatus = 2	**KFlops** = 145811
StdOut = "sim.out"	**LoadAvg** = 0.220000
Owner = "tannenba"	**Machine** = "nostos.cs.wisc.edu"
ProcId = 64	**Memory** = 511
QDate = 971377131	**Mips** = 732
RemoteSysCpu = 0.000000	**OpSys** = "LINUX"
RemoteUserCpu = 0.000000	**Start** = (LoadAvg <= 0.300000) &&
RemoteWallClockTime = 2401399.000000	(KeyboardIdle > (15 * 60))
TransferFiles = "NEVER"	**State** = "Unclaimed"
WantCheckpoint = FALSE	**Subnet** = "128.105.165"
WantRemoteSyscalls = FALSE	**TotalVirtualMemory** = 787144
⋮	⋮

Figure 14.1
Examples of ClassAds in Condor.

Requirements expression for the job ad specified in Figure 14.1 refers to `Arch`, `OpSys`, and `Disk`, which are all attributes found in the machine ad.

What happens if Condor finds more than one machine ClassAd that satisfies the constraints specified by **Requirements**? That is where the **Rank** expression comes into play. The **Rank** expression specifies the desirability of the match (where higher numbers mean better matches). For example, the job ad in Figure 14.1 specifies

```
Requirements = ((Arch=="INTEL" && OpSys=="LINUX") && Disk > DiskUsage)
Rank         = (Memory * 100000) + KFlops
```

In this case, the job requires a computer running the Linux operating system and more local disk space than it will use. Among all such computers, the user prefers those with large physical memories and fast floating-point CPUs (`KFlops` is a metric of floating-point performance). Since the **Rank** is a user-specified metric, *any* expression may be used to specify the perceived desirability of the match. Condor's matchmaking algorithms deliver the best resource (as defined by the `Rank` expression) while satisfying other criteria.

14.2 Using Condor

The road to using Condor effectively is a short one. The basics are quickly and easily learned.

14.2.1 Roadmap to Using Condor

The following steps are involved in running jobs using Condor:

Prepare the Job to Run Unattended. An application run under Condor must be able to execute as a batch job. Condor runs the program unattended and in the background. A program that runs in the background will not be able to perform interactive input and output. Condor can redirect console output (`stdout` and `stderr`) and keyboard input (`stdin`) to and from files. You should create any needed files that contain the proper keystrokes needed for program input. You should also make certain the program will run correctly with the files.

Select the Condor Universe. Condor has five runtime environments from which to choose. Each runtime environment is called a *Universe*. Usually the Universe you choose is determined by the type of application you are asking Condor to run. There are six job Universes in total: two for serial jobs (Standard and Vanilla), one for parallel PVM jobs (PVM), one for parallel MPI jobs (MPI), one for Grid applications (Globus), and one for meta-schedulers (Scheduler). Section 14.2.4 provides more information on each of these Universes.

Create a Submit Description File. The details of a job submission are defined in a *submit description* file. This file contains information about the job such as what executable to run, which Universe to use, the files to use for `stdin, stdout,` and `stderr`, requirements and preferences about the machine which should run the program, and where to send e-mail when the job completes. You can also tell Condor how many times to run a program; it is simple to run the same program multiple times with different data sets.

Submit the Job. Submit the program to Condor with the `condor_submit` command.

Once a job has been submitted, Condor handles all aspects of running the job. You can subsequently monitor the job's progress with the `condor_q` and `condor_status` commands. You may use `condor_prio` to modify the order in which Condor will run your jobs. If desired, Condor can also record what is being done with your job at every stage in its lifecycle, through the use of a log file specified during submission.

When the program completes, Condor notifies the owner (by e-mail, the user-specified log file, or both) the exit status, along with various statistics including time used and I/O performed. You can remove a job from the queue at any time with `condor_rm`.

14.2.2   Submitting a Job

To submit a job for execution to Condor, you use the `condor_submit` command. This command takes as an argument the name of the submit description file, which contains commands and keywords to direct the queuing of jobs. In the submit description file, you define everything Condor needs to execute the job. Items such as the name of the executable to run, the initial working directory, and command-line arguments to the program all go into the submit description file. The `condor_submit` command creates a job ClassAd based on the information, and Condor schedules the job.

The contents of a submit description file can save you considerable time when you are using Condor. It is easy to submit multiple runs of a program to Condor. To run the same program 500 times on 500 different input data sets, the data files are arranged such that each run reads its own input, and each run writes its own output. Every individual run may have its own initial working directory, `stdin`, `stdout`, `stderr`, command-line arguments, and shell environment.

The following examples illustrate the flexibility of using Condor. We assume that the jobs submitted are serial jobs intended for a cluster that has a shared file system across all nodes. Therefore, all jobs use the Vanilla Universe, the simplest one for running serial jobs. The other Condor Universes are explored later.

Example 1.   Example 1 is the simplest submit description file possible. It queues up one copy of the program 'foo' for execution by Condor. A log file called 'foo.log' is generated by Condor. The log file contains events pertaining to the job while it runs inside of Condor. When the job finishes, its exit conditions are noted in the log file. We recommend that you always have a log file so you know what happened to your jobs. The *queue* statement in the submit description file tells Condor to use all the information specified so far to create a job ClassAd and place the job into the queue. Lines that begin with a pound character (#) are comments and are ignored by `condor_submit`.

```
# Example 1 : Simple submit file
universe = vanilla
executable = foo
log = foo.log
queue
```

Example 2. Example 2 queues two copies of the program 'mathematica'. The first copy runs in directory 'run_1', and the second runs in directory 'run_2'. For both queued copies, 'stdin' will be 'test.data', 'stdout' will be 'loop.out', and 'stderr' will be 'loop.error'. Two sets of files will be written, since the files are each written to their own directories. This is a convenient way to organize data for a large group of Condor jobs.

```
# Example 2: demonstrate use of multiple
# directories for data organization.
universe = vanilla
executable = mathematica
# Give some command line args, remap stdio
arguments = -solver matrix
input = test.data
output = loop.out
error = loop.error
log = loop.log

initialdir = run_1
queue
initialdir = run_2
queue
```

Example 3. The submit description file for Example 3 queues 150 runs of program 'foo'. This job requires Condor to run the program on machines that have greater than 128 megabytes of physical memory, and it further requires that the job not be scheduled to run on a specific node. Of the machines that meet the requirements, the job prefers to run on the fastest floating-point nodes currently available to accept the job. It also advises Condor that the job will use up to 180 megabytes of memory when running. Each of the 150 runs of the program is given its own process number, starting with process number 0. Several built-in macros can be used in a submit description file; one of them is the *$(Process)* macro which Condor expands to be the process number in the job cluster. This causes files 'stdin', 'stdout', and 'stderr' to be 'in.0', 'out.0', and 'err.0' for the first run of the program, 'in.1', 'out.1', and 'err.1' for the second run of the program, and so forth. A single log file will list events for all 150 jobs in this job cluster.

```
# Example 3: Submit lots of runs and use the
# pre-defined $(Process) macro.
universe = vanilla
executable = foo
requirements = Memory > 128  && Machine != "server-node.cluster.edu"
rank = KFlops
image_size = 180

Error   = err.$(Process)
Input   = in.$(Process)
Output  = out.$(Process)
Log = foo.log

.queue 150
```

Note that the **requirements** and **rank** entries in the submit description file will become the requirements and rank attributes of the subsequently created ClassAd for this job. These are arbitrary expressions that can reference any attributes of either the machine or the job; see Section 14.1.2 for more on requirements and rank expressions in ClassAds.

14.2.3   Overview of User Commands

Once you have jobs submitted to Condor, you can manage them and monitor their progress. Table 14.1 shows several commands available to the Condor user to view the job queue, check the status of nodes in the pool, and perform several other activities. Most of these commands have many command-line options; see the Command Reference chapter of the Condor manual for complete documentation. To provide an introduction from a user perspective, we give here a quick tour showing several of these commands in action.

When jobs are submitted, Condor will attempt to find resources to service the jobs. A list of all users with jobs submitted may be obtained through **condor_status** with the *-submitters* option. An example of this would yield output similar to the following:

```
% condor_status -submitters

Name                    Machine      Running IdleJobs HeldJobs

ballard@cs.wisc.edu     bluebird.c         0       11        0
nice-user.condor@cs.    cardinal.c         6      504        0
wright@cs.wisc.edu      finch.cs.w         1        1        0
jbasney@cs.wisc.edu     perdita.cs         0        0        5
```

Command	Description
condor_checkpoint	Checkpoint jobs running on the specified hosts
condor_compile	Create a relinked executable for submission to the Standard Universe
condor_glidein	Add a Globus resource to a Condor pool
condor_history	View log of Condor jobs completed to date
condor_hold	Put jobs in the queue in hold state
condor_prio	Change priority of jobs in the queue
condor_qedit	Modify attributes of a previously submitted job
condor_q	Display information about jobs in the queue
condor_release	Release held jobs in the queue
condor_reschedule	Update scheduling information to the central manager
condor_rm	Remove jobs from the queue
condor_run	Submit a shell command-line as a Condor job
condor_status	Display status of the Condor pool
condor_submit_dag	Manage and queue jobs within a specified DAG for interjob dependencies.
condor_submit	Queue jobs for execution
condor_userlog	Display and summarize job statistics from job log files

Table 14.1
List of user commands.

	RunningJobs	IdleJobs	HeldJobs
ballard@cs.wisc.edu	0	11	0
jbasney@cs.wisc.edu	0	0	5
nice-user.condor@cs.	6	504	0
wright@cs.wisc.edu	1	1	0
Total	7	516	5

Checking on the Progress of Jobs. The condor_q command displays the status of all jobs in the queue. An example of the output from condor_q is

```
% condor_q

-- Schedd: uug.cs.wisc.edu : <128.115.121.12:33102>
ID       OWNER       SUBMITTED    RUN_TIME ST PRI SIZE CMD
55574.0  jane        6/23 11:33  4+03:35:28 R  0   25.7 seycplex seymour.d
55575.0  jane        6/23 11:44  0+23:24:40 R  0   26.8 seycplexpseudo sey
83193.0  jane        3/28 15:11 48+15:50:55 R  0   17.5 cplexmip test1.mp
83196.0  jane        3/29 08:32 48+03:16:44 R  0   83.1 cplexmip test3.mps
83212.0  jane        4/13 16:31 41+18:44:40 R  0   39.7 cplexmip test2.mps
```

```
5 jobs; 0 idle, 5 running, 0 held
```

This output contains many columns of information about the queued jobs. The
ST column (for status) shows the status of current jobs in the queue. An R in
the status column means the the job is currently running. An I stands for idle.
The status H is the hold state. In the hold state, the job will not be scheduled
to run until it is released (via the condor_release command). The RUN_TIME
time reported for a job is the time that job has been allocated to a machine as
DAYS+HOURS+MINS+SECS.

Another useful method of tracking the progress of jobs is through the user log. If
you have specified a log command in your submit file, the progress of the job may be
followed by viewing the log file. Various events such as execution commencement,
checkpoint, eviction, and termination are logged in the file along with the time at
which the event occurred. Here is a sample snippet from a user log file

```
000 (8135.000.000) 05/25 19:10:03 Job submitted from host: <128.105.146.14:1816>
...
001 (8135.000.000) 05/25 19:12:17 Job executing on host: <128.105.165.131:1026>
...
005 (8135.000.000) 05/25 19:13:06 Job terminated.
        (1) Normal termination (return value 0)
                        Usr 0 00:00:37, Sys 0 00:00:00  -  Run Remote Usage
                        Usr 0 00:00:00, Sys 0 00:00:05  -  Run Local Usage
                        Usr 0 00:00:37, Sys 0 00:00:00  -  Total Remote Usage
                        Usr 0 00:00:00, Sys 0 00:00:05  -  Total Local Usage
        9624  -  Run Bytes Sent By Job
        7146159  -  Run Bytes Received By Job
        9624  -  Total Bytes Sent By Job
        7146159  -  Total Bytes Received By Job
...
```

The condor_jobmonitor tool parses the events in a user log file and can use the
information to graphically display the progress of your jobs. Figure 14.2 contains
a screenshot of condor_jobmonitor in action.

You can locate all the machines that are running your job with the condor_status
command. For example, to find all the machines that are running jobs submitted
by breach@cs.wisc.edu, type

```
% condor_status -constraint 'RemoteUser == "breach@cs.wisc.edu"'

Name        Arch    OpSys      State      Activity    LoadAv Mem  ActvtyTime

alfred.cs.  INTEL   LINUX      Claimed    Busy        0.980  64   0+07:10:02
```

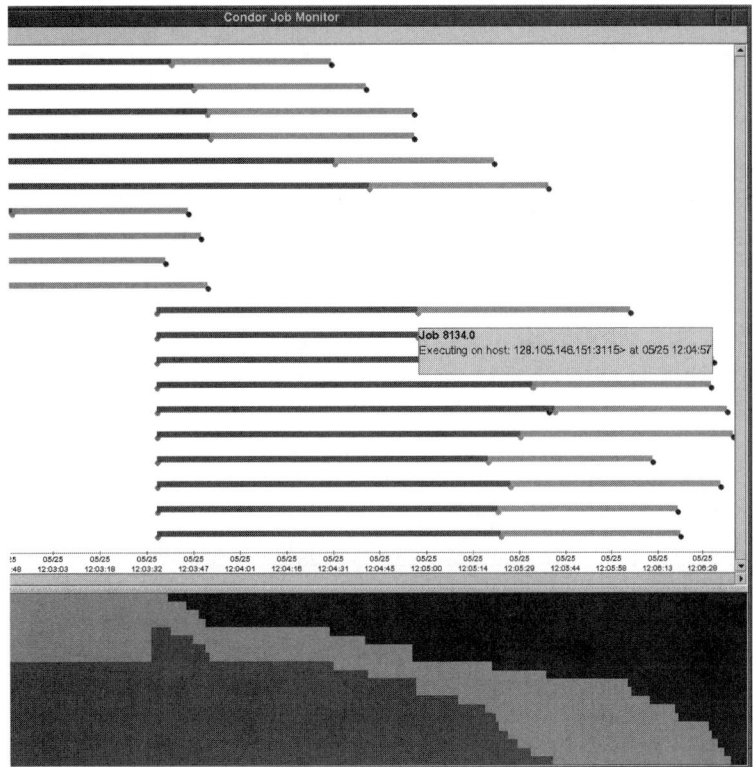

Figure 14.2
Condor jobmonitor tool.

biron.cs.w	INTEL	LINUX	Claimed	Busy	1.000	128	0+01:10:00
cambridge.	INTEL	LINUX	Claimed	Busy	0.988	64	0+00:15:00
falcons.cs	INTEL	LINUX	Claimed	Busy	0.996	32	0+02:05:03
happy.cs.w	INTEL	LINUX	Claimed	Busy	0.988	128	0+03:05:00
istat03.st	INTEL	LINUX	Claimed	Busy	0.883	64	0+06:45:01
istat04.st	INTEL	LINUX	Claimed	Busy	0.988	64	0+00:10:00
istat09.st	INTEL	LINUX	Claimed	Busy	0.301	64	0+03:45:00
...							

To find all the machines that are running any job at all, type

```
% condor_status -run
```

Name	Arch	OpSys	LoadAv	RemoteUser	ClientMachine
adriana.cs	INTEL	LINUX	0.980	hepcon@cs.wisc.edu	chevre.cs.wisc.

```
alfred.cs. INTEL    LINUX       0.980  breach@cs.wisc.edu   neufchatel.cs.w
amul.cs.wi INTEL    LINUX       1.000  nice-user.condor@cs. chevre.cs.wisc.
anfrom.cs. INTEL    LINUX       1.023  ashoks@jules.ncsa.ui jules.ncsa.uiuc
anthrax.cs INTEL    LINUX       0.285  hepcon@cs.wisc.edu   chevre.cs.wisc.
astro.cs.w INTEL    LINUX       1.000  nice-user.condor@cs. chevre.cs.wisc.
aura.cs.wi INTEL    LINUX       0.996  nice-user.condor@cs. chevre.cs.wisc.
balder.cs. INTEL    LINUX       1.000  nice-user.condor@cs. chevre.cs.wisc.
bamba.cs.w INTEL    LINUX       1.574  dmarino@cs.wisc.edu  riola.cs.wisc.e
bardolph.c INTEL    LINUX       1.000  nice-user.condor@cs. chevre.cs.wisc.
...
```

Removing a Job from the Queue.   You can remove a job from the queue at any time using the condor_rm command. If the job that is being removed is currently running, the job is killed without a checkpoint, and its queue entry is removed. The following example shows the queue of jobs before and after a job is removed.

```
% condor_q

-- Submitter: froth.cs.wisc.edu : <128.105.73.44:33847> : froth.cs.wisc.edu
 ID      OWNER           SUBMITTED     RUN_TIME  ST PRI SIZE CMD
 125.0   jbasney         4/10 15:35   0+00:00:00 I  -10 1.2  hello.remote
 132.0   raman           4/11 16:57   0+00:00:00 R  0   1.4  hello

2 jobs; 1 idle, 1 running, 0 held

% condor_rm 132.0
Job 132.0 removed.

% condor_q

-- Submitter: froth.cs.wisc.edu : <128.105.73.44:33847> : froth.cs.wisc.edu
 ID      OWNER           SUBMITTED     RUN_TIME  ST PRI SIZE CMD
 125.0   jbasney         4/10 15:35   0+00:00:00 I  -10 1.2  hello.remote

1 jobs; 1 idle, 0 running, 0 held
```

Changing the Priority of Jobs.   In addition to the priorities assigned to each user, Condor provides users with the capability of assigning priorities to any submitted job. These job priorities are local to each queue and range from -20 to $+20$, with higher values meaning better priority.

The default priority of a job is 0. Job priorities can be modified using the condor_prio command. For example, to change the priority of a job to -15, type

```
% condor_q raman
```

```
-- Submitter: froth.cs.wisc.edu : <128.105.73.44:33847> : froth.cs.wisc.edu
 ID      OWNER           SUBMITTED     RUN_TIME  ST PRI SIZE CMD
 126.0   raman           4/11 15:06    0+00:00:00 I  0   0.3  hello

1 jobs; 1 idle, 0 running, 0 held

% condor_prio -p -15 126.0

% condor_q raman


-- Submitter: froth.cs.wisc.edu : <128.105.73.44:33847> : froth.cs.wisc.edu
 ID      OWNER           SUBMITTED     RUN_TIME  ST PRI SIZE CMD
 126.0   raman           4/11 15:06    0+00:00:00 I -15  0.3  hello

1 jobs; 1 idle, 0 running, 0 held
```

We emphasize that these *job* priorities are completely different from the *user* priorities assigned by Condor. Job priorities control only which one of *your* jobs should run next; there is no effect whatsoever on whether your jobs will run before another user's jobs.

Determining Why a Job Does Not Run. A specific job may not run for several reasons. These reasons include failed job or machine constraints, bias due to preferences, insufficient priority, and the preemption throttle that is implemented by the condor_negotiator to prevent thrashing. Many of these reasons can be diagnosed by using the *-analyze* option of condor_q. For example, the following job submitted by user jbasney had not run for several days.

```
% condor_q

-- Submitter: froth.cs.wisc.edu : <128.105.73.44:33847> : froth.cs.wisc.edu
 ID      OWNER           SUBMITTED     RUN_TIME  ST PRI SIZE CMD
 125.0   jbasney         4/10 15:35    0+00:00:00 I -10  1.2  hello.remote

1 jobs; 1 idle, 0 running, 0 held
```

Running condor_q's analyzer provided the following information:

```
% condor_q 125.0 -analyze

-- Submitter: froth.cs.wisc.edu : <128.105.73.44:33847> : froth.cs.wisc.edu
---
125.000:  Run analysis summary.  Of 323 resource offers,
```

```
323 do not satisfy the request's constraints
  0 resource offer constraints are not satisfied by this request
  0 are serving equal or higher priority customers
  0 are serving more preferred customers
  0 cannot preempt because preemption has been held
  0 are available to service your request

WARNING:  Be advised:
  No resources matched request's constraints
  Check the Requirements expression below:

Requirements = Arch == "INTEL" && OpSys == "IRIX6" &&
  Disk >= ExecutableSize && VirtualMemory >= ImageSize
```

The `Requirements` expression for this job specifies a platform that does not exist. Therefore, the expression always evaluates to FALSE.

While the analyzer can diagnose most common problems, there are some situations that it cannot reliably detect because of the instantaneous and local nature of the information it uses to detect the problem. The analyzer may report that resources are available to service the request, but the job still does not run. In most of these situations, the delay is transient, and the job will run during the next negotiation cycle.

If the problem persists and the analyzer is unable to detect the situation, the job may begin to run but immediately terminates and return to the idle state. Viewing the job's error and log files (specified in the submit command file) and Condor's `SHADOW_LOG` file may assist in tracking down the problem. If the cause is still unclear, you should contact your system administrator.

Job Completion. When a Condor job completes (either through normal means or abnormal means), Condor will remove it from the job queue (therefore, it will no longer appear in the output of `condor_q`) and insert it into the job history file. You can examine the job history file with the `condor_history` command. If you specified a log file in your submit description file, then the job exit status will be recorded there as well.

By default, Condor will send you an e-mail message when your job completes. You can modify this behavior with the `condor_submit` "notification" command. The message will include the exit status of your job or notification that your job terminated abnormally.

14.2.4 Submitting Different Types of Jobs: Alternative Universes

A Universe in Condor defines an execution environment. Condor supports the following Universes on Linux:

- Vanilla
- MPI
- PVM
- Globus
- Scheduler
- Standard

The `Universe` attribute is specified in the submit description file. If the Universe is not specified, it will default to Standard.

Vanilla Universe. The Vanilla Universe is used to run serial (nonparallel) jobs. The examples provided in the preceding section use the Vanilla Universe. Most Condor users prefer to use the Standard Universe to submit serial jobs because of several helpful features of the Standard Universe. However, the Standard Universe has several restrictions on the types of serial jobs supported. The Vanilla Universe, on the other hand, has no such restrictions. Any program that runs outside of Condor will run in the Vanilla Universe. Binary executables as well as scripts are welcome in the Vanilla Universe.

A typical Vanilla Universe job relies on a shared file system between the submit machine and all the nodes in order to allow jobs to access their data. However, if a shared file system is not available, Condor can transfer the files needed by the job to and from the execute machine. See Section 14.2.5 for more details on this.

MPI Universe. The MPI Universe allows parallel programs written with MPI to be managed by Condor. To submit an MPI program to Condor, specify the number of nodes to be used in the parallel job. Use the `machine_count` attribute in the submit description file, as in the following example:

```
# Submit file for an MPI job which needs 8 large memory nodes
universe = mpi
executable = my-parallel-job
requirements = Memory >= 512
machine_count = 8
queue
```

Further options in the submit description file allow a variety of parameters, such as the job requirements or the executable to use across the different nodes.

By late 2001, Condor expects your MPI job to be linked with the MPICH implementation of MPI configured with the `ch_p4` device (see Section 9.6.1). Support for different devices and MPI implementations is expected, however, so check the documentation included with your specific version of Condor for additional information on how your job should be linked with MPI for Condor.

If your Condor pool consists of both dedicated compute machines (that is, Beowulf cluster nodes) and opportunistic machines (that is, desktop workstations), by default Condor will schedule MPI jobs to run on the dedicated resources only.

PVM Universe. Several different parallel programming paradigms exist. One of the more common is the "master/worker" or "pool of tasks" arrangement. In a master/worker program model, one node acts as the controlling master for the parallel application and sends out pieces of work to worker nodes. The worker node does some computation and sends the result back to the master node. The master has a pool of work that needs to be done, and it assigns the next piece of work out to the next worker that becomes available.

The PVM Universe allows master/worker style parallel programs written for the Parallel Virtual Machine interface (see Chapter 11) to be used with Condor. Condor runs the master application on the machine where the job was submitted and will not preempt the master application. Workers are pulled in from the Condor pool as they become available.

Specifically, in the PVM Universe, Condor acts as the resource manager for the PVM daemon. Whenever a PVM program asks for nodes via a `pvm_addhosts()` call, the request is forwarded to Condor. Using ClassAd matching mechanisms, Condor finds a machine in the Condor pool and adds it to the virtual machine. If a machine needs to leave the pool, the PVM program is notified by normal PVM mechanisms, for example, the `pvm_notify()` call.

A unique aspect of the PVM Universe is that PVM jobs submitted to Condor can harness both dedicated and nondedicated (opportunistic) workstations throughout the pool by dynamically adding machines to and removing machines from the parallel virtual machine as machines become available.

Writing a PVM program that deals with Condor's opportunistic environment can be a tricky task. For that reason, the MW framework has been created. MW is a tool for making master-worker style applications in Condor's PVM Universe. For more information, see the MW Home page online at `www.cs.wisc.edu/condor/mw`.

Submitting to the PVM Universe is similar to submitting to the MPI Universe, except that the syntax for `machine_count` is different to reflect the dynamic nature of the PVM Universe. Here is a simple sample submit description file:

```
# Require Condor to give us one node before starting
# the job, but we'll use up to 75 nodes if they are
# available.
universe = pvm
executable = master.exe
machine_count = 1..75
queue
```

By using `machine_count = <min>..<max>`, the submit description file tells Condor that before the PVM master is started, there should be at least `<min>` number of machines given to the job. It also asks Condor to give it as many as `<max>` machines.

More detailed information on the PVM Universe is available in the Condor manual as well as on the Condor-PVM home page at URL `www.cs.wisc.edu/condor/pvm`.

Globus Universe. The Globus Universe in Condor is intended to provide the standard Condor interface to users who wish to submit jobs to machines being managed by Globus (`www.globus.org`).

Scheduler Universe. The Scheduler Universe is used to submit a job that will immediately run on the *submit* machine, as opposed to a remote execution machine. The purpose is to provide a facility for job *meta-schedulers* that desire to manage the submission and removal of jobs into a Condor queue. Condor includes one such meta-scheduler that utilizes the Scheduler Universe: the DAGMan scheduler, which can be used to specify complex interdependencies between jobs. See Section 14.2.6 for more on DAGMan.

Standard Universe. The Standard Universe requires minimal extra effort on the part of the user but provides a serial job with the following highly desirable services:

- Transparent process *checkpoint* and *restart*
- Transparent process migration
- Remote system calls
- Configurable file I/O buffering
- On-the-fly file compression/inflation

Process Checkpointing in the Standard Universe. A checkpoint of an executing program is a snapshot of the program's current state. It provides a way for the program to be continued from that state at a later time. Using checkpoints gives Condor the freedom to reconsider scheduling decisions through preemptive-resume scheduling. If the scheduler decides to rescind a machine that is running a

Condor job (for example, when the owner of that machine returns and reclaims it or when a higher-priority user desires the same machine), the scheduler can take a checkpoint of the job and preempt the job without losing the work the job has already accomplished. The job can then be resumed later when the Condor scheduler allocates it a new machine. Additionally, periodic checkpoints provide fault tolerance. Normally, when performing long-running computations, if a machine crashes or must be rebooted for an administrative task, all the work that has been done is lost. The job must be restarted from the beginning, which can mean days, weeks, or even months of wasted computation time. With checkpoints, Condor ensures that progress is always made on jobs and that only the computation done since the last checkpoint is lost. Condor can be take checkponts periodically, and after an interruption in service, the program can continue from the most recent snapshot.

To enable taking checkpoints, you do not need to change the program's source code. Instead, the program must be relinked with the Condor system call library (see below). Taking the checkpoint of a process is implemented in the Condor system call library as a signal handler. When Condor sends a checkpoint signal to a process linked with this library, the provided signal handler writes the state of the process out to a file or a network socket. This state includes the contents of the process's stack and data segments, all CPU state (including register values), the state of all open files, and any signal handlers and pending signals. When a job is to be continued using a checkpoint, Condor reads this state from the file or network socket, restoring the stack, shared library and data segments, file state, signal handlers, and pending signals. The checkpoint signal handler then restores the CPU state and returns to the user code, which continues from where it left off when the checkpoint signal arrived. Condor jobs submitted to the Standard Universe will automatically perform a checkpoint when preempted from a machine. When a suitable replacement execution machine is found (of the same architecture and operating system), the process is restored on this new machine from the checkpoint, and computation is resumed from where it left off.

By default, a checkpoint is written to a file on the local disk of the submit machine. A Condor checkpoint server is also available to serve as a repository for checkpoints.

Remote System Calls in the Standard Universe. One hurdle to overcome when placing an job on a remote execution workstation is data access. In order to utilize the remote resources, the job must be able to read from and write to files on its submit machine. A requirement that the remote execution machine be able to access these files via NFS, AFS, or any other network file system may significantly limit the number of eligible workstations and therefore hinder the ability of an environment to achieve high throughput. Therefore, in order to maximize throughput, Condor strives to be able to run any application on any remote workstation of a given platform without relying upon a common administrative setup. The enabling technology that permits this is Condor's Remote System Calls mechanism. This mechanism provides the benefit that Condor does not require a user to possess a login account on the execute workstation.

When a Unix process needs to access a file, it calls a file I/O system function such as `open()`, `read()`, or `write()`. These functions are typically handled by the standard C library, which consists primarily of stubs that generate a corresponding system call to the local kernel. Condor users link their applications with an enhanced standard C library via the `condor_compile` command. This library does not duplicate any code in the standard C library; instead, it augments certain system call stubs (such as the ones that handle file I/O) into remote system call stubs. The remote system call stubs package the system call number and arguments into a message that is sent over the network to a `condor_shadow` process that runs on the submit machine. Whenever Condor starts a Standard Universe job, it also starts a corresponding shadow process on the initiating host where the user originally submitted the job (see Figure 14.3). This shadow process acts as an agent for the remotely executing program in performing system calls. The shadow then executes the system call on behalf of the remotely running job in the normal way. The shadow packages up the results of the system call in a message and sends it back to the remote system call stub in the Condor library on the remote machine. The remote system call stub returns its result to the calling procedure, which is unaware that the call was done remotely rather than locally. In this fashion, calls in the user's program to `open()`, `read()`, `write()`, `close()`, and all other file I/O calls transparently take place on the machine that submitted the job instead of on the remote execution machine.

Relinking and Submitting for the Standard Universe.   To convert a program into a Standard Universe job, use the `condor_compile` command to relink with the Condor libraries. Place `condor_compile` in front of your usual link command. You do not need to modify the program's source code, but you do need access to its unlinked object files. A commercial program that is packaged as a single executable file cannot be converted into a Standard Universe job.

For example, if you normally link your job by executing

```
% cc main.o tools.o -o program
```

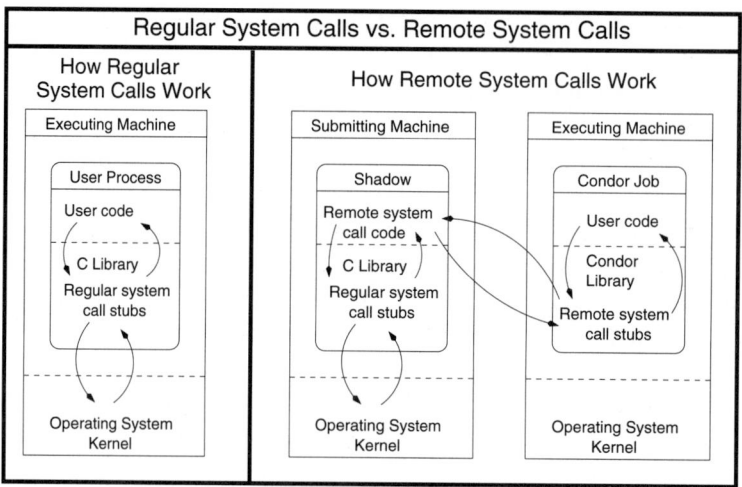

Figure 14.3
Remote System calls in the Standard Universe.

You can relink your job for Condor with

```
% condor_compile cc main.o tools.o -o program
```

After you have relinked your job, you can submit it. A submit description file for the Standard Universe is similar to one for the Vanilla Universe. However, several additional submit directives are available to perform activities such as on-the-fly compression of data files. Here is an example:

```
# Submit 100 runs of my-program to the Standard Universe
universe = standard
executable = my-program.exe
# Each run should take place in a seperate subdirectory: run0, run1, ...
initialdir = run$(Process)
# Ask the Condor remote syscall layer to automatically compress
# on-the-fly any writes done by my-program.exe to file data.output
compress_files = data.output
queue 100
```

Standard Universe Limitations.   Condor performs its process checkpoint and migration routines strictly in user mode; there are no kernel drivers with Condor. Because Condor is not operating at the kernel level, there are limitations on what process state it is able to checkpoint. As a result, the following restrictions are imposed upon Standard Universe jobs:

1. Multiprocess jobs are not allowed. This includes system calls such as `fork()`, `exec()`, and `system()`.

2. Interprocess communication is not allowed. This includes pipes, semaphores, and shared memory.

3. Network communication must be brief. A job *may* make network connections using system calls such as `socket()`, but a network connection left open for long periods will delay checkpoints and migration.

4. Multiple kernel-level threads are not allowed. However, multiple user-level threads (green threads) *are* allowed.

5. All files should be accessed read-only or write-only. A file that is both read and written to can cause trouble if a job must be rolled back to an old checkpoint image.

6. On Linux, your job must be statically linked. Dynamic linking is allowed in the Standard Universe on some other platforms supported by Condor, and perhaps this restriction on Linux will be removed in a future Condor release.

14.2.5 Giving Your Job Access to Its Data Files

Once your job starts on a machine in your pool, how does it access its data files? Condor provides several choices.

If the job is a Standard Universe job, then Condor solves the problem of data access automatically using the Remote System call mechanism described above. Whenever the job tries to open, read, or write to a file, the I/O will actually take place on the submit machine, whether or not a shared file system is in place.

Condor can use a shared file system, if one is available and permanently mounted across the machines in the pool. This is usually the case in a Beowulf cluster. But what if your Condor pool includes nondedicated (desktop) machines as well? You could specify a `Requirements` expression in your submit description file to require that jobs run only on machines that actually do have access to a common, shared file system. Or, you could request in the submit description file that Condor transfer your job's data files using the Condor File Transfer mechanism.

When Condor finds a machine willing to execute your job, it can create a temporary subdirectory for your job on the execute machine. The Condor File Transfer mechanism will then send via TCP the job executable(s) and input files from the submitting machine into this temporary directory on the execute machine. After the input files have been transferred, the execute machine will start running the job with the temporary directory as the job's current working directory. When the job completes or is kicked off, Condor File Transfer will automatically send back to the submit machine any output files created or modified by the job. After the files have been sent back successfully, the temporary working directory on the execute machine is deleted.

Condor's File Transfer mechanism has several features to ensure data integrity in a nondedicated environment. For instance, transfers of multiple files are performed atomically.

Condor File Transfer behavior is specified at job submission time using the submit description file and `condor_submit`. Along with all the other job submit description parameters, you can use the following File Transfer commands in the submit description file:

transfer_input_files = < file1, file2, file... >: Use this parameter to list all the files that should be transferred into the working directory for the job before the job is started.

transfer_output_files = < file1, file2, file... >: Use this parameter to explicitly list which output files to transfer back from the temporary working directory on the execute machine to the submit machine. Most of the time, however, there is no need to use this parameter. If `transfer_output_files` is not specified, Condor will automatically transfer in the job's temporary working directory all files that have been modified or created by the job.

transfer_files = <ONEXIT | ALWAYS | NEVER>: If `transfer_files` is set to `ONEXIT`, Condor will transfer the job's output files back to the submitting machine only when the job completes (exits). Specifying `ALWAYS` tells Condor to transfer back the output files when the job completes *or* when Condor kicks off the job (preempts) from a machine prior to job completion. The `ALWAYS` option is specifically intended for fault-tolerant jobs that periodocially write out their state to disk and can restart where they left off. Any output files transferred back to the submit machine when Condor preempts a job will automatically be sent back out again as input files when the job restarts.

14.2.6 The DAGMan Scheduler

The DAGMan scheduler within Condor allows the specification of dependencies between a set of programs. A directed acyclic graph (DAG) can be used to represent a set of programs where the input, output, or execution of one or more programs is dependent on one or more other programs. The programs are nodes (vertices) in the graph, and the edges (arcs) identify the dependencies. Each program within the DAG becomes a job submitted to Condor. The DAGMan scheduler enforces the dependencies of the DAG.

An input file to DAGMan identifies the nodes of the graph, as well as how to submit each job (node) to Condor. It also specifies the graph's dependencies and describes any extra processing that is involved with the nodes of the graph and must take place just before or just after the job is run.

A simple diamond-shaped DAG with four nodes is given in Figure 14.4.

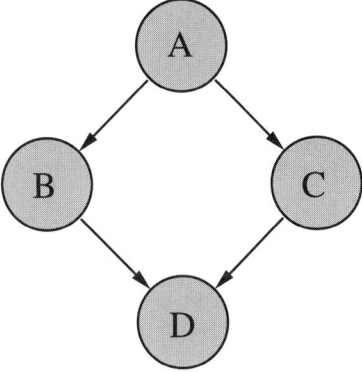

Figure 14.4
A directed acyclic graph with four nodes.

A simple input file to DAGMan for this diamond-shaped DAG may be

```
# file name: diamond.dag
Job  A  A.condor
Job  B  B.condor
Job  C  C.condor
Job  D  D.condor
PARENT A CHILD B C
PARENT B C CHILD D
```

The four nodes are named A, B, C, and D. Lines beginning with the keyword Job identify each node by giving it a name, and they also specify a file to be used as a submit description file for submission as a Condor job. Lines with the keyword PARENT identify the dependencies of the graph. Just like regular Condor submit description files, lines with a leading pound character (#) are comments.

The DAGMan scheduler uses the graph to order the submission of jobs to Condor. The submission of a child node will not take place until the parent node has successfully completed. No ordering of siblings is imposed by the graph, and therefore DAGMan does not impose an ordering when submitting the jobs to Condor. For the diamond-shaped example, nodes B and C will be submitted to Condor in parallel.

Each job in the example graph uses a different submit description file. An example submit description file for job A may be

```
# file name: A.condor
executable    = nodeA.exe
output        = A.out
error         = A.err
log           = diamond.log
universe      = vanilla
queue
```

An important restriction for submit description files of a DAG is that each node of the graph use the same log file. DAGMan uses the log file in enforcing the graph's dependencies.

The graph for execution under Condor is submitted by using the Condor tool `condor_submit_dag`. For the diamond-shaped example, submission would use the command

```
condor_submit_dag diamond.dag
```

14.3   Condor Architecture

A Condor pool comprises a single machine that serves as the *central manager* and an arbitrary number of other machines that have joined the pool. Conceptually, the pool is a collection of resources (machines) and resource requests (jobs). The role of Condor is to match waiting requests with available resources. Every part of Condor sends periodic updates to the central manager, the centralized repository of information about the state of the pool. The central manager periodically assesses the current state of the pool and tries to match pending requests with the appropriate resources.

14.3.1 The Condor Daemons

In this subsection we describe all the daemons (background server processes) in Condor and the role each plays in the system.

`condor_master`: This daemon's role is to simplify system administration. It is responsible for keeping the rest of the Condor daemons running on each machine in a pool. The master spawns the other daemons and periodically checks the timestamps on the binaries of the daemons it is managing. If it finds new binaries, the master will restart the affected daemons. This allows Condor to be upgraded easily. In addition, if any other Condor daemon on the machine exits abnormally, the `condor_master` will send e-mail to the system administrator with information about the problem and then automatically restart the affected daemon. The `condor_master` also supports various administrative commands to start, stop, or reconfigure daemons remotely. The `condor_master` runs on every machine in your Condor pool.

`condor_startd`: This daemon represents a machine to the Condor pool. It advertises a machine ClassAd that contains attributes about the machine's capabilities and policies. Running the `startd` enables a machine to execute jobs. The `condor_startd` is responsible for enforcing the policy under which remote jobs will be started, suspended, resumed, vacated, or killed. When the `startd` is ready to execute a Condor job, it spawns the `condor_starter`, described below.

`condor_starter`: This program is the entity that spawns the remote Condor job on a given machine. It sets up the execution environment and monitors the job once it is running. The starter detects job completion, sends back status information to the submitting machine, and exits.

`condor_schedd`: This daemon represents jobs to the Condor pool. Any machine that allows users to submit jobs needs to have a `condor_schedd` running. Users submit jobs to the `condor_schedd`, where they are stored in the *job queue*. The various tools to view and manipulate the job queue (such as `condor_submit`, `condor_q`, or `condor_rm`) connect to the `condor_schedd` to do their work.

`condor_shadow`: This program runs on the machine where a job was submitted whenever that job is executing. The shadow serves requests for files to transfer, logs the job's progress, and reports statistics when the job completes. Jobs that are linked for Condor's Standard Universe, which perform remote system calls, do so via the `condor_shadow`. Any system call performed on the remote execute machine is sent over the network to the `condor_shadow`. The shadow performs the system call (such as file I/O) on the submit machine and the result is sent back over the network to the remote job.

`condor_collector`: This daemon is responsible for collecting all the information about the status of a Condor pool. All other daemons periodically send ClassAd updates to the collector. These ClassAds contain all the information about the state of the daemons, the resources they represent, or resource requests in the pool (such as jobs that have been submitted to a given `condor_schedd`). The `condor_collector` can be thought of as a dynamic database of ClassAds. The `condor_status` command can be used to query the collector for specific information about various parts of Condor. The Condor daemons also query the collector for important information, such as what address to use for sending commands to a remote machine. The `condor_collector` runs on the machine designated as the central manager.

`condor_negotiator`: This daemon is responsible for all the matchmaking within the Condor system. The negotiator is also responsible for enforcing user priorities in the system.

14.3.2   The Condor Daemons in Action

Within a given Condor installation, one machine will serve as the pool's central manager. In addition to the `condor_master` daemon that runs on every machine in a Condor pool, the central manager runs the `condor_collector` and the `condor_negotiator` daemons. Any machine in the installation that should be capable of running jobs should run the `condor_startd`, and any machine that should maintain a job queue and therefore allow users on that machine to submit jobs should run a `condor_schedd`.

Condor allows any machine simultaneously to execute jobs and serve as a submission point by running both a `condor_startd` and a `condor_schedd`. Figure 14.5 displays a Condor pool in which every machine in the pool can both submit and run jobs, including the central manager.

The interface for adding a job to the Condor system is `condor_submit`, which reads a job description file, creates a job ClassAd, and gives that ClassAd to the `condor_schedd` managing the local job queue. This triggers a *negotiation cycle*. During a negotiation cycle, the `condor_negotiator` queries the `condor_collector` to discover all machines that are willing to perform work and all users with idle jobs. The `condor_negotiator` communicates *in user priority order* with each

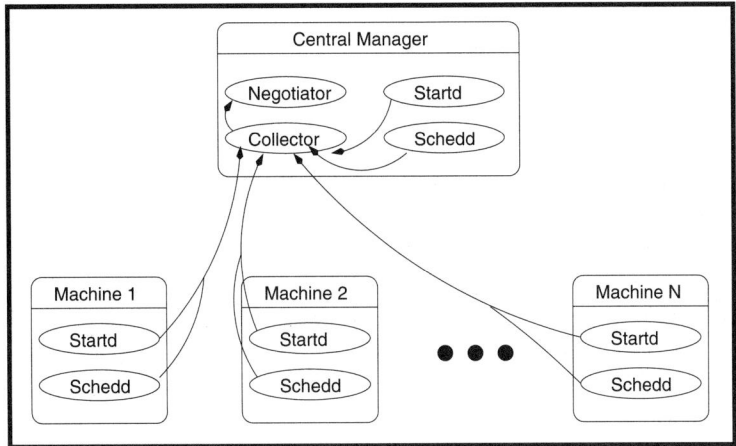

Figure 14.5
Daemon layout of an idle Condor pool.

condor_schedd that has idle jobs in its queue, and performs matchmaking to match jobs with machines such that both job and machine ClassAd requirements are satisfied and preferences (rank) are honored.

Once the condor_negotiator makes a match, the condor_schedd claims the corresponding machine and is allowed to make subsequent scheduling decisions about the order in which jobs run. This hierarchical, distributed scheduling architecture enhances Condor's scalability and flexibility.

When the condor_schedd starts a job, it spawns a condor_shadow process on the submit machine, and the condor_startd spawns a condor_starter process on the corresponding execute machine (see Figure 14.6). The shadow transfers the job ClassAd and any data files required to the starter, which spawns the user's application.

If the job is a Standard Universe job, the shadow will begin to service remote system calls originating from the user job, allowing the job to transparently access data files on the submitting host.

When the job completes or is aborted, the condor_starter removes every process spawned by the user job, and frees any temporary scratch disk space used by the job. This ensures that the execute machine is left in a clean state and that resources (such as processes or disk space) are not being leaked.

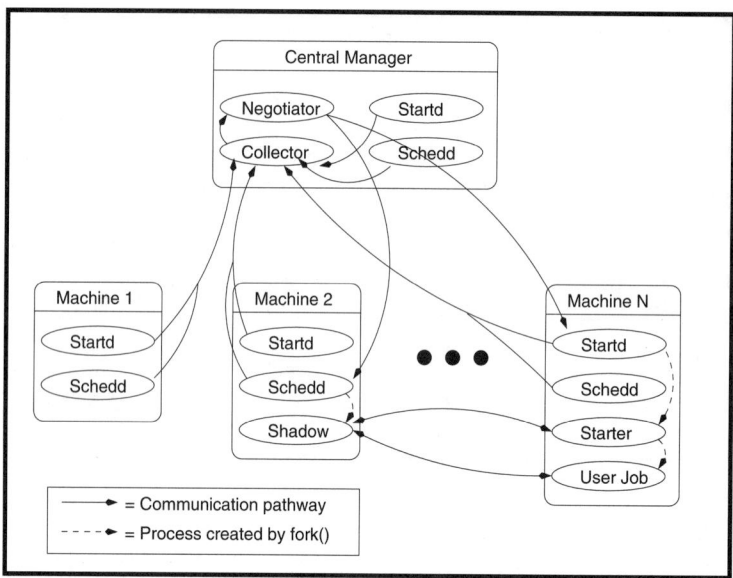

Figure 14.6
Daemon layout when a job submitted from Machine 2 is running.

14.4   Installing Condor under Linux

The first step toward the installation of Condor is to download the software from the Condor Web site at `www.cs.wisc.edu/condor/downloads`. There is no cost to download or use Condor.

On the Web site you will find complete documentation and release notes for the different versions and platforms supported. You should take care to download the appropriate version of Condor for your platform (the operating system and processor architecture).

Before you begin the installation, there are several issues you need to consider and actions to perform.

Creation of User Condor. For both security and performance reasons, the Condor daemons should execute with root privileges. However, to avoid running as root except when absolutely necessary, the Condor daemons will run with the privileges of user condor on your system. In addition, the user condor simplifies installation, since files owned by the user condor will be created, and the home directory of the user condor can be used to specify file locations. For Linux clusters, we highly recommend that you create the user condor on all machines before installation begins.

Location. Administration of your pool is eased when the release directory (which includes all the binaries, libraries, and configuration files used by Condor) is placed on a shared file server. Note that one set of binaries is needed for each platform in your pool.

Administrator. Condor needs an e-mail address for an administrator. Should Condor need assistance, this is where e-mail will be sent.

Central Manager. The central manager of a Condor pool does matchmaking and collects information for the pool. Choose a central manager that has a good network connection and is likely to be online all the time (or at least rebooted quickly in the event of a failure).

Once you have decided the answers to these questions (and set up the condor user) you are ready to begin installation. The tool called condor_install is executed to begin the installation. The configuration tool will ask you a short series of questions, mostly related to the issues addressed above. Answer the questions appropriately for your site, and Condor will be installed.

On a large Linux cluster, you can speed the installation process by running condor_install once on your fileserver node and configuring your entire pool at the same time. If you use this configuration option, you will need to run only the condor_init script (which requires no input) on each of your compute nodes.

The default Condor installation will configure your pool to assume nondedicated resources. Section 14.5 discusses how to configure and customize your pool for a dedicated cluster.

After Condor is installed, you will want to customize a few security configuration right away. Condor implements security at the host (or machine) level. A set of configuration defaults set by the installation deal with access to the Condor pool by host. Given the distributed nature of the daemons that implement Condor, access to these daemons is naturally host based. Each daemon can be given the ability to allow or deny service (by host) within its configuration. Within the access levels available, *Read*, *Write*, *Administrator*, and *Config* are important to set correctly for each pool of machines.

Read: allows a machine to obtain information from Condor. Examples of information that may be read are the status of the pool and the contents of the job queue.

Write: allows a machine to provide information to Condor, such as submit a job or join the pool.

Administrator: allows a user on the machine to affect privileged operations such as changing a user's priority level or starting and stopping the Condor system from running.

Config: allows a user on the machine to change Condor's configuration settings remotely using the `condor_config_val` tool's *-set* and *-rset* options. This has very serious security implications, so we recommend that you not enable Config access to any hosts.

The defaults during installation give all machines read and write access. The central manager is also given administrator access. You will probably wish to change these defaults for your site. Read the Condor Administrator's Manual for details on network authorization in Condor and how to customize it for your wishes.

14.5   Configuring Condor

This section describes how to configure and customize Condor for your site. It discusses the configuration files used by Condor, describes how to configure the policy for starting and stopping jobs in your pool, and recommends settings for using Condor on a cluster.

A number of configuration files facilitate different levels of control over how Condor is configured on each machine in a pool. The top-level or global configuration file is shared by all machines in the pool. For ease of administration, this file should be located on a shared file system. In addition, each machine may have multiple local configuration files allowing the local settings to override the global settings. Hence, each machine may have different daemons running, different policies for when to start and stop Condor jobs, and so on.

All of Condor's configuration files should be owned and writable only by root. It is important to maintain strict control over these files because they contain security-sensitive settings.

14.5.1   Location of Condor's Configuration Files

Condor has a default set of locations it uses to try to find its top-level configuration file. The locations are checked in the following order:

1.   The file specified in the `CONDOR_CONFIG` environment variable.

2. '/etc/condor/condor_config', if it exists.

3. If user condor exists on your system, the 'condor_config' file in this user's home directory.

If a Condor daemon or tool cannot find its global configuration file when it starts, it will print an error message and immediately exit. Once the global configuration file has been read by Condor, however, any other local configuration files can be specified with the LOCAL_CONFIG_FILE macro.

This macro can contain a single entry if you want only two levels of configuration (global and local). If you need a more complex division of configuration values (for example, if you have machines of different platforms in the same pool and desire separate files for platform-specific settings), LOCAL_CONFIG_FILE can contain a list of files.

Condor provides other macros to help you easily define the location of the local configuration files for each machine in your pool. Most of these are special macros that evaluate to different values depending on which host is reading the global configuration file:

- HOSTNAME: The hostname of the local host.
- FULL_HOSTNAME: The fully qualified hostname of the local host.
- TILDE: The home directory of the user condor on the local host.
- OPSYS: The operating system of the local host, such as "LINUX," "WINNT4" (for Windows NT), or "WINNT5" (for Windows 2000). This is primarily useful in heterogeneous clusters with multiple platforms.
- RELEASE_DIR: The directory where Condor is installed on each host. This macro is defined in the global configuration file and is set by Condor's installation program.

By default, the local configuration file is defined as

```
LOCAL_CONFIG_FILE = $(TILDE)/condor_config.local
```

14.5.2 Recommended Configuration File Layout for a Cluster

Ease of administration is an important consideration in a cluster, particularly if you have a large number of nodes. To make Condor easy to configure, we highly recommend that you install all of your Condor configuration files, even the per-node local configuration files, on a shared file system. That way, you can easily make changes in one place.

You should use a subdirectory in your release directory for holding all of the local configuration files. By default, Condor's release directory contains an 'etc' directory for this purpose.

You should create separate files for each node in your cluster, using the hostname as the first half of the filename, and ".local" as the end. For example, if your cluster nodes are named "n01", "n02" and so on, the files should be called 'n01.local', 'n02.local', and so on. These files should all be placed in your 'etc' directory.

In your global configuration file, you should use the following setting to describe the location of your local configuration files:

```
LOCAL_CONFIG_FILE = $(RELEASE_DIR)/etc/$(HOSTNAME).local
```

The central manager of your pool needs special settings in its local configuration file. These attributes are set automatically by the Condor installation program. The rest of the local configuration files can be left empty at first.

Having your configuration files laid out in this way will help you more easily customize Condor's behavior on your cluster. We discuss other possible configuration scenarios at the end of this chapter.

Note: We recommend that you store all of your Condor configuration files under a version control system, such as CVS. While this is not required, it will help you keep track of the changes you make to your configuration, who made them, when they occurred, and why. In general, it is a good idea to store configuration files under a version control system, since none of the above concerns are specific to Condor.

14.5.3   Customizing Condor's Policy Expressions

Certain configuration expressions are used to control Condor's policy for executing, suspending, and evicting jobs. Their interaction can be somewhat complex. Defining an inappropriate policy impacts the throughput of your cluster and the happiness of its users. If you are interested in creating a specialized policy for your pool, we recommend that you read the Condor Administrator's Manual. Only a basic introduction follows.

All policy expressions are ClassAd expressions and are defined in Condor's configuration files. Policies are usually poolwide and are therefore defined in the global configuration file. If individual nodes in your pool require their own policy, however, the appropriate expressions can be placed in local configuration files.

The policy expressions are treated by the condor_startd as part of its machine ClassAd (along with all the attributes you can view with condor_status -long).

They are always evaluated against a job ClassAd, either by the condor_negotiator when trying to find a match or by the condor_startd when it is deciding what to do with the job that is currently running. Therefore, all policy expressions can reference attributes of a job, such as the memory usage or owner, in addition to attributes of the machine, such as keyboard idle time or CPU load.

Most policy expressions are ClassAd Boolean expressions, so they evaluate to TRUE, FALSE, or UNDEFINED. UNDEFINED occurs when an expression references a ClassAd attribute that is not found in either the machine's ClassAd or the ClassAd of the job under consideration. For some expressions, this is treated as a fatal error, so you should be sure to use the ClassAd meta-operators, described in Section 14.1.2 when referring to attributes which might not be present in all ClassAds.

An explanation of policy expressions requires an understanding of the different stages that a job can go through from initially executing until the job completes or is evicted from the machine. Each policy expression is then described in terms of the step in the progression that it controls.

The Lifespan of a Job Executing in Condor. When a job is submitted to Condor, the condor_negotiator performs matchmaking to find a suitable resource to use for the computation. This process involves satisfying both the job and the machine's requirements for each other. The machine can define the exact conditions under which it is willing to be considered available for running jobs. The job can define exactly what kind of machine it is willing to use.

Once a job has been matched with a given machine, there are four states the job can be in: running, suspended, graceful shutdown, and quick shutdown. As soon as the match is made, the job sets up its execution environment and begins running.

While it is executing, a job can be suspended (for example, because of other activity on the machine where it is running). Once it has been suspended, the job can resume execution or can move on to preemption or eviction.

All Condor jobs have two methods for preemption: graceful and quick. Standard Universe jobs are given a chance to produce a checkpoint with graceful preemption. For the other universes, graceful implies that the program is told to get off the system, but it is given time to clean up after itself. On all flavors of Unix, a SIGTERM is sent during graceful shutdown by default, although users can override this default when they submit their job. A quick shutdown involves rapidly killing all processes associated with a job, without giving them any time to execute their own cleanup procedures. The Condor system performs checks to ensure that processes are not left behind once a job is evicted from a given node.

Condor Policy Expressions.   Various expressions are used to control the policy for starting, suspending, resuming, and preempting jobs.

START: when the condor_startd is willing to start executing a job.

RANK: how much the condor_startd prefers each type of job running on it. The RANK expression is a floating-point instead of a Boolean value. The condor_startd will preempt the job it is currently running if there is another job in the system that yields a higher value for this expression.

WANT_SUSPEND: controls whether the condor_startd should even consider suspending this job or not. In effect, it determines which expression, SUSPEND or PREEMPT, should be evaluated while the job is running. WANT_SUSPEND does not control when the job is actually suspended; for that purpose, you should use the SUSPEND expression.

SUSPEND: when the condor_startd should suspend the currently running job. If WANT_SUSPEND evaluates to TRUE, SUSPEND is periodically evaluated whenever a job is executing on a machine. If SUSPEND becomes TRUE, the job will be suspended.

CONTINUE: if and when the condor_startd should resume a suspended job. The CONTINUE expression is evaluated only while a job is suspended. If it evaluates to TRUE, the job will be resumed, and the condor_startd will go back to the Claimed/Busy state.

PREEMPT: when the condor_startd should preempt the currently running job. This expression is evaluated whenever a job has been suspended. If WANT_SUSPEND evaluates to FALSE, PREEMPT is checked while the job is executing.

WANT_VACATE: whether the job should be evicted gracefully or quickly if Condor is preempting a job (because the PREEMPT expression evaluates to TRUE). If WANT_VACATE is FALSE, the condor_startd will immediately kill the job and all of its child processes whenever it must evict the application. If WANT_VACATE is TRUE, the condor_startd performs a graceful shutdown, instead.

KILL: when the condor_startd should give up on a graceful preemption and move directly to the quick shutdown.

PREEMPTION_REQUIREMENTS: used by the condor_negotiator when it is performing matchmaking, not by the condor_startd. While trying to schedule jobs on resources in your pool, the condor_negotiator considers the priorities of the various users in the system (see Section 14.6.3 for more details). If a user with a better priority has jobs waiting in the queue and no resources are currently idle, the matchmaker will consider preempting another user's jobs and giving those resources to the user with the better priority. This process is known as *priority preemption*. The PREEMPTION_REQUIREMENTS expression must evaluate to TRUE for such a preemption to take place.

PREEMPTION_RANK: a floating-point value evaluated by the condor_negotiator. If the matchmaker decides it must preempt a job due to user priorities, the macro PREEMPTION_RANK determines which resource to preempt. Among the set of all resources that make the PREEMPTION_REQUIREMENTS expression evaluate to TRUE, the one with the highest value for PREEMPTION_RANK is evicted.

14.5.4 Customizing Condor's Other Configuration Settings

In addition to the policy expressions, you will need to modify other settings to customize Condor for your cluster.

DAEMON_LIST: the comma-separated list of daemons that should be spawned by the condor_master. As described in Section 14.3.1 discussing the architecture of Condor, each host in your pool can play different roles depending on which daemons are started on it. You define these roles using the DAEMON_LIST in the appropriate configuration files to enable or disable the various Condor daemons on each host.

DedicatedScheduler: the name of the dedicated scheduler for your cluster. This setting must have the form

```
DedicatedScheduler = "DedicatedScheduler@full.host.name.here"
```

14.6   Administration Tools

Condor has a rich set of tools for the administrator. Table 14.2 gives an overview of the Condor commands typically used solely by the system administrator. Of course, many of the "user-level" Condor tools summarized in Table 14.2 can be helpful for cluster administration as well. For instance, the condor_status tool can easily display the status for all nodes in the cluster, including dynamic information such as current load average and free virtual memory.

14.6.1   Remote Configuration and Control

All machines in a Condor pool can be remotely managed from a centralized location. Condor can be enabled, disabled, or restarted remotely using the condor_on,

Command	Description
condor_checkpoint	Checkpoint jobs running on the specified hosts
condor_config_val	Query or set a given Condor configuration variable
condor_master_off	Shut down Condor and the condor_master
condor_off	Shut down Condor daemons
condor_on	Start up Condor daemons
condor_reconfig	Reconfigure Condor daemons
condor_restart	Restart the condor_master
condor_stats	Display historical information about the Condor pool
condor_userprio	Display and manage user priorities
condor_vacate	Vacate jobs that are running on the specified hosts

Table 14.2
Commands reserved for the administrator.

condor_off, and condor_restart commands, respectively. Additionally, any aspect of Condor's configuration file on a node can be queried or changed remotely via the condor_config_val command. Of course, not everyone is allowed to change your Condor configuration remotely. Doing so requires proper authorization, which is set up at installation time (see Section 14.4).

Many aspects of Condor's configuration, including its scheduling policy, can be changed on the fly without requiring the pool to be shut down and restarted. This is accomplished by using the condor_reconfig command, which asks the Condor daemons on a specified host to reread the Condor configuration files and take appropriate action—on the fly if possible.

14.6.2 Accounting and Logging

Condor keeps many statistics about what is happening in the pool. Each daemon can be asked to keep a detailed log of its activities; Condor will automatically rotate these log files when they reach a maximum size as specified by the administrator.

In addition to the condor_history command, which allows users to view job ClassAds for jobs that have previously completed, the condor_stats tool can be used to query for historical usage statistics from a poolwide accounting database. This database contains information about how many jobs were being serviced for each user at regular intervals, as well as how many machines were busy. For instance, condor_stats could be asked to display the total number of jobs running at five-minute intervals for a specified user between January 15 and January 30.

The condor_view tool takes the raw information obtainable with condor_stats and converts it into HTML, complete with interactive charts. Figure 14.7 shows a sample display of the output from `condor_view` in a Web browser. The site administrator, using `condor_view`, can quickly put detailed, real-time usage statistics about the Condor pool onto a Web site.

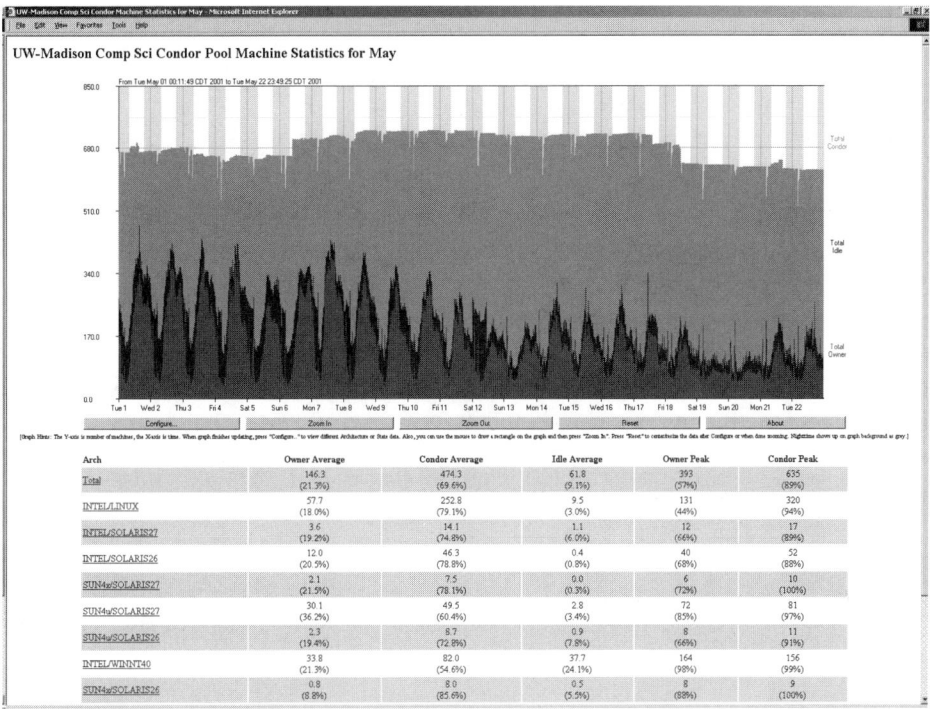

Figure 14.7
CondorView displaying machine usage.

14.6.3 User Priorities in Condor

The job queues in Condor are not strictly first-in, first-out. Instead, Condor implements *priority queuing*. Different users will get different-sized allocations of machines depending on their current user priority, regardless of how many jobs from a competing user are "ahead" of them in the queue. Condor can also be configured to perform *priority preemption* if desired. For instance, suppose user A is using all the nodes in a cluster, when suddenly a user with a superior priority submits jobs. With priority preemption enabled, Condor will preempt the jobs of the lower-priority user in order to immediately start the jobs submitted by the higher-priority user.

Starvation of the lower-priority users is prevented by a fair-share algorithm, which attempts to give all users the same amount of machine allocation time over a specified interval. In addition, the priority calculations in Condor are based on *ratios* instead of absolutes. For example, if Bill has a priority that is twice as good as that of Fred, Condor will not starve Fred by allocating all machines to Bill. Instead, Bill will get, on average, twice as many machines as will Fred because Bill's priority is twice as good.

The `condor_userprio` command can be used by the administrator to view or edit a user's priority. It can also be used to override Condor's default fair-share policy and explicitly assign users a better or worse priority in relation to other users.

14.7   Cluster Setup Scenarios

This section explores different scenarios for how to configure your cluster. Five scenarios are presented, along with a basic idea of what configuration settings you will need to modify or what steps you will need to take for each scenario:

1.   A uniformly owned, dedicated compute cluster, with a single front-end node for submission, and support for MPI applications.

2.   A cluster of multiprocessor nodes.

3.   A cluster of distributively owned nodes. Each node prefers to run jobs submitted by its owner.

4.   Desktop submission to the cluster.

5.   Expanding the cluster to nondedicated (desktop) computing resources.

Most of these scenarios can be combined. Each scenario builds on the previous one to add further functionality to the basic cluster configuration.

14.7.1   Basic Configuration: Uniformly Owned Cluster

The most basic scenario involves a cluster where all resources are owned by a single entity and all compute nodes enforce the same policy for starting and stopping jobs. All compute nodes are dedicated, meaning that they will always start an idle job and they will never preempt or suspend until completion. There is a single front-end node for submitting jobs, and dedicated MPI jobs are enabled from this host.

In order to enable this basic policy, your global configuration file must contain these settings:

```
START = True
SUSPEND = False
CONTINUE = False
PREEMPT = False
KILL = False
WANT_SUSPEND = True
WANT_VACATE = True
RANK = Scheduler =?= $(DedicatedScheduler)
DAEMON_LIST = MASTER, STARTD
```

The final entry listed here specifies that the default role for nodes in your pool is execute-only. The DAEMON_LIST on your front-end node must also enable the condor_schedd. This front-end node's local configuration file will be

```
DAEMON_LIST = MASTER, STARTD, SCHEDD
```

14.7.2   Using Multiprocessor Compute Nodes

If any node in your Condor pool is a symmetric multiprocessor machine, Condor will represent that node as multiple virtual machines (VMs), one for each CPU. By default, each VM will have a single CPU and an even share of all shared system resources, such as RAM and swap space. If this behavior satisfies your needs, you do not need to make any configuration changes for SMP nodes to work properly with Condor.

Some sites might want different behavior of their SMP nodes. For example, assume your cluster was composed of dual-processor machines with 1 gigabyte of RAM, and one of your users was submitting jobs with a memory footprint of 700 megabytes. With the default setting, all VMs in your pool would only have 500 megabytes of RAM, and your user's jobs would never run. In this case, you would want to unevenly divide RAM between the two CPUs, to give half of your VMs 750 megabytes of RAM. The other half of the VMs would be left with 250 megabytes of RAM.

There is more than one way to divide shared resources on an SMP machine with Condor, all of which are discussed in detail in the Condor Administrator's Manual. The most basic method is as follows. To divide shared resources on an SMP unevenly, you must define different *virtual machine types* and tell the condor_startd how many virtual machines of each type to advertise. The simplest method to define a virtual machine type is to specify what fraction of all shared resources each type should receive.

For example, if you wanted to divide a two-node machine where one CPU received one-quarter of the shared resources, and the other CPU received the other three-quarters, you would use the following settings:

```
VIRTUAL_MACHINE_TYPE_1 = 1/4
VIRTUAL_MACHINE_TYPE_2 = 3/4
NUM_VIRTUAL_MACHINES_TYPE_1 = 1
NUM_VIRTUAL_MACHINES_TYPE_2 = 1
```

If you want to divide certain resources unevenly but split the rest evenly, you can specify separate fractions for each shared resource. This is described in detail in the Condor Administrator's Manual.

14.7.3   Scheduling a Distributively Owned Cluster

Many clusters are owned by more than one entity. Two or more smaller groups might pool their resources to buy a single, larger cluster. In these situations, the group that paid for a portion of the nodes should get priority to run on those nodes.

Each resource in a Condor pool can define its own RANK expression, which specifies the kinds of jobs it would prefer to execute. If a cluster is owned by multiple entities, you can divide the cluster's nodes up into groups, based on ownership. Each node would set Rank such that jobs coming from the group that owned it would have the highest priority.

Assume there is a 60-node compute cluster at a university, shared by three departments: astronomy, math, and physics. Each department contributed the funds for 20 nodes. Each group of 20 nodes would define its own Rank expression. The astronomy department's settings, for example, would be

```
Rank = Department == "Astronomy"
```

The users from each department would also add a Department attribute to all of their job ClassAds. The administrators could configure Condor to add this attribute automatically to all job ads from each site (see the Condor Administrator's Manual for details).

If the entire cluster was idle and a physics user submitted 40 jobs, she would see all 40 of her jobs start running. If, however, a user in math submitted 60 jobs and a user in astronomy submitted 20 jobs, 20 of the physicist's jobs would be preempted, and each group would get 20 machines out of the cluster.

If all of the astronomy department's jobs completed, the astronomy nodes would go back to serving math and physics jobs. The astronomy nodes would continue to run math or physics jobs until either some astronomy jobs were submitted, or all the jobs in the system completed.

14.7.4 Submitting to the Cluster from Desktop Workstations

Most organizations that install a compute cluster have other workstations at their site. It is usually desirable to allow these machines to act as front-end nodes for the cluster, so users can submit their jobs from their own machines and have the applications execute on the cluster. Even if there is no shared file system between the cluster and the rest of the computers, Condor's remote system calls and file transfer functionality can enable jobs to migrate between the two and still access their data (see Section 14.2.5 for details on accessing data files).

To enable a machine to submit into your cluster, run the Condor installation program and specify that you want to setup a *submit-only* node. This will set the DAEMON_LIST on the new node to be

```
DAEMON_LIST = MASTER, SCHEDD
```

The installation program will also create all the directories and files needed by Condor.

Note that you can have only one node configured as the dedicated scheduler for your pool. Do not attempt to add a second submit node for MPI jobs.

14.7.5 Expanding the Cluster to Nondedicated (Desktop) Computing Resources

One of the most powerful features in Condor is the ability to combine dedicated and opportunistic scheduling within a single system. *Opportunistic scheduling* involves placing jobs on nondedicated resources under the assumption that the resources might not be available for the entire duration of the jobs. Opportunistic scheduling is used for all jobs in Condor with the exception of dedicated MPI applications.

If your site has a combination of jobs and uses applications other than MPI, you should strongly consider adding all of your computing resources, even desktop workstations, to your Condor pool. With checkpointing and process migration, suspend and resume capabilities, opportunistic scheduling and matchmaking, Condor can harness the idle CPU cycles of any machine and put them to good use.

To add other computing resources to your pool, run the Condor installation
program and specify that you want to configure a node that can both submit and
execute jobs. The default installation sets up a node with a policy for starting,
suspending, and preempting jobs based on the activity of the machine (for example,
keyboard idle time and CPU load). These nodes will not run dedicated MPI jobs,
but they will run jobs from any other universe, including PVM.

14.8   Conclusion

Condor is a powerful tool for scheduling jobs across platforms, both within and
beyond the boundaries of your Beowulf clusters. Through its unique combination of
both dedicated and opportunistic scheduling, Condor provides a unified framework
for high-throughput computing.

15 Maui Scheduler: A Multifunction Cluster Scheduler

David B. Jackson

In this chapter we describe the Maui scheduler, a job-scheduling component that can interact with a number of different resource managers.

Like virtually every major development project, Maui grew out of a pressing need. In Maui's case, various computing centers including the Maui High-Performance Computing Center, Pacific Northwest National Laboratory, San Diego Supercomputer Center, and Argonne National Laboratory were investing huge sums of money in new, top-of-the-line hardware, only to be frustrated by the inability to use these new resources in an efficient or controlled manner. While existing resource management systems allowed the basic ability to submit and run jobs, they did not empower the site to maximize the use of the cluster. Sites could not *translate* local mission policies into scheduling behavior, and the scheduling decisions that were made were often quite suboptimal. Worse, the resulting system was often so complex that management, administrators, and users were unable to tell how well the system was running or what could be done to improve it.

Maui was designed to address these issues and has been developed and tested over the years at many leading-edge computing centers. It was built to enable sites to control, understand, and use their clusters effectively. Maui picks up where many scheduling systems leave off, providing a suite of advanced features in the areas of reservations, backfill, fairshare, job prioritization, quality of service, metascheduling, and more.

15.1 Overview

Maui is an *external* scheduler, meaning it does not include a resource manager but rather extends the capabilities of the existing resource manager. Maui uses the native scheduling APIs of OpenPBS, PBSPro and Loadleveler to obtain system information and direct cluster scheduling activities. While the underlying resource manager continues to maintain responsibility for managing nodes and tracking jobs, Maui controls the decisions of when, where, and how jobs will run.

System administrators control Maui via a master config file, `maui.cfg`, and text or Web-based administrator commands. On the other hand, end users are not required to learn any new commands or job submission language, and need not even know that Maui has been installed. While Maui provides numerous commands to provide users with additional job information and control, these commands are optional and may be introduced to the users as needed.

15.2 Installation and Initial Configuration

The Maui scheduler is available in many of the most popular cluster-building tool-kits, including *Rocks* and *OSCAR*. For the most recent version of Maui, you can download the code from the Maui home page at `supercluster.org/maui`. This site also contains online documentation, FAQs, links to the Maui users mailing list, and other standard open source utilities. To build the code once it has been downloaded, you need simply to issue the standard `configure`, `make`, and `make install`.

15.2.1 Basic Configuration

The `configure` script will prompt you for some basic information regarding the `install` directory and desired resource manager type. It then creates the Maui home directory, builds executables in the `bin` subdirectory, and copies these to the `install` directory. Finally, the script creates an initial `maui.cfg` file using templates located in the `samples` subdirectory and user-supplied information. This file is a *flat text* config file used for virtually all scheduler configuration and contains a number of parameters that should be verified, particularly, `SERVERHOST`, `SERVERMODE`, and `ADMIN1`. Initially, these should be set to the name of the host where Maui will run, `NORMAL`, and the user name of the Maui administrator, respectively. At any time when Maui is running, the `schedctl` command can be used with the '`-l`' flag to *list* the value of any parameter whether explicitly set or not, while the '`-m`' flag can be used to dynamically *modify* parameter values. The online `parameters` documentation provides further details about these and all other Maui parameters.

15.2.2 Simulation and Testing

With the initial configuration complete, the next step is testing the scheduler to become familiar with its capabilities and to verify basic functionality. Maui can be run in a completely *safe* manner by setting `SERVERMODE` to `TEST`. In *test* mode, Maui contacts the resource manager to obtain up-to-date configuration, node, and job information; however, in this mode, interfaces to start or modify these jobs are disabled. To start Maui, you must make the parameter changes and issue the command `maui`. You may also use commands such as `showq`, `diagnose`, and `checknode` to verify proper scheduler-resource manager communication and scheduler functionality. Full details on the suite of Maui commands are available online or in documentation included with your distribution.

15.2.3 Production Scheduling

Once you've taken the scheduler for a test drive and have verified its proper behavior, you can run Maui *live* by disabling the default scheduler and changing the
SERVERMODE parameter to NORMAL. Information on disabling the default resource
manager scheduler is provided in the resource manager's documentation and in the
online Maui migration guides located at supercluster.org/documentation/maui.
These changes will allow Maui to start, modify, and cancel jobs according to the
specified scheduling policies.

Out of the box, Maui essentially duplicates the behavior of a vanilla cluster scheduler, providing first-in, first-out scheduling with backfill enabled. The parameters
documentation explains in detail each of the parameters needed to enable advanced
scheduling features. In most cases, each site will require only a small subset of the
available parameters to meet local needs.

15.3 Advanced Configuration

With the initial configuration and testing completed, you can now configure Maui
to end your administration pilgrimage and reach the long-sought cluster mecca—
running the right jobs at the right time, in the right way, at the right place. To
this end, Maui can be thought of as an integrated scheduling toolkit providing
a number of capabilities that may be used individually or together to obtain the
desired system behavior. These include

- job prioritization,
- node allocation policies,
- throttling policies,
- fairshare,
- reservations,
- allocation management,
- quality of service,
- backfill,
- node sets, and
- preemption policies.

Each of these is described below. While this coverage will be adequate to introduce and initially configure these capabilities, you should consult the online Maui
Administrators Manual for full details. We reiterate that while Maui possesses a

wide range of features and associated parameters, most capabilities are disabled by default; thus, a site need configure only the features of interest.

15.3.1   Assigning Value: Job Prioritization and Node Allocation

In general, prioritization is the process of determining which of many options best fulfills overall goals. n the case of scheduling, a site will often have multiple, independent goals that may include maximizing system utilization, giving preference to users in specific projects, or making certain that no job sits in the queue for more than a given period of time. One approach to representing a multifaceted set of site goals is to assign weights to the various objectives so an overall value or priority can be associated with each potential scheduling decision. With the jobs prioritized, the scheduler can roughly fulfill site objectives by starting the jobs in priority order.

Maui was designed to allow component and subcomponent weights to be associated with many aspects of a job. To realize this fine-grained control, Maui uses a simple priority-weighting hierarchy where the contribution of a priority factor is calculated as `PRIORITY-FACTOR-VALUE * SUBFACTORWEIGHT * FACTORWEIGHT`. Component and subcomponent weights are listed in Table 15.1. Values for all weights may be set in the `maui.cfg` file by using the associated component-weight parameter specified as the name of the weight followed by the string `WEIGHT` (e.g., `SERVICEWEIGHT` or `PROCWEIGHT`).

By default, Maui runs jobs in order of actual submission, using the `QUEUETIME`. By using priority components, however, you can incorporate additional information, such as current level of service, service targets, resources requested, and historical usage. You can also limit the contribution of any component, by specifying a priority component *cap*, such as `RESOURCECAP`. A job's priority is equivalent to the sum of all enabled priority factors.

Each component or subcomponent may be used for different purposes. `WALLTIME` can be used to favor (or disfavor) jobs based on their duration; `ACCOUNT` can be used to favor jobs associated with a particular project; `QUEUETIME` can be used to favor those jobs that have been waiting the longest. By mixing and matching priority weights, sites generally obtain the desired job-start behavior. At any time, you can issue the `diagnose -p` command to determine the impact of the current priority-weight settings on idle jobs.

While most subcomponents are metric based (i.e., number of seconds queued or number of nodes requested), the credential subcomponents are based on priorities specified by the administrator. Maui allows you to use the `*CFG` parameters to rank

Component	Subcomponent
SERVICE (Level of Service)	QUEUETIME (Current queue time in minutes)
	XFACTOR (Current expansion factor)
	BYPASS (Number of times jobs were bypassed via backfill)
TARGET (Proximity to Service Target - Exponential)	TARGETQUEUETIME (Delta to queue-time target in minutes)
	TARGETXFACTOR (Delta to Xfactor target)
RESOURCE (Resources Requested)	PROC (Processors)
	MEM (Requested memory in MBytes)
	SWAP (Requested virtual memory in MBytes)
	DISK (Requested local disk in MBytes)
	NODE (Requested number of nodes)
	WALLTIME (Requested wall time in seconds)
	PS (Requested processor-seconds)
	PE (Requested processor-equivalents)
FS (Fairshare)	FSUSER (User fairshare percentage)
	FSGROUP (Group fairshare percentage)
	FSACCOUNT (Account fairshare percentage)
	FSCLASS (Class fairshare percentage)
	FSQOS (QoS fairshare percentage)
CRED (Credential)	USER (User priority)
	GROUP (Group priority)
	ACCOUNT (Account priority)
	CLASS (Class priority)
	QOS (QoS priority)

Table 15.1
Maui priority components.

jobs by individual job credentials. For example, to favor jobs submitted by users **bob** and **john** and members of the group **staff**, a site might specify the following:

```
USERCFG[bob]           PRIORITY=100
USERCFG[john]          PRIORITY=500
GROUPWEIGHT[staff] PRIORITY=1000
USERWEIGHT             1
GROUPWEIGHT            1
CREDWEIGHT             1
```

Note that both component and subcomponent weights are specified to enable these credential priorities to take effect. Further details about the use of these component factors, as well as anecdotal usage information, are available in the Maui Administrators Manual.

Complementing the issue of job prioritization is that of node allocation. When the scheduler selects a job to run, it must also determine which resources to allocate to the job. Depending on the use of the cluster, you can specify different policies by using NODEALLOCATIONPOLICY. Legal parameter values include the following:

- MINRESOURCE: This algorithm selects the nodes with the minimum configured resources which still meet the requirements of the job. The algorithm leaves more richly endowed nodes available for other jobs that may specifically request these additional resources.
- LASTAVAILABLE: This algorithm is particularly useful when making reservations for backfill. It determines the earliest time a job can run and then selects the resources available at a time such that, whenever possible, currently idle resources are left unreserved and are thus available for backfilling.
- NODEPRIORITY: This policy allows a site to create its own node allocation prioritization scheme, taking into account issues such as installed software or other local node configurations.
- CPULOAD: This policy attempts to allocate the most lightly loaded nodes first.

15.3.2 Fairness: Throttling Policies and Fairshare

The next issue most often confronting sites is *fairness*. Fairness seems like a simple concept but can be terribly difficult to map onto a cluster. Should all users get to run the same number of jobs or use the same number of nodes? Do these usage constraints cover the present time only or a specified time frame? If historical information is used, what is the metric of consumption? What is the time frame? Does fair consumption necessarily mean equal consumption? How should resources be allocated if user X bought two-thirds of the nodes and user Y purchased the other third? Is fairness based on a static metric, or is it conditional on current resource demand?

While Maui is not able to address all these issues, it does provide some flexible tools that help with 90 percent of the battle. Specifically, these tools are *throttling policies* and *fairshare* used to control immediate and historical usage, respectively.

Throttling Policies. The term "throttling policies" is collectively applied to a set of policies that constrain instantaneous resource consumption. Maui supports limits on the number of processors, nodes, proc-seconds, jobs, and processor equivalents allowed at any given time. Limits may be applied on a per user, group, account, QoS, or queue basis via the *CFG set of parameters. For example, specifying USERCFG[bob] MAXJOB=3 MAXPROC=32 will constrain user bob to running no more than 3 jobs and 32 total processors at any given time. Specifying GROUPCFG[DEFAULT] MAXNODE=64 will limit each group to using no more than 64 nodes simultaneously unless overriding limits for a particular group are specified. ACCOUNTCFG, QOSCFG, and CLASSCFG round out the *CFG family of parameters providing a means to throttle instantaneous use on accounts, QoS's, and classes, respectively.

With each of the parameters, *hard* and *soft* limits can be used to apply a form of *demand*-sensitive limits. While hard limits cannot be violated under any conditions, soft limits may be violated if no other jobs can run. For example, specifying USERCFG[DEFAULT] MAXNODE=16,24 will allow each user to cumulatively allocate up to 16 nodes while jobs from other users can use available resources. If no other jobs can use these resources, a user may run on up to 24 nodes simultaneously.

Throttling policies are effective in preventing cluster "hogging" by an individual user or group. They also provide a simple mechanism of fairness and cycle distribution. Such policies may lead to lower overall system utilization, however. For instance, resources might go unused if these policies prevent all queued jobs from running. When possible, throttling policies should be set to the highest feasible level, and the cycle distribution should be managed by tools such as fairshare, allocation management systems, and QoS-based prioritization.

Fairshare. A typical fairshare algorithm attempts to deliver a fair resource distribution over a given time frame. As noted earlier, however, this general statement leaves much to interpretation. In particular, how is the distribution to be measured, and what time frame should be used?

Maui provides the parameter FSPOLICY to allow each site to determine how resource distribution is to be measured, and the parameters FSINTERVAL, FSDEPTH, and FSDECAY to determine how historical usage information is to be weighted.

To control resource distribution, Maui uses fairshare targets that can be applied to users, groups, accounts, queues, and QoS mechanisms with both default and specific targets available. Each target may be one of four different types: *target*, *floor*, *ceiling*, or *cap*. In most cases, Maui adjusts job priorities to meet fairshare targets. With the standard target, Maui attempts to adjust priorities at all times in an attempt to meet the target. In the case of floors, Maui will increase job priority only to maintain *at least* the targeted usage. With ceilings, the converse occurs. Finally, with fairshare caps, job eligibility rather than job priority is adjusted to prevent jobs from running if the cap is exceeded during the specified fairshare interval.

The example below shows a possible fairshare configuration.

```
# maui.cfg
FSPOLICY    DEDICATEDPS
FSDEPTH     7
FSINTERVAL  24:00:00
FSDECAY     0.80


USERCFG[DEFAULT]    FSTARGET=10.0
USERCFG[john]       FSTARGET=25.0+
GROUPCFG[staff]     FSTARGET=20.0-
```

In this case, fairshare usage will track delivered system *processor seconds* over a seven-day period with a 0.8 decay factor. All users will have a fairshare *target* of 10 percent of these processor seconds—with the exception of john, who will have a *floor* of 25 percent. Also, the group staff will have a fairshare *ceiling* of 20 percent. At any time, you can examine the fairshare status of the system by using the diagnose -f command.

15.3.3 Managing Resource Access: Reservations, Allocation Managers, and Quality of Service

In managing any cluster system, half of the administrative effort involves configuring it to handle the *steady-state* situation. The other half occurs when a very important user has a special one-time request. Maui provides two features, advance reservations and QoS, to handle many types of such special requests.

Advance Reservations. Reservations allow a site to set aside a block of resources for various purposes such as cluster maintenance, special user projects, or benchmarking nodes. In order to create a reservation, a start and end time must be determined, as well as the resources to be reserved and a list of those who can access these resources. Reservations can be created dynamically by scheduler administrators using the setres command or managed directly by Maui via config file parameters.

For example, to reserve nodeA and nodeB for a four-hour maintenance at 2:30 P.M., you could issue the following command:

```
> setres -s 14:30 -d 4:00:00 'node[AB]'
```

A reservation request can specify allocation of particular resources or a given quantity of resources. The following reservation will allocate 20 processors to users john and sam starting on April 14 at 5:00 P.M.

```
> setres -u john:sam -s 17:00_04/14 TASKS==20
```

With no duration or end time specified, this reservation will default to an infinite length and will remain in place until removed by a scheduler administrator using the releaseres command.

Access to reservations is controlled by an access control list (ACL). Reservation access is based on job credentials, such as user or group, and job attributes, such as wall time requested. Reservation ACLs can include multiple access types and individuals. For example, a reservation might reserve resources for users A and B, jobs in class C, and jobs that request less than 30 minutes of wall time. Reservations may also overlap each other if desired, in which case access is granted only if the job meets the access policies of all active reservations.

At many sites, reservations are used on a permanent or periodic basis. In such cases, it is best to use *standing* reservations. Standing reservations allow a site to apply reservations as an ongoing part of cluster policies. The parameter SRPERIOD can be set to DAY, WEEK, or INFINITE to indicate the periodicity of the reservation, with additional parameters available to determine what time of the day or week the reservation should be enabled. For example, the following configuration will create a reservation named development that, during primetime hours, will set aside 16 nodes for exclusive use by jobs requiring less than 30 minutes.

```
SRPERIOD[development]     DAY
SRDAYS[development]       Mon Tue Wed Thu Fri
SRSTARTTIME[development]  8:00:00
SRENDTIME[development]    17:00:00
SRMAXTIME[development]    00:30:00
SRTASKCOUNT[development]  16
```

At times, a site may want to allow access to a set of resources only if there are no other resources available. Maui enables this conditional usage through reservation *affinity*. When specifying any reservation access list, each access value can be associated with positive, negative, or neutral affinity by using the '+', '-', or '=' characters. If nothing is specified, positive affinity is assumed. For example, consider the following reservation line:

```
SRUSERLIST[special]   bob john steve= bill-
```

With this specification, `bob` and `john`'s jobs receive the default positive affinity and are essentially *attracted* to the reservation. For these jobs, Maui will attempt to use resources in the `special` reservation first, before considering any other resources. Jobs belonging to `steve`, on the other hand, can use these resources but are not attracted to them. Finally, `bill`'s jobs will use resources in the `special` reservation only if no other resources are available. You can get detailed information about reservations by using the `showres` and `diagnose -r` commands.

Allocation Managers. Allocation management systems allow a site to control total resource access in real time. While interfaces to support other systems exist, the allocation management system most commonly used with the Maui scheduler is QBank (`http://www.emsl.pnl.gov:80/mscf/docs/qbank-2.9`), provided by Pacific Northwest National Laboratory. This system and others like it allow sites to provide distinct resource allocations much like the creation of a bank account. As jobs run, the resources used are translated into a charge and debited from the appropriate account. In the case of QBank, expiration dates may be associated with allocations, private and shared accounts maintained, per machine allocations created, and so forth.

Within Maui, the allocation manager interface is controlled through a set of `BANK*` parameters such as in the example below:

```
BANKTYPE              QBANK
BANKHOST              bank.univ.edu
BANKCHARGEPOLICY      DEBITSUCCESSFULWC
BANKDEFERJOBONFAILURE TRUE
BANKFALLBACKACCOUNT   freecycle
```

This configuration enables a connection to an allocation manager located on `bank.univ.edu` using the QBank interface. The unit of charge is configured to be *dedicated processor-seconds* and users will be charged only if their job completes successfully. If the job does not have adequate allocations in the specified account, Maui will attempt to redirect the job to use allocations in the `freecycle` account. In many cases, a *fallback* account is configured so as to be associated with lower priorities and/or additional limitations. If the job is not approved by the allocation manager, Maui will defer the job for a period of time and try it again later.

Quality of Service. Maui's QoS feature allows sites to control access to special functions, resources, and service levels. Each QoS consists of an access control list controlling which users, groups, accounts, and job queues can access the QoS privileges. Associated with each QoS are special service-related priority weights and service targets. Additionally, each QoS can be configured to span resource partitions, preempt other jobs, and the like.

Maui also enables a site to charge a premium rate for the use of some QoS services. For example, the following configuration will cause user john's jobs to use QoS hiprio by default and allow members of the group bio to access it by request:

```
USERCFG[john]  QLIST=hiprio:normal QDEF=hiprio
GROUPCFG[bio]  QLIST=hiprio:medprio:development QDEF=medprio
QOSCFG[hiprio] PRIORITY=50 QTTARGET=30 FLAGS=PREEMPTOR:IGNMAXJOB \
    MAXPROC=150
```

Jobs using QoS hiprio receive the following privileges and constraints:

- A priority boost of 50 * QOSWEIGHT * DIRECTWEIGHT
- A queue-time target of 30 minutes
- The ability to preempt lower priority PREEMPTEE jobs
- The ability to ignore MAXJOB policy limits defined elsewhere
- A cumulative limit of 150 processors allocated to QoS hiprio jobs

A site may have dozens of QoS objects described and may allow users access to any number of these. Depending on the type of service desired, users may then choose the QoS that best meets their needs.

15.3.4   Optimizing Usage: Backfill, Node Sets, and Preemption

The Maui scheduler provides several features to optimize performance in terms of system utilization, job throughput, and average job turnaround time.

Backfill.   Backfill is a now common method used to improve both system utilization and average job turnaround time by running jobs out of order. Backfill, simply put, enables the scheduler to run any job so long as it does not delay the start of jobs of higher priority. Generally, the algorithm prevents delay of high-priority jobs through some form of reservation. Backfill can be thought of as a process of filling in the resource *holes* left by the high priority jobs. Since holes are being filled, it makes sense that the jobs most commonly backfilled are the ones requiring the least time and/or resources. With backfill enabled, sites typically report system utilization improvements of 10 to 25% and a slightly lower average job queue time.

By default, backfill scheduling is enabled in Maui under control of the parameter BACKFILLPOLICY. While the default configuration generally is adequate, sites may want to adjust the job selection policy, the reservation policy, the depth of reservations, or other aspects of backfill scheduling. You should consult the online documentation for details about associated parameters.

Allocation Based on Node Set.   While backfill improves the scheduler's performance, this is only half the battle. The efficiency of a cluster, in terms of actual work accomplished, is a function of both scheduling performance and individual job efficiency. In many clusters, job efficiency can vary from node to node as well as with the *node mix* allocated. Since most parallel jobs written in popular languages such as MPI or PVM do not internally load balance their workload, they run only as fast as the slowest node allocated. Consequently, these jobs run most effectively on homogeneous sets of nodes. While many clusters start out as homogeneous, however, they quickly evolve as new generations of compute nodes are integrated into the system. Research has shown that this integration, while improving scheduling performance due to increased scheduler selection, can actually decrease average job efficiency.

A feature called *node sets* allows jobs to request sets of common resources without specifying exactly what resources are required. Node set policy can be specified globally or on a per job basis and can be based on node processor speed, memory, network interfaces, or locally defined node attributes. In addition to forcing jobs onto homogeneous nodes, these policies may also be used to guide jobs to one or more types of nodes on which a particular job performs best, similar to job preferences available in other systems. For example, an I/O-intensive job may run best on a certain range of processor speeds, running slower on slower nodes while wasting cycles on faster nodes. A job may specify `ANYOF:PROCSPEED:450:500:650` to request nodes in the range of 450 to 650 MHz. Alternatively, if a simple procspeed-homogeneous node set is desired, `ONEOF:PROCSPEED` may be specified. On the other hand, a communication-sensitive job may request a network-based node set with the configuration `ONEOF:NETWORK:via:myrinet:ethernet`, in which case Maui will first attempt to locate adequate nodes where all nodes contain VIA network interfaces. If such a set cannot be found, Maui will look for sets of nodes containing the other specified network interfaces. In highly heterogeneous clusters, the use of node sets has been found to improve job throughput by 10 to 15 percent.

Preemption.   Many sites possess workloads of varying importance. While it may be critical that some jobs obtain resources immediately, other jobs are less sensitive to turnaround time but have an insatiable hunger for compute cycles, consuming every available cycle for years on end. These latter jobs often have turnaround times on the order of weeks or months. The concept of *cycle stealing*, popularized by systems such as Condor, handles such situations well and enables systems to run low-priority preemptible jobs whenever something more pressing is not running. These other systems are often employed on compute farms of desktops where the jobs must vacate whenever interactive system use is detected.

Maui's QoS-based preemption system allows a dedicated, noninteractive cluster to be used in much the same way. Certain QoS objects may be marked with the flag PREEMPTOR and others with the flag PREEMPTEE. With this configuration, low-priority "preemptee" jobs can be started whenever idle resources are available. These jobs will be allowed to run until a "preemptor" job arrives, at which point the preemptee job will be checkpointed if possible and vacated. This strategy allows almost immediate resource access for the preemptor job. Using this approach, a cluster can maintain nearly 100 percent system utilization while still delivering excellent turnaround time to the jobs of greatest value.

Use of the preemption system need not be limited to controlling low-priority jobs. Other uses include optimistic scheduling and development job support.

15.3.5 Evaluating System Performance: Diagnostics, Profiling, Testing, and Simulation

High-performance computing clusters are complicated. First, such clusters have an immense array of attributes that affect overall system performance, including processor speed, memory, networks, I/O systems, enterprise services, and application and system software. Second, each of these attributes is evolving over time, as is the usage pattern of the system's users. Third, sites are presented with an equally immense array of buttons, knobs, and levers which they can push, pull, kick, and otherwise manipulate. How does one evaluate the success of a current configuration? And how does one establish a causal effect between pushing one of the many provided buttons and improved system performance when the system is constantly changing in multiple simultaneous dimensions?

To help alleviate this problem, Maui offers several useful features.

Diagnostics. Maui possesses many internal diagnostic functions that both locate problems and present system state information. For example, the *priority* diagnostic aggregates priority relevant information, presenting configuration settings and their impact on the current idle workload; administrators can see the contribution associated with each priority factor on a per job and systemwide average basis. The *node* diagnostic presents significant node-relevant information together with messages regarding any unexpected conditions. Other diagnostics are available for jobs, reservations, QoS, fairshare, priorities, fairness policies, users, groups, and accounts.

Profiling Current and Historical Usage. Maui maintains internal statistics and records detailed information about each job as it completes. The `showstats` command provides detailed usage information for users, groups, accounts, nodes, and the system as a whole. The `showgrid` command presents scheduler performance statistics in a job size/duration matrix to aid in analyzing the effectiveness of current policies.

The completed job statistics are maintained in a flat file located in the `stats` directory. These statistics are useful for two primary purposes: driving simulations (described later) and profiling actual system usage. The `profiler` command allows the processing of these historical scheduler statistics and generation of usage reports for specific time frames or for selected users, groups, accounts, or types of jobs.

Testing. To test new policies, you can run a `TEST` mode instance of Maui concurrently with the production scheduler. This allows a site to analyze the effects of the new policies on the scheduling behavior of the test instance, while safely running the production workload under tried and true policies. When running an instance of Maui in test mode, it is often best to create a second Maui directory with associated `log` and `stats` subdirectories. To run multiple, concurrent Maui instances, you should take the following into account:

• **Configuration file:** The test version of Maui should have its own `maui.cfg` file to allow specification of the `SERVERMODE` parameter and allow policy differences as needed by the test.

• **User interface port:** To avoid conflicts between different scheduler instances and client commands, the test version of the `maui.cfg` file should specify a unique parameter value for `SERVERPORT`.

• **Log and statistics files:** Both production and test runs will create and update log and statistics files. To avoid file conflicts, each instance of the scheduler should point to different files using the `LOGDIR` and `STATDIR` parameters.

• **Home directory:** When Maui was initially installed, the `configure` script prompted for a home directory where the default `maui.cfg` file could be found. To run multiple instances of Maui, you should override this default by using the `-c` command line flag or by specifying the environment variable `MAUIHOMEDIR`. The latter approach is most often used, with the variable set to the new home directory before starting the test version of the scheduler or running test version client commands.

Once the test version is started, all scheduler behavior will be identical to the production system with the exception that Maui's ability to start, cancel, or otherwise modify jobs is disabled. You can, however, observe Maui's behavior under the new set of policies and validate the scheduler either directly via client commands or indirectly by analyzing the Maui log files.

Simulation. Simulation allows a site to specify a workload and resource configuration trace file. These traces, specified via the `SIMWORKLOADTRACEFILE` and `SIMRESOURCETRACEFILE`, can accurately and reproducibly replicate the workload and resources recorded at the site. To run a simulation, an adjusted `maui.cfg` file is created with the policies of interest in place and the parameter `SERVERMODE` set to `SIMULATION`. Once started, Maui can be stepped through simulated time using the `schedctl` command. All Maui commands continue to function as before, allowing interactive querying of status, adjustment to parameters, or even submission or cancellation of jobs.

This feature enables sites to analyze the impact of different scheduling policies on their own workload and system configuration. The effects of new reservations or job prioritizations can be evaluated in a *zero-exposure* environment, allowing sites to determine ideal policies without experimenting on a production system. Sites can also evaluate the impact of additional or modified workloads or changes in available resources. What impact will removing a block of resources for maintenance have on average queue time? How much benefit will a new reservation dedicated exclusively to development jobs have on development job turnaround time? How much pain will it cause nondevelopment jobs? Using simulation makes it easier to obtaining answers to such questions.

This same simulation feature can be used to test a new algorithm against workload and resource traces from various supercomputing centers. Moreover, with the simulator, you can create and plug in modules to emulate the behavior of various job types on different hardware platforms, across bottlenecking networks, or under various data migration conditions.

The capabilities and use of simulation cannot be adequately covered in a chapter of this size. Further information is given in the Simulation section of the Maui Administrators Manual.

15.4   Steering Workload and Improving Quality of Information

A good scheduler can improve the use of a cluster significantly, but its effectiveness is limited by the scheduling environment in which it must work and the quality of information it receives. Often, a cluster is underutilized because users overestimate a job's resource requirements. Other times, inefficiencies crop up when users request job constraints in terms of job duration or processors required that are not easily packed onto the cluster. Maui provides tools to allow fine tuning of job resource requirement information and steering of cluster workload so as to allow maximum utilization of the system.

One such tool is a *feedback* interface, which allows a site to report detailed job usage statistics to users. This interface provides information about the resources requested and those actually used. Using the FEEDBACKPROGRAM parameter, local scripts can be executed that use this information to help users improve resource requirement estimates. For example, a site with nodes with various memory configurations may choose to create a script such as the following that automates the mailing of notices at job completion:

```
Job 1371 completed successfully}.  Note that it requested nodes
with 512 MBytes of RAM yet used  only 112 MBytes.  Had the job provided a
more accurate estimate, it would have, on average, started 02:27:16
earlier.
```

Such notices can be used to improve memory, disk, processor, and wall-time estimates. Another route that is often used is to set the allocation manager charge policy so that users are charged for requested resources rather than used resources.

The showbf command is designed to help tailor jobs that can run immediately. This command allows you to specify details about your desired job (such as user, group, queue, and memory requirements) and returns information regarding the quantity of available nodes and the duration of their availability.

A final area of user feedback is job scaling. Often, users will submit parallel jobs that scale only moderately scale, hoping that by requesting more processors, their job will run faster and provide results sooner. A job's completion time is simply the sum of its queue time plus its execution time. Users often fail to realize that a larger job may be more difficult to schedule, resulting in a longer queue time, and may run less efficiently, with a *sublinear* speedup. The increased queue-time delay, together with the limitations in execution time improvements, generally results in larger jobs having a greater average turnaround time than smaller jobs performing the same work. Maui commands such as showgrid can provide real-time job efficiency and average queue-time stats correlated to job size. The output of the profiler command can also be used to provide per user job efficiency and average queue time correlated by job size and can alert administrators and users to this problem.

15.5 Troubleshooting

When troubleshooting scheduling issues, you should start with Maui's diagnostic and informational commands. The `diagnose` command together with `checknode` and `checkjob` provides detailed state information about the scheduler, including its various facilities, nodes, and jobs. Additionally, each of these commands initiates an extensive internal sanity check in the realm of interest. Results of this check are reported in the form of `WARNING` messages appended to the normal command output. Use of these commands typically identifies or resolves 95 percent of all scheduling issues.

If you need further information, Maui writes out detailed logging information in the directory pointed to by the `LOGFILE` parameter (usually in `${MAUIHOME}/log/maui.log`). Using the `LOGLEVEL` and `LOGFACILITY` parameters, you can control the verbosity and focus of these logs. (Note, however, that these logs can become *very* verbose, so keeping the LOGLEVEL below 4 or so unless actually tracking problems is advised.) These logs contain a number of entries, including the following:

`INFO:` provides status information about normal scheduler operations.

`WARNING:` indicates that an unexpected condition was detected and handled.

`ALERT:` indicates that an unexpected condition occurred that could not be fully handled.

`ERROR:` indicates that problem was detected that prevents Maui from fully operating. This may be a problem with the cluster that is outside of Maui's control or may indicate corrupt internal state information.

`Function header:` indicates when a function is called and the parameters passed.

A simple `grep` through the log file will usually indicate whether any serious issues have been detected and is of significant value when obtaining support or locally diagnosing problems. If neither commands nor logs point to the source of the problem, you may consult the Maui users list (`mauiusers@supercluster.org`) or directly contact Supercluster support at `support@supercluster.org`.

15.6 Conclusions

This chapter has introduced some of the key Maui features currently available. With hundreds of sites now using and contributing to this open source project, Maui is evolving and improving faster than ever. To learn about the latest developments and to obtain more detailed information about the capabilities described above, see the Maui home page at `www.supercluster.org/maui`.

16 PBS: Portable Batch System

James Patton Jones

The Portable Batch System (PBS) is a flexible workload management and job scheduling system originally developed to manage aerospace computing resources at NASA. PBS has since become the leader in supercomputer workload management and the de facto standard job scheduler for Linux.

Today, growing enterprises often support hundreds of users running thousands of jobs across different types of machines in different geographical locations. In this distributed heterogeneous environment, it can be extremely difficult for administrators to collect detailed, accurate usage data or to set systemwide resource priorities. As a result, many computing resources are left underused, while others are overused. At the same time, users are confronted with an ever-expanding array of operating systems and platforms. Each year, scientists, engineers, designers, and analysts waste countless hours learning the nuances of different computing environments, rather than being able to focus on their core priorities. PBS addresses these problems for computing-intensive industries such as science, engineering, finance, and entertainment.

PBS allows you to unlock the potential in the valuable assets you already have, while at the same time reducing demands on system administrators, freeing them to focus on other activities. PBS can also help you effectively manage growth by tracking use levels across your systems and enhancing effective utilization of future purchases.

16.1 History of PBS

In the past, computers were used in a completely interactive manner. Background jobs were just processes with their input disconnected from the terminal. As the number of processors in computers continued to increase, however, the need to be able to schedule tasks based on available resources rose in importance. The advent of networked compute servers, smaller general systems, and workstations led to the requirement of a networked batch scheduling capability. The first such Unix-based system was the Network Queueing System (NQS) from NASA Ames Research Center in 1986. NQS quickly became the de facto standard for batch queuing.

Over time, distributed parallel systems began to emerge, and NQS was inadequate to handle the complex scheduling requirements presented by such systems. In addition, computer system managers wanted greater control over their compute resources, and users wanted a single interface to the systems. In the early 1990s

NASA needed a solution to this problem, but after finding nothing on the market that adequately addressed their needs, led an international effort to gather requirements for a next-generation resource management system. The requirements and functional specification were later adopted as an IEEE POSIX standard (1003.2d). Next, NASA funded the development of a new resource management system compliant with the standard. Thus the Portable Batch System was born.

PBS was quickly adopted on distributed parallel systems and replaced NQS on traditional supercomputers and server systems. Eventually the entire industry evolved toward distributed parallel systems, taking the form of both special-purpose and commodity clusters. Managers of such systems found that the capabilities of PBS mapped well onto cluster systems.

The latest chapter in the PBS story began when Veridian (the research and development contractor that developed PBS for NASA) released the Portable Batch System Professional Edition (PBS Pro), a complete workload management solution. The cluster administrator can now choose between two versions of PBS: OpenPBS, an older Open Source release of PBS; and PBS Pro, the new hardened and enhanced commercial version.

This chapter gives a technical overview of PBS and information on installing, using, and managing both versions of PBS. However, it is not possible to cover all the details of a software system the size and complexity of PBS in a single chapter. Therefore, we limit this discussion to the recommended configuration for Linux clusters, providing references to the various PBS documentation where additional, detailed information is available.

16.1.1 Acquiring PBS

While both OpenPBS and PBS Pro are bundled in a variety of cluster kits, the best sources for the most current release of either product are the official Veridian PBS Web sites: `www.OpenPBS.org` and `www.PBSpro.com`. Both sites offers downloads of the software and documentation, as well as FAQs, discussion lists, and current PBS news. Hardcopy documentation, support services, training and PBS Pro software licenses are available from the PBS Online Store, accessed through the PBS Pro Web site.

16.1.2 PBS Features

PBS Pro provides many features and benefits to the cluster administrator. A few of the more important features are the following:

Enterprisewide resource sharing provides transparent job scheduling on any PBS system by any authorized user. Jobs can be submitted from any client system, both local and remote, crossing domains where needed.

Multiple user interfaces provide a graphical user interface for submitting batch and interactive jobs; querying job, queue, and system status; and monitoring job progress. Also provided is a traditional command line interface.

Security and access control lists permit the administrator to allow or deny access to PBS systems on the basis of username, group, host, and/or network domain.

Job accounting offers detailed logs of system activities for charge-back or usage analysis per user, per group, per project, and per compute host.

Automatic file staging provides users with the ability to specify any files that need to be copied onto the execution host before the job runs and any that need to be copied off after the job completes. The job will be scheduled to run only after the required files have been successfully transferred.

Parallel job support works with parallel programming libraries such as MPI, PVM, and HPF. Applications can be scheduled to run within a single multiprocessor computer or across multiple systems.

System monitoring includes a graphical user interface for system monitoring. PBS displays node status, job placement, and resource utilization information for both standalone systems and clusters.

Job interdependency enables the user to define a wide range of interdependencies between jobs. Such dependencies include execution order, synchronization, and execution conditioned on the success or failure of another specific job (or set of jobs).

Computational Grid support provides an enabling technology for meta-computing and computational Grids, including support for the Globus Toolkit.

Comprehensive API includes a complete application programming interface for sites that wish to integrate PBS with other applications or to support unique job-scheduling requirements.

Automatic load-leveling provides numerous ways to distribute the workload across a cluster of machines, based on hardware configuration, resource availability, keyboard activity, and local scheduling policy.

Distributed clustering allows customers to use physically distributed systems and clusters, even across wide area networks.

Common user environment offers users a common view of the job submission, job querying, system status, and job tracking over all systems.

Cross-system scheduling ensures that jobs do not have to be targeted to a specific computer system. Users may submit their job and have it run on the first available system that meets their resource requirements.

Job priority allows users the ability to specify the priority of their jobs; defaults can be provided at both the queue and system level.

User name mapping provides support for mapping user account names on one system to the appropriate name on remote server systems. This allows PBS to fully function in environments where users do not have a consistent username across all the resources they have access to.

Full configurability makes PBS easily tailored to meet the needs of different sites. Much of this flexibility is due to the unique design of the scheduler module, which permits complete customization.

Broad platform availability is achieved through support of Windows 2000 and every major version of Unix and Linux, from workstations and servers to supercomputers. New platforms are being supported with each new release.

System integration allows PBS to take advantage of vendor-specific enhancements on different systems (such as supporting `cpusets` on SGI systems and interfacing with the global resource manager on the Cray T3E).

For a comparison of the features available in the latest versions of OpenPBS and PBS Pro, visit the PBS Product Comparison Web page: `www.OpenPBS.org/product_comparison.html`.

16.1.3 PBS Architecture

PBS consists of two major component types: user-level commands and system daemons. A brief description of each is given here to help you make decisions during the installation process.

PBS supplies both command-line programs that are POSIX 1003.2d conforming and a graphical interface. These are used to submit, monitor, modify, and delete jobs. These *client commands* can be installed on any system type supported by PBS and do not require the local presence of any of the other components of PBS. There are three classifications of commands: user commands that any authorized user can use, operator commands, and manager (or administrator) commands. Operator and manager commands require specific access privileges. (See also the security sections of the PBS Administrator Guide.)

The *job server* daemon is the central focus for PBS. Within this document, it is generally referred to as the *Server* or by the execution name `pbs_server`. All commands and the other daemons communicate with the Server via an Internet Protocol (IP) network. The Server's main function is to provide the basic batch services such as receiving or creating a batch job, modifying the job, protecting the job against system crashes, and running the job. Typically, one Server manages a given set of resources.

The *job executor* is the daemon that actually places the job into execution. This daemon, `pbs_mom`, is informally called *MOM* because it is the mother of all executing jobs. (MOM is a reverse-engineered acronym that stands for Machine Oriented Mini-server.) MOM places a job into execution when it receives a copy of the job from a Server. MOM creates a new session as identical to a user login session as possible. For example, if the user's login shell is `csh`, then MOM creates a session in which `.login` is run as well as `.cshrc`. MOM also has the responsibility for returning the job's output to the user when directed to do so by the Server. One MOM daemon runs on each computer that will execute PBS jobs.

The *job scheduler* daemon, `pbs_sched`, implements the site's policy controlling when each job is run and on which resources. The Scheduler communicates with the various MOMs to query the state of system resources and with the Server to learn about the availability of jobs to execute. The interface to the Server is through the same API (discussed below) as used by the client commands. Note that the Scheduler interfaces with the Server with the same privilege as the PBS manager.

16.2 Using PBS

From the user's perspective, a workload mangement system enables you to make more efficient use of your time by allowing you to specify the tasks you need run on the cluster. The system takes care of running these tasks and returning the results to you. If the cluster is full, then it holds your tasks and runs them when the resources are available.

With PBS you create a *batch job* that you then submit to PBS. A batch job is a shell script containing the set of commands you want run on the cluster. It also contains directives that specify the resource requirements (such as memory or CPU time) that your job needs. Once you create your PBS job, you can reuse it, if you wish, or you can modify it for subsequent runs. Example job scripts are shown below.

PBS also provides a special kind of batch job called *interactive batch*. This job is treated just like a regular batch job (it is queued up and must wait for resources to become available before it can run). But once it is started, the user's terminal input and output are connected to the job in what appears to be an `rlogin` session. It appears that the user is logged into one of the nodes of the cluster, and the resources requested by the job are reserved for that job. Many users find this feature useful for debugging their applications or for computational steering.

PBS provides two user interfaces: a command-line interface (CLI) and a graphical user interface (GUI). You can use either to interact with PBS: both interfaces have the same functionality.

16.2.1 Creating a PBS Job

Previously we mentioned that a PBS job is simply a shell script containing resource requirements of the job and the command(s) to be executed. Here is what a sample PBS job might look like the following:

```
#!/bin/sh
#PBS -l walltime=1:00:00
#PBS -l mem=400mb
#PBS -l ncpus=4
#PBS -j oe


cd ${HOME}/PBS/test
mpirun -np 4 myprogram
```

This script would then be submitted to PBS using the *qsub* command.

Let us look at the script for a moment. The first line tells what shell to use to interpret the script. Lines 2–4 are resource directives, specifying arguments to the "resource list" ("-l") option of qsub. Note that all PBS directives begin with #PBS. These lines tell PBS what to do with your job. Any qsub option can also be placed inside the script by using a #PBS directive. However, PBS stops parsing directives with the first blank line encountered.

Returning to our example above, we see a request for 1 hour of wall-clock time, 400 MBytes of memory and 4 CPUs. The fifth line is a request for PBS to merge the stdout and stderr file streams of the job into a single file. The last two lines are the commands the user wants executed: change directory to a particular location, then execute an MPI program called 'myprogram'.

This job script could have been created in one of two ways: using a text editor, or using the *xpbs* graphical interface (see below).

16.2.2 Submitting a PBS Job

The command used to submit a job to PBS is qsub. For example, say you created a file containing your PBS job called 'myscriptfile'. The following example shows how to submit the job to PBS:

```
% qsub myscriptfile
12322.sol.pbspro.com
```

The second line in the example is the job identifier returned by the PBS server. This unique identifier can be used to act on this job in the future (before it completes running). The next section of this chapter discusses using this "job id" in various ways.

The **qsub** command has a number of options that can be specified either on the command-line or in the job script itself. Note that any command-line option will override the same option within the script file.

Table 16.1 lists the most commonly used options to **qsub**. See the PBS User Guide for the complete list and full description of the options.

Option	Purpose
-l list	List of resources needed by job
-q queue	Queue to submit job to
-N name	Name of job
-S shell	Shell to execute job script
-p priority	Priority value of job
-a datetime	Delay job under after datetime
-j oe	Join output and error files
-h	Place a hold on job

Table 16.1
PBS commands.

The "**-l resource_list**" option is used to specify the resources needed by the job. Table 16.2 lists all the resources available to jobs running on clusters.

16.2.3 Getting the Status of a PBS Job

Once the job has been submitted to PBS, you can use either the **qstat** or **xpbs** commands to check the job status. If you know the job identifier for your job, you can request the status explicitly. Note that unless you have multiple clusters, you need only specify the sequence number portion of the job identifier:

```
% qstat 12322
Job id        Name          User   Time Use S Queue
------------- ------------- ------ -------- - -----
12322.sol     myscriptfile jjones 00:06:39 R submit
```

Resource	Meaning
arch	System architecture needed by job
cput	CPU time required by all processes in job
file	Maximum single file disk space requirements
mem	Total amount of RAM memory required
ncpus	Number of CPUs (processors) required
nice	Requested "nice" (Unix priority) value
nodes	Number and/or type of nodes needed
pcput	Maximum per-process CPU time required
pmem	Maximum per-process memory required
wall time	Total wall-clock time needed
workingset	Total disk space requirements

Table 16.2
PBS resources.

If you run the `qstat` command without specifing a job identifier, then you will receive status on all jobs currently queued and running.

Often users wonder why their job is not running. You can query this information from PBS using the "-s" (status) option of `qstat`, for example,

```
% qstat 12323
Job id          Name          User    Time Use S Queue
------------    ------------  ------  -------- - -----
12323.sol     myscriptfile jjones 00:00:00 Q submit
    Requested number of CPUs not currently available.
```

A number of options to `qstat` change what information is displayed. The PBS User Guide gives the complete list.

16.2.4   PBS Command Summary

So far we have seen several of the PBS user commands. Table 16.3 is provided as a quick reference for all the PBS user commands. Details on each can be found in the PBS manual pages and the PBS User Guide.

16.2.5   Using the PBS Graphical User Interface

PBS provides two GUI interfaces: a TCL/TK-based GUI called **xpbs** and an optional Web-based GUI.

The GUI xpbs provides a user-friendly point-and-click interface to the PBS commands. To run **xpbs** as a regular, nonprivileged user, type

Command	Purpose
qalter	Alter job(s)
qdel	Delete job(s)
qhold	Hold job(s)
qmsg	Send a message to job(s)
qmove	Move job(s) to another queue
qrls	Release held job(s)
qrerun	Rerun job(s)
qselect	Select a specific subset of jobs
qsig	Send a signal to job(s)
qstat	Show status of job(s)
qsub	Submit job(s)
xpbs	Graphical Interface (GUI) to PBS commands

Table 16.3
PBS commands.

```
setenv DISPLAY your_workstation_name:0
xpbs
```

To run xpbs with the additional purpose of terminating PBS Servers, stopping and starting queues, or running or rerunning jobs, type

```
xpbs -admin
```

Note that you must be identified as a PBS operator or manager in order for the additional "-admin" functions to take effect.

The optional Web-based user interface provides access to all the functionality of xpbs via almost any Web browser. To access it, you simply type the URL of your PBS Server host into your browser. The layout and usage are similar to those of xpbs. For details, see The PBS User Guide.

16.2.6   PBS Application Programming Interface

Part of the PBS package is the PBS Interface Library, or IFL. This library provides a means of building new PBS clients. Any PBS service request can be invoked through calls to the interface library. Users may wish to build a PBS job that will check its status itself or submit new jobs, or they may wish to customize the job status display rather than use the qstat command. Administrators may use the interface library to build new control commands.

The IFL provides a user-callable function that corresponds to each PBS client command. There is (approximately) a one-to-one correlation between commands and PBS service requests. Additional routines are provided for network connection management. The user-callable routines are declared in the header file 'PBS_ifl.h'. Users request service of a batch server by calling the appropriate library routine and passing it the required parameters. The parameters correspond to the options and operands on the commands. The user must ensure that the parameters are in the correct syntax. Each function will return zero upon success and a nonzero error code on failure. These error codes are available in the header file 'PBS_error.h'. The library routine will accept the parameters and build the corresponding batch request. This request is then passed to the server communication routine. (The PBS API is fully documented in the PBS External Reference Specification.)

16.3   Installing PBS

PBS is able to support a wide range of configurations. It may be installed and used to control jobs on a single system or to load balance jobs on a number of systems. It may be used to allocate nodes of a cluster or parallel system to both serial and parallel jobs. It can also deal with a mix of these situations. However, given the topic of this book, we focus on the recommended configuration for clusters. The PBS Administrator Guide explains other configurations.

When PBS is installed on a cluster, a MOM daemon must be on each execution host, and the Server and Scheduler should be installed on one of the systems or on a front-end system.

For Linux clusters, PBS is packaged in the popular *RPM* format (Red Hat's Package Manager). (See the PBS Administrator Guide for installation instructions on other systems.) PBS RPM packages are provided as a single tar file containing

- the PBS Administrator Guide in both Postscript and PDF form,
- the PBS User Guide in both Postscript and PDF form (PBS Pro only),
- multiple RPM packages for different components of PBS (see below),
- a full set of Unix-style manual pages, and
- supporting text files: software license, README, release notes, and the like.

When the PBS tar file is extracted, a subtree of directories is created in which all these files are created. The name of the top-level directory of this subtree will reflect the release number and patch level of the version of PBS being installed. For example, the directory for PBS Pro 5.1 will be named 'PBSPro_5_1_0'.

To install PBS Pro, change to the newly created directory, and run the installation program:

```
cd PBSPro_5_1_0
./INSTALL
```

The installation program will prompt you for the names of directories for the different parts of PBS and the type of installation (full, server-only, execution host only). Next, you will be prompted for your software license key(s). (See Section 16.1.1 if you do not already have your software license key.)

For OpenPBS, there are multiple RPMs corresponding to the different installation possibilities: full installation, execution host only, or client commands only. Select the correct RPM for your installation; then install it manually:

```
cd pbspro_v5.1
rpm -i RPMNAME...
```

Note that in OpenPBS, the RPMs will install into predetermined locations under '/usr/pbs' and '/usr/spool/PBS'.

16.4 Configuring PBS

Now that PBS has been installed, the Server and MOMs can be configured and the scheduling policy selected. Note that further configuration of may not be required since PBS Pro comes preconfigured, and the default configuration may completely meet your needs. However, you are advised to read this section to determine whether the defaults are indeed complete for you or whether any of the optional settings may apply.

16.4.1 Network Addresses and PBS

PBS makes use of fully qualified host names for identifying the jobs and their location. A PBS installation is known by the host name on which the Server is running. The name used by the daemons or used to authenticate messages is the canonical host name. This name is taken from the primary name field, h_name, in the structure returned by the library call gethostbyaddr(). According to the IETF RFCs, this name must be fully qualified and consistent for any IP address assigned to that host.

16.4.2 The Qmgr Command

The PBS manager command, qmgr, provides a command-line administrator interface. The command reads directives from standard input. The syntax of each directive is checked and the appropriate request sent to the Server(s). A `qmgr` directive takes one of the following forms:

```
command server [names] [attr OP value[,...]]
command queue  [names] [attr OP value[,...]]
command node   [names] [attr OP value[,...]]
```

where `command` is the command to perform on an object. The `qmgr` commands are listed in Table 16.4.

Command	Explanation
active	Set the active objects.
create	Create a new object, applies to queues and nodes.
delete	Destroy an existing object (queues or nodes).
set	Define or alter attribute values of the object.
unset	Clear the value of the attributes of the object.
list	List the current attributes and values of the object.
print	Print all the queue and server attributes.

Table 16.4
`qmgr` commands.

The `list` or `print` subcommands of `qmgr` can be executed by the general user. Creating or deleting a queue requires PBS Manager privilege. Setting or unsetting `server` or `queue` attributes requires PBS Operator or Manager privilege.

Here are several examples that illustrate using the `qmgr` command. These and other `qmgr` commands are fully explained below, along with the specific tasks they accomplish.

```
% qmgr
Qmgr: create node mars np=2,ntype=cluster
Qmgr: create node venus properties="inner,moonless"
Qmgr: set node mars properties = inner
Qmgr: set node mars properties += haslife
Qmgr: delete node mars
Qmgr: d n venus
```

Commands can be abbreviated to their minimum unambiguous form (as shown in the last line in the example above). A command is terminated by a new line character or a semicolon. Multiple commands may be entered on a single line. A command may extend across lines by marking the new line character with a backslash. Comments begin with a pound sign and continue to the end of the line. Comments and blank lines are ignored by qmgr. See the qmgr manual page for detailed usage and syntax description.

16.4.3 Nodes

Where jobs will be run is determined by an interaction between the Scheduler and the Server. This interaction is affected by the contents of the PBS 'nodes' file and the system configuration onto which you are deploying PBS. Without this list of nodes, the Server will not establish a communication stream with the MOM(s), and MOM will be unable to report information about running jobs or to notify the Server when jobs complete. In a cluster configuration, distributing jobs across the various hosts is a matter of the Scheduler determining on which host to place a selected job.

Regardless of the type of execution nodes, each node must be defined to the Server in the PBS nodes file, (the default location of which is '/usr/spool/PBS/server_priv/nodes'). This is a simple text file with the specification of a single node per line in the file. The format of each line in the file is

```
node_name[:ts] [attributes]
```

The node name is the network name of the node (host name), it does not have to be fully qualified (in fact, it is best kept as short as possible). The optional ":ts" appended to the name indicates that the node is a timeshared node.

Nodes can have attributes associated with them. Attributes come in three types: properties, name=value pairs, and name.resource=value pairs.

Zero or more properties may be specified. The property is nothing more than a string of alphanumeric characters (first character must be alphabetic) without meaning to PBS. Properties are used to group classes of nodes for allocation to a series of jobs.

Any legal node name=value pair may be specified in the node file in the same format as on a qsub directive: attribute.resource=value. Consider the following example:

```
NodeA resource_available.ncpus=3 max_running=1
```

The expression np=N may be used as shorthand for resources_available.ncpus=N, which can be added to declare the number of virtual processors (VPs) on the node. This syntax specifies a numeric string, for example, np=4. This expression will allow the node to be allocated up to N times to one job or more than one job. If np=N is not specified for a cluster node, it is assumed to have one VP.

You may edit the nodes list in one of two ways. If the server is not running, you may directly edit the nodes file with a text editor. If the server is running, you should use qmgr to edit the list of nodes.

Each item on the line must be separated by white space. The items may be listed in any order except that the host name must always be first. Comment lines may be included if the first nonwhite space character is the pound sign.

The following is an example of a possible nodes file for a cluster called "planets":

```
# The first set of nodes are cluster nodes.
# Note that the properties are provided to
# logically group certain nodes together.
# The last node is a timeshared node.
#
mercury     inner moonless
venus       inner moonless np=1
earth       inner np=1
mars        inner np=2
jupiter     outer np=18
saturn      outer np=16
uranus      outer np=14
neptune     outer np=12
pluto:ts
```

16.4.4 Creating or Adding Nodes

After pbs_server is started, the node list may be entered or altered via the qmgr command:

```
create node node_name [attribute=value]
```

where the attributes and their associated possible values are shown in Table 16.5.

Below are several examples of setting node attributes via qmgr:

```
% qmgr
Qmgr: create node mars np=2,ntype=cluster
Qmgr: create node venus properties="inner,moonless"
```

Once a node has been created, its attributes and/or properties can be modified by using the following qmgr syntax:

```
set node node_name [attribute[+|-]=value]
```

Attribute	Value
state	`free`, `down`, `offline`
properties	any alphanumeric string
ntype	`cluster`, `time-shared`
`resources_available.ncpus` (np)	number of virtual processors > 0
`resources_available`	list of resources available on node
`resources_assigned`	list of resources in use on node
`max_running`	maximum number of running jobs
`max_user_run`	maximum number of running jobs per user
`max_group_run`	maximum number of running jobs per group
queue	queue name (if any) associated with node
reservations	list of reservations pending on the node
comment	general comment

Table 16.5
PBS node syntax.

where attributes are the same as for `create`, for example,

```
% qmgr
Qmgr: set node mars properties=inner
Qmgr: set node mars properties+=haslife
```

Nodes can be deleted via `qmgr` as well, using the `delete node` syntax, as the following example shows:

```
% qmgr
Qmgr: delete node mars
Qmgr: delete node pluto
```

Note that the `busy` state is set by the execution daemon, `pbs_mom`, when a load-average threshold is reached on the node. See `max_load` in MOM's config file. The `job-exclusive` and `job-sharing` states are set when jobs are running on the node.

16.4.5 Default Configuration

Server management consist of configuring the Server and establishing queues and their attributes. The default configuration, shown below, sets the minimum server settings and some recommended settings for a typical PBS cluster.

```
% qmgr
Qmgr: print server
# Create queues and set their attributes
```

```
#
# Create and define queue workq
#
create queue workq
set queue workq queue_type = Execution
set queue workq enabled = True
set queue workq started = True
#
# Set Server attributes
#
set server scheduling = True
set server default_queue = workq
set server log_events = 511
set server mail_from = adm
set server query_other_jobs = True
set server scheduler_iteration = 600
```

16.4.6   Configuring MOM

The execution server daemons, MOMs, require much less configuration than does
the Server. The installation process creates a basic MOM configuration file that
contains the minimum entries necessary in order to run PBS jobs. This section
describes the MOM configuration file and explains all the options available to customize the PBS installation to your site.

The behavior of MOM is controlled via a configuration file that is read upon
daemon initialization (startup) and upon reinitialization (when **pbs_mom** receives a
SIGHUP signal). The configuration file provides several types of runtime information to MOM: access control, static resource names and values, external resources
provided by a program to be run on request via a shell escape, and values to pass to
internal functions at initialization (and reinitialization). Each configuration entry
is on a single line, with the component parts separated by white space. If the line
starts with a pound sign, the line is considered to be a comment and is ignored.

A minimal MOM configuration file should contain the following:

```
$logevent 0x1ff
$clienthost server-hostname
```

The first entry, **$logevent**, specifies the level of message logging this daemon should
perform. The second entry, **$clienthost**, identifies a host that is permitted to

connect to this MOM. You should set the *server-hostname* variable to the name of the host on which you will be running the PBS Server (`pbs_server`). Advanced MOM configuration options are described in the PBS Administrator Guide.

16.4.7 Scheduler Configuration

Now that the Server and MOMs have been configured, we turn our attention to the PBS Scheduler. As mentioned previously, the Scheduler is responsible for implementing the local site policy regarding which jobs are run and on what resources. This section discusses the recommended configuration for a typical cluster. The full list of tunable Scheduler parameters and detailed explanation of each is provided in the PBS Administrator Guide.

The PBS Pro Scheduler provides a wide range of scheduling policies. It provides the ability to sort the jobs in several different ways, in addition to FIFO order. It also can sort on user and group priority. The queues are sorted by queue priority to determine the order in which they are to be considered. As distributed, the Scheduler is configured with the defaults shown in Table 16.6.

Option	Default Value
round_robin	False
by_queue	True
strict_fifo	False
load_balancing	False
load_balancing_rr	False
fair_share	False
help_starving_jobs	True
backfill	True
backfill_prime	False
sort_queues	True
sort_by	shortest_job_first
smp_cluster_dist	pack
preemptive_sched	True

Table 16.6
Default scheduling policy parameters.

Once the Server and Scheduler are configured and running, job scheduling can be initiated by setting the Server attribute scheduling to a value of true:

```
# qmgr -c "set server scheduling=true"
```

The value of scheduling is retained across Server terminations or starts. After the Server is configured, it may be placed into service.

16.5   Managing PBS

This section is intended for the PBS administrator: it discusses several important aspects of managing PBS on a day-to-day basis.

During the installation of PBS Pro, the file '/etc/pbs.conf' was created. This configuration file controls which daemons are to be running on the local system. Each node in a cluster should have its own '/etc/pbs.conf' file.

16.5.1   Starting PBS Daemons

The daemon processes (pbs_server, pbs_sched, and pbs_mom) must run with the real and effective uid of root. Typically, the daemons are started automatically by the system upon reboot. The boot-time start/stop script for PBS is '/etc/init.d/pbs'. This script reads the '/etc/pbs.conf' file to determine which daemons should be started.

The startup script can also be run by hand to get status on the PBS daemons, and to start/stop all the PBS daemons on a given host. The command line syntax for the startup script is

> /etc/init.d/pbs [status | stop | start]

Alternatively, you can start the individual PBS daemons manually, as discussed in the following sections. Furthermore, you may wish to change the options specified to various daemons, as discussed below.

16.5.2   Monitoring PBS

The node monitoring GUI for PBS is xpbsmon. It is used for displaying graphically information about execution hosts in a PBS environment. Its view of a PBS environment consists of a list of sites where each site runs one or more Servers and each Server runs jobs on one or more execution hosts (nodes).

The system administrator needs to define the site's information in a global X resources file, 'PBS_LIB/xpbsmon/xpbsmonrc', which is read by the GUI if a personal '.xpbsmonrc' file is missing. A default 'xpbsmonrc' file is created during installation defining (under *sitesInfo resource) a default site name, the list of Servers that run on the site, the set of nodes (or execution hosts) where jobs on a particular Server run, and the list of queries that are communicated to each node's pbs_mom.

If node queries have been specified, the host where 'xpbsmon' is running must have been given explicit permission by the pbs_mom daemon to post queries to it; this is done by including a $restricted entry in the MOM's config file.

16.5.3   Tracking PBS Jobs

Periodically you (or the user) will want track the status of a job. Or perhaps you want to view all the log file entries for a given job. Several tools allow you to track a job's progress, as Table 16.7 shows.

Command	Explanation
qstat	Shows status of jobs, queues, and servers
xpbs	Can alert user when job starts producing output
tracejob	Collates and sorts PBS log entries for specified job

Table 16.7
Job-tracking commands.

16.5.4   PBS Accounting Logs

The PBS Server daemon maintains an accounting log. The log name defaults to '/usr/spool/PBS/server_priv/accounting/yyyymmdd' where yyyymmdd is the date. The accounting log files may be placed elsewhere by specifying the -A option on the pbs_server command line. The option argument is the full (absolute) path name of the file to be used. If a null string is given, for example

```
# pbs_server -A ""
```

then the accounting log will not be opened, and no accounting records will be recorded.

The accounting file is changed according to the same rules as the log files. If the default file is used, named for the date, the file will be closed and a new one opened every day on the first event (write to the file) after midnight. With either the default file or a file named with the -A option, the Server will close the accounting log and reopen it upon the receipt of a SIGHUP signal. This strategy allows you to rename the old log and start recording anew on an empty file. For example, if the current date is December 1, the Server will be writing in the file '20011201'. The following actions will cause the current accounting file to be renamed 'dec1' and the Server to close the file and starting writing a new '20011201'.

```
# mv 20011201 dec1
# kill -HUP (pbs_server's PID)
```

16.6 Troubleshooting

The following is a list of common problems and recommended solutions. Additional information is always available on the PBS Web sites.

16.6.1 Clients Unable to Contact Server

If a client command (such as **qstat** or **qmgr**) is unable to connect to a Server there are several possible errors to check. If the error return is 15034, *No server to connect to*, check (1) that there is indeed a Server running and (2) that the default Server information is set correctly. The client commands will attempt to connect to the Server specified on the command line if given or, if not given, the Server specified in the default server file, '**/usr/spool/PBS/default_server**'.

If the error return is 15007, *No permission*, check for (2) as above. Also check that the executable **pbs_iff** is located in the search path for the client and that it is **setuid** root. Additionally, try running **pbs_iff** by typing

```
pbs_iff server_host 15001
```

where **server_host** is the name of the host on which the Server is running and 15001 is the port to which the Server is listening (if started with a different port number, use that number instead of 15001). The executable **pbs_iff** should print out a string of garbage characters and exit with a status of 0. The garbage is the encrypted credential that would be used by the command to authenticate the client to the Server. If **pbs_iff** fails to print the garbage and/or exits with a nonzero status, either the Server is not running or it was installed with a different encryption system from that used for **pbs_iff**.

16.6.2 Nodes Down

The PBS Server determines the state of nodes (up or down), by communicating with MOM on the node. The state of nodes may be listed by two commands: **qmgr** and **pbsnodes**.

```
% qmgr
Qmgr: list node @active

% pbsnodes -a
Node jupiter
        state = down, state-unknown
        properties = sparc, mine
```

```
ntype = cluster
```

A node in PBS may be marked **down** in one of two substates. For example, the state above of node "jupiter" shows that the Server has not had contact with MOM on that since the Server came up. Check to see whether a MOM is running on the node. If there is a MOM and if the MOM was just started, the Server may have attempted to poll her before she was up. The Server should see her during the next polling cycle in ten minutes. If the node is still marked **down, state-unknown** after ten minutes, either the node name specified in the Server's node file does not map to the real network hostname or there is a network problem between the Server's host and the node.

If the node is listed as

```
% pbsnodes -a
Node jupiter
        state = down
        properties = sparc, mine
        ntype = cluster
```

then the Server has been able to communicate with MOM on the node in the past, but she has not responded recently. The Server will send a **ping** PBS message to every free node each ping cycle (10 minutes). If a node does not acknowledge the ping before the next cycle, the Server will mark the node **down**.

16.6.3 Nondelivery of Output

If the output of a job cannot be delivered to the user, it is saved in a special directory '/usr/spool/PBS/undelivered' and mail is sent to the user. The typical causes of nondelivery are the following:

- The destination host is not trusted and the user does not have a .rhost file.
- An improper path was specified.
- A directory in the specified destination path is not writable.
- The user's .cshrc on the destination host generates output when executed.

The '/usr/spool/PBS/spool' directory on the execution host does not have the correct permissions. This directory must have mode 1777 (drwxrwxrwxt).

16.6.4 Job Cannot Be Executed

If a user receives a mail message containing a job identifier and the line "Job cannot be executed," the job was aborted by MOM when she tried to place it into execution. The complete reason can be found in one of two places: MOM's log file or the standard error file of the user's job.

If the second line of the message is "See Administrator for help," then MOM aborted the job before the job's files were set up. The reason will be noted in MOM's log. Typical reasons are a bad user/group account or a system error.

If the second line of the message is "See job standard error file," then MOM had already created the job's file, and additional messages were written to standard error.

17 PVFS: Parallel Virtual File System

Walt Ligon and Rob Ross

An increasing number of cluster-based systems are being used for applications that involve not only a significant computational component but also a large amount of I/O. These applications consume or produce very large data sets, generate large checkpoint dumps, or use very large databases. In these situations, a Beowulf computer may be especially attractive because each node of the cluster includes a fully functional I/O subsystem. By using all of the available I/O hardware as a parallel I/O system, you can realize serious performance gains at low cost. As is typically the case in Beowulf systems, the key ingredient is software that allows these hardware resources to be orchestrated for use in high-performance applications. In this chapter we discuss parallel file systems—software that allows all of the disks in a cluster to be used as a single high-performance storage resource. In particular, we present details of the Parallel Virtual File Systems (PVFS), an open source implementation of a parallel file system designed for use on Beowulf computers.

17.1 Introduction

In this section we discuss in general terms what a parallel file system is, what one can do, and when it might be appropriate to use one. We also cover ways to use a parallel file system in parallel applications and issues that might affect performance. Subsequent sections present the details of installing and using PVFS.

17.1.1 Parallel File Systems

A parallel file system (PFS) is system software for a parallel computer that provides data distribution and parallel access. Data distribution allows file data to be distributed among disks attached to different nodes of the computer. Parallel access facilitates coordinated access to that file data by the multiple tasks of a parallel application. The primary goal of a parallel file system is to provide very high performance I/O access to large data sets for parallel applications. This point is as important in what it does *not* say as in what it does say. In particular, parallel file systems may *not* provide especially good performance for single-task applications. Parallel file systems may *not* provide especially low latency for small random accesses. Parallel file systems may *not* provide redundancy or other means of security or reliability. That said, the designer of any file system strives to incorporate these features to the extent possible, but in the case of a parallel file system these considerations are typically secondary to the goal of high-performance access to large data sets.

For purposes of this discussion, a parallel computer is a collection of processor nodes connected with an interconnection network. Some of these nodes have I/O devices attached. A parallel application consists of a number of *tasks* that are distributed among some of the nodes for processing. We call nodes that have attached I/O devices *I/O nodes* and nodes that run an application task *compute nodes*. These sets of nodes may be distinct or may overlap, even to the extent that all nodes are both I/O nodes and compute nodes.

A parallel file system generally consists of two software components: *client code*, which runs on the compute nodes; and *server code*, which runs on the I/O nodes. Application tasks, or clients, present I/O requests to the client code on the compute node where the task is running. The client code decomposes the request and sends it to each of the I/O nodes where the affected data resides. The server code on the I/O nodes transfers data between the network and the storage devices. In a typical I/O request, communication between the compute nodes and I/O nodes is an "all-to-all" pattern. For a read operation, data from each I/O node must be scattered to the various compute nodes, and on the compute nodes, data from the various I/O nodes must be gathered into the read buffer. A write request is similar, but the data flow is reversed.

The other critical component of a parallel file system is the file metadata. All file systems must maintain file metadata, which indicates important properties of the file such as its name, owner, access permissions, and type. In a parallel file system, additional information relating the physical distribution of the data must also be maintained. This includes which I/O nodes hold the file data and how the data is split among the I/O nodes. Special files such as directories and symbolic links more closely resemble metadata than true files and may be stored as such. At least one node on a parallel computer must act as a *manager node* where file metadata is stored. Metadata can be stored in a single location or distributed much as file data is distributed. Generally, all metadata for a single file is stored in a single location and is not distributed as file data is.

How is PFS different from NFS or Samba? In many ways a parallel file system is like a network file system such as NFS [30] or Samba [2]. These systems allow applications running on one system, the client system, to access file data stored on another system, the server. While it is possible to use more than one server with NFS or Samba, only one server manages a given file system (or subdirectory) for the client at a time. Individual files are stored entirely on the one server, along with their metadata. See Chapter 6 for more information on file systems such as these.

In a parallel file system, on the other hand, the data representing a single file is distributed among several servers. In addition, the file metadata may be stored on yet another server. This feature allows a parallel file system to take advantage of multiple I/O subsystems to achieve a performance gain. A parallel file system may provide various interfaces that allow the programmer to access file data in different ways. Moreover, a parallel file system may provide a choice of access semantics that affect how multiple tasks coordinate access to file data. This aspect is significant in that it determines when and where data read or written by multiple tasks is stored in the file and how concurrent update of a file is coordinated or synchronized. In contrast, the semantics and interfaces implemented for network file systems such as NFS and Samba generally do not allow for efficient and deterministic access in the presence of concurrent accesses.

Another important difference between general-purpose network file systems and a parallel file system is in the performance characteristics relative to different workloads. Typical network file systems are designed for interactive workloads. Policies for such features as the minimum transfer unit and local caching are relatively conservative and favor frequent small accesses with high locality. A parallel file system, on the other hand, is more typically designed to provide high throughput for relatively large accesses and optimizes transfers based on the access patterns of parallel applications. Thus, while a parallel file system may functionally serve as a general-purpose network file system, the performance of a PFS in this role may be poor.

What is PVFS?   The Parallel Virtual File System is an open source implementation of a parallel file system developed specifically for Beowulf clusters and the Linux operating system [3]. PVFS runs as a set of user-level daemons and libraries and includes an optional Linux kernel module that allows standard utilities to access PVFS files. PVFS provides a simple striping distribution that allows the user to specify the stripe size and the number of I/O nodes on which data is striped on a per file basis. PVFS also provides a POSIX-like interface that allows transparent access to PVFS files and a number of other interfaces that offer more powerful and flexible access to the PVFS request mechanism. These interfaces are accessed via user-level libraries to provide the best access performance. Additionally, there is at least one implementation of the MPI-IO interface for PVFS.

The PVFS software consists of three daemons. The first is the `mgr` daemon, which maintains metadata for a file system. One copy of this daemon runs for a given file system. Second is the `iod` daemon, which services requests to read and write file data. One of these daemons runs on each node that will act as an I/O node. The third daemon, `pvfsd`, works with the optional kernel module to perform PVFS requests for the kernel. One of these daemons is needed on each client node if and only if that node will make use of the optional kernel module interface.

The PVFS client interface is a library in both shared (`libpvfs.so`) and static (`libpvfs.a`) versions. This library also includes the other user interfaces such as the multidimensional block interface (MDBI) and the partitioned file interface (discussed in Section 17.2.1). These are needed on the node(s) used to compile PVFS applications and, in the case of the shared library, on each client node. The optional PVFS kernel module allows a PVFS file system to be mounted to provide transparent use by client applications. All file system requests are relayed via the `pvfsd` on the client node. This module must be loaded into the kernel on each client node that will have non-PVFS applications access PVFS file systems. A good example of such applications are utilities such as `ls`, `cat`, `cp`, and `mv`.

PVFS uses the Berkeley sockets interface to communicate between the clients and servers via TCP/IP (see Chapter 6 for more information on sockets and TCP/IP). In general, a PVFS application will establish a TCP connection with each `iod` for each open file. The `iods` store file data on the I/O nodes under one subdirectory, using whatever file system that subdirectory is implemented with to store the actual data. File metadata is stored on the node running the `mgr` daemon in standard Unix files, one per file in the PVFS file system. Each file in this metadata directory has a unique `inode` number on that node. That `inode` number is used to identify each segment of the file data on each of the I/O nodes.

Clients access the PVFS manager in order to obtain metadata for PVFS files. Using this metadata, they can then directly access data stored on I/O servers. The interface used by the application defines the semantics of this access and constrains how data might be described; we will cover interface options later in this and the following sections.

17.1.2 Setting Up a Parallel File System

The first step in configuring a PFS is deciding what role each node in the system will play, that is, which nodes will act as I/O nodes, which node will serve the metadata, and which nodes will be compute nodes. While assigning these roles may seem to be fairly straightforward, in fact several different approaches are possible. As is often the case, different approaches may be more suitable to different applications. This section outlines the concepts related to setting up a parallel file system. Specific details of administering PVFS are covered in Section 17.3.

How do I decide on a configuration? Typically, the first consideration in configuring a parallel file system is deciding how many I/O nodes will be used. This can reasonably vary from selecting a single I/O node to using all of the nodes in the system as I/O nodes. The primary consideration for a node to be an I/O node is that each I/O node must have at least one disk drive. Technically an I/O node can serve data from a remote mounted disk, but this approach will create unneeded network traffic. For many clusters, each node has a disk installed, and in this case it is reasonable to make every node an I/O node. Note that files need not be distributed to every I/O node in the network, but making each node an I/O node allows every node to be used for I/O. Alternatively, some cluster designs may include larger disks or additional disks on a subset of the nodes or may include disks on only a few of the nodes. In these cases it is more reasonable to limit the set of I/O nodes to those nodes that naturally lend themselves to that role because of their available resources.

A related issue is whether the applications intend to use some or all of the nodes as both I/O nodes and compute nodes at the same time. Here, one extreme is to use every node in the system in both roles, and the other extreme is to have two distinct sets of nodes: one for computation and one for I/O. This choice may reflect having the budget available to build specialized nodes and having a strong sense of the needs of the application(s). Ideally, these considerations can be addressed at the time the cluster is built so that node hardware will suitably match the role that is planned for each node.

What are the key components of an I/O node? If node hardware is to be tuned to the role of the node, hardware that may impact a node's role includes the disks, device bus, network interface, processors, and memory. The guidelines given here should be considered in light of the material in Chapter 3, where a detailed discussion of hardware issues for Beowulf machines is given. An I/O node needs to provide a certain amount of disk I/O throughput, which depends on both the ratio of I/O nodes to compute nodes and the required I/O throughput needed by the applications. In selecting an I/O node, the choice of SCSI versus IDE disks, number of disks, number of disk controllers, and configuration of the peripheral bus (such as PCI) are all important. An I/O node also needs enough network throughput to deliver the available disk throughput to all of the compute nodes. In fact, it is often desirable that an I/O node be able to deliver more throughput via the network than is available at the disk subsystem, because caching often allows for bursts of traffic that exceed the throughput limits of the disk subsystem. This implies not only that the network interface can provide the required throughput but that the peripheral bus can support both the network and disk I/O load. This also has implications for the choice of network itself.

For dedicated I/O nodes, less powerful CPUs than used in compute nodes might be more cost effective. On the other hand, nodes that serve as both compute and I/O nodes tend to need even more CPU performance, since a certain amount of CPU load is required by the I/O servers in addition to the computational load. Experimental results have shown that having dual CPUs can be advantageous in both dedicated I/O nodes and nodes performing both roles.

17.1.3   Programming with a Parallel File System

Once a parallel file system is operational, data can be stored and accessed by using normal programs and utilities. To really take advantage of a parallel file system, however, you must understand some concepts key to efficient parallel file access and must use these concepts when implementing applications.

The POSIX I/O interface [18] is the standard for file and directory access on Linux systems. With this interface you may seek specific byte positions within a file and access contiguous regions of data at these positions. The semantics of the POSIX I/O interface defines what happens when applications write to overlapping regions as well, placing guarantees on the resulting file. This interface was created to serve as a standard for uniprocessing applications running on Unix machines accessing local file systems.

With parallel file systems, the costs associated with access are often different from those with local access. In particular, performing a single write or read operation often involves a noticeable amount of overhead required to initiate the operation. Thus, when large numbers of small accesses are performed in a parallel I/O environment, performance often suffers. Parallel applications often divide data among processes. This division often leads to situations where different processes want to read from a file a number of records that are not located in a contiguous block [24]. Since each access involves substantial overhead, it would be more efficient to access these regions with a single operation [33] and also more convenient for the programmer. To address this situation, parallel file systems typically offer an interface that allows a large number of noncontiguous regions to be accessed with a single I/O request.

Many parallel applications alternate between I/O and computation. In these types of application a large number of I/O-related operations occur simultaneously, often to the same file. If the operations are all performed independently, it is difficult for the underlying file system to identify and optimize for the access pattern. Grouping these accesses into a "collective access" can allow for further optimization.

Collective I/O is a mechanism provided by many parallel file systems where a single global request to the file system allows each task to access different data in the same file. Collective I/O has been provided in a number of special-purpose interfaces such as PASSION [33] and Panda [28] and is provided in MPI-IO [11]. Collective I/O to PVFS file systems is currently supported through the use of the ROMIO MPI-IO interface [34] (also discussed later in this chapter).

The POSIX semantics also imposes strict requirements on the order in which operations may be completed on I/O servers in a parallel environment. The semantics cripples the ability to perform I/O in parallel in many situations. Interfaces with more relaxed semantics provide more opportunities for parallelism by eliminating the overhead associated with atomicity of access; the application programmer ensures consistency instead.

All of these concepts, aggregating requests, collective I/O, and access semantics boil down to making the best use of available interfaces. We cover these next.

What other interfaces do I have to work with? Many interfaces and optimizations have been proposed and implemented to address the three issues of noncontiguous access, collective I/O, and the semantics of parallel access. These interfaces can be categorized into POSIX-like interfaces, general-purpose parallel I/O interfaces, and specialized (or application-specific) interfaces.

POSIX-like interfaces use the POSIX interface as their basis and provide various extensions in order to better describe parallel access. One such extension is file partitioning. File partitioning allows the interface to create a "view" of a file that contains of some subset of the data in the file. Partitions are usually based on some systematic subsetting of the file, for example, "Starting with the second byte of the file, view every fourth byte of the file." A more useful view might consider the file as a sequence of n byte records and take every pth record starting with record k. If there are p parallel tasks, and each creates a partition with the same value of n but with a different value of k ranging from 0 to $p - 1$, then the set of partitions will cover the entire file, and none of the partitions will overlap. This is one way to evenly distribute file data among p tasks.

With an interface that supports partitioning, once the partition is defined, the program accesses the data in the partition as if it is the only thing in the file. In other words, any data not in the partition no longer appears in the file, and the data in the partition appears to be contiguous in the partitioned file. This is a convenient abstraction in that all of the information regarding the distribution of data among the tasks in located only in the part of the program that creates the partition. This can be especially nice in converting sequential programs to parallel programs because sometimes all that is needed is to set up the partition and then let the program run as originally written. Partitioning is also one way that the programmer can specify a large set of noncontiguous accesses with a single request, which may allow the file system opportunities for optimization. This optimization would be impossible if instead `seek()` were used to access each contiguous region one at a time.

File partitioning has been included in the Vesta interface [5] and MPI-IO [11] (as *file views*), among others, and is supported by PVFS. Some partitioning interfaces require all tasks accessing a file to specify a common partitioning scheme that provides no overlap and complete file coverage. Other interfaces, such as the one implemented for PVFS, may allow individual tasks to specify different partitions, including those that overlap or that do not cover all of the data in the file. Details of the PVFS partitioning interface are given in Section 17.2.

Some applications require that output data from different tasks be interleaved, and yet cannot predict how much data each task will produce for each output. In this case a shared file pointer can be an effective mechanism for coordinating file I/O. With a shared file pointer, sequential access proceeds not from the last location accessed by the task performing I/O but from the last location accessed by any task. In one variation, a shared file pointer can be used with a collective operation, and each task's data is stored in the file in task order.

Shared file pointer interfaces are useful for low-volume I/O such as log messages and infrequent tracing data. A collective shared file pointer interface can also be useful for applications that synchronize well but generate data of varying size. Care must be taken in using a shared file pointer interface, however, since some implementations entail substantial overhead or result in serialized access. Shared file pointers have been provided by the Intel PFS, Vesta [5], and MPI-IO [11]. PVFS does not currently support shared file pointers.

Extensions or modifications to the POSIX interface such as partitioning and shared file pointers can help in providing more usable and higher-performance interfaces for some applications. However, more flexible interfaces can allow for even more convenient access and higher performance for a broader range of applications. One such interface is MPI-IO.

MPI-IO is a parallel I/O interface defined as part of the MPI-2 specification [11]. It is supported by a number of parallel file systems and provides all of the features described above: partitioning, collective operations, a mechanism to create noncontiguous I/O requests, and relaxed access semantics. MPI-IO is a very powerful application-independent interface and is probably the interface of choice for MPI programs. PVFS supports MPI-IO through the use of ROMIO, an MPI-IO implementation built on top of MPI [34]. Details of MPI-IO are given in Chapter 10 and in [14, Chapter 3].

A number of I/O interfaces also have been designed for special purposes. Examples include Panda [28], HDF5, and PVFS's multidimensional block interface (MDBI) [4]. MDBI provides special methods to allow you to define a regularly spaced n-dimensional data set that will be stored in the file. This description is similar to that of an n-dimensional array of some base type. Once this definition is in place, you can access any element of the data set with its corresponding coordinates. Additional methods allow you to control buffering of elements from the data set. Details of MDBI are given below in Section 17.2.1.

How do I tune my application for high performance?   Parallel applications that use a parallel file system typically work by distributing the data in the file among the application's tasks. Exactly how this is done will vary from application to application, but in many cases there are natural divisions in the data. For example, a file may contain an array of records each of which includes several scalar data values. The records may represent a linear sequence or may represent a matrix of two or more dimensions. In the former case, the record boundaries are natural divisions. Thus most tasks will read a multiple of the record size (in bytes) from the file. In the latter case, the rows and columns are perhaps more natural divisions. Thus a task may read one or more whole rows at a time.

With such an application it is important to consider how the data will be distributed. Often this means considering these natural boundaries when selecting a stripe size for file distribution (assuming a striped physical data distribution). If the stripe size is matched to the natural boundaries in the data set, accesses by applications tend to be more uniformly distributed across the I/O servers. One pitfall is that many files include a header that is not the same size as a record. In this case the presence of the header can force the data not to align properly on the I/O nodes, and poor performance can result. The most common solution is to pad the header with blank space to the next physical boundary (depending on the distribution) so that the records will align. Another solution is to store the header information in a separate file or at the end of the file instead of the beginning.

PVFS performs better when multiple clients are accessing the *same* file, rather than each client accessing its own file. This is because the underlying storage systems respond better to single-file traffic. Thus, for PVFS it is best to aggregate output data into a single file; luckily this is often the most convenient option.

The next consideration is how the data accessed by each task is spread across the I/O nodes. When using PVFS, it is often best to store and access data distributed across multiple I/O servers with single requests. This approach makes the best use of the underlying network by moving data through multiple TCP streams. This same approach applies in the case of multiple simultaneous accesses as well; just as PVFS clients perform more efficiently when exchanging data with multiple servers, PVFS servers perform at their best when servicing multiple clients simultaneously. What this means is that some experimentation is often necessary to determine the optimal matching of natural boundaries to the stripe; sometimes it is more efficient to place multiple rows, for example, in a single stripe. All that said, there are also advantages to accessing data residing locally when an overlapped compute/server environment is in place, especially when the interconnect in the cluster is relatively slow.

We discussed the coordination of access and the advantages of collective I/O earlier in this section. It is important to note, however, that there are cases when collective I/O *doesn't* pay off. In particular, if an application spends a great majority of its time computing, it might be more optimal to stagger the tasks' accesses to the I/O system. This approach lightens the load on the I/O servers and simultaneously allows more time for the I/O as a whole to take place. In all cases it is important to attempt to keep all I/O servers busy.

We emphasize that not all parallel file systems share these characteristics. Many such systems do not perform well with large numbers of clients simultaneously accessing single servers or simultaneously accessing the same file [19]. You should consider these issues when moving an application from one platform to another.

What is out-of-core computation?   Another issue to consider is how the file system will be used in a computation. Some applications tend to read an input data file and produce an output data file. Other applications might not do much I/O at all, except that they require an extremely large amount of storage for their data structures and cannot keep everything in memory. In this case, the parallel file system can be used as a large shared-memory region using a technique known as out-of-core (OOC) computation. OOC techniques are similar to virtual memory use in that data is moved between disk and memory as needed for computation. Unlike virtual memory, however, OOC requires the programmer to explicitly read and write data rather than doing it transparently via a demand paged memory management system. While using virtual memory is much easier than OOC, a well-designed OOC program will outperform a virtual memory program by better utilizing memory and by moving data in and out of memory in large blocks, rather than moving a page at a time as demand paging would.

Facilities that support OOC allow the programmer to describe the data structures stored in the parallel file and then access them in a manner consistent with that logical view of the data. For example, the MDBI provided by PVFS (discussed in Section 17.2.1) allows the program to describe a file as a multidimensional array and then read and write blocks of that array by using array subscripts.

Could you give me a tuning example? Many parallel applications involve regularly structured data that is evenly distributed to the tasks. Records can be assigned to tasks in groups. These groups may consist of contiguous records or non-contiguous but regularly spaced records. For example, consider an image-processing application. Each scan line of the image can be considered a record. Suppose the image has 512 scan lines, and you are using 16 processors. One distribution would be to assign the first 32 scan lines to the first processor, the second 32 to the second processor, and so on. Another distribution would be to assign one of each of the first 16 scan lines to each processor, in order, and then start over again and assign a second scan line from the second set of 16. A third option might be to assign 8 scan lines to each processor until the first 128 scan lines are assign, and then start over and assign the next 128, 8 at a time. In each case each processor gets 32 scan lines. The advantages and disadvantages of each depend on the algorithm being implemented and are beyond the scope of this book. Suffice it say each is a potentially useful distribution.

This example illustrates the concept known as "strided access." In strided access, a task accesses a contiguous region of data (in this case one or more scan lines), skips a region, and then accesses another region of the same size as the first, skips a region the same size as the first, and so on. Strided access can be used to access rows in a matrix, groups of rows in a matrix, columns in a matrix, groups of columns in a matrix, and other patterns. Because this is such a common distribution, many interfaces, including the PVFS library and MPI-IO, provide mechanisms to issue requests for strided accesses.

As alluded to above, the choice of distribution can affect algorithm performance, but it can also have an impact on I/O performance in that it can affect how I/O requests are distributed among the I/O nodes. Continuing the above example, assume each scan line of the image has 512 pixels and each pixel is 4 bytes. Thus an image is a total of 1 MByte. Suppose the file system uses a striped distribution, and you choose a 32 KByte strip size, which results in stripes of 512 KBytes.

The the image will be evenly distributed to all 16 disks, two 32 KByte blocks per node. Now consider the three distributions discussed above for the computational tasks. In the first, each task will access 32 scan lines of 2 KBytes each, which will be evenly distributed across 2 disks; 2 tasks will share 2 disks (consider disks 0 and

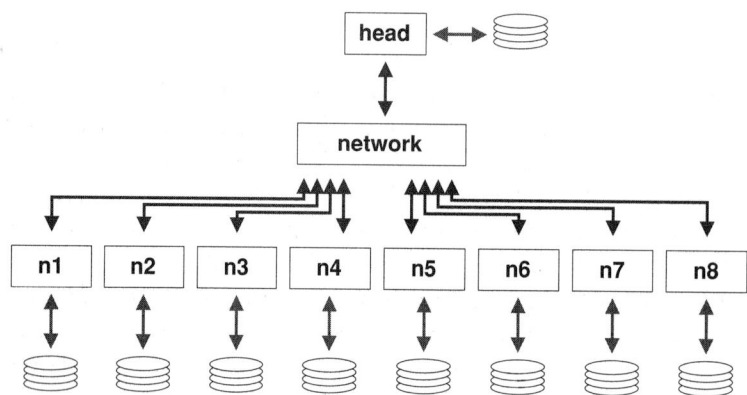

Figure 17.1
Example system.

1, which hold scan lines 0 to 15, 16 to 31, 128 to 143, and 144 to 159, which will map to tasks 0, 0, 8, and 8, respectively). In the second distribution, each task will access 2 scan lines from each of all 16 disks. Thus all 16 disks will service requests from all 16 tasks. In the third distribution, each task's data will map to 4 disks, and each disk will service 4 tasks. Thus the choice of distribution and stripe size affects how requests are spread across disks.

17.2   Using PVFS

In this section we discuss the options for accessing PVFS file systems from applications. We assume that a PVFS file system is already configured and available for use.

For the purposes of discussion we will pretend that PVFS is running on a small cluster of nine machines. In our example system, shown in Figure 17.1, there is one "head" node, called head, and eight other nodes, n1–n8. Each of these systems has a local disk, they are connected via some switch or hub, IP is up and running, and they can talk to each other via these short names. We will come back to this example throughout this chapter in order to clarify installation, configuration, and usage issues. This section, and the following one, are rife with example shell interactions in order to show exactly how things are configured.

17.2.1   Writing PVFS Programs

Programs written to use normal Unix I/O will work fine with PVFS without any changes. Files created this way will be striped according to the file system defaults set at compile time, usually set to a 256 KByte stripe size across all of the I/O nodes, starting with the first node listed in the .iodtab file. We note that use of Unix system calls `read()` and `write()` results in exactly the data specified being exchanged with the I/O nodes each time the call is made. Large numbers of small accesses performed with these calls will not perform well at all. In contrast, the buffered routines of the standard I/O library `fread()` and `fwrite()` locally buffer small accesses and perform exchanges with the I/O nodes in chunks of at least some minimum size. Utilities such as `tar` have options (e.g., `--block-size`) for setting the I/O access size as well. Generally PVFS will perform better with larger buffer sizes.

For applications using stdio routines to access PVFS files, you may want to increase the buffer size used by `fread()` and `fwrite()`. The `setvbuf()` call may be used to specify the buffering characteristics of a stream (`FILE *`) after opening. This call must be made before any other operations are performed, for example,

```
FILE *fp;
fp = fopen("foo", "r+");
setvbuf(fp, NULL, _IOFBF, 256*1024);
/* now we have a 256K buffer and are fully buffering I/O */
```

See the man page on `setvbuf()` for more information.

This transparent access involves significant overhead both due to data movement through the kernel and due to our user-space client-side daemon (`pvfsd`). To get around this, the PVFS libraries can be used either directly (via the native PVFS calls) or indirectly (through the ROMIO MPI-IO interface, the MDBI interface, or some higher-level interface such as HDF5).

In this section we begin by covering how to write and compile programs with the PVFS libraries. Next we cover how to specify the physical distribution of a file and how to set logical partitions. Following this we cover the MDBI interface. Finally we touch upon the use of ROMIO with PVFS. In addition to these interfaces, it is important to know how to control the physical distribution of files. In the next three sections, we will discuss how to specify the physical partitioning, or striping, of a file, how to set logical partitions on file data, and how the PVFS multidimensional block interface can be used.

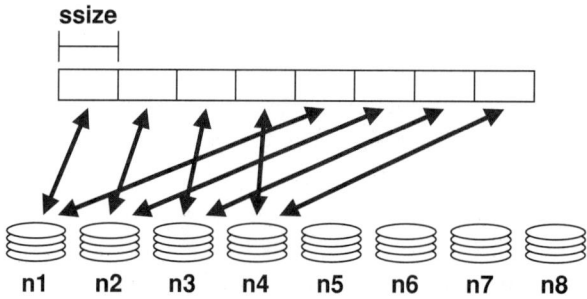

Figure 17.2
Striping example with base of 0 and `pcount` of 4

Preliminaries. When compiling programs to use PVFS, you should include in the source the PVFS `include` file, typically installed in `/usr/local/include/`, by

```
#include <pvfs.h>
```

To link to the PVFS library, typically installed in `/usr/local/lib/`, you should add `-lpvfs` to the link line and possibly `-L/usr/local/lib` to ensure that the directory is included in the library search.

The PVFS interface calls will also operate correctly on standard, non-PVFS, files, including the MDBI interface. When you are debugging code, this feature can help isolate application problems from bugs in the PVFS system.

Specifying Striping Parameters. The current physical distribution mechanism used by PVFS is a simple striping scheme. The distribution of data is described with three parameters:

base — index of the starting I/O node, with 0 being the first in the file system

pcount — number of servers on which data will be stored (partitions, a misnomer)

ssize — strip size, the size of the contiguous chunks stored on I/O servers

In Figure 17.2 we show an example where the base node is 0 and the `pcount` is 4 for a file stored on our example PVFS file system. As you can see, only four of the I/O servers will hold data for this file, because of the striping parameters.

Physical distribution is determined when the file is first created. Using `pvfs_open()`, you can specify the following parameters:

```
pvfs_open(char *pathname, int flag, mode_t mode);
pvfs_open(char *pathname, int flag, mode_t mode,
          struct pvfs_filestat *dist);
```

If the first set of parameters is used, a default distribution will be imposed. If, instead, a structure defining the distribution is passed in and the O_META flag is OR'd into the flag parameter, you can define the physical distribution via the pvfs_filestat structure passed in by reference as the last parameter. This structure is defined in the PVFS header files as follows:

```
struct pvfs_filestat {
    int base;   /* The first iod node to be used */
    int pcount; /* The number of iod nodes for the file */
    int ssize;  /* stripe size */
    int soff;   /* NOT USED */
    int bsize;  /* NOT USED */
}
```

The soff and bsize fields are artifacts of previous research and are not in use at this time. Setting the pcount value to -1 will use all available I/O daemons for the file. Setting -1 in the ssize and base fields will result in the default values being used (see Section 17.3.4 for more information on default values).

To obtain information on the physical distribution of a file, you should use pvfs_ioctl() on an open file descriptor:

```
pvfs_ioctl(int fd, GETMETA, struct pvfs_filestat *dist);
```

It will fill in the pvfs_filestat structure with the physical distribution information for the file. On the command line the pvstat utility can be used to obtain this information (see Section 17.2.2).

Setting a Logical Partition.   The PVFS logical partitioning system allows you to describe the regions of interest in a file and subsequently access those regions efficiently. Access is more efficient because the PVFS system allows disjoint regions that can be described with a logical partition to be accessed as single units. The alternative would be to perform multiple seek-access operations, which is inferior because of both the number of separate operations and the reduced data movement per operation. PVFS logical partitioning is an implementation of file partitioning; it is named "logical" because it is independent of any physical characteristics of the file (such as the stripe size).

If applicable, logical partitioning can also ease parallel programming by simplifying data access to a shared data set by the tasks of an application. Each task can set up its own logical partition, and once this is done all I/O operations will "see" only the data for that task.

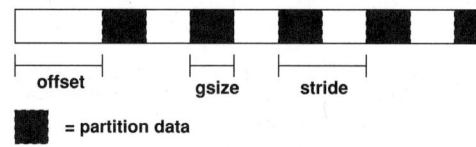

Figure 17.3
Partitioning parameters.

With the current PVFS partitioning mechanism, partitions are defined with three parameters: *offset*, group size (*gsize*), and *stride*. The offset is the distance in bytes from the beginning of the file to the first byte in the partition. Group size is the number of contiguous bytes included in the partition. Stride is the distance from the beginning of one group of bytes to the next. Figure 17.3 shows these parameters.

To set the file partition, the program uses a `pvfs_ioctl()` call. The parameters are as follows:

```
pvfs_ioctl(fd, SETPART, &part);
```

where **part** is a structure defined as follows:

```
struct fpart {
    int offset;
    int gsize;
    int stride;
    int gstride; /* NOT USED */
    int ngroups; /* NOT USED */
};
```

The last two fields, `gstride` and `ngroups`, are remnants of previous research, are no longer used, and should be set to zero. The `pvfs_ioctl()` call can also be used to get the current partitioning parameters by specifying the `GETPART` flag. Note that whenever the partition is set, the file pointer is reset to the beginning of the new partition. Also note that setting the partition is a purely local call; it does not involve contacting any of the PVFS daemons. Thus it is reasonable to reset the partition as often as needed during the execution of a program. When a PVFS file is first opened, a "default partition" is imposed on it that allows the process to see the entire file.

As an example, suppose a file contains 40,000 records of 1,000 bytes each, there are four parallel tasks, and each task needs to access a partition of 10,000 records each for processing. In this case you would set the group size to 10,000 records

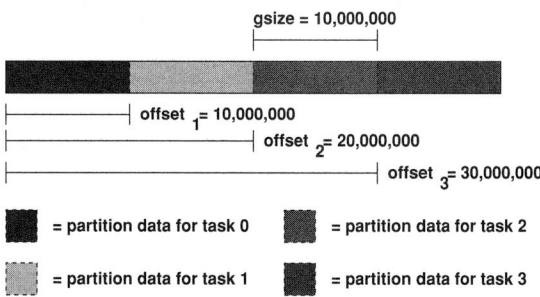

Figure 17.4
Partitioning Example 1, block distribution.

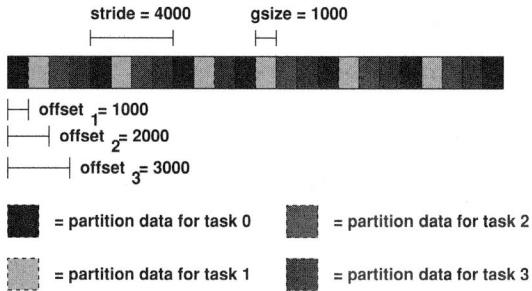

Figure 17.5
Partitioning Example 2, cyclic distribution.

times 1,000 bytes, or 10,000,000 bytes. Then each task would set its offset so that it would access a disjoint portion of the data. This is shown in Figure 17.4.

Alternatively, suppose you want to allocate the records in a cyclic, or "round-robin," manner. In this case the group size would be set to 1,000 bytes, the stride would be set to 4,000 bytes, and the offsets would again be set to access disjoint regions, as shown in Figure 17.5.

Setting the partition for one task has no effect whatsoever on any other tasks. There is also no reason for the partitions set by each task to be distinct; the partitions of different tasks can be overlapped, if desired. Finally, no direct relationship exists between partitioning and striping for a given file; while it is often desirable to match the partition to the striping of the file, you have the option of selecting any partitioning scheme independent of the striping of a file.

Simple partitioning is useful for one-dimensional data and simple distributions of two-dimensional data. More complex distributions and multidimensional data are often more easily partitioned by using the multidimensional block interface.

Using Multidimensional Blocking.   The PVFS multidimensional block interface provides a slightly higher level view of file data than does the native PVFS interface. With the MDBI, file data is considered as an n-dimensional array of records. This array is divided into "blocks" of records by specifying the dimensions of the array and the size of the blocks in each dimension. The parameters used to describe the array are as follows:

D — number of dimensions

rs — record size

nb_n — number of blocks (in each dimension)

ne_n — number of elements in a block (in each dimension)

bf_n — blocking factor (in each dimension), described later

Once you have defined the view of the data set, blocks of data can be read with single function calls, greatly simplifying the act of accessing these types of data sets. This is done by specifying a set of *index* values, one per dimension.

Five basic calls are used for accessing files with MDBI:

```
int open_blk(char *path, int flags, int mode);
```

```
int set_blk(int fd, int D, int rs, int ne1, int nb1, ..., int nen,
       int nbn);
```

```
int read_blk(int fd, char *buf, int index1, ..., int indexn);
```

```
int write_blk(int fd, char *buf, int index1, ..., int indexn);
```

```
int close_blk(int fd);
```

The open_blk() and close_blk() calls operate similarly to the standard Unix open() and close(). The call set_blk() is used to set the blocking parameters for the array before reading or writing; this process will be described in a moment. It can be used as often as necessary and does not entail communication. The two calls read_blk() and write_blk() are used to read blocks of records once the blocking has been set.

Figure 17.6 gives an example of blocking. Here a file has been described as a two-dimensional array of blocks, with blocks consisting of a two by three array of records. Records are shown with dotted lines, with groups of records organized into blocks denoted with solid lines.

In this example, the array would be described with a call to set_blk() as follows:

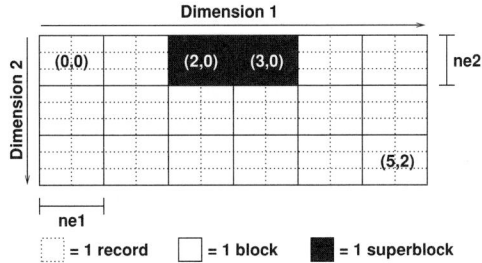

Figure 17.6
MDBI Example 1.

```
set_blk(fd, 2, 500, 2, 6, 3, 3);
```

If you wanted to read block $(2, 0)$ from the array, you could then

```
read_blk(fd, &buf, 2, 0);
```

Similarly, to read block $(5, 2)$, you could use

```
write_blk(fd, &blk, 5, 2);
```

A final feature of the MDBI is block buffering. Sometimes multidimensional blocking is used to set the size of the data that the program wants to read and write from disk. Other times the block size has some physical meaning in the program and is set for other reasons. In this case, individual blocks may be rather small, resulting in poor I/O performance and underutilization of memory. MDBI provides a buffering mechanism that causes multiple blocks to be read and written from disk and stored in a buffer in the program's memory address space. Subsequent transfers using `read_blk()` and `write_blk()` result in memory-to-memory transfers unless a block outside of the current buffer is accessed.

Since it is difficult to predict what blocks should be accessed when, PVFS relies on user cues to determine what to buffer. This is done by defining "blocking factors" that group blocks together. The *blocking factor* indicates how many blocks in the given dimension should be buffered. A single function is used to define the blocking factor: `int buf_blk(int fd, int` bf_1`, ..., int` bf_n`)`.

Looking at Figure 17.6 again, we can see how blocking factors can be defined. In the example, the call

```
buf_blk(fd, 2, 1);
```

is used to specify the blocking factor. We denote the larger resulting buffered blocks as *superblocks* (a poor choice of terms in retrospect), one of which is shaded in the example.

Whenever a block is accessed, if its superblock is not in the buffer, the current superblock is written back to disk (if dirty), and the new superblock is read in its place; then the desired block is copied into the given buffer. The default blocking factor for all dimensions is 1, and any time the blocking factor is changed the buffer is written back to disk if dirty.

We emphasize that no cache coherency is performed here; if application tasks are sharing superblocks, unexpected results will occur if writes are performed. The user must ensure that this does not happen. A good strategy for buffering is to develop a program with buffering turned off, and then enable it later in order to improve performance.

Using the ROMIO MPI-IO Implementation. The MPI specification provides a de facto standard for message passing in parallel programs. The MPI-2 specification, which builds on the successful MPI-1 specification, includes a section on I/O that is commonly referred to as MPI-IO [14, 11]. Just as MPI has become the interface of choice for message passing in parallel applications, the MPI-IO interface has become a prominent low-level interface for I/O access in parallel applications.

ROMIO is one implementation of the MPI-IO interface [34]. ROMIO is unique in that it implements an abstract I/O device (ADIO) layer that aids in porting ROMIO to new underlying I/O systems. The success of this design is evident in the number of systems for which ROMIO provides MPI-IO support, including HP, IBM, NEC, SGI, and Linux.

In addition to merely mapping MPI-IO operations into the correct underlying operations, ROMIO implements two important optimizations that can be of great benefit in a number of scenarios. The first of these is *data sieving* [33], which allows ROMIO to take advantage of MPI-IO noncontiguous requests by accessing larger, contiguous regions containing desired data with single calls. Combining many small accesses into a single large one is a very effective optimization in many I/O systems. The second of these optimizations is a collective optimization termed *two-phase I/O* [32]. The goal of two-phase I/O is to more optimally access the disk. In collective operations, multiple processes often will read small adjoining regions from a single server. Two-phase I/O combines these adjoining accesses into a single access by a single process. Data for the access is then scattered (in the read case) or first gathered (in the write case) in order to attain the desired distribution.

In Linux clusters ROMIO can be configured to operate on top of PVFS, providing applications using the MPI-IO interface direct access to PVFS file systems. This strategy allows applications to use this high-performance I/O option without constraining application programmers to using the PVFS interface. Chapter 10 includes details on using MPI-IO in applications.

The MPI hints mechanism may be used to pass striping information to PVFS through the MPI-IO interface. Hints are passed by the "info" object that is an argument to MPI_File_open(). The following three keywords are valid for PVFS:

striping_unit — ssize value

striping_factor — pcount value

start_iodevice — base value

When using ROMIO with PVFS, you must be aware of three important cases. First, if ROMIO was not compiled with PVFS support, it will access files only through the kernel-supported interface (i.e., a mounted PVFS file system). If PVFS support was compiled into ROMIO and you attempt to access a PVFS-mounted volume, the PVFS library will detect that these are PVFS files (if the pvfstab file is correct) and use the library calls to avoid the kernel overhead. If PVFS support is compiled into ROMIO and you attempt to access a PVFS file for which there is *no* mounted volume, the file name *must* be prefixed with pvfs: to indicate that the file is a PVFS file; otherwise ROMIO will not be able to find the file.

17.2.2 PVFS Utilities

A few utilities are provided for dealing with PVFS files and file systems.

Copying Files to PVFS. While the cp utility can copy files onto a PVFS file system, the user then loses control over the physical distribution of the file (the default is used). Instead, the u2p command supplied with PVFS can be used to copy an existing Unix file to a PVFS file system while specifying physical distribution parameters. The syntax for u2p is

```
u2p -s <stripe size> -b <base> -n <# of nodes> <srcfile> <destfile>
```

This function is most useful in converting pre-existing data files to PVFS so that they can be used in parallel programs. The u2p command relies on the existence of the /etc/pvfstab file to operate correctly.

Examining PVFS File Distributions.   The `pvstat` utility will print out the physical distribution parameters for a PVFS file. After earlier creating a file on our example PVFS file system, we see

```
[root@head /root]# /usr/local/bin/pvstat /pvfs/foo
/pvfs/foo: base = 0, pcount = 8, ssize = 65536
```

The `pvstat` utility relies on the existence of the `/etc/pvfstab` file to operate correctly.

Checking on Server Status.   The `iod-ping` utility can be used to determine whether a given I/O server is running:

```
[root@head /root]# /usr/local/bin/iod-ping -h n1 -p 7000
n1:7000 is responding.
[root@head /root]# /usr/local/bin/iod-ping -h head -p 7000
head:7000 is down.
```

In this case, we have started the I/O server on n1, so it is up and running. We are not running an I/O server on the head, so it is reported as down. Likewise the `mgr-ping` utility can be used to check the status of metadata servers:

```
[root@head /root]# /usr/local/bin/mgr-ping -h head -p 3000
head:3000 is responding.
[root@head /root]# /usr/local/bin/mgr-ping -h n1 -p 3000
n1:3000 is down.
```

The `mgr` is up and running on head, but we're not running one on n1.

These two utilities also set their exit values appropriately for use with scripts; in other words, they set their exit value to 0 on success (responding) and 1 on failure (down). If no additional parameters are specified, the program will automatically check for a server on `localhost` at the default port for the server type (7000 for I/O server, 3000 for metadata server). If the "-p" option is not specified, the default port is used.

No `fsck` currently exists for PVFS, although arguably there should be one.

17.3   Administering PVFS

In this section we cover the specifics of administering PVFS, first building the PVFS components, then installing and configuring the servers, next installing and configuring client software, and finally starting things up and verifying that the system is operating. We continue to rely on the system described in Section 17.2 and shown in Figure 17.1 as an example.

17.3.1   Building the PVFS Components

The PVFS package has come a long way in the past few versions in terms of ease of compilation. The process is now fairly simple.

Two tar files are needed for compiling PVFS:

- `pvfs` (e.g., `pvfs-1.5.0.tgz`)
- `pvfs-kernel` (e.g., `pvfs-kernel-0.9.0.tgz`)

The first of these contains code for the PVFS servers and for the PVFS library. The second contains code specific to the Linux VFS support, which allows PVFS file systems to be mounted on Linux PCs. This code is not essential for using PVFS, but it makes accessing PVFS files much more convenient.

Obtaining the Source.   PVFS is open source and is freely available on the Web. Currently there are two consistent sources for obtaining PVFS via the FTP protocol:

- `ftp://ftp.parl.clemson.edu:/pub/pvfs/`
- `ftp://mirror.chpc.utah.edu:/pub/pvfs/` (mirror site)

Within one of these directories are the files `pvfs-v1.tgz` and `pvfs-kernel-v2.tgz`, where `v1` and `v2` are version numbers. These files are `tar` archives of the PVFS source that have subsequently been compressed with the `gzip` tool. You should download the latest versions of each; the version numbers of the two packages will not match each other. (At the time of writing, the newest version of the pvfs archive was 1.5.1, and the newest version of the pvfs-kernel archive was 0.9.1.)

Untarring the Packages.   It is a bit easier to perform the compilations if both the archives are untarred in the same directory, since the pvfs-kernel source relies on `include` files from the `pvfs` source tree. In our example, we will untar into `/usr/src/` on the head node:

```
[root@head /root]# cp pvfs-1.5.0.tgz pvfs-kernel-0.9.0.tgz /usr/src
[root@head /usr/src]# cd /usr/src
[root@head /usr/src]# tar xzf pvfs-1.5.0.tgz
[root@head /usr/src]# tar xzf pvfs-kernel-0.9.0.tgz
[root@head /usr/src]# ln -s pvfs-1.5.0 pvfs
[root@head /usr/src]# ls -lF
total 476
lrwxrwxrwx   1 root   root        15 Dec 14 17:42 pvfs -> pvfs-1.5.0/
```

```
drwxr-xr-x  12 root    root       512 Dec 14 10:11 pvfs-1.5.0/
-rw-r--r--   1 root    root    371535 Dec 14 17:41 pvfs-1.5.0.tgz
drwxr-xr-x   6 root    root      1024 Dec 14 10:10 pvfs-kernel-0.9.0/
-rw-r--r--   1 root    root    105511 Dec 14 17:41 pvfs-kernel-0.9.0.tgz
```

The symbolic link allows the pvfs-kernel package easily to find the include files it needs. Once this is finished, the source is ready to be compiled.

Compiling the Packages. Next we will compile the two packages. We also will discuss how to install the packages on the local system; however, most users will wish to wait and distribute the files to the correct machines after compiling is complete. In the Section 17.3.2 we discuss what components need to be where.

First we will compile the `pvfs` package (leaving out the output):

```
[root@head /usr/src]# cd pvfs
[root@head /usr/src/pvfs-1.5.0]# ./configure
[root@head /usr/src/pvfs-1.5.0]# make
```

Then the components can be installed:

```
[root@head /usr/src/pvfs-1.5.0]# make install
```

The following are installed by default:

- `mgr`, `iod` in `/usr/local/sbin/`
- `libpvfs.a` in `/usr/local/lib/`
- include files in `/usr/local/include/`
- test programs and utilities in `/usr/local/bin/`
- man pages in `/usr/local/man/`

These installation directories can be changed via options to `configure`. See `configure --help` in the package source directory.

The PVFS-kernel package will perform tests for features based on header files and the running kernel, so it is important that the desired the kernel be running and the matching header files available on the machine on which the compilation will take place. With the matching headers, compiling is easy. Again we omit the output of the compile process:

```
[root@head /usr/src/pvfs-1.5.0]# cd ../pvfs-kernel-0.9.0
[root@head /usr/src/pvfs-kernel-0.9.0]# ./configure \
--with-libpvfs-dir=../pvfs/lib
[root@head /usr/src/pvfs-kernel-0.9.0]# make
```

The configure option here lets the package know where it can find the PVFS I/O library `libpvfs.a`, which is used by this package. The `README` and `INSTALL` files in the source directory contain hints for working around common compilation problems.

Once these steps are complete, the kernel components can be installed:

```
[root@head /usr/src/pvfs-kernel-0.9.0]# make install
```

The following are installed by default:

- `/usr/local/sbin/pvfsd`
- `/sbin/mount.pvfs`

The program `mount.pvfs` is put in that location because that is the only location the system utility `mount` will look in for a file system-specific executable; this is covered in more detail in Section 17.3.5.

You must install `pvfs.o` in the right place. This is usually
`/lib/modules/<kernel-version>/misc/`.

17.3.2 Installation

PVFS is a somewhat complicated package to get up and running. The reason is, in part, because it is a multicomponent system, but also because the configuration is a bit unintuitive. The purpose of this section is to shed light on the process of installing, configuring, starting, and using the PVFS system.

It is important to have in mind the roles that machines (a.k.a. nodes) will play in the PVFS system. Remember that there are three potential roles that a machine might play: metadata server, I/O server, and client. A machine can fill one, two, or all of these roles simultaneously. Each role requires a specific set of binaries and configuration information. There will be one metadata server for the PVFS file system. There can be many I/O servers and clients. In this section we discuss the components and configuration files needed to fulfill each role.

Again, we configure our example system so that the "head" node provides metadata service, the eight other nodes provide I/O service, and all nodes can act as clients.

For additional information on file system default values and other configuration options, see Section 17.3.4.

Directories Used by PVFS.   In addition to the roles that a machine may play, three types of directories are used in PVFS. A great deal of confusion seems to surround these, so before we begin our example installation we will attempt to dispel this confusion. The three types of directories are metadata directory, data directory, and mount point.

There is a single metadata directory for a PVFS file system. It exists on the machine that is filling the role of the metadata server. In this directory information is stored describing the files stored on the PVFS file system, including the owner of files, the permissions, and the way the files are distributed across I/O servers. Additionally, two special files are stored in this directory, .iodtab and .pvfsdir, which are used by the metadata server to find I/O servers and PVFS files.

There is a data directory on each I/O server. This directory is used to store the data that makes up PVFS files. The data is stored in individual files in a subdirectory hierarchy.

Finally there is a mount point on each client. This is an empty directory on which the PVFS file system is mounted and at which pvfstab files point (see Section 17.3.4). This empty directory is identical to any other mount point.

Installing and Configuring the PVFS Servers.   Three files are necessary for a metadata server to operate:

- mgr executable
- .iodtab file
- .pvfsdir file

The mgr executable is the daemon that provides metadata services in the PVFS system. It normally runs as root. It must be started before clients attempt to access the system.

The .iodtab file contains an ordered list of IP addresses and ports for contacting I/O daemons (iods). Since this list is ordered, once it is created it must not be modified, because this can destroy the integrity of data stored on PVFS.

The .pvfsdir file describes the permissions of the directory in which the metadata is stored.

Both the .iodtab and .pvfsdir files may be created with the mkmgrconf script. In our example we will use the directory /pvfs-meta as our metadata directory.

```
[root@head /usr/src/pvfs-kernel-0.9.0]# cd /
[root@head /]# mkdir /pvfs-meta
[root@head /]# cd /pvfs-meta

[root@head /pvfs-meta]# /usr/local/bin/mkmgrconf
This script will make the .iodtab and .pvfsdir files
in the metadata directory of a PVFS file system.
```

```
Enter the root directory:
/pvfs-meta
Enter the user id of directory:
root
Enter the group id of directory:
root
Enter the mode of the root directory:
777
Enter the hostname that will run the manager:
localhost
Searching for host...success
Enter the port number on the host for manager:
(Port number 3000 is the default)
3000
Enter the I/O nodes:  (can use form node1, node2, ...  or
nodename#-#,#,#)
n1-8
Searching for hosts...success
I/O nodes:  n1 n2 n3 n4 n5 n6 n7 n8
Enter the port number for the iods:
(Port number 7000 is the default)
7000
Done!

[root@head /pvfs-meta]# ls -al
total 9
drwxr-xr-x    2 root     root              82 Dec 17 15:01 ./
drwxr-xr-x   21 root     root             403 Dec 17 15:01 ../
-rwxr-xr-x    1 root     root              84 Dec 17 15:01 .iodtab*
-rwxr-xr-x    1 root     root              43 Dec 17 15:01 .pvfsdir*
```

The mkmgrconf script is installed with the rest of the utilities.

I/O servers have their own executable and configuration file, distinct from client and metadata server files:

- iod executable
- iod.conf file

The iod executable is the daemon that provides I/O services in the PVFS system. It normally is started as root, after which time it changes its group and user to some nonsuperuser ids. These iods must be running in order for file I/O to take place.

The iod.conf file describes the iod's environment. In particular it describes the location of the PVFS data directory on the machine and the user and group under which iod should run. There should be a comparable configuration file for the mgr, but there is not at this time.

In our example we're going to run our I/O server as user nobody and group nobody, and we're going to have it store data in a directory called /pvfs-data (this could be a mount point or a subdirectory and doesn't have to be this name). Lines that begin with a pound sign are comments. Here's our iod.conf file:

```
# iod.conf file for example cluster
datadir /pvfs-data
user nobody
group nobody
```

We then create the data directory and change the owner, group, and permissions to protect the data from inappropriate access while allowing the iod to store and retrieve data. We'll do this on our first I/O server (n1) first:

```
[root@n1 /]# cd /
[root@n1 /]# mkdir /pvfs-data
[root@n1 /]# chmod 700 /pvfs-data
[root@n1 /]# chown nobody.nobody /pvfs-data
[root@n1 /]# ls -ald /pvfs-data
drwx------    2 nobody    nobody           35 Dec  1 09:41 /pvfs-data/
```

This must be repeated on each I/O server. In our example case, the /etc/iod.conf file is exactly the same on each server, and we create the /pvfs-data directory in the same way as well.

Installing and Configuring Clients.   Five files and one directory are necessary for a client to access PVFS file systems:

- pvfsd executable
- pvfs.o kernel module (compiled to match kernel)
- /dev/pvfsd device file
- mount.pvfs executable
- pvfstab file

- mount point

As mentioned in Section 17.2.1 there are two approaches to client access: direct library access and kernel support. The first four items in the above list are specifically for kernel access and may be ignored if this method of access is not desired.

The pvfsd executable is a daemon that performs network transfers on behalf of client programs. It is normally started as root. It must be running before a PVFS file system is mounted on the client.

The pvfs.o kernel module registers the PVFS file system type with the Linux kernel, allowing PVFS files to be accessed with system calls. This is what allows existing programs to access PVFS files once a PVFS file system is mounted.

The /dev/pvfsd device file is used as a point of communication between the pvfs.o kernel module and the pvfsd daemon. It must exist before the pvfsd is started. It need be created only once on each client machine.

The mount.pvfs executable is used by mount to perform the PVFS-specific mount process. Alternatively it can be used in a standalone manner to mount a PVFS file system directly. This will be covered in Section 17.3.3.

The pvfstab file provides an fstab-like entry that describes to applications using the PVFS libraries how to access PVFS file systems. This is *not* needed by the kernel client code. It is used only if code is directly or indirectly linked to libpvfs. This includes using the ROMIO MPI-IO interface.

The mount point, as mentioned earlier, is just an empty directory. In our example we are placing our mount point in the root directory so that we can mount our PVFS file system to /pvfs. We then create the PVFS device file. The mknod program is used to create device files, which are special files used as interfaces to system resources. The mknod program takes four parameters: a name for the device, a type ("c" for character special file in our case), and a major and minor number. We have somewhat arbitrarily chosen 60 for our major number for now.

We'll do this first on the head machine:

```
[root@head /]# mkdir /pvfs
[root@head /]# ls -ald /pvfs
drwxr-xr-x   2 root    root            35 Dec  1 09:37 /pvfs/
[root@head /]# mknod /dev/pvfsd c 60 0
[root@head /]# ls -l /dev/pvfsd
crw-r--r--   1 root    root        60,   0 Dec  1 09:45 /dev/pvfsd
```

If one is using the devfs system, it is not necessary to create the /dev/pvfsd file, but it will not hurt to do so.

In our example system we are going to use the PVFS libraries on our nodes, so we will also create the `pvfstab` file using `vi` or `emacs`. It's important that users be able to read this file. Here's what it looks like:

```
[root@head /]# chmod 644 /etc/pvfstab
[root@head /]# ls -al /etc/pvfstab
-rw-r--r--    1 root      root              46 Dec 17 15:19 /etc/pvfstab
[root@head /]# cat /etc/pvfstab
head:/pvfs-meta  /pvfs  pvfs  port=3000  0  0
```

This process must be repeated on each node that will be a PVFS client. In our example we would need to copy out these files to each node and create the mount point.

Installing PVFS Development Components. A few components should also be installed if applications are going to be compiled for PVFS:

- `libpvfs.a` library
- `include` files
- `man` pages
- `pvfstab` file

The `libpvfs.a` library and `include` files are used when compiling programs to access the PVFS system directly (what we term "native access"). The man pages are useful for reference. The `pvfstab` file was described in the preceding section; it is necessary for applications to access PVFS file systems without going through the kernel.

In our example we expect to compile some programs that use native PVFS access on our "head" node. By performing a `make install` in the PVFS source on the head, everything is automatically installed.

Configuring ROMIO to Use PVFS. In order for ROMIO to access PVFS files most optimally, it must be configured with PVFS support. Since ROMIO is typically installed as part of the MPICH package, a full coverage of the configuration, compilation, and installation process is outside the scope of this section. One should instead reference Section 9.6.1 for this information.

In short, when compiling ROMIO either as a standalone package or as part of MPICH, two important additional flags must be provided:

- `-file_system=pvfs+ufs+nfs`
- `-lib=/usr/local/lib/libpvfs.a`

The first of these specifies that ROMIO support regular Unix files, PVFS files, and NFS files. The second indicates the location of the PVFS library for linking to the ROMIO package.

17.3.3 Startup and Shutdown

At this point all the binaries and configuration files should be in place. Now we will start up the PVFS file system and verify that it is working. First we will start the server daemons. Then we will initialize the client software and mount the PVFS file system. Next we will create some files to show that things are working. Following this we will discuss unmounting file systems. Finally we will discuss shutting down the components.

Starting PVFS Servers. First we need to get the servers running. It doesn't matter what order we start them in as long as they are all running before we start accessing the system.

Going back to our example, we'll start the metadata server daemon first. It stores its log file in /tmp/ by default:

```
[root@head /root]# /usr/local/sbin/mgr
[root@head /root]# ls -l /tmp
total 5
-rwxr-xr-x    1 root     root            0 Dec 18 18:22 mgrlog.MupejR
```

The characters at the end of the log filename are there to ensure a unique name. A new file will be created each time the server is started.

Next we start the I/O server daemon on each of our I/O server nodes:

```
[root@n1 /root]# /usr/local/sbin/iod
[root@n1 /root]# ls -l /tmp
total 5
-rwxr-xr-x    1 root     root           82 Dec 18 18:28 iolog.n2MjK4
```

This process must be repeated on each node.

Getting a Client Connected. With the servers started, we can now start up the client-side components. First we load the module, then we start the client daemon pvfsd, and then we mount the file system:

```
[root@head /root]# insmod pvfs.o
[root@head /root]# lsmod
Module                    Size  Used by
```

```
pvfs                      32816    0   (unused)
eepro100                  17104    1   (autoclean)
[root@head /root]# /usr/local/sbin/pvfsd
[root@head /root]# ls -l /tmp
total 7
-rwxr-xr-x    1 root    root            0 Dec 18 18:22 mgrlog.MupejR
-rwxr-xr-x    1 root    root          102 Dec 18 18:22 pvfsdlog.WtOw7g
[root@head /root]# /sbin/mount.pvfs head:/pvfs-meta /pvfs
[root@head /root]# ls -al /pvfs
total 1
drwxrwxrwx    1 root    root           82 Dec 18 18:33 ./
drwxr-xr-x   20 root    root          378 Dec 17 15:01 ../
[root@head /root]# df -h /pvfs
Filesystem            Size  Used Avail Use% Mounted on
head:/pvfs-meta       808M   44M  764M   5% /pvfs
```

Now we should be able to access the file system. As an aside, we note that the -h
option to df simply prints things in more human-readable form.

Checking Things Out. Let's create a couple of files:

```
[root@head /root]# cp /etc/pvfstab /pvfs/
[root@head /root]# dd if=/dev/zero of=/pvfs/zeros bs=1M count=10
[root@head /root]# ls -l /pvfs
total 10240
-rw-r--r--    1 root    root           46 Dec 18 18:41 pvfstab
-rw-r--r--    1 root    root     10485760 Dec 18 18:41 zeros
[root@head /root]# cat /pvfs/pvfstab
head:/pvfs-meta /pvfs pvfs port=3000  0  0
```

Everything looks good. Now we must repeat this on the other nodes so that they
can access the file system as well.

Unmounting File Systems and Shutting Down Components. As with any
other file system type, if a client is not accessing files on a PVFS file system, you
can simply unmount it:

```
[root@head /root]# umount /pvfs
[root@head /root]# ls -al /pvfs
total 1
drwxrwxrwx    1 root    root           82 Dec 18 18:33 ./
```

```
drwxr-xr-x    20 root     root          378 Dec 17 15:01 ../
```

You could then remount to the same mount point or some other mount point. It is not necessary to restart the `pvfsd` daemon or reload the `pvfs.o` module in order to change mounts.

For clean shutdown, all clients should unmount PVFS file systems before the servers are shut down. The preferred order of shutdown is as follows:

- unmount PVFS file systems on clients
- stop `pvfsd` daemons using `kill` or `killall`
- unload `pvfs.o` module using `rmmod`
- stop `mgr` daemon using `kill` or `killall`
- stop `iod` daemons using `kill` or `killall`

17.3.4   Configuration Details

As the preceding discussion suggests, the current PVFS configuration system is a bit complex. Here we try to shed more light on configuration file formats, file system defaults, and other options. This information is all supplementary, but it might be useful in the event of an error.

The `.pvfsdir` and `.iodtab` Files.   In Section 17.3.2, we discussed the creation of both the `.pvfsdir` and the `.iodtab` files. In this section we cover the details of the file formats. The `.pvfsdir` file holds information for the metadata server for the file system. The `.iodtab` file holds a list of the I/O daemon locations and port numbers that make up the file system. Both of these files can be created by using the `mkmgrconf` script, whose use is also described in Section 17.3.2.

The `.pvfsdir` file is in text format and includes the following information in this order, with an entry on each line:

- `inode` number of the directory in which the `.pvfsdir` resides
- userid for the directory
- groupid for the directory
- permissions for the directory
- port number for metadata server
- hostname for the metadata server
- metadata directory name
- name of this subdirectory (for the `.pvfsdir` file in the metadata directory this will be "/")

Here's a sample `.pvfsdir` file that might have been produced for our example file system:

```
116314
0
0
0040775
3000
head
/pvfs-meta
/
```

This file would reside in the metadata directory, which in our example case is `/pvfs-meta`. There will be a `.pvfsdir` file in each subdirectory under this as well. The metadata server will automatically create these new files when subdirectories are created.

The `.iodtab` file is also created by the system administrator. It consists simply of an ordered list of hosts (or IP addresses) and optional port numbers. Lines beginning with `#` are comments and are ignored by the system. It is stored in the metadata directory of the PVFS file system.

An example of a `.iodtab` file is as follows:

```
# example .iodtab file using IP addresses and explicit ports
192.168.0.1:7000
192.168.0.2:7000
192.168.0.3:7000
192.168.0.4:7000
192.168.0.5:7000
192.168.0.6:7000
192.168.0.7:7000
192.168.0.8:7000
```

Another example, assuming the default port (7000) and using hostnames (as in our example system), is the following:

```
# example .iodtab file using hostnames and default port (7000)
n1
n2
n3
n4
```

```
n5
n6
n7
n8
```

Manually creating .iodtab files, especially for large systems, is encouraged. However, once files are stored on a PVFS file system, it is no longer safe to modify this file.

iod.conf **Files.** The iod will look for an optional configuration file named iod.conf in the /etc directory when it is started. This file can specify a number of configuration parameters for the I/O daemon, including changing the data directory, the user and group under which the I/O daemon runs, and the port on which the I/O daemons operate.

Every line consists of two fields: a key field and a value field. These two fields are separated by one or more spaces or tabs. The key field specifies a configuration parameter whose value should be changed. The key is followed by this new value. Lines starting with a pound sign and empty lines are ignored. Keys are case insensitive. If the same key is used again, it will override the first instance. The valid keys are as follows:

port — specifies the port on which the iod should accept requests. Default is 7000.

user — specifies the user under which the iod should run. Default is nobody.

group — specifies the group under which the iod should run. Default is nobody.

rootdir — gives the directory the iod should use as its rootdir. The iod uses chroot(2) to change to this directory before accessing files. Default is /.

logdir — gives the directory in which the iod should write log files. Default is /tmp.

datadir — gives the directory the iod should use as its data directory. The iod uses chdir(2) to change to this directory after changing the root directory. Default is /pvfs_data.

debug — sets the debugging level; currently zero means don't log debug info and nonzero means do log debug info. This is useful mainly for helping find bugs in PVFS.

The `rootdir` keyword allows you to create a chroot jail for the `iod`. Here is a list of the steps the `iod` takes on startup:

1. read `iod.conf`

2. open log file in `logdir`

3. `chroot()` to `rootdir`

4. `chdir()` to `datadir`

5. `setuid()` and `setgid()`

The log file is always opened with the entire file system visible, while the datadir is changed into after the `chroot()` call. In almost all cases this option should be left as the default value.

Here is an example `iod.conf` file that could have been used for our example system:

```
# IOD Configuration file, iod.conf

port 7000
user nobody
group nobody
rootdir /
datadir /pvfs-data
logdir /tmp
debug 0
```

An alternative location for the `iod.conf` file may be specified by passing the filename as the first parameter on the command line to `iod`. Thus, running "`iod`" is equivalent to running "`iod /etc/iod.conf`".

pvfstab Files.   When the client library is used, it will search for a `/etc/pvfstab` file in order to discover the local directories for PVFS files and the locations of the metadata server responsible for each of these file systems. The format of this file is the same as that of the `fstab` file:

```
head:/pvfs-meta  /pvfs  pvfs  port=3000  0  0
```

Here we have specified that the metadata server is called head, that the directory the server is storing metadata in is `/pvfs-meta`, that this PVFS file system should be considered as "mounted" on the mount point /pvfs on the client (local) system, and that the TCP port on which the server is listening is 3000. The third field (the file system type) should be set to "pvfs" and the last two fields to 0. The fourth field is for options; the only valid option at this time is port.

It is occasionally convenient to be able to specify an alternative location for the information in this file. For example, if you want to use PVFS calls but cannot create a file in /etc, you might instead want to store the file in your home directory.

The PVFSTAB_FILE environment variable may be set before running a program to specify another location for the pvfstab file. In a parallel processing environment it may be necessary to define the variable in a .cshrc, .bashrc, or .login file to ensure that all tasks get the correct value.

Compile-Time Options. The majority of file system configuration values are defined in pvfs_config.h in the PVFS distribution. You can modify these values and recompile in order to obtain new default parameters such as ports, directories, and data distributions. Here are some of the more important ones:

__ALWAYS_CONN__ — if defined, all connections to all I/O servers will be established immediately when a file is opened. This is poor use of resources but makes performance more consistent.

PVFSTAB_PATH — default path to pvfstab file.

PVFS_SUPER_MAGIC — magic number for PVFS file systems returned by statfs().

CLIENT_SOCKET_BUFFER_SIZE — send and receive size used by clients.

MGR_REQ_PORT — manager request port. This should be an option to the manager, but it isn't at the moment.

DEFAULT_SSIZE — default strip size.

__RANDOM_BASE__ — if defined, the manager will pick a random base number (starting I/O server) for each new file. This can help with disk utilization. There is also a manager command line parameter to enable this.

Additionally a --with-log-dir option to configure has recently been added to the PVFS package. This option specifies a new subdirectory in which to place log files. It has the side effect of turning off the use of unique strings on the end of log file names, making it easier to manage the log files.

17.3.5 Miscellanea

This section contains some notes on options to the `mgr` and on using `mount` with PVFS.

Currently the only important option to `mgr` is "-r", which enables random selection of base nodes for new PVFS files. The `mgr` by default logs a message any time a file is opened. Here is an example:

```
i 2580, b 0, p 4, s 65536, n 1, /pvfs-meta/foo
```

The fields printed are as follows:

i — `inode` number/handle

b — base node number

p — `pcount`

s — strip size

n — number of processes which have this file open

Finally the name of the metadata file is listed. This information is particularly helpful when debugging applications using parallel I/O.

We mentioned earlier that the `mount.pvfs` program is used to mount PVFS file systems. This is a little bit different from most file systems, in that usually the `mount` program can be used to mount any kind of file system. Some versions of the Linux `mount`, which is distributed as part of the util-linux package, will automatically look in `/sbin` for an external file system-specific mount program to use for a given file system type. At the time of writing all versions later than 2.10f seem to have this feature enabled. If this is enabled, then `mount` will automatically call `/sbin/mount.pvfs` when a PVFS file system mount is attempted. Using our example, we have

```
[root@head /root]# /sbin/mount -t pvfs head:/pvfs-meta /pvfs
```

If this works, then the administrator can also add entries into `/etc/fstab` for PVFS file systems. However, it is important to remember that the module must be loaded, the `pvfsd` daemon must be running, and the server daemons must be running on remote systems before a PVFS file system can be mounted.

17.4   Final Words

PVFS is an ever-developing system. As the system evolves, it's fairly likely that documentation updates will trail software development.

The PVFS development team is open to suggestions and contributions to the project. We are especially interested in scripts and tools that people develop to make managing PVFS easier. Users who have developed utilities to help manage their system are encouraged to contact us. We'll try to include such programs into the next PVFS release.

Lots of development is taking place in PVFS, particularly to help handle issues such as redundancy, more interesting data distributions, and the use of zero-copy network protocols (described in Chapter 6). For the newest information on PVFS, check the Web site: `www.parl.clemson.edu/pvfs`.

18 Chiba City: The Argonne Scalable Cluster

Remy Evard

With 256 dual-CPU computing nodes, Chiba City is the largest cluster in the Argonne scalable clusters project.

Chiba City was designed with a unique purpose in mind: to support scalable computer science and the development of scalable systems software. We believe that advances in the state of system software for high-performance computing are critical in order to improve the performance and reliability of high-end machines. Yet the developers and researchers who will bring about those advances often find it very difficult to gain access to the largest systems because those computers are dedicated to running large code. With the advent of commodity clusters, the solution to this problem became clear: using relatively inexpensive parts, it was now possible to build a system that could be used to support activities that required development and testing at large scale without the usual large price tag. This was the basis of the idea for Chiba City.

In addition, Chiba City was built to support a wide range of parallel computational science applications. In the Mathematics and Computer Science (MCS) Division of Argonne National Laboratory, we collaborate with hundreds of researchers around the world who use our computing facilities in partnership with the scientists in our division. Chiba City was meant to be used by these scientists in order to tackle real scientific problems while they simultaneously worked with computer scientists to expand the scope of problem that they could address.

In essence, Chiba City is intended to support two distinct goals that are occasionally in conflict: scalable computer science research, which needs a dynamic and interactive testbed, and computational science, which has historically used stable, batch-oriented systems. We believe that Chiba City has achieved a comfortable balance between these two worlds and has helped promote good science in both.

The difference in requirements between experimentation and classic production computing has kept us—Chiba City's designers and administrators—living in two worlds at once, trying to keep the cluster both stable and interesting. We hope that this case study will achieve both goals as well.

18.1 Chiba City Configuration

In this section, we describe the configuration of the cluster from multiple perspectives. We cover not only what has gone into the cluster but why it is there and how it is used.

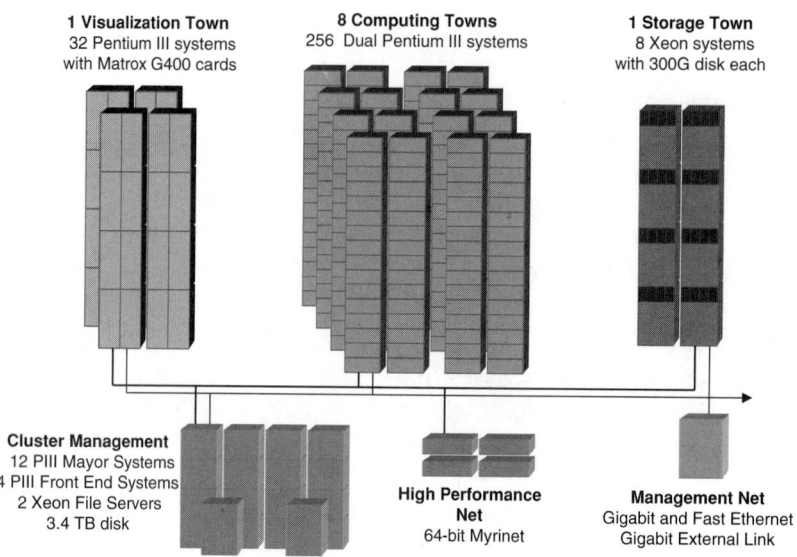

1 Visualization Town
32 Pentium III systems
with Matrox G400 cards

8 Computing Towns
256 Dual Pentium III systems

1 Storage Town
8 Xeon systems
with 300G disk each

Cluster Management
12 PIII Mayor Systems
4 PIII Front End Systems
2 Xeon File Servers
3.4 TB disk

High Performance Net
64-bit Myrinet

Management Net
Gigabit and Fast Ethernet
Gigabit External Link

Figure 18.1
Chiba City schematic.

18.1.1 Node Configuration

Chiba City includes the following computing components (see Figure 18.1):

- 256 computing nodes
- 32 visualization nodes
- 8 storage nodes
- 18 management nodes

Computing Nodes. The 256 computing nodes are the workhorse portion of the cluster. These are the primary nodes that run the user's programs.

CPU. Each computing node has two 550 MHz Pentium III CPUs. This lets us play the game of sometimes referring to the system as a "512-CPU computer" rather than a "256-node computer." (Of course, some people actually include every CPU on the system when they count, not just the ones available to the users. In Chiba's case, this would be 574 CPUs, not including the CPUs in the networking equipment.)

One of the more hotly debated issue throughout the design phase of Chiba was the question of how many CPUs each node should have. From a pure performance viewpoint, it makes the most sense to have only one CPU per system, for several reasons. First, the memory bandwidth on Pentium IIIs is quite limited; thus one CPU alone can easily saturate the memory bus, making any more than the first one potentially useless. Second, in order to most efficiently use all of the CPUs in the system with an MPI job, the communication between processes must use both network and shared-memory communication, which is difficult. Third, at the time of the installation, Linux didn't run on more than one CPU particularly well.

On the other hand, from a price/performance perspective, it makes much more sense to have multiple CPUs on each node—and in fact, four would have been better than two from this viewpoint. It's typically cheaper to buy a dual-CPU system than to buy two of the same system, each with only one CPU. Furthermore, it's far cheaper to install a network for 256 nodes than for 512 nodes. (On the other hand, if the network is the bottleneck, then some people who use multi-CPU systems end up installing two or more network interfaces per computer.)

On Chiba City, we decided to go with dual-CPUs for flexibility. We wanted to be able to support experiments and development on both types of MPI programming. Those wishing to go for maximal node performance could ignore the second CPU. Alternatively, those wishing to use or experiment with mixed-mode MPI programming would have that option as well.

In retrospect, this is exactly what has happened. Some users find that their code is more efficient if they use only one processor. Others find that two processors work well for them. And developers have needed access to both types of configurations.

Computing Node Memory. Each computing node has 512 megabytes of RAM. We felt that this was a minimum for dual CPUs at the time. We do occasionally see applications run out of free memory and start swapping, particularly when using both CPUs, but in general this has proven to be sufficient.

Computing Node Footprint. The nodes themselves are 2U units. (Equipment that can be housed in computer racks is measured in the unit U, where 1U is 1.75 inches. A standard rack is 42U.) We went with these because they were the smallest system we could find at the time. In fact, the size of the units was a major driver: one of the initial proposals we received from vendors had 3U and 5U units, which would essentially doubled the floor space required for the cluster. We simply didn't have that much space in our machine room.

Ironically, 1U Pentium systems hit the market a few months after we installed Chiba City. We knew they were likely be available around then, but renegotiating the cluster purchase to have 1Us was simply not an option.

Computing Node Disks. Some cluster builders include disks in all nodes. Others go completely diskless. Diskless nodes have a number of advantages in a cluster. First, it's a little easier to configure the operating systems on the nodes when they're diskless, because those configurations are stored on management nodes. (This advantage can be negated if adequate configuration tools are used to manage diskful nodes.) Also, disks tend to break. If the nodes don't have disks, that's one less thing on each node that may require service. On large clusters, it's a good idea to eliminate any situation that involves touching the nodes.

On Chiba City, we have 9 gigabyte hard drives on each node. We decided to install disks in each node for maximum flexibility. Some applications that the scientists run make extensive use of local disk. We also anticipated that system-software experiments or alternative operating systems might need to use the local disk. It has turned out that, for us, this was the right choice. Many, many uses of the system rely on or take advantage of the local disk. And while we do occasionally have drives that fail, this has been much less of an issue than many other hardware components, particularly the fans.

Other Computing Node Hardware. In addition to the CPUs, the RAM, and the hard drive, each computing node has

- one 32-bit PCI slot that is used for a Myrinet card,
- a 10/100 Ethernet port on the motherboard,
- a floppy drive (because that was included), and
- serial, parallel, keyboard, and the other usual PC ports.

Computing Node Connections. Looking at the back of a node can be instructive. Each connection plugs into another component of the cluster, all of which are described in detail in following sections of this chapter.

- The Myrinet card is a part of the Myrinet network. Each node has one fairly large Myrinet cable that runs under the floor to a Myrinet Clos64 switch.
- The Ethernet port is used for to connect to the Ethernet network. Each node connects to an Ethernet switch in its rack or in a neighboring rack.
- The serial port that Linux uses as the console plugs into a serial concentrator in the rack, which enables remote access to all of the consoles.

- The "management" serial port on each node plugs into a separate serial concentrator, to be used for low-level hardware and management. This is a motherboard-specific management interface, and we've never needed to use it.
- The power cable runs to a Baytech power control unit that allows us to remotely monitor and control the power to each node.
- The keyboard and video ports are left vacant. In rare situations, such as hardware diagnosis or BIOS upgrades, we may plug a keyboard and monitor into them. In an ideal world, we would never use these at all. Other clusters built since Chiba use daisy-chain mechanisms to allow somewhat remote access to the keyboard and video.

Visualization Nodes. The 32 visualization nodes are used by computer scientists for research into cluster-based image synthesis and computer graphics. They are sometimes used as their own independent 32-node cluster and sometimes used in conjunction with the computing nodes as part of one large program.

The primary feature of the visualization nodes is that they include high-end video cards that can be used for graphics and image synthesis. Ideally, these cards can be used in two ways:

- Simply as video cards. In our environment, we have a remote console infrastructure for graphics systems that allows us to connect the display port of graphics systems located in one spot to display systems located in a laboratory. This means that the visualization nodes can be housed in the machine room and still be used to drive the CAVE or our 15-projector Powerwall, both of which are in other rooms.
- As pipelines for generating images.

The world of commodity PC graphics cards is still far more focused on the first application than the second, so we end up using the nodes more as drivers for high-end display devices than as graphics computing engines.

These video cards typically require an AGP slot. The requirement for the AGP slot drives every other detail of the visualization nodes. For example, computers with AGP slots are usually desktop systems or workstations rather than servers. Our visualization nodes are workstation-style systems that don't fit into racks well and are actually kept on shelves. The systems that were available at the time we purchased Chiba City were 550 MHz Pentium III systems configured with 13 GBytes of disk and 384 MBytes of RAM. We manage them the same way that we do the compute nodes, including remote serial and power control.

The video cards were originally Matrox Millenium 32 MBytes G400Max cards. Since installing Chiba City, we've upgraded the video cards to NVidea GEFORCE3 cards.

Storage Nodes. The eight storage nodes are not accessed directly by most of the users of Chiba City. Instead, they provide file system service to the computing nodes, as described in Section 18.3.1.

Each storage node has a 500 MHz Xeon, 512 MBytes of RAM, and, most important, 300 Gbytes of SCSI-attached disk. So, in aggregate, the storage nodes provide 2.4 TBytes of raw disk space to the computing nodes.

The storage nodes are a part of the Myrinet network. In some cases, cluster builders will choose to put their storage nodes exclusively on the Ethernet network. This choice is primarily an issue of performance versus cost. With an even order of two number of computing nodes (i.e., 64, 128, 256, etc.), one can often build an interconnect network with a lot less hardware than would be required for those same compute nodes plus a few storage nodes. The difference may be negligible or may be substantial. In our case, getting the storage nodes onto the Myrinet meant that we needed to purchase several additional Myrinet switches. Because I/O performance and experiments are important to our user community, we felt the cost was worth it.

The storage nodes interface with the rest of the cluster in the same way that the rest of nodes on the cluster do. In addition to being available over Myrinet, they're also on the Ethernet. They also have remote power and console control.

Under normal conditions users don't have direct access to the storage nodes. However, scientists working on a project specifically related to I/O research may have access to the I/O servers. In this case, it's possible that their programs will run simultaneously on both the compute nodes and the storage nodes.

Management Nodes and Servers. The nodes used for cluster management come in several different flavors:

- 12 systems used as the cluster "mayors," or monitor systems
- 4 front ends
- 2 file servers

The mayors provide a scalable management mechanism, which is described in greater detail in Section 18.1.2.

Mayor systems: Every set of 32 computers in the cluster is associated with a computer, called their "mayor," that monitors and manages them. The mayors are never used as part of any computation or experiment running on the cluster but are instead used to configure the cluster for that experiment and recover from any problems it might cause. Each mayor is system with a single 550 MHz Pentium

III, 512 MBytes of RAM, 10/100 Ethernet, Gigabit Ethernet, and 200 GBytes of SCSI disk. Two of the mayor units have special functions. One serves as the "city mayor" and is used to control the other mayors. The other runs the scheduler for the cluster.

Front ends: Chiba City was originally configured with four front ends: systems that users could login to in order to build their programs and launch them onto the compute nodes. Since these systems are identical to the compute nodes, the users' build environment would be the same as program's execution environment. In practice we found that two front ends was sufficient, and we have used the other two nodes as test systems.

File servers: The two file servers provide file systems via NFS to the login nodes and to the mayors. They house all of the user's home file systems and all of the configuration files (kernels, RPMs, config files, and so on) for the nodes. They do not export file systems directly to the nodes—that's the job of the storage nodes. The file servers have exactly the same hardware configuration as the storage nodes. Each has 500 GBytes of disk.

Nodes We Missed. After a few years of running the cluster, we've concluded that the configuration that we put together is almost correct, but we missed a few pieces.

First, we could use more test systems. Linux kernels, file systems, system software, and applications all change rapidly. Having between four and eight test machines for testing individual pieces of code and cluster functions would be extremely helpful. At present, we usually allocate some of the compute nodes in order to test new software. This procedure works okay, but since it reduces the pool of compute nodes the users can access, it tends to be a short-term solution.

Second, we could use a few spare nodes. We always seem to have a small handful of nodes with hardware problems, which makes it difficult to reliably be able to run jobs on all 256 nodes. We would like to have a pool of spare nodes that we would swap in for a node with broken hardware. Then, once that node was repaired, it would go into the pool of spare nodes. Four spare nodes would probably cover most situations.

We actually considered both of these in the original plan, but for financial reasons they were removed. It's difficult to justify between eight and twelve computers that aren't really being used most of the time.

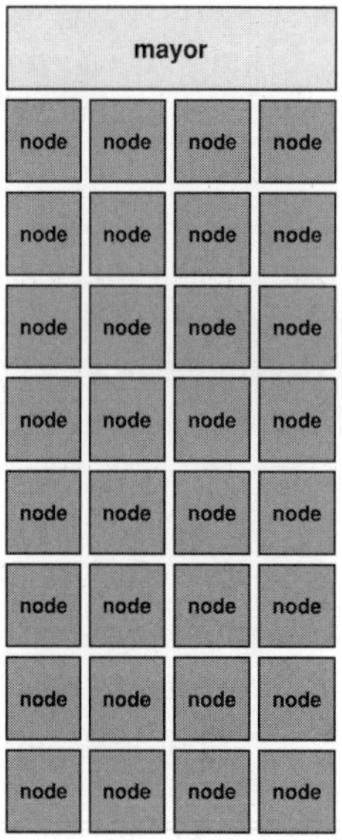

Figure 18.2
A Chiba City town.

18.1.2   Logical Configuration

Chiba City is conceptually divided into cluster building units which we call "towns."
In our definition, a town consists of a set of computers and a single "mayor" node
that manages them. For example, each of the eight towns of computing nodes in
Chiba City includes one mayor and thirty-two computing nodes.

In Chiba City, there are eleven towns:

- 8 computing towns, each with 32 computing nodes
- 1 visualization town of 32 visualization nodes
- 1 storage town with the 8 storage nodes
- 1 server/mayor town with the 10 mayors, login nodes, and file servers

The towns are a mechanism to allow scalable management (see Figure 18.2). From a
systems administration perspective, we would like to be able to completely manage
every node in a town by interacting with its mayor. So, in order to manage the
256 computing nodes in Chiba, one merely needs to manage the 8 mayors of those
computing nodes. To accomplish this, the mayor provides boot service, operating
system configuration, console management, and file services to each of the other

nodes in its town. It monitors those nodes to make sure that they're running correctly. The mayor performs management functions only and never participates in the computing activity of the nodes, so the users of the cluster never work with the mayors directly.

In most cases on Chiba City, each mayor monitors 32 nodes. In a few cases, such as the storage town, there are fewer nodes in the town. We chose 32 clients for a number of reasons:

- Our tests indicated that NFS performed reasonably with 32 clients. Thus, NFS would be an option within a town if we so chose.
- In a 1024-node cluster, there would be 32 towns of 32 nodes.
- The hardware for a 32-node town fit nearly perfectly into two racks.

The town relationship is hierarchical. A collection of mayors can be managed by a higher-level mayor in the same way that a collection of nodes is managed by a mayor. In Chiba City, we have one node, which we refer to as the City Mayor, that is responsible for managing each of the mayors. This gives us a single point of control from which the entire cluster can be managed.

The concept of building the larger system out of smaller replicated systems, each with their own server, wasn't a new one. Beyond being a classic computer science technique, it was used to some degree in the IBM SP, has been a standard approach for years in the systems administration community, and was demonstrated on clusters by the Sandia National Laboratories CPlant project.

We've made a number of observations about the mayor/town concept while operating the cluster:

- The mayor concept has proven its worth over and over. We could not manage the cluster without some sort of hierarchical approach.
- Some network services already have scalability mechanisms built in, or scale to the size of the cluster. The Dynamic Host Configuration Protocol (DHCP) is one of these. Breaking these down so that it runs on each mayor and supports only the local town isn't worth the time. In other words, some services for the cluster can and should be global.
- The ratio of clients to mayor is highly dependent on what those clients are doing. With 32 nodes, we're comfortable supporting network booting and remote operating system installation. If we were also supporting high-capacity file systems or other services, we might need to scale down. On the other hand, if every node was largely independent except for monitoring and time service, for example, then we could probably shift to 64 nodes per mayor.

We have often been asked why we call the building blocks "towns." In the early design phases of Chiba City, we talked to a lot of people in a lot of companies who had never heard of clusters before. We had trouble explaining that we wanted to build the cluster out of these subclusters that had a monitoring agent, so we started to call them "towns" as a part of the city metaphor. This explanation helped quite a bit even though, of course, real cities aren't made up of towns that look identical—they're made up of neighborhoods that are usually very different. But the metaphor helped explain the concept, and the name stuck.

18.1.3 Network Configuration

Chiba City has two types of networks—Myrinet and Ethernet. In this section, we describe their configuration and their use.

Myrinet.   The Myrinet network is used to support high-speed communication between nodes as part of a user's program, usually related to computation or I/O.

On Chiba City, a high-performance network is essential. Many of the jobs that run on the cluster are bound by the performance of the network: the faster the network, the better the performance of their code. Also, a lot of the computer science research on Chiba is related to communication.

We chose to use Myrinet, a product of Myricom, because it was the most cost-effective high-performance networking solution on the market at the time we purchased the cluster. Myrinet has a number of nice characteristics. It can deliver a full bisection bandwith network between all of the nodes of a cluster. The network cards that we installed can support a theoretical 1.28 Gbps transfer rate, with latencies from process to process in the 10–15 microsecond range.

The specific Myrinet hardware on Chiba City includes 4 Myrinet spine switches, 5 CLOS-64 switches, and 320 Lanai 7.2 NICs. The hosts that usually participate on the Myrinet network include the computing nodes, the visualization nodes, the storage nodes, and the login nodes. In other words, everything except the management nodes and the file servers is typically on Myrinet. At different times over the life of the cluster, we have connected the file servers and mayors to support experiments.

It is possible to run IP over Myrinet, and we do. From an IP standpoint, the Myrinet network is a flat IP subnet and is not accessible from outside of the cluster.

Ethernet.   The Ethernet network is used for everything that the Myrinet network isn't. For the most part, this means management functions, remote access, and

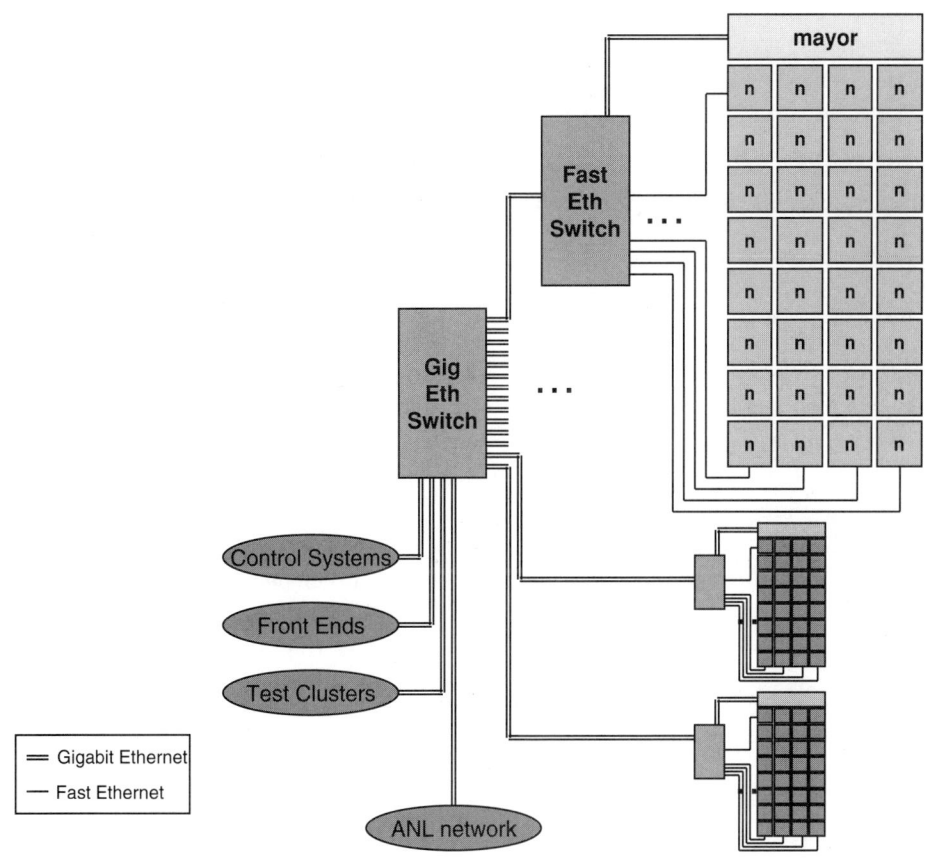

Figure 18.3
The Chiba City Ethernet.

a fallback communications network for applications if the Myrinet network isn't available.

Figure 18.3 is a diagram of the Ethernet network, which is arranged in a simple tree structure. Each computing, visualization, and storage node is connected via Fast Ethernet to an Ethernet switch near that node. There are 10 Cisco Catalyst 4000s distributed around the cluster, each connecting approximately 32 nodes.

A central Gigabit Ethernet switch, a Cisco Catalyst 6509, is connected to each of the Catalyst 4000s with two channel bonded Gigabit Ethernet links. The remaining computers—the front end nodes, the file servers, and the mayors—all connect directly to the Catalyst 6509. Also, Chiba City's link to the outside world comes in through the Catalyst 6509.

In essence, Chiba City has a completely switched Ethernet. The IP network layered on top of this Ethernet is one flat subnet with no routing. Every node in the cluster is at most three Ethernet switch hops away from every other node.

18.1.4 Physical Configuration

The physical layout of a cluster is particularly important space is limited, as is the case for us. Chiba City occupies twenty-seven standard 19-inch racks arranged into two rows (see Figure 18.4). The racks include

- 16 racks of computing nodes. Each computing town fits precisely into two racks. This include the 32 compute nodes, the mayor and its disk, the serial and power management systems, and the Ethernet switch for the town.
- 4 racks of storage nodes. The storage nodes and their associated disk each take up half of a rack.
- 2 double-layer shelving units for the visualization nodes. Because of cable length limits for the video systems, these are located in another part of our machine room from the rest of Chiba City.
- 3 racks for the Myrinet switches. These racks have the heaviest cable density in Chiba, because every node has a cable that runs to some port in these racks.
- 1 rack for the file servers and their disk.
- 1 rack for the Gigabit Ethernet switch and remaining servers.

18.2 Chiba City Timeline

In this section of the case study, we examine the phases of activity that Chiba City has gone through, starting with the early seeds of the idea up through full-time operation. These are similar to the phases that most other clusters go through.

18.2.1 Phase 1: Motivation

As noted at the beginning of this chapter, the primary driver for Chiba City was to create a testbed that could be used to support scalability testing and research into scalability issues. We believe that this area is the most important aspect of computing to address in order to advance the state of high-performance computing.

Furthermore, we felt that it was important to build a system that could be used for general computer science and development, rather than on applications and simulations, which is typically what large computers are used for.

Figure 18.4
One of two rows of Chiba City.

We had been building and running small clusters for several years, including clusters based on Windows NT, Linux, and FreeBSD. We had used those to support research into communication, visualization, and several other areas of experimentation. But, by fall of 1998, we still had not yet been convinced that the large system in MCS would be a cluster.

However, once we considered the issues of scalability, the need for a computer science testbed, and the price/performance of commodity clusters, it became clear that a large-scale cluster could probably address all of these needs as well as become the next major MCS platform for simulation and computational science.

We originally considered installing a 1024-node system. However, we decided to start with a 256-node system in order to test many of the concepts. Thus, Chiba City was started as the first step toward a thousand-node (or larger) cluster, with a primary goal of supporting scalable computer science and a secondary goal of supporting scientific applications.

18.2.2 Phase 2: Design and Purchase

Having convinced ourselves that a large cluster was the right direction for MCS, we started, in December 1998, to design the system and arrange to purchase it.

We spent the next several months repeating this cycle over and over:

1. Think about what we needed and how we would use it.

2. Talk to vendors, integrators, and the cluster community in order to find out what would be available on our time frame.

3. Consider various funding options and match those with design and availability.

We discovered, among other things, that the traditional set of high-performance computing vendors were all trying to decide what to do about clusters (and what to do about Linux). At the time, it was possible to buy an actual cluster from Compaq and from a number of small integrators, but none of the larger vendors had yet created cluster product lines. No one was selling anything like what we wanted for Chiba City.

Eventually we put together a presentation to use to explain to vendors what we wanted to buy. The presentation explained what clusters were, what the cluster would be used for, how we wanted to operate it, and what we thought the necessary parts might be. As we updated our internal designs for the system software, we updated the purchasing presentation. We talked to a lot of different vendors and then went through the formal purchasing process. Eventually we agreed to buy the system through IBM. IBM arranged to provide subsets of the system from other vendors, including the Ethernet hardware from Cisco, the Myrinet from Myricom, and the 2U compute nodes from VA Linux.

These days, the purchasing phase is a lot easier. Almost every vendor can sell you a small or medium cluster without much thought, and even large clusters are relatively simple. However, the very large clusters with focused requirements still require a great deal of interaction with the vendor.

Throughout this period, we continued the design of the management infrastructure and system software for Chiba City, developing and testing it on a small cluster. (We called the nodes in the small cluster "the freakies." No one seems to knows why. That small cluster is long gone, but the name continues to live on in code references and machine configurations. Be warned.)

18.2.3 Phase 3: Installation

In October 1999, we installed the cluster.

During the preceding month, truck after truck had backed up to our loading dock and dropped off boxes. We had piles of computers, racks, cables, network boxes, disks, and miscellaneous hardware stacked everywhere. Fortunately we had been through large computer installations before, so we were careful to keep rigorous track of which boxes arrived from which vendor on which truck on which day. Despite this, there were still a few missing boxes that took weeks to locate.

During the purchase phase of the system, we realized that the installation of the cluster would be interesting. While the vendors were willing to provide installation technicians as part of the package, we were the ones who knew how the cluster should be connected. We needed to be actively involved in the installation.

Once we realized this, we decided this was an opportunity rather than a problem. Many of the scientists at Argonne are interested in the details of the computers, and we felt that they would probably enjoy being able to help install the system. We decided to assemble the cluster in the style of an old-fashioned barnraising, inviting everyone to join in. Everyone was enthusiastic about the idea. Over forty people signed up to help.

Before the installation, the MCS Systems Group built one of the computing towns. We took detailed notes on what we did and then put together a twelve-page installation manual. Based on the amount of time it took us and the space to work in the machine room, we estimated that we could build the entire cluster in two days. We spent the day before the barnraising working with technicians from VA to assemble the racks and to put the Ethernet and serial cables under the floor.

The barnraising itself was great fun. We divided the volunteers into teams of four people. Each team was led by a member of the Systems Group or a VA technician. We ran four teams at a time. Each team took half a day to assemble one rack, and each rack was half a town. So, by the end of the first day, four computing towns—half of Chiba City—was assembled.

While the teams worked, lots of other things were going on. IBM engineers assembled the storage nodes. The Chiba development team fine-tuned the software for some initial testing. And, most important, Janet Sayre of the Systems Group created just the right kind of atmosphere by sitting in the middle of all the activity and playing the banjo.

At the end of the second day, we connected all of the towns and booted every node. There were a few minor hardware problems with a few systems, so we weren't able to bring them all up, but we were able to run an MPI job on 248 of the nodes.

A time-lapse video of the barnraising is available on the Chiba City Web page
www.mcs.anl.gov/chiba/barnraising/video.html.

18.2.4   Phase 4: Final Development

For the next four months, the cluster was primarily in development mode. While we
had demonstrated that the nodes were running an operating system and connected
to each other at the end of the barnraising, a lot of work had to be completed before
the system was ready for users.

Among other things, we needed to finish the cluster environment: to get a cluster
schedule installed, arrange for data management, and tune the communications
networks. We also had to get the management system working, including the
ability to create user accounts, push out node configuration changes, and so on.

During this time, we asked a few users to try various tests on the system, but it
was not available to more than three or four users.

18.2.5   Phase 5: Early Users

Starting in March 2000, we opened up the cluster to the first set of early application
users. There were around four early users at first, all of whom were trying to use
the cluster but were also providing detailed feedback to us so that we could fix
problems they found.

Once things were relatively stable for them, we opened up the cluster to a few
more users, and then a few more, and so on. By the end of the early user phase,
we had around sixty user accounts on the cluster.

The majority of the problems that we had to address during this time were related
to the scheduler and to the Myrinet communication libraries.

18.2.6   Phase 6: Full Operation

In June 2000, we felt that we had eliminated most of problems that would impact
users of the system, and we opened up the cluster for general use.

From this point on, account requests for Chiba City were handled in the same
way that requests are handled for other MCS computing facilities—the account
request is approved based on whether the use matches the mission (and therefore
the funding) of the system. These decisions are made by a group of MCS scientists
who are responsible for the activities on the MCS systems.

Chiba City has been in full operation mode since that point. In the future, Chiba
will no doubt go through the next phase: upgrade or become obsolete. We will see
how that turns out.

18.3   Chiba City Software Environment

In this section we examine two aspects of the Chiba City software environment: computing and management.

18.3.1   The Computing Environment

The computing environment on Chiba City is, like the rest of the cluster, optimized to support computer science yet intended to support other uses. In this section, we describe the standard computing environment on the cluster as well as the special modifications we've made to support computer science and scalability research.

The Default Node Environment.   The "node computing environment" is the set of programs and services available on the user-accessible nodes of the system, that is, the computing nodes, the visualization nodes, and the login nodes.

All machines in the cluster run Linux by default. The original distribution that we started with when building the node operating system was Red Hat 6.2. Over time, we've added and removed RPMs, changed much of the default behavior, and added software from all over. The nodes are still vaguely recognizable as Red Hat, but they could just as easily have been another distribution.

The specific kernel installed on these nodes varies over time—and varies a bit more than we would like. In an ideal world, we would have a stable kernel installed that meets all of the requirements of our users, but we have yet to find one.

The compilers available on the front end include C, C++, and Fortran 90. Some users also program in Java, Perl, Python, and PHP.

The Default Cluster Environment.   The software glue that we use to turn the pile of nodes into a functional cluster includes a number of different packages.

Communications libraries: The vast majority of jobs on Chiba City use MPI for communication. Our preferred version of MPI is MPICH. We have multiple versions of MPICH installed in order to allow users to choose their favorite compiler and flavor of network. To use generic messages over Myrinet, you must link with MPICH-GM from Myricom.

The set of MPICH installations on Chiba got so large, in fact, that we built a small tool that lists all of the MPICH installations and allows you to pick the one you will be working with by default. The number of MPICH installations inspired the MPICH group to provide an alternative for handling multiple compilers; see Section 9.6.6.

Scheduling: We use the Portable Batch Scheduler (PBS) for queue management (see Chapter 16 for a detailed discussion of PBS). Since we Chiba was built, PBS has been picked up by Veridian Systems, and the open source version of PBS has become known as OpenPBS. In other words, we are running OpenPBS on Chiba City.

OpenPBS wasn't designed for environments as large or distributed as Chiba City and therefore has some scalability issues. Most of the problems that users of the cluster have are related to OpenPBS. We believe that many of these are being tackled by the community (we have worked on some of them ourselves) and that a set of patches will be available in the future that address many of these problems.

OpenPBS can be interfaced with an external scheduler that makes the decisions about which jobs in the queue will run at what time. We use the Maui scheduler for this purpose (see Chapter 15 for a detailed discussion of the Maui scheduler). We've been quite happy with Maui.

Global file systems: A global file system is one that is available on every node of the cluster and presents the same view of the data in the file system. It is not necessarily capable of supporting high-performance use, but at least provides a common name space. This normally is used for home directories, common applications, and so on.

One of the early design decisions on Chiba City was that we would not use NFS as a global file system on the cluster. NFS performs badly and scales worse. We felt that if it were really necessary, NFS could be made to work on the 256+ nodes of Chiba City, perhaps by using an optimized NFS server such as a Network Appliance box. However, Chiba City is meant in part to be a prototype of a much larger cluster of 1024 nodes or more, and at that level we expect NFS to be useless. Therefore, we decided to try to run the cluster without a global NFS file system to see how it worked out.

This has been an experiment with mixed results.

One approach to avoiding NFS is to use some other networked file system as a global file system. We have toyed with several but have found nothing that instills any confidence in us. Several network file systems have just recently become open source or will be released in the near future, so we have some hope that this situation will improve.

Another approach to avoiding NFS is to simply not have a global file system. This is what we have done. It's fairly simple to survive without a global file system for administration purposes—one simply uses `rdist` or other file synchronization mechanisms. On the user side, though, we've had two primary problems:

- *Job staging.* The user's program, support files, and data must be copied out to that user's nodes at the beginning of their job. After the job has completed, any output files that were created must be staged off the nodes before the nodes can be used by the next user. We've tackled this problem from a number of angles and have a solution in place that works but is not as fast as we would like. We believe that multicast file copying is the right solution to this problem and will be investigating it in the near future.
- *Confusion.* Users tend to expect that the cluster will have a global file system. When they log in to their nodes and look around, they don't see the files they expect in their home file system on that node. Even when the entire environment is explained, it is difficult to use the data transfer tools to copy in the right files and copy out the right files.

It's fairly clear that a nicely scalable global file system would be the best solution.

Parallel file systems: In contrast to a global file system, a parallel file system is specifically meant to provide high-performance access to application data for large parallel jobs. For example, one might store a very large input dataset on a parallel file system and subsequently start an application consisting of a few hundred tasks, all of which simultaneously access portions of this dataset. The parallel file system provides both a single logical space for application processes to look for data files and also the performance necessary for these parallel applications to have timely access to their data.

The only parallel file system available on Linux clusters is the Parallel Virtual File System (PVFS), which is described in detail in Chapter 17. PVFS and Chiba have a comfortable relationship, and over the years Chiba has become the primary development platform for PVFS. In this environment PVFS has been proven to scale to hundreds of I/O servers and compute processes, and peak aggregate throughput of over 3 GBytes per second has been shown. Running at these scales also served to highlight some reliability issues in PVFS that were not evident when running in smaller configurations. As these problems have been addressed and PVFS has begun to stabilize, we have begun to make a PVFS file system available as a full-time resource for the users of Chiba City. This has two benefits for users: it provides a high-performance data storage space for use by applications, and it gives users a single place to store datasets that can be accessed from any node.

Job invocation: Job startup of hundreds of processes using MPICH with its default `ch_p4` device is slow. Especially for interactive jobs, something more scalable is needed. Chiba provided some of the motivation for the `ch_p4mpd` device described in Section 9.6.2. Chiba City has provided a valuable testbed for the development of the MPD system and the version of MPICH that relies on it for job startup. The MPD daemons can run as root, and we have been experimenting with using them to run a mix of user jobs. Our long-term plan is to eventually transition to using MPD as our primary process manager.

Parallel Unix commands: Chiba City is also serving as testbed for the Scalable Unix Commands [10], which provide parallel versions of the common Unix commands such as `ps` and `cp`. A new version of these [25] is now available at `www.mcs.anl.gov/sut`. The new version implements these interactive commands as MPI applications, so the fast startup of MPI jobs made possible by MPD is critical. We plan to make these familiar commands available to all users as part of the Chiba environment.

Support for Computer Science. Computer scientists have a few general requirements that conflict with running applications on a system: interactivity, a license to crash the system, and the need to modify the system software.

Interactivity: Computer scientists, as well as developers of all types, often want to use the computer in "interactive" mode. They want to edit code, compile it, and then test it immediately. The test, and even the production run, may last only for a few seconds, but it often needs to use the entire system.

If the computer scientist has to submit a test job in a queue and wait until it can be scheduled, it can take hours or even days to complete a one-minute run. If the scheduler is optimized to allow access to the entire machine quickly, the resulting schedule will have huge numbers of unused node time. Production sites and computers that have real dollars tied to machine utilization simply can't afford to have that type of scheduling policy.

This need for interactivity is not unique to computer scientists, of course. Application developers need interactive test cycles while building code that will eventually run for hours. But many of these developers can get away with testing on a small set of nodes, which is easier to acquire, and computer scientists may never need the entire cluster for more than a few minutes at a time.

On Chiba City, we do run a batch scheduler because we have not yet found a better way to equitably share the system between many users. But we clear the cluster of all jobs every day for a two-hour period, during which time no job longer than five minutes can run. This gives computer scientists a two-hour window every day for quick turnaround. Long-running jobs have to wait until the weekend, when we allow jobs to go from Friday evening until Monday morning.

Also, it's possible to schedule a number of nodes and then simply use them in interactive mode during that timeslot.

License to crash: Some computer scientists and developers work on low-level pieces of code that can have bugs that impact the entire operating system on a node. In some cases, such as in file systems and job managers, they may even crash the entire cluster. It's important to have some kind of facility where code like this can be tested in a real-world environment.

Crashing a node on Chiba, even to the point of requiring a rebuild, is fairly minor. We have remote power control, remote monitoring, and the ability to rebuild a node from scratch. (All of these systems are described in Section 18.3.2.) If a node needs to be rebuilt, we simply set a flag in the City database for that node, and that node's mayor will initiate a rebuild the next time that node reboots. If necessary, the mayor can force the reboot.

Crashing the entire cluster is a bigger problem. Still, we set the expectation that we actively support development of the cluster's system software and that we expect things will occasionally crash. We try to minimize the frequency of these large-scale problems and try to minimize their impact. But in a worst-case situation, we can rebuild all the nodes and reboot in 20–30 minutes.

Modifiable node environment: A small number of developers actually need a completely different node environment. They might be testing a set of device drivers that are unusual, or comparing FreeBSD to Windows 2000 to Linux. In any of these cases, the scientists may need to have root access on their nodes or may want to replace the node operating system entirely for the duration of their job.

We support the ability to arbitrarily modify the node computing environment. The mayors build their nodes from a node "image," where an image is a set of files or binary file system data. The mayor will write that to the node's disk, then boot it.

You can build an image of any operating system desired, as long as it boots. During the time that the nodes are reserved for you by the scheduler, you can do whatever is necessary on those nodes. Once your scheduled time is up, the mayor power cycles the node, catches the booting system, and reinstalls the Chiba City default Linux image on the node. This process is illustrated in Figure 18.5.

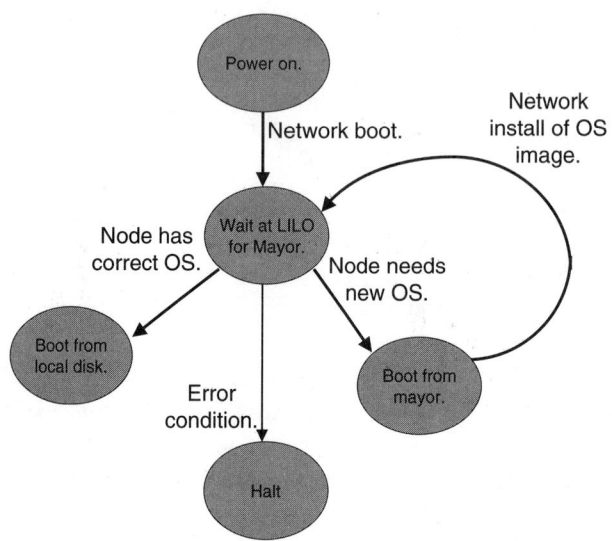

Figure 18.5
Node image management.

18.3.2 Management Environment

Starting with the very first design for the cluster, we put a great deal of emphasis on scalable management of Chiba City. For example, one of our goals was never to have to physically touch a node unless it was having hardware problems.

We emphasized scalable administration because we must. All management functions of a very large system, of which Chiba City is a prototype, must scale for obvious reasons. Furthermore, we need scalable management for Chiba itself. The management team for Chiba City consists of three people who are responsible for all aspects of the administration of the cluster, all user support, the development of management tools and system software, involvement in experiments, and other aspects of the MCS computing environment.

The management approach for Chiba City incorporates a number of philosophies:

• Support all the needs of the diverse user community, ranging from stable batch-oriented computing to letting individual users have root access on their nodes.
• Don't change the model too much, because our scientists need to work in the common model to make their tools applicable to others. For example, we couldn't switch over to a shared-memory model of the cluster.

- Manage from a central point. The mayor/town architecture—in which the city mayor presides over the mayors, each of whom manages a set of nodes—is designed to strongly support central management.
- Use open source and existing tools as much as possible. As much as we like to invent cooler wheels, we don't have time.

The remainder of this section describes the individual components of the management environment.

City Database. The city mayor keeps a database of relatively static cluster information. We call this database the City Database or "citydb." The database describes the node/mayor relationship, keeps track of which nodes have what types of hardware, and knows which nodes should have which operating system image at which time.

The City Database is different from the database kept by the scheduler, which is much more dynamic. The dynamic database includes job information, which users own which nodes, and which nodes are currently up. Optimally, both databases would be more closely related, but in practice it has been easier for us to keep the functionality split.

The City Database is authoritative. If the database and reality don't match, then reality must be wrong. Using this philosophy, we can describe the desired cluster configuration in the database and then tell the mayors to make sure the cluster conforms to the configuration. The configuration management tools described below take care of this.

Citydb is built on MySQL using standard SQL.

Configuration Management. At the highest level, the configuration model works this way:

- The configuration for every node is described on the city mayor. Since many nodes are identical, this is not as bad as it might seem.
- The city mayor is the source for all configuration files, images, and RPMs. All mayors keep a mirror image of those files.
- When a configuration change is necessary, the administrator makes a change on the city mayor and then invokes a process to push that change out.
- The nodes themselves are checked at boot up and after user jobs run to make sure that they have the correct configuration.

The primary configuration management tool that we use on Chiba City is a program called `sanity`. The idea behind `sanity` is that it can install RPMs, modify

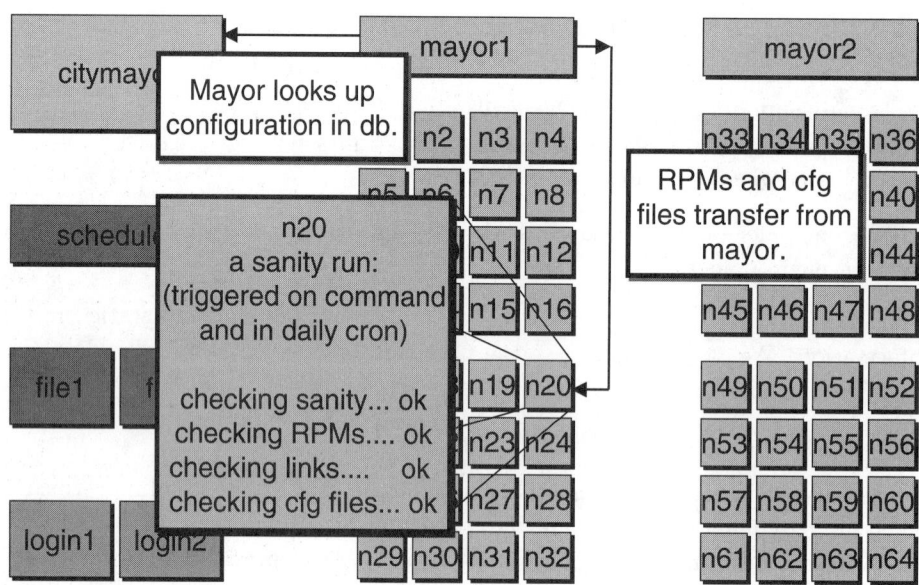

Figure 18.6
OS image management.

configuration files, and execute scripts. It decides what to do based on a configuration file that can be general or very specific to a node. Once it has established that the node matches the configuration in that file, the node is pronounced sane.

The mayors have the ability to invoke `sanity` on each of their nodes. The nodes also run `sanity` when they first boot and after a user job completes. The configuration for `sanity` is an aspect of the image on that node, and the image for each node is recorded in the citydb on the city mayor.

In order to make a change to all of the nodes on the system, one would modify the `sanity` configuration file for the default image, then invoke a global `sanity` push on the city mayor. It tells each mayor to kick off a `sanity` run, and each mayor in turn tells each node to run `sanity`.

This process is illustrated in Figure 18.6.

Serial Infrastructure. Another tool in the management arsenal is remote console management. The console of every system in Chiba City is available over the network. The system works in the following way:

• The console port on each node is connected to a serial concentrator for that town.

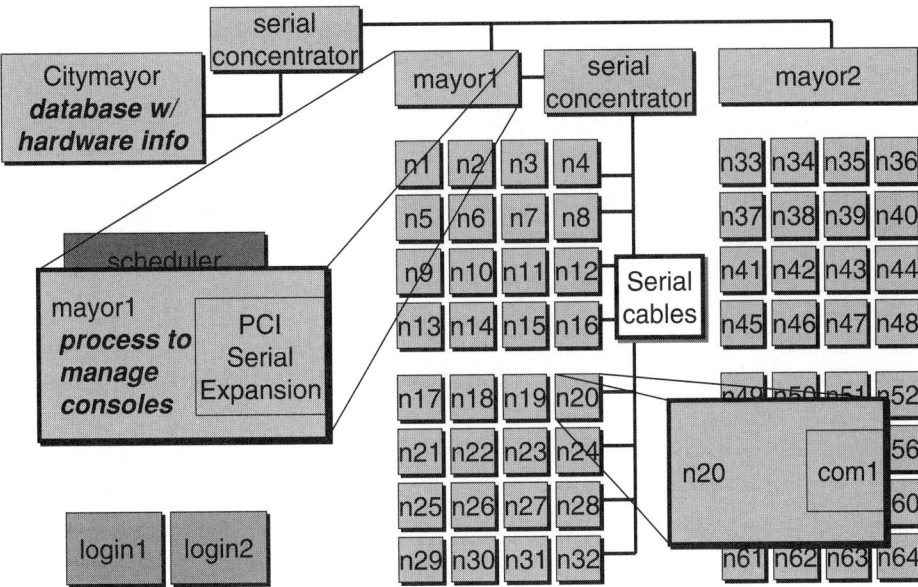

Figure 18.7
Serial infrastructure.

- The serial concentrator is connected to the mayor.
- The mayor runs a daemon called `conserver` that enables remote access to the console from anywhere on the network that has permission. This daemon is an open source tool that is widely used in the system administration community.
- From any point on the MCS network, an administrator can type `console <node>` and get access to the console of that node.

This process is illustrated in Figure 18.7.

In practice, we use this feature only when debugging. Ideally we don't want to actually have to go to all the consoles of all the nodes. Sometimes, though, a node will quit responding for no reason. It's frequently possible to recover the node via the console—or at least get a hint from the console messages what might have gone wrong.

The `conserver` daemon has another feature of console management that is also critical to Chiba City. It can log all of the output of any console to a file or to a process. We wrote a program called `chex` that monitors the output of each console, looking for particular strings. Among other things, this lets us know whether a node is rebooting, whether it has panicked, or whether some other error condition has taken place.

We take advantage of this console monitoring to capture node-specific information such as the node's MAC address. See the section below entitled "The First Boot Process" for an example of why this is useful.

Low-Level Diagnostics. Some motherboards have the ability to provide useful information about the hardware, such as the temperature of the node and the fan speed. Some can also control the power of the system.

The nodes that we are using have this ability. Initially, however, this functionality was accessible only if you used a Windows NT system to monitor the node remotely. Since then, people have created open source software that runs on Linux to manage these ports.

Unfortunately, we have never taken advantage of this system. It would be nice, but we haven't had time to get to it.

Power Control. We do, however, have remote power control for every component of Chiba City. The power control system works as follows:

- Every computer and network box is plugged into a Baytech power unit. There are, on average, five Baytech units per town.
- The Baytech unit is somewhat like a power strip with an Ethernet port. It's possible to telnet to the Baytech and then power on, power off, or query the power status of anything plugged into it.
- We have a simple tool called `city_power` that allows a Chiba City administrator to control the power of any device or set of devices in Chiba City.

The Baytechs are connected to their own network, which is built of very simple Ethernet hubs. We could connect them using the Chiba City Ethernet, but then, if something went wrong with the network, we couldn't access the Baytechs to reset the Ethernet devices. The power network is accessible only via the City Mayor.

The power configuration is shown in detail in Figure 18.8.

The First Boot Process. To explain how the management tools work together, we give an example. One of the more complicated scenarios on a cluster is when a node is booted for the very first time. The cluster software needs to be made aware of that process, and the node needs to get the right operating system. Many people ignore this situation and take care of the details by hand.

Here is what happens on Chiba City when a completely new node is installed in the cluster:

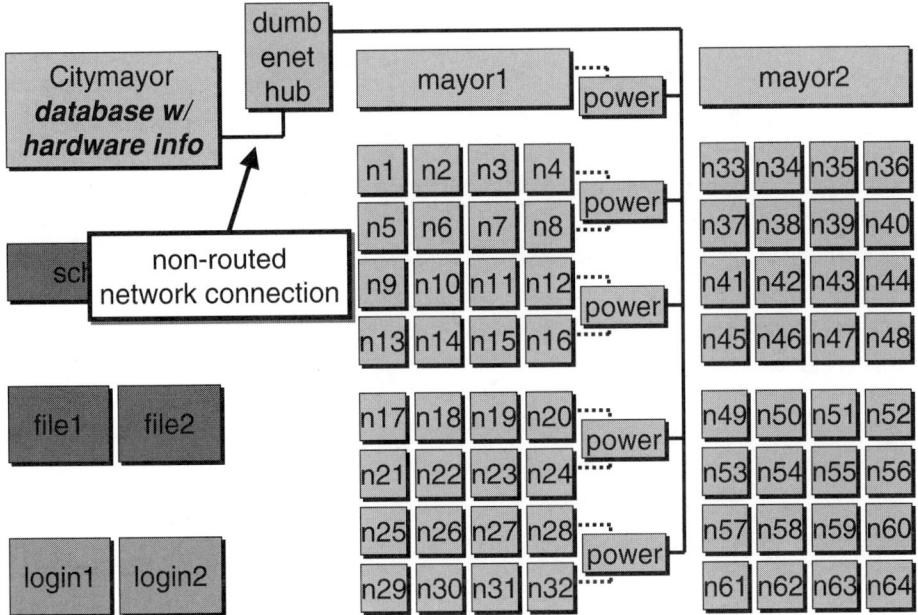

Figure 18.8
Power infrastructure.

1. We set a flag in the City Database indicating that this is a new node.

2. The node is installed in the correct spot in the rack and cabled appropriately.

3. We install the correct BIOS in the node. This, unfortunately, is still done manually, although we are looking into a boot floppy approach that will do the right thing. Among other things, the BIOS is set to boot using PXE, a type of network booting. This means that on all subsequent power cycles, the node will boot from the network.

4. The node is turned on, and it boots from the network. Some server on the net, usually that node's mayor, responds with the boot image.

5. The boot code is a Linux boot image that includes LILO and a kernel. LILO is configured to launch and then wait forever at its boot prompt, occasionally reissuing the prompt.

6. The LILO boot prompt is issued over the serial line.

7.   The node's mayor sees the Boot prompt. It knows which node this is because it knows which serial lines it is watching. Thus, at this point, the mayor knows that it node15 (for example) is waiting to boot.

8.   The mayor checks the City Database to see what image should be on that node. It discovers that this is a new node.

9.   Based on this information, it issues a boot command over the serial line to the node, handing it a set of boot parameters. This command tells the node to boot from the mayor from the Build Image.

10.   The node receives the command and boots the Build Image kernel that was transferred back in Step 4.

11.   As a part of booting the Build Image, the setup scripts partition the node's disk and install the correct image files.

12.   At the end of the Build Image, the node displays certain relevant pieces of information to its console, including its Ethernet MAC address.

13.   The mayor, which is monitoring the console, now knows that this new node has successfully built. Furthermore, it has the MAC address of that node.

14.   The mayor updates the DHCP tables on the city mayor with the new MAC address and queues a DHCP restart request.

15.   The mayor updates Citydb with a flag saying that the node has the correct image installed.

16.   The node waits for a minute and then reboots. Once again, it PXE boots and loads the boot image from the mayor. It issues the LILO boot prompt to the serial console and waits.

17.   The mayor checks Citydb and notes that this node has already built the correct image onto its local disk. It issues a "boot from local disk" command to the LILO boot prompt over the serial line.

18.   The node boots from the local disk. Among other things, it will send out a DHCP request to get its IP address and will be sent the correct IP address for the node in that spot of the cluster.

19.   After rebooting, the node runs `sanity`. It installs any modifications necessary for that operating system image.

20. Finally, the node is ready to run. The scheduler notes that the node is up and adds it to the pool of allocatable resources.

This whole process is long to describe but fast to run. The only slow part is the operating system build in Step 11, when the bits are being installed on the local disk. That can take 10–15 minutes, with the exact time dependent on the size of the image and the activity on the network. Once the node has been installed and the BIOS updated, the process requires no intervention from an administrator.

18.4   Chiba City Use

The average user of Chiba City interacts with it just like any other cluster of distributed supercomputer. Consider the following scenario.

A user logs into the front end node using SSH. She compiles her code on that system, or perhaps copy in precompiled code. If she wants to test the code on several nodes before submitting a large job, she can choose nodes on the 32 nodes of the cluster that we refer to as the interactive town. This set of nodes is configured in the same way as the standard computing nodes, but is never scheduled. It is always available specifically for testing purposes. It's quite possible that two users' codes will conflict with each other, so it's not useful for performance testing or long-running code. Once she is confident that her code will run successfully, she prepares her code and her job data to be copied out to the nodes that she will eventually be allocated. She does this by putting everything together in a directory. Finally, she submits her job to the PBS queue using the qsub command. She can check on the status of her job with qstat. Eventually she will be assigned a set of nodes for the duration of her timeslot, and her job will be invoked on those nodes. During this time, she will be able to login to her nodes, which she will want to do if she's running an interactive job. If there are any errors with her job, she will be notified by e-mail. Once her job has completed or her time is up, whichever comes first, the datafiles she created are copied back to her home directory on the front end node.

Nonstandard use of Chiba City can entail endless variations of this scenario. A user might arrange to have dedicated access to the cluster for a long period of time—this requires administrator and, in some cases, management approval. Or a user might have a custom image to be tested and then arranged for installation on that user's nodes. Some people use the storage nodes as part of I/O experiments. Others use the visualization nodes, sometimes in conjunction with the jobs on the computing nodes, and other times as a completely separate activity.

Currently, we have about one hundred active users on Chiba City. We expect to add several hundred more in the next few months as a result of changes in the allocation policies on some of our other supercomputers.

Since its installation, Chiba has been used for many different types of activities. Notable among these are the following:

- Monte Carlo simulations in nuclear physics
- Computational optimization
- Parallel and numerical library development
- Distributed supercomputing development
- Communication library development
- File system development
- Astrophysical simulation
- Scalable system software development
- Visualization
- Genomics
- Automated reasoning
- Climate modeling of both Earth and Mars
- Molecular dynamics simulations
- Scalability testing of open source tools

A detailed description of these projects is beyond the scope of this chapter; this list is merely meant to give a feel for the different types of use that the cluster enables.

18.5   Final Thoughts

In this case study, we have described in detail the kinds of issues that we encounter when designing, building, and running a multipurpose large cluster. We hope that the topics discussed here will be useful to others who may find themselves in a similar situation.

18.5.1   Lessons Learned

This entire case study is about lessons that we've learned while running Chiba City. We still have a few that are worth mentioning.

- It is surprisingly difficult to run a job on the entire cluster. Most users don't care about this, but management would always like to confirm that a job has used every possible resource on the system. It seems like there is always at least one node that is down for hardware maintenance, or one network interface this is flaky, or a node that just isn't in the mood to play. We have actually run jobs on all of the nodes using both types of network, but these jobs take focused effort and are relatively rare.

- In a cluster, the hardware gets stressed beyond what any vendor expects because it is always being used, sometimes in ways that the designer never anticipated. We've had bad AGP and PCI slots, large-scale memory problems, fan lossage, bad cables, and everything else. Furthermore, when buying commodity hardware, one gets commodity quality. This hardware doesn't take abuse the way high-end supercomputing equipment does. It's a very good idea to invest in a three-year hardware maintenance option.

- When running a cluster like Chiba City, it is essential to have at least one person who lives in the Linux world. Two or three people is even better. Those people should follow the important Linux mailing lists, track bugs, and follow discussions on Web sites. The success of the cluster often rides on figuring out exactly which version of the kernel works best with which set of applications, or knowing that a particular feature will be available (or removed) in a few weeks.

18.5.2 Future Directions

Chiba City has largely been a success. We would like for some portions of the system, notably the scheduler and the I/O system, to be more reliable and functional, but despite these failings, good science has been accomplished on the computer, both in the realm of computer science and in scientific simulation. The model that we use to manage and operate the cluster has worked well and shows every sign of scaling to a much larger cluster. We have a number of plans for software modifications to improve the system and to support new capabilities.

In the near future, the scalability work that has been started on Chiba City must continue to expand to larger and larger testbed systems. Many open scientific questions require systems that can deliver sustained petaflops of computation. It is not yet clear what the path to building a petaflop system is, but it is very likely that such a computer will be built from many tens or hundreds of thousands of individual computing components. As a community, in order to build such a system, we must have systems software that can operate a machine of that scale, and we must have algorithms and applications that can make reasonable use of it. Thus, while the computing industry forges ahead with building better and faster processors, we must have a strategy for connecting them together and making them run well. Scalability testbeds such as Chiba City are an important part of this plan, and we hope that research and activities in this space will continue to be expanded.

For more information on Chiba City and the software used to drive it, see `www.mcs.anl.gov/chiba`.

19 Conclusions

Thomas Sterling

This book represents the practical state of the art in hardware and software for Beowulf cluster computing. But it also exemplifies the extreme rate at which commodity clusters are maturing and in so doing, gaining utility across ever-broader domains of application. Only two years ago our first work in this area, *How to Build a Beowulf,* was published by MIT Press. But in the short interval since then, the art and practice of cluster computing have evolved dramatically. Then, such systems were used in rather restrictive ways with limited software support beyond the basic node operating systems and message-passing libraries. System size rarely exceeded a hundred processors. Today, systems exceeding a thousand processors are employed for both technical and commercial computing. But more significant is the array of software tools available and under development to manage the implementation, maintenance, administration, and resource allocation of workloads on Beowulf clusters both large and small. Thus, in the brief period between this offering and our original modest work, Beowulf commodity cluster computing has come of age. Then, Beowulf systems were only a narrow element of the parallel computing domain. Today, they are often the system of choice and are rapidly coming to dominate even the highest end of computing. It is telling that at the most recent Supercomputing conference, the industrial exhibits included more commodity clusters on the floor than all other forms of parallel computing systems combined.

In spite of these enormous gains, Beowulf cluster computing is very much a field in transition. There is no one universally accepted distributed environment or, for that matter, hardware foundation on which the cluster community relies. Of course, the flexibility this implies is part of its strength and invulnerability to vendor changes. Indeed, both hardware and software are in a state of flux, with continued changes foreseen for the next one to three years. It is worth considering where these likely changes will occur.

19.1 Future Directions for Hardware Components

Processor technology is witnessing three areas of change. The first is continued growth of processor capability, most notably in clock speed. Predictions to the contrary, clock rates continue to grow. At the time of this writing, the Pentium 4 with a clock rate of 1.7 GHz is available in consumer-grade packages. Memory enhancements and cache size also expand to attempt to match the processor peak performance. The second change is a new generation of 64-bit architecture with the commercial release of the Intel IA-64 64-bit family of processors. The third area of change is the likely integration of multiple processors per chip in SMP configurations. Should this trend become reality, then nodes of commodity clusters could all be SMP structures of two or more processors. All of these advances are driven by the continued reduction of integration feature size, with logic moving below 0.18 micron.

Network technology is expected to make significant strides as gigahertz per node channels become commonplace and costs continue to drop. Myrinet and Ethernet dominate Beowulf cluster configurations, but other network technologies are having significant impact. The Quadrics QSW networks are providing a high-bandwidth framework for the highest end of the Compaq Alpha processor-based systems, and larger configurations have been proposed that could yield clusters capable of over 100 teraflops peak performance. The VIA architecture continues to make inroads in the cluster market delivering gigabit per second throughputs and latencies well below 10 microseconds. Foremost among these is the Emulex cLAN network. But perhaps the most interesting advance is the emergence of the new industry Infiniband architecture (IBA) standard (well over 1,500 pages). Infiniband provides a new tightly integrated strategy and technology for all I/O needs including cluster interconnection networks. Instead of connecting to an intermediary I/O interface such as PCI, Infiniband will be tied more directly to the processor communications, increasing I/O bandwidth and reducing latencies down toward a microsecond. Already specified are several levels of bandwidth including the use of optical media that will work in the 10 Gbps regime. Infiniband is supported by a large industrial consortium and may become the new dominant I/O interface. Products based on IBA should be available within the next eighteen months. However, in spite of wide optimism, costs to customers have yet to be determined. It is interesting to note that the external network bandwidths are approaching the main memory bandwidths of the processing nodes. With another order of magnitude gain in bandwidth anticipated in the next few years, it may be that network bandwidth will cease to be the dominant bottleneck to realizable performance.

Although less widely discussed, significant advances in mass storage are expected. These are being fueled by the rapidly growing PDA, digital camera, and cellular phone markets that require high-capacity storage in small, lightweight, and low-power components. "Matchbox" disk drives will provide multigigabyte capacities in the near future. For larger units, advanced EIDE drives will provide hundreds of gigabytes per unit at a cost of less than $10 per gigabyte. For many technical and commercial problems, mass storage is the bottleneck, both in capacity and in bandwidth. Commodity clusters provide a rich tradeoff space within which to configure and operate large disk farms. But reliability and software support for distributed file spaces continue to offer considerable challenges that have not been fully resolved.

Packaging of systems will continue to evolve and have impact on Beowulf clusters in two important ways. Historically, Beowulfs have taken up a lot of room. Although the very first Beowulf was custom packaged with 16 motherboards in a half-height rack, the majority of systems leveraged the low-cost, high-reliability PC tower packages with power supply. But the density of this class of package is low. For all but the smallest systems, floor space has become a problem. Because the market for Beowulf-class clusters has become significant, however, vendors are providing new packaging options with high-density rack-mounted units available such that 40 or more processors can now be installed in a single floor standing rack. As higher-degree SMPs are built into such units, the number of processors per rack will continue to expand allowing larger systems to be installed in modest machine rooms. But this also leads to the second way future machines will be impacted and that is the scale of the largest Beowulf-clusters. In the near future, the largest systems in the world will be commodity clusters comprising 10,000 processors or more. Within the lifetime of this edition of this book, clusters delivering as much as 100 teraflops may be implemented on this scale.

19.2   Future Directions for Software Components

While enormous strides have been made in the area of cluster middleware within the past few years, the general consensus is that continued advances are required to bring this class of system to a level of usability and robustness equivalent to other server technology. Key attributes sought are completeness, commonality, usability, generality, and reliability.

Completeness relates to the need for a comprehensive software environment that spans all aspects of the distributed cluster system and supports the major activities associated with the operation of a commodity cluster, large or small. These activities include installation, configuration and initialization, status monitoring and maintenance, administration, and resource scheduling.

Commonality is the property of such an environment to be broadly used across the majority of Beowulf clusters throughout the community. Linux, Windows, and MPI all exhibit this property, which has been an important enabler to the wide dissemination of Beowulf systems. To that extent, if you've used one Beowulf, you are likely to be able, with little trouble, to work with any other. But at the middleware level, there is not such uniformity of environments. This is partly intentional and partly due to history. As vendors have successfully advanced into the arena, middleware has been one area in which they could provide product differentiation, to enhance the apparent value of their respective offerings. Historically, low-level tools—especially for monitoring system status, operation, and health—have been developed in house with only limited sharing. As we have seen, however, other tools such as schedulers have seen much wider use.

Usability combined with *generality* relates to the ease of system operation through the abstraction presented by the middleware environment. A highly valued attribute, perceived to strongly contribute to usability, is "single-system image." Originally, Beowulf clusters were treated as an ensemble of separate loosely coupled processing systems, each being managed individually. In the earliest days, there would even be some kind of a switchbox connecting the operator's keyboard and monitor to any designated processor node. While this can work for small, dedicated systems, it is untenable for larger, multiuser clusters and undesirable in any case. A system includes a number of name spaces with which the user must contend. Some of these include the user application's global variables, the file space, the set of process IDs and jobs, and I/O. In the worst case, these all need to be dealt with on a per node basis. As systems grow to the scale of a thousand or more processors, this too can prove untenable. Even for much smaller systems, such explicit per node control is prone to operator error. Single-system image is the property by which the entire cluster presents only a single name space for each class of named object for the entire system, independent of the number of processors employed. The user sees one process ID space, one distributed file space, and the same for others. Generality extends the property of usability to include a broad range of operating modes from dedicated single user to multi-user, multiprogram operation.

System reliability is critical to long-term acceptance of Beowulf clusters by the information processing market. Opinions differ widely concerning the actual reliability of Beowulf systems. Infant mortality lasting weeks for moderate-sized systems can be high with fans, power supplies, disk drives, and even memories breaking in a short time interval. After this period, however, systems often experience long stable operation, potentially of many months between required maintenance. After two to three years, age begins to take its toll, and failures begin to escalate. But for very large systems on the order of thousands of processors, single point failures can be significantly more prevalent. For either class of system, rapid detection, diagnosis, repair, restart, and recovery are essential to high availability. Software tools to aid in all facets of reliability are essential as well, but little work has been done in this area, and no accepted general set of tools is in use, although some experimental systems have been explored. One important capability is checkpoint and restart, and some tools exist but involve direct application programmer intervention. Tools for logging and reporting soft errors can be used to identify likely future failures, directing preemptive controlled replacement of system components without disrupting application execution. Much more work is required in this area.

A valuable effort is the collection and integration of a critical subset of existing tools to build a useful environment meeting at least some of the requirements above. OSCAR led out of Oak Ridge National Lab, Rocks being done at the San Diego Supercomputing Center, the integrated tool set at the Cornell Theory Center (CTC), and the integrated software system provided by Scyld are all examples of such efforts. OSCAR is a collaboration of a number of organizations including industry partners and is worth watching as it evolves. The tool set from CTC is one of the most comprehensive to be based on Windows. The Scyld software environment provides a good example of a user level single system image. While most Beowulf cluster software supports full operating systems on every node, each operating semi-independently, the Scyld model is different. By employing a logical structure of a master processor and multiple slave processors, all name spaces are managed through the master processor, presenting a single system image to the user. Processes are controlled by the master but delegated to the slave processors to be executed. The slave node kernels are very limited and lightweight and are downloaded by the master. This can be performed very efficiently, much more quickly than on conventional clusters, and solves the problem of version consistency control. Nevertheless, while the Scyld software environment exhibits many desirable properties, there is a question regarding scalability. A single master processor can create a bottleneck, and the coordination of multiple masters is nontrivial.

With increased prevalence of SMP nodes in cluster systems, means of exploiting this class of tightly coupled unit is called for. OpenMP has been developed as one way to apply these resources within a shared-memory paradigm. But between nodes is still the fragmented name space so typical of most clusters. Ironically, even on systems with distributed shared memory hardware support, the majority of parallel programmers today use MPI with its message-passing model. The underlying mechanisms supporting the MPI implementation take advantage of the shared-memory hardware support, thereby making at least some of its operators more efficient than between cluster nodes, and this is done in a way that is transparent to the user. But a clean way of using shared memory within a node and distributed memory between nodes has not found a satisfactory solution in common practice. A class of programming models sometimes referred to as "put-get" models may provide at least a partial solution. Inspired in part by the Cray T3E programming model, this approach gives the impression of a distributed shared memory but assumes no cache coherence. Within an SMP node, conventional load/store operations are used, but for remote accesses the corresponding get and put operators are used within the same programming model. Examples of this include UPC developed at IDA CCS and the experimental Earth-C developed at the University of Delaware.

19.3   Final Thoughts

It is hard to forecast where such a volatile technology as parallel computing will take us, as so many factors and trends influence the final outcome. A decade ago, clusters were in their infancy, and Beowulf was still in the future. A decade from now will see as many changes. Nonetheless, at least some of the possibilities can be considered. Extrapolating both the Top500 list and the Semiconductor Industry Association roadmap implies that the largest computers in the world, in all likelihood commodity clusters, will achieve a peak performance of 1 petaflops by the year 2010. Integrated circuits of a billion devices most likely comprising a number of processors will be capable of a performance on the order of 100 Gflops or more. DRAM densities will grow a factor of a hundred in that same timeframe. And if optical communications are employed to their fullest, per channel bandwidths of 1 Tbps or more are possible. In such a scenario, almost every small Beowulf will be a teraflops machine by 2010.

As long as there is a need for servers of one type or another, there will be the opportunity for performance gains through commodity clusters. But a number of trends in the market are not aligned with a future with clusters. Portable computing devices including personal digital assistants, laptop computers, and soon to be released (probably) electronic books all have built-in human interfaces including screens and keyboards that make them unsuitable for clustering. It is true that their technology push helps reduce cost, power, and size, which can have a positive influence on cluster nodes. But the mass-market products themselves are not likely to be used in clusters generally. Admittedly, there have already been cases of clustering laptops. But these are not cost effective. Desktop (or desk side) computers in their ungainly tower cases may already be becoming extinct. A growing number of users have simply migrated their complete user environment onto their laptops. The laptop is everything, their entire world. With wireless interconnect in the office and home, even cellular Internet connections on the road, and disk capacities that will shortly exceed 100 Gbytes, the desktop is rapidly becoming a dinosaur. But it was from these devices that the first Beowulfs were devised. Beowulf-class systems exploited the existing mass-market devices, and now these may disappear.

But this is no longer a problem because the value of clusters to the market has been proven. Vendors are now manufacturing processor nodes explicitly for the purpose of building high-density clusters. Thus the components are no longer hand-me-downs from other markets but optimized for this purpose. In a sense, the day of Beowulf classic is passing—not yet, but eventually. Commodity clusters were offered as a cheap alternative to MPPs to help offload these more expensive machines of at least part of their workload. But with the next-generation high-bandwidth networks and their tight integration with the processor/memory core, much of the distinction between MPPs and clusters is beginning to disappear. And with efficient implementations of such operations as put and get, a shared memory space (without cache coherence) model may be available, further eroding the distinction between cluster and MPP. If this happens, we will have truly witnessed the convergence of parallel architecture.

And yet, that will not be the end of the story. The programming models described so far are still primitive and require a close and explicit relationship between the physical system and the programmer. In the limit, the programmer should be responsible for describing the application's parallel algorithm, but not responsible for hand manipulating the management of the physical resources and their direct association to the application task and data objects. As processors become ubiquitous in the tens of thousands and the critical resource is recognized to be memory bandwidth, these parallel systems will motivate the development of a new family of programming models where once again, as in the earliest days of computing, the programmer will treat the computer as a single system and not a distributed collection of many machines. We have had only tantalizing glimpses of what such models might contain, but already researchers are considering just such new paradigms. Beowulf cluster computing is leading parallel processing into the future. Each step is an accomplishment in its own right and the foundation for progress to the next.

A Glossary of Terms

AFS: Andrew File System

AMD: Advanced Micro Devices

ASIC: Application Specific Integrated Circuits

ASRAM: Asynchronous Static Random Access Memory

ATM: Asynchronous Transfer Mode; a network and protocol for wide area networks (WAN); while employed as the interconnection medium for some commodity clusters, it has not seen wide use for clusters because it is not optimized for this use and is fairly expensive

BDA: BIOS Data Area

Beowulf-class system: commodity cluster employing personal computers or low-cost SMP servers to achieve excellent price-performance initially developed by the Beowulf project at the NASA Goddard Space Flight Center

BIOS: Basic Input Output System

bit: the fundamental unit of information representing a two-state value; a digital circuit capable of storing a two-state value

BLAS: basic linear algebra subroutines

BOOTP: Bootstrap Protocol

bps: bits per second, a unit measure of data transfer rate

byte: a commonly addressed quantity of digital information storage of eight bits reflecting one of 256 distinct values

CD-ROM: Compact Disc Read Only Memory

CERT: Computer Emergency Response Team

cluster: in the general sense, any interconnected ensemble of computers capable of independent operation but employed to service a common workload

CMOS: Complimentary Metal Oxide Semiconductor

commodity cluster: a cluster of commercial computing nodes integrated with a commercial system area network

Condor: a software package developed at the University of Wisconson to manage the scheduling of a job workload across a distributed computing system including clusters

constellation: a cluster of large DSM, SMP, or MPP computing nodes incorporating more microprocessors per node than there are nodes in the system

CORBA: Common Object Request Broker Architecture

COW: cluster of workstations; an early project at the University of Wisconsin

CPU: Central Processing Unit

CRC: Cyclic Redundancy Check

DCE: Distributed Computing Environment

DCOM: Distributed Component Object Model

DDR: Double Data Rate

DFS: Distributed File System

DHCP: Dynamic Host Configuration Protocol

DRAM: Dynamic Random Access Memory

DSM: distributed shared memory multiprocessor, tightly coupled cache coherent multiprocessor with non-uniform memory access

DVD: Digital Versatile Disc

EDO: Extended Data Out

EEPROM: Electrically Erasable Programmable Read Only Memory

EIDE: Enhanced Integrated Drive Electronics

Emulex: vendor, distributor, and developer of the cLAN network for commodity clusters

EPIC: Explicitly Parallel Instruction Computing

Ethernet: the first widely used and truly ubiquitous local area network operating at 10 Mbps

Fast Ethernet: a cost effective local area network based on the original Ethernet protocol that has become very popular with low end Beowulf-class systems; providing 100 Mbps

FDD: Floppy Disk Drive

FHS: File system Hierarchy Standard

FSSTND: File System Standard

FTP: File Transfer Protocol

Gigabit Ethernet: a LAN that is the successor of Fast Ethernet providing peak bandwidth of 1 Gbps. While employed for some clusters, its use is limited by its relatively high cost

GNU: a project resulting in a number of open source and free software tools including the GNU C compiler and Emacs

GPL: GNU Public License; a legal framework protecting open source software

HDD: Hard Disk Drive

HDF: Hierarchical data format, both a file format and high level interface for I/O access in both sequential and parallel applications

HPL: High Performance Linpack

I/O: Input/Output

IBM: International Business Machines

IDE: Integrated Drive Electronics

IDL: Interface Definition Language

IP: Internet Protocol

IPv4: Internet Protocol, version 4

IPv6: Internet Protocol, version 6

IRQ: Interrupt Request

JIT: Just In Time

JVM: Java Virtual Machine

LAN: Local Area Network; a network employed within a single administrative domain such as a laboratory or office complex, connecting PCs and workstations together to file servers, printers and other peripherals, and to the Internet. Low cost LAN technology has been adopted to provide Beowulf-class systems with inexpensive moderate bandwidth interconnect

LED: Light Emitting Diode

Linux: the dominant Unix-like cross-platform operating system developed by a broad international community enabled by an open source code framework

LOBOS: Lots of Boxes on Shelves

LPT: Line Printer

MAC: Media Access Controller

MAU: Medium Attachment Unit

Mbps: 1 million bits per second data transfer rate or bandwidth

Mega: prefix meaning 1 million or in the case of storage 2^{20}

message passing: An approach to parallelism based on communicating data between processes running (usually) on separate computers.

metadata: Used in the context of file systems, this is the information describing the file, including owner, permissions, and location of data

MPI: message passing interface, a community derived logical standard for the transfer of program messages between separate concurrent processes

MPP: or Massively Parallel Processors

MTBF: Mean Time Between Failure

Myricom: vendor, distributor, and developer of the Myrinet network for commodity clusters

NAT: Network Address Translator

network: the combination of communication channels, switches, and interface controllers that transfer digital messages between Beowulf cluster nodes

NFS: Network File System

NIC: network interface controller; usually the combination of hardware and software that matches the network transport layer to the computer node of a cluster

NIH: National Institutes of Health

NIS: Network Information System

NOW: network or workstations, and early influential commodity cluster project at UC Berkeley

OMG: Object Management Group

ONC: Open Network Computing

ORB: Object Request Broker

PC: see Personal Computer

PCI: the dominant external interface standard for PCs and workstations to support I/O controllers including NICs

Personal Computer or PC: mass market microprocessor based computer employed by both commercial and consumer users for everything from games to spreadsheets and internet browsers; emphasizing performance/cost for maximum market share, these nodes are the basis for low cost Beowulf-class clusters

PLS: Physical Line Signaling

PnP: Plug 'n Play

POST: Power On Self Test

PROM: Programmable Read Only Memory

PVFS: Parallel virtual file system

PVM: Parallel Virtual Machine, a library of functions supporting an advanced message-passing semantics

QSW: high bandwidth network employed in very large clusters, specifically the SC series developed by Compaq

Quadrics: commercial vendor of networking hardware and software. See QSW

RAM: Random Access Memory

RFC: Request For Comments

RISC: Reduced Instruction Set Computer

RMI: Remote Method Invocation

ROM: Read Only Memory

ROMIO: Portable implementation of MPI-IO interface (not an acronym)

RPC: Remote Procedure Call

RSH: Remote SHell

RTC: Real Time Clock

RWCP: major Japanese initiative to develop robust and sophisticated cluster software environment

SAN: System Area Network; a network optimized for use as a dedicated communication medium within a commodity cluster

SBSRAM: Synchronous Burst Static Random Access Memory

Scheduler: a software tool which is part of the node operating system or system middleware that manages the assignment of tasks to cluster nodes and determines the timing of their execution

SCI: Scalable Coherent Interconnect

SCSI: Small Computer System Interface

SDRAM: Synchronous Dynamic Random Access Memory

SMP: Symmetric MultiProcessor, tightly coupled cache coherent multiprocessor with uniform memory access

SQL: Structured Query Language

SRAM: Static Random Access Memory

SSH: Secure SHell

TCP: Transmission Control Protocol

TFTP: Trivial File Transfer Protocol

TLA: Three Letter Acronym

UDP: Unreliable Datagram Protocol

VGA: Video Graphics Array

VIA: Virtual Interface Architecture

WAN: Wide Area Networks used to connect distant sites, even on a continental scale

XDR: eXternal Data Representation

XTI: X/Open Transport Interface

B Annotated Reading List

This appendix contains an annotated reading list of books and papers of interest to builders and users of Beowulf clusters.

Ian Foster. *Designing and Building Parallel Programs.* Addison-Wesley, 1995. Also at: `http://www.mcs.anl.gov/dbpp/`. A general introduction to the process of creating parallel applications. It includes short sections on MPI and HPF.

William Gropp, Steven Huss-Lederman, Andrew Lumsdaine, Ewing Lusk, Bill Nitzberg, William Saphir, and Marc Snir. *MPI—The Complete Reference: Volume 2, The MPI-2 Extensions.* MIT Press, Cambridge, MA, 1998. An annotated version of the MPI Standard; this contains additional examples and discussion about MPI-2.

William Gropp, Ewing Lusk, and Anthony Skjellum. *Using MPI: Portable Parallel Programming with the Message Passing Interface,* 2nd edition. MIT Press, 1999. A tutorial introduction to the MPI Standard, with examples in C and Fortran.

William Gropp, Ewing Lusk, and Rajeev Thakur. *Using MPI-2: Advanced Features of the Message-Passing Interface.* MIT Press, Cambridge, MA, 1999. A tutorial introduction to the MPI-2 Standard, with examples in C and Fortran. This is the best place to find information on using MPI I/O in applications.

Brian W. Kernighan and Dennis M. Ritchie. *The C Programming Language.* PTR Prentice Hall, 2nd edition, 1988. The original book describing the C programming language.

John M. May. *Parallel I/O for High Performance Computing.* Morgan Kaufmann, 2001. A thorough introduction to parallel I/O including MPI I/O and higher-level libraries such as HDF.

Evi Nemeth, Garth Snyder, Scott Seebass, and Trent R. Hein. *Unix System Administration Handbook.* Prentice Hall PTR, 3rd edition, 2001. A comprehensive and practical book on Unix system administration, it covers all major varieties of Unix, not just Linux.

Peter S. Pacheco. *Parallel Programming with MPI.* Morgan Kaufman, 1997. A good introductory text on parallel programming using MPI.

Gregory F. Pfister. *In Search of Clusters: The Ongoing Battle in Lowly Parallel Computing, 2nd ed.* Prentice Hall, Englewood Cliffs, NJ, 1995 edition, 1998. A delightful book advocating clusters for many problems, including for commercial computing. It has nice sections on parallel programming and (as part of his argument for clusters) a good discussion of shared-memory systems and the issues of correctness and performance that are often brushed under the rug. See Pfister's annotated bibliography for more books and articles on clusters.

Marc Snir, Steve W. Otto, Steven Huss-Lederman, David W. Walker, and Jack Dongarra. *MPI—The Complete Reference: Volume 1, The MPI Core,* 2nd edition. MIT Press, Cambridge, MA, 1998. An annotated version of the MPI-1 Standard, it contains more examples than the official copy and is a good reference on MPI.

Thomas L. Sterling, John Salmon, Donald J. Becker, and Daniel F. Savarese. *How to Build a Beowulf.* MIT Press, 1999. The original and best-selling Beowulf book.

W. Richard Stevens. *Advanced Programming in the UNIX Environment.* Addison-Wesley, Reading, MA, USA, 1992. A thorough and highly readable reference on programming under Unix.

W. Richard Stevens. *UNIX Network Programming: Interprocess Communications,* volume 2. Prentice-Hall, Upper Saddle River, NJ 07458, USA, second edition, 1998. A companion to Stevens' excellent book on sockets and XTI, this book covers POSIX and System V interprocess communication mechanisms including shared memory, remote procedure calls, and semaphores.

W. Richard Stevens. *UNIX Network Programming: Networking APIs: Sockets and XTI,* volume 1. Prentice-Hall PTR, Upper Saddle River, NJ 07458, USA, second edition, 1998. An excellent reference for network programming under Unix; it provides a highly readable and detailed description of all aspects of Unix socket programming.

David Wright, editor. *Beowulf.* Penguin Classics, 1957. A highly regarded translation (into prose) of the Beowulf Epic.

C Annotated URLs

Below is a sampling of URLs that are helpful for those building or using a Beowulf. This is not an exhaustive list, and we encourage the reader to browse the Web for other sites. A good place to start is the general Beowulf Web sites.

C.1 General Beowulf Information

`www.beowulf.org`: The original Beowulf Web site.

`beowulf-underground.org`: The Beowulf Underground provides "unsanctioned and unfettered information on building and using Beowulf systems." It is a site that allows the Beowulf community to post brief articles about software, documentation, and announcements related to Beowulf computing. Each article includes links to Web sites and downloads for the various items. A separate commercial and vendor area keeps free software well delineated. Moderators work to keep the material brief and on topic and to prevent abuses. This is the one stop for all things Beowulf.

C.2 Node and Network Hardware

`www.cs.virginia.edu/stream`: The STREAM Benchmark provides a simple measure of the performance of the memory system on a node. This site also includes results for a wide variety of platforms, from PC nodes suitable for a Beowulf, to workstations, to supercomputers.

`www.tomshardware.com`: Aimed at hobbyists building their own computers, this is a good site for general background on node hardware and includes up-to-date instructions on building your own node.

C.3 Performance Tools

`www.netlib.org/benchmark/hpl`: Home of the High Performance Linpack Benchmark

C.4 Parallel Programming and Software

`www.mpi-forum.org`: The official MPI Forum Web site, contains Postscript and HTML versions of the MPI-1 and MPI-2 Standards.

`www.mcs.anl.gov/mpi`: A starting point for information about MPI, including libraries and tools that use MPI and papers about the implementation or use of MPI.

`www.mcs.anl.gov/mpich`: Home of the MPICH implementation of MPI. Download source, documentation, and Unix and Windows versions of MPI from here. Also check the bug list page for patches and announcements of releases.

`www.mcs.anl.gov/mpi/mpptest`: Performance tests for MPI, including a guide for how *not* to measure communication performance.

`www.netlib.org`: A valuable collection of mathematical software and related information.

`www.csm.ornl.gov/pvm`: PVM home page.

`www.mcs.anl.gov/romio`: Home of the ROMIO implementation of the I/O chapter from MPI-2. ROMIO is included in MPICH and LAM but can also be downloaded separately. Information on tuning ROMIO for performance can be found here.

`hdf.ncsa.uiuc.edu`: Home of HDF. Included here are I/O libraries; tools for analyzing, visualizing, and converting scientific data; and software downloads, documentation, and support information.

`www.parl.clemson.edu/pvfs`: Home of PVFS, a parallel file system designed for Beowulf. This site includes online documentation, FAQ, source code downloads, mailing lists, developer's area, and research papers about PVFS.

`www.cs.dartmouth.edu/pario`: Home of the Parallel I/O Archive. This includes a list of projects in parallel I/O, people working in parallel I/O, and conferences on parallel I/O. Its biggest claim to fame is an extensive annotated bibliography of parallel I/O resources.

C.5   Scheduling and Management

`www.openpbs.org`: The OpenPBS site is the official Web site for the open source version of PBS. Maintained by Veridian, it offers downloads of software, patches, and documentation, and it hosts FAQs, discussion lists, searchable archives, and general PBS community announcements.

`www.pbspro.com`: Focused on the Professional Version of PBS, the PBS Pro Web site includes software downloads, documentation, evaluation versions, beta releases of new software, news, and information for the PBS administrator.

`www.supercluster.org`: The Supercluster Web site contains documentation for the Maui scheduler and Silver metascheduler. It also includes cluster-relevant research in areas of simulation, metascheduling, data staging, allocation management, and resource optimization.

References

[1] Sridhar Anandakrishnan. Penguins everywhere: GNU/Linux in Antarctica. *IEEE Software*, 16(6):90–96, Nov/Dec 1999.

[2] John D. Blair. *Samba: Integrating UNIX and Windows*. Specialized Systems Consultants, Inc., 1998.

[3] Philip H. Carns, Walter B. Ligon III, Robert B. Ross, and Rajeev Thakur. PVFS: A parallel file system for Linux clusters. In *Proceedings of the 4th Annual Linux Showcase and Conference*, pages 317–327, Atlanta, GA, October 2000. USENIX Association.

[4] Matthew Cettei, Walter Ligon, and Robert Ross. Support for parallel out of core applications on beowulf workstations. In *Proceedings of the 1998 IEEE Aerospace Conference*, March 1998.

[5] Peter F. Corbett and Dror G. Feitelson. The Vesta parallel file system. *ACM Transactions on Computer Systems*, 14(3):225–264, August 1996.

[6] Cray Research. *Application Programmer's Library Reference Manual*, 2nd edition, November 1995. Publication SR-2165.

[7] Chris DiBona, Sam Ockman, and Mark Stone. *Open Sources: Voices from the Open Source Revolution*. O'Reilly & Associates, Inc., 1999.

[8] Jack Dongarra. Performance of various computers using standard linear equations software. Technical Report Number CS-89-85, University of Tennessee, Knoxville TN, 37996, 2001. http://www.netlib.org/benchmark/performance.ps.

[9] G. C. Fox, S. W. Otto, and A. J. G. Hey. Matrix algorithms on a hypercube I: Matrix multiplication. *Parallel Computing*, 4:17–31, 1987.

[10] W. Gropp and E. Lusk. Scalable Unix tools on parallel processors. In *Proceedings of the Scalable High-Performance Computing Conference, May 23–25, 1994, Knoxville, Tennessee*, pages 56–62, 1109 Spring Street, Suite 300, Silver Spring, MD 20910, USA, 1994. IEEE Computer Society Press.

[11] William Gropp, Steven Huss-Lederman, Andrew Lumsdaine, Ewing Lusk, Bill Nitzberg, William Saphir, and Marc Snir. *MPI—The Complete Reference: Volume 2, The MPI-2 Extensions*. MIT Press, Cambridge, MA, 1998.

[12] William Gropp, Ewing Lusk, Nathan Doss, and Anthony Skjellum. A high-performance, portable implementation of the MPI Message-Passing Interface standard. *Parallel Computing*, 22(6):789–828, 1996.

[13] William Gropp, Ewing Lusk, and Anthony Skjellum. *Using MPI: Portable Parallel Programming with the Message Passing Interface*, 2nd edition. MIT Press, Cambridge, MA, 1999.

[14] William Gropp, Ewing Lusk, and Rajeev Thakur. *Using MPI-2: Advanced Features of the Message-Passing Interface*. MIT Press, Cambridge, MA, 1999.

[15] William D. Gropp and Ewing Lusk. Reproducible measurements of MPI performance characteristics. In Jack Dongarra, Emilio Luque, and Tomàs Margalef, editors, *Recent Advances in Parallel Virtual Machine and Message Passing Interface*, volume 1697 of *Lecture Notes in Computer Science*, pages 11–18. Springer Verlag, 1999. 6th European PVM/MPI Users' Group Meeting, Barcelona, Spain, September 1999.

[16] Don Heller. Rabbit: A performance counters library for Intel/AMD processors and Linux. `www.scl.ameslab.gov/Projects/Rabbit/`.

[17] J. M. D. Hill, B. McColl, D. C. Stefanescu, M. W. Goudreau, K. Lang, S. B. Rao, T. Suel, T. Tsantilas, and R. H. Bisseling. BSPlib: The BSP programming library. *Parallel Computing*, 24(14):1947–1980, December 1998.

[18] IEEE/ANSI Std. 1003.1. Portable operating system interface (POSIX)–part 1: System application program interface (API) [C language], 1996 edition.

[19] John Krystynak and Bill Nitzberg. Performance characteristics of the iPSC/860 and CM-2 I/O systems. In *Proceedings of the Seventh International Parallel Processing Symposium*, pages 837–841, Newport Beach, CA, 1993. IEEE Computer Society Press.

[20] Josip Loncaric. Linux 2.2.12 TCP performance fix for short messages. `www.icase.edu/coral/LinuxTCP2.html`.

[21] Message Passing Interface Forum. MPI: A Message-Passing Interface standard. *International Journal of Supercomputer Applications*, 8(3/4):165–414, 1994.

[22] Message Passing Interface Forum. MPI2: A message passing interface standard. *International Journal of High Performance Computing Applications*, 12(1–2):1–299, 1998.

[23] P. Mucci, S. Brown, C. Deane, and G. Ho. Papi: A portable interface to hardware performance counters. `icl.cs.utk.edu/projects/papi/`.

[24] Nils Nieuwejaar, David Kotz, Apratim Purakayastha, Carla Schlatter Ellis, and Michael Best. File-access characteristics of parallel scientific workloads. *IEEE Transactions on Parallel and Distributed Systems*, 7(10):1075–1089, October 1996.

[25] Emil Ong, Ewing Lusk, and William Gropp. Scalable Unix commands for parallel processors: A high-performance implementation. In Jack Dongarra and Yiannis Cotronis, editors, *Proceedings of Euro PVM/MPI*. Springer Verlag, 2001. To appear.

[26] OpenMP Web page. `www.openmp.org`.

[27] R. Reussner, P. Sanders, L. Prechelt, and M Müller. SKaMPI: A detailed, accurate MPI benchmark. In Vassuk Alexandrov and Jack Dongarra, editors, *Recent advances in Parallel Virtual Machine and Message Passing Interface*, volume 1497 of *Lecture Notes in Computer Science*, pages 52–59. Springer, 1998. 5th European PVM/MPI Users' Group Meeting.

[28] Kent E. Seamons and Marianne Winslett. Multidimensional array I/O in Panda 1.0. *Journal of Supercomputing*, 10(2):191–211, 1996.

[29] Marc Snir, Steve W. Otto, Steven Huss-Lederman, David W. Walker, and Jack Dongarra. *MPI—The Complete Reference: Volume 1, The MPI Core,* 2nd edition. MIT Press, Cambridge, MA, 1998.

[30] Hal Stern. *Managing NFS and NIS*. O'Reilly & Associates, Inc., 1991.

[31] W. Richard Stevens. *UNIX network programming: Networking APIs: Sockets and XTI*, volume 1. Prentice-Hall PTR, Upper Saddle River, NJ 07458, USA, second edition, 1998.

[32] Rajeev Thakur and Alok Choudhary. An Extended Two-Phase Method for Accessing Sections of Out-of-Core Arrays. *Scientific Programming*, 5(4):301–317, Winter 1996.

[33] Rajeev Thakur, Alok Choudhary, Rajesh Bordawekar, Sachin More, and Sivaramakrishna Kuditipudi. Passion: Optimized I/O for parallel applications. *IEEE Computer*, 29(6):70–78, June 1996.

[34] Rajeev Thakur, William Gropp, and Ewing Lusk. On implementing MPI-IO portably and with high performance. In *Proceedings of the 6th Workshop on I/O in Parallel and Distributed Systems*, pages 23–32. ACM Press, May 1999.

[35] Rajeev Thakur, Ewing Lusk, and William Gropp. A case for using MPI's derived datatypes to improve I/O performance. In *Proceedings of SC98: High Performance Networking and Computing*, November 1998.

[36] TotalView Multiprocess Debugger/Analyzer, 2000. `www.etnus.com/Products/TotalView`.

[37] J. L. Traeff, R. Hempel, H. Ritzdoff, and F. Zimmermann. Flattening on the fly: Efficient handling of MPI derived datatypes. Number 1697 in Lecture Notes in Computer Science, pages 109–116, Berlin, Germany / Heidelberg, Germany / London, UK / etc., 1999. Springer-Verlag.

[38] Mitch Wagner. Google keeps pace with demand, May 2001. `www.internetweek.com/infrastructure01/infra050701.htm`.

[39] Omer Zaki, Ewing Lusk, William Gropp, and Deborah Swider. Toward scalable performance visualization with Jumpshot. *High Performance Computing Applications*, 13(2):277–288, Fall 1999.

Index